Notes on Spain and the Spaniards,

in the Summer of 1859, with a Glance at Sardinia

SOUTHERN CLASSICS SERIES

Mark M. Smith and Peggy G. Hargis, Series Editors

NOTES ON SPAIN
and THE SPANIARDS,
in the Summer of 1859, with
a Glance at Sardinia

JAMES JOHNSTON PETTIGREW

New Introduction by
Clyde N. Wilson

THE UNIVERSITY OF SOUTH CAROLINA PRESS
*Published in Cooperation with the Institute for
Southern Studies of the University of South Carolina*

New material © 2010 University of South Carolina

Cloth edition published by the Presses of Evans & Cogswell, Charleston, South Carolina, 1861
Paperback edition published by the University of South Carolina Press, Columbia, South Carolina 29208

www.sc.edu/uscpress

Manufactured in the United States of America

19 18 17 16 15 14 13 12 11 10
10 9 8 7 6 5 4 3 2 1

Library of Congress Cataloging-in-Publication Data
Pettigrew, James Johnston, 1828–1863.
  Notes on Spain and the Spaniards, in the summer of 1859, with a glance at Sardinia / James Johnston Pettigrew ; new introduction by Clyde N. Wilson.
      p. cm.
  "Published in Cooperation with the Institute for Southern Studies of the University of South Carolina."
  Originally published: Charleston, S.C. : Presses of Evans & Cogswell, 1861.
  ISBN 978-1-57003-904-1 (pbk : alk. paper)
  1. Spain—Description and travel. 2. Pettigrew, James Johnston, 1828–1863—Travel—Spain. 3. Spain—Civilization. I. University of South Carolina. Institute for Southern Studies. II. Title.
  DP41.P49 2010
  946'.072092—dc22
                                        2009043191

This book was printed on Glatfelter Natures, a recycled paper with 30 percent postconsumer waste content.

Publication of the Southern Classics series is made possible in part by the generous support of the Watson-Brown Foundation.

CONTENTS

CHAPTER XII. — BULL FIGHTS.

CHAPTER XIII. — ENVIRONS. — HISTORICAL.

CHAPTER XIV. — SOCIAL LIFE.

CHAPTER XV. — CORDOVA.

CHAPTER XVI. — CORDOVA, BY MALAGA AND ALHAMA TO GRANADA.

CHAPTER XVII. — GRANADA.

SERIES EDITORS' PREFACE

Sometimes a book's title serves to confuse rather than clarify and can almost doom a work to perpetual obscurity. Such was the case with James Johnston Pettigrew's *Notes on Spain and the Spaniards, in the Summer of 1859, with a Glance at Sardinia,* as Clyde N. Wilson points out in his enlightening introduction to this important reprint. *Notes on Spain and the Spaniards* was, rightly maintains Wilson, first and foremost, a product of a first-rate Southern mind and can—and should—be read profitably in that context. Erudite, cosmopolitan, informed, and elegant, Pettigrew's *Notes* reaffirms what a growing number of scholars have recently argued: that the life of the mind in the antebellum South was intellectually impressive, engaged with the world, and far from provincial. Students will find the book both engrossing and helpful as they continue to ponder the texture and meaning of the Old South's intellectual history.

Southern Classics returns to general circulation books of importance dealing with the history and culture of the American South. Sponsored by the Institute for Southern Studies, the series is advised by a board of distinguished scholars who suggest titles and editors of individual volumes to the series editors and help establish priorities in publication.

Chronological age alone does not determine a title's designation as a Southern Classic. The criteria also include significance in contributing to a broad understanding of the region, timeliness in relation to events and moments of peculiar interest to the American South, usefulness in the classroom, and suitability for inclusion in personal and institutional collections on the region.

MARK M. SMITH
PEGGY G. HARGIS
Series Editors

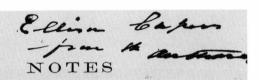

NOTES

ON

SPAIN AND THE SPANIARDS,

IN THE SUMMER OF 1859,

WITH A

GLANCE AT SARDINIA.

BY

A CAROLINIAN.

(J. J. P.)

(James Johnston Pettigrew)

FOR PRIVATE CIRCULATION.

Quid dignum memorare tuis, Hispania, terris
Vox humana valet?

CHARLESTON:
STEAM-POWER PRESSES OF EVANS & COGSWELL,
No. 3 Broad and 103 East Bay Street.
1861.

Title page of the 1861 edition of *Notes on Spain and the Spaniards*

INTRODUCTION

This is James Johnston Pettigrew's only book, privately printed in Charleston during the first weeks of the War between the States and here for the first time reprinted. In the opening passage, the author describes himself crossing the Alps on his way to seek service in the army of the king of Sardinia. His mission was to take part in a struggle for liberty, the liberation of Italy from the yoke of Austria.

That was 1859. By pure chance it was the Fourth of July, not only the birthday of American independence but also, as it happened, Pettigrew's own birthday, his thirty-first. Exactly four years later (July 4, 1863), he was beside the Emmitsburg road near a Pennsylvania town called Gettysburg nursing a useless right arm that had been smashed by grapeshot and waiting for an enemy counterattack that never came.

All around him were the surviving North Carolina soldiers who the day before he had led through a mile of frontal and flank fire to within a few yards of the now eternally famous stone wall on Cemetery Ridge. Pettigrew was, by his own lights, engaged in another struggle for liberty, that of his own people from a Union that had grown hateful. Two weeks later he died after being wounded in a minor skirmish that occurred when the rear guard of the Army of Northern Virginia recrossed the Potomac back to the Confederacy.

In 1859, just a few days after the decisive Battle of Solferino, Pettigrew caught up with the allied Sardinian and French forces in northern Italy. In that battle the French had broken the Austrian center, posted on a ridge, with an attack across a wide expanse of open land—an uncanny resemblance in terrain and action to the third day at Gettysburg. The open ground covered by the French charge was a bit steeper, but also shorter, than that to be covered by Confederates on July 3, 1863. And of course, unlike the Confederates at Gettysburg, the French were successful.

The author's early death, along with the time and circumstances of the book's printing, explains in part why *Notes on Spain and the Spaniards* has been nearly unknown. Another reason is its title, which does not indicate that it belongs in the domain of Southern literature, but places it, apparently, in the rather perishable category of travel books. *Notes on Spain and the Spaniards* is, in fact, an extremely interesting product of the intellect of the late antebellum South, which accounts for its publication in this series.

THE AUTHOR

James Johnston Pettigrew was born on July 4, 1828, at the Bonarva plantation in Tyrrell County, North Carolina. He was the sixth of seven children born to Ebenezer Pettigrew, a pious, hardworking, and very successful planter, and Ann Blount Shepard Pettigrew, who came from a prominent New Bern mercantile family. There is an apocryphal story about a proud man who refused to serve in Congress because it was no place for a gentleman. This was quite literally true of Ebenezer Pettigrew, who, after one term in the House of Representatives, never set foot in Washington again. Johnston (as he was usually called) inherited his father's idealism but not his disdain for public action.

While he was still a child, his relatives observed that Johnston enjoyed exceptional mental gifts. The end result was that, while two older brothers inherited plantations, his legacy was the best available education and a portion of capital sufficient to allow him to become established in a profession.

He attended Robert Bingham's academy in Hillsborough, considered the best school in the state, and the university in Chapel Hill, graduating first in his class with a perfect academic record at age eighteen. Among the visiting dignitaries at the Chapel Hill commencement of 1847 were alumnus President James K. Polk and the internationally distinguished astronomer and oceanographer Lieutenant Matthew F. Maury of the U.S. Navy. They were so impressed with the mathematical genius of the valedictorian that Pettigrew was on the spot offered a "professorship" at the Naval (or National) Observatory, of which Maury was superintendent. Maury later referred to Pettigrew as "the most promising young man of the South."[1]

After six months as an astronomer at the observatory (now the official residence of the vice president), Pettigrew moved to Baltimore to study law under a son-in-law of Chief Justice Roger B.

Taney. In 1849 he was offered a position as a junior partner in the Charleston practice of James Louis Petigru, one of the foremost members of the South Carolina bar and his father's first cousin.

Before he began his professional career, there occurred the period of the author's life most pertinent to the present occasion. From January 1850 until August 1852, Pettigrew traveled throughout Europe, enjoying experiences unavailable to most Americans, and of which he made the most.

He spent his first year at the University of Berlin earning a degree in civil law. For the rest of his time in the Old World, the young Carolinian went native, traveling and living in Germany, Austria, Bohemia, Hungary, Italy, France, Britain, and Spain. Much of his travel was off the beaten track of tourists, afoot or on horseback. For long periods of time, Pettigrew cut himself off from all American contact and mingled solely with European people.

As is documented in his diaries and letters, abundantly preserved at Chapel Hill, Pettigrew became proficient in German, French, Spanish, and Italian, both spoken and written, and in written Arabic and Hebrew. He immersed himself, as is clear from his book, not only in the history and culture of Europe—the relics of antiquity and the Middle Ages, the scholarship, art, architecture, and battlefields—but also in the contemporary life of various classes and countries.

His time abroad left him with a lasting admiration for the Latin peoples, especially the Italians and Spanish, which was quite unusual for an English-speaking tourist of the time. "In proportion as we approached Italy," he once wrote, "my feeling of satisfaction arose; I felt as I used to do on leaving the Yankee land on the way to the South. At almost every railway station, one could perceive an increase in the beauty of the women, in the sociability of the men, and in the smiling genial aspect of the country."[2] (One is reminded a bit of Faulkner's Quentin Compson crossing Mason and Dixon's line on the train from Harvard.) So well did Pettigrew fit in that he found, to his delight, Englishmen often mistook him for a Frenchman or a Spaniard.

He spent his last months in Europe in southern Spain, describing this time as the happiest of his life. There Pettigrew formed the project of writing a scholarly history of Arab contributions to the civilization of Europe. The work was never written, but *Notes on Spain and the Spaniards* contains many intimations of what it might have been. This is another characteristic that makes reissuing this book timely, as we live today amid a renewed conflict between the West and Islam. Another of his historical enthusiasms was the career of the Carlist general Tomás de Zumalacárregui, a sort of Spanish Francis Marion.

On his departure from Europe, in an inaccurate prophecy but a revealing sentiment, Pettigrew wrote his sister: "Alas! Romantic Spain, I shall never see thee again. By the bye I have not a portion of heart remaining as large as a pea. The whole is left in Andalusia."[3]

Pettigrew spent the rest of the 1850s in Charleston, a city that, as a modest North Carolinian, he at first found distastefully fashionable and self-important. But as he was adopted by the extended family of James Louis Petigru, Charleston became more congenial. He practiced law, engaged in politics, wrote for the newspapers, nearly died of yellow fever, was a second in a notable duel, and established a reputation as an eccentric genius and a somewhat eligible bachelor. He pursued intellectual interests in the company of historian William Henry Trescot and theologian and linguist James Warley Miles. In 1856 and 1857, he served a term in the South Carolina House of Representatives. At that time he acquired a brief national reputation for writing a committee report that killed a foolish and provocative proposal for reopening the African slave trade that Governor James H. Adams had put forward.

Pettigrew's family politics was Whig, critical of fire-eaters and secessionists and inclined to ignore, rather than respond in kind, to Northern attacks. But, characteristically for his generation, he became convinced that sectional war was inevitable and undertook to prepare himself for a creditable part in it. He participated actively in the militia and studied it closely. This led him to write "The Militia System of South Carolina"—probably his most important work after *Notes on Spain and the Spaniards*—which was published anonymously in *Russell's Magazine*.[4] It was an extended, good-natured but biting satire of the delusion that South Carolina was prepared for military defense. At the same time, Pettigrew took every opportunity to make himself a model officer, not neglecting artillery, engineering, ordnance, sanitation, supply, or cookery.

In 1859, when news was received of war in Italy, Pettigrew made his will, purchased equipment, and hastened to New York to take ship. He reached Italy as he describes herein. He obtained an interview with a secretary of Count Cavour, the Sardinian prime minister, declaring that he wanted to serve as a volunteer in action with no expectation of commission or pay. Unfortunately for him, a truce had been declared just a few days earlier, after Solferino, when the allies had achieved their immediate goal of releasing Lombardy from the Austrian grasp.

Disappointed in the hope of participating in, or even witnessing, battle, Pettigrew went to Paris and spent some time learning from French officers as much as he could about military art and science. Then he went again to Spain, the pilgrimage he records in *Notes on Spain and the Spaniards.*

From the secession of South Carolina in December 1860 until the surrender of Fort Sumter the following April, Pettigrew was active in Charleston Harbor as colonel of the South Carolina First Regiment of Rifles, the elite infantry formation of the new state army. Soon after, he was informed of his election as colonel of what became the Twenty-second North Carolina Regiment, which he hastened to Raleigh to join. This regiment guarded the Potomac in the vicinity of Fredericksburg from the summer of 1861 to the spring of 1862. In March 1862 Pettigrew learned that he was appointed a brigadier general. He refused promotion, arguing that no person without combat experience should hold that rank. He was called to Richmond for a conference with an amused President Jefferson Davis, who remarked this was the first time anyone had ever refused a promotion on the grounds of inexperience.

He was finally persuaded to accept the post. The impression Pettigrew had made is indicated by the fact that there were very few generals at that time who were as young and who were not former U.S. Army officers or powerful politicians. On May 31, 1862, Pettigrew went into action at the Battle of Seven Pines, the first engagement of the Peninsular campaign. Leading an attack, he received three wounds and was left for dead on the field behind enemy lines. Though unconscious, he was not dead and was picked up by a party of federal soldiers that included future U.S. Supreme Court justice Oliver Wendell Holmes Jr. Imprisoned at Fort Delaware, Pettigrew was believed dead by the Confederacy and had the unique experience of reading his own obituaries.

Some weeks later he was exchanged and, though still partly disabled, returned immediately to duty. He assumed command of a newly formed North Carolina brigade, which, from the summer of 1862 until the spring of 1863, took part in a number of small battles against federal occupying forces in eastern North Carolina. On June 1 the brigade joined the Army of Northern Virginia on the move to Pennsylvania. On the march north Pettigrew wrote to Governor Zebulon B. Vance about his hope that "peace is to be conquered this summer." To a relative he wrote of the Confederacy: "In the midst of all our trials it is a consolation to reflect, that our reputation, next to Greece, will be the most heroic of nations."[5]

Pettigrew's role in the Battle of Gettysburg is significant enough to guarantee him at least a small place in history. His brigade made the first, unexpected contact with the federal army near the town on June 30. The next day it played the key part in a bloody advance that drove the enemy from McPherson's and Seminary ridges and in the process smashed out of existence the Iron Brigade, thought to be the best in the Union army. On July 3, Pettigrew's men were called upon again to advance against a heavily defended position, a failed action that they carried off as bravely as Pickett's previously unbloodied division, leaving a somewhat misleading popular name for the historical charge. The casualties in his brigade were among the heaviest for a few days' fighting in the entire war on either side.

During the withdrawal, on July 14, Pettigrew was shot in the stomach when a straggling company of federal cavalry accidentally rode into a group of officers of the rear guard at Falling Waters, Maryland, on the north bank of the Potomac. Pettigrew was told that his only chance of survival was to remain behind, immobilized, under the care of enemy surgeons. He insisted on staying with his army and was carried for three days in a litter, dying on July 17 at Bunker Hill, (West) Virginia.

"None had more deeply at heart than he the cause for which he shed his blood," wrote a former British army officer who served under Pettigrew. "I tell you the truth when I say that I have never met with one who fitted more entirely my 'beau ideal' of the patriot, the soldier, the man of genius, and the accomplished gentleman." According to Douglas Southall Freeman: "For none who fought so briefly in the Army of Northern Virginia was there more praise while living or laments when dead."[6]

THE BOOK

By the author's own account, *Notes on Spain and the Spaniards* was begun in Charleston in the spring of 1860 in time spared from law practice and militia drill. He regarded the writing to be chiefly for his own benefit, "an offering in memoriam of the happiest days of my life." By June 1860 the manuscript was completed and put aside. Exactly a year later, in the interim between the surrender of Fort Sumter and his departure for the Virginia front, Pettigrew took out the manuscript and had it printed at his own expense, using his salary from service as colonel in the state army. Three hundred copies were printed. One hundred of these were bound, to be given to relatives and friends.[7]

At this stage the work was intended for private circulation, though the author's introductory note seems to suggest he intended future printings. The title page identified the author only by his initials and the title "A Carolinian." According to the bibliographic research of Patricia T. Thompson and Alexander Moore, about fourteen institutions (including two in Boston) hold copies, with multiple copies at the University of North Carolina. One of the copies at UNC is a set of unbound pages with corrections possibly made by the author. It seems likely that most of the unbound copies have perished, for Charleston suffered two major fires and a 587-day bombardment and siege in the few years following the printing. The work has been microfilmed and is part of the large (145 reels) microfilm edition of *Confederate Imprints, 1861–1865*, published by Research Publications in 1974. *Notes on Spain* is found on reel 89, item number 2675.

A few scholars in the two Carolinas—both could claim Pettigrew —of the author's generation and the one following noticed and wrote about the book. Their comments were cogent, specific, and complimentary, making it all the more surprising that the work dropped totally out of sight after the early years of the twentieth century.

Reading and critical comment began with some of those who received copies. "Very clever and very like himself," wrote one relative of Pettigrew. James Louis Petigru, a man of considerable learning, said that his opinion of the work rose on each rereading.[8] William Henry Trescot, one of the friends who received a copy, wrote in a memorial of Pettigrew soon after the war: "This book is admirably written. The country and the people whom he described had for him a romantic charm, and his enthusiastic sympathy for their history and character gives to his descriptions a warmth and truthfulness which a colder observation could never have imparted. His thorough knowledge of Spanish history and his familiarity with the language taught him both what to observe and how to observe."[9]

In 1875 Theodore Bryant Kingsbury, who had been a student with Pettigrew at Chapel Hill and who was, like Pettigrew, a seasoned

European traveler, wrote an appreciation of the work for a Southern magazine. "On every page is revealed the scholar, thinker, and keen observer," said Kingsbury, "whilst we have frequent glimpses of a statesman and philosopher at home among the social and political systems of the Old World."

He described *Notes on Spain,* correctly, as "fresh, witty, vivacious, thoughtful, kindly" and "distinguished by a catholic and generous spirit quite uncommon among travelers." Further the "book has been rather a surprise to us. . . . There are occasional passages of a humorous turn that we were not prepared to meet with. It is, besides more artistic, hearty and eloquent, than we anticipated." Kingsbury doubtless had in mind such humorous passages as Pettigrew's treatment of Charlemagne as a filibusterer and his self-satirical description of renting a mule from villagers in the Pyrenees. Kingsbury proposed that *Notes on Spain* was more lively and learned and less prejudiced than any of the popular travel books by Northerners.[10]

In 1887 Cornelia Phillips Spencer, a well-known North Carolina writer of the time whose father and brother had taught Pettigrew at Chapel Hill, published an essay called "General Pettigrew's Book." She had evidently been presented with a copy by the general's brother William. While complimentary, she was somewhat irritated at Pettigrew's fondness for the Latins and contempt for the Mother Country, Britain, of which, she said, "to deride and depreciate which he omits no opportunity."[11]

Notes on Spain and the Spaniards was next noticed by Ludwig Lewisohn, a minor critic, while writing a series on South Carolina literature for the *Charleston News* in 1903. "Pettigrew's single book is as interesting a volume of its kind as one can well imagine," he wrote. Lewisohn observed that Pettigrew had a very high potential as a writer and regarded it as a flaw of the old regime in the South that he had not developed his talent further.[12] In this, Lewisohn was keeping with the scholarly consensus of the time. William Peterfield Trent had put forward a similar theory in an 1892 biography of William Gilmore Simms.

In the multivolume *Library of Southern Literature* (1908–13), Pettigrew was included, with excerpts from the book and a critical sketch by Nathan W. Walker, a professor at the University of North Carolina. Walker wrote: "That the author had the temperament of the man of letters, and possessed literary ability and skill of a high order, will readily be seen by even a glance at his work. Large tolerance and intellectual flexibility are everywhere apparent, and one realizes here and there the touch of the master's hand and feels that nothing could be finer than some of his descriptive passages. Deep poetic feeling and imagination, delicate humor, refined wit, a 'rare gift for the happy word' are some of the author's earmarks."[13] Walker's selections reflected the artistic, descriptive passages of the book: ranging from the author's reaction to the Seville cathedral and the Catholic piety observed there to the charms of Spanish ladies and to the Alhambra, the last a subject already made familiar to American readers by Washington Irving.

Other than my study of Pettigrew (dissertation, 1971; book, 1990), Walker's seems to be the last notice taken of this book, with one exception. A 1973 novel, *The Killer Angels,* describes an intellectual General Pettigrew presenting a copy of a book he had written to General James Longstreet during the Battle of Gettysburg. This scene, entirely fictional and extremely unlikely, was included in the film *Gettysburg.*

The testimony of these critics should be enough to establish *Notes on Spain and the Spaniards* as a work deserving attention. It does what every good book does—presents an interesting mind at work on interesting material. It is readable and gives nourishment for thought. Pettigrew records a journey that is not only geographical and contemporary. It is an odyssey that is historical, aesthetic, intellectual, political, and spiritual. His experiences, impressions, and judgments are sincere and rendered with considerable art. The work is at the same time a travelogue, an exploration of Spanish history and manners, and a defense of Spain from the prejudices of "Anglo-Saxons." For him, the Anglo-Saxons were the North, and the Spaniards, the South.

More important, the book exhibits the well-developed social philosophy and worldview of a late antebellum Southerner, an exhibition of elements different from those usually assumed to characterize Pettigrew's society.

About 1970, when I first began to study James Johnston Pettigrew and his forgotten book, I remember feeling strongly the existing scholarly neglect and condescension in regard to the intellectual life of the Old South. Few scholars, it seemed, took Southern thought seriously, with some exceptions in regard to a few conspicuous proslavery writers. Despite the inherent implausibility that nothing of interest had been written during the time between Thomas Jefferson and William Faulkner, the intellectual life of the nineteenth century was dismissed as of insufficient quantity and quality to merit consideration.

The case is rather different nearly forty years later. In the intervening period, a number of historians have undertaken examinations of the mental life of the Old South—its creative literature, theology, education, and political, social, and economic thought. The preponderance of scholars who know something about the subject are now aware that the Old South had an intellectual culture interesting in kind and amount and that no sharp division could be drawn between the antebellum South and Revolutionary and early national ideas. Pettigrew is an example of the latter fact, being in sum as much an early Republic classicist as a nineteenth-century romantic. The South had men and women, not insignificant in numbers and talents, actively reading and writing, abreast of the world of ideas past and current, and thinking about subjects other than the immediate politics of their peculiar region.

Neglect, if not condescension, has disappeared, and the intellectual life of the antebellum South is now, in fact, a substantial element in Southern historiography. Such writers and thinkers as William Gilmore Simms, James Henry Hammond, Henry Timrod, George Frederick Holmes, Beverly Tucker, George Tucker, Henry Hughes, Louisa Cheves McCord, Mary Boykin Chesnut, Augusta Jane Evans Wilson, James Henley Thornwell, Robert Lewis Dabney, and others have received extended treatments.

Much, though not all, of this literature is characterized by the same implicit assumptions that have always dominated fashionable writing about Southern history. That everything, even what appears to be intellectual or creative accomplishment, is to be explained in terms of irrelevance, evil motives, warped personalities, guilt, self-delusion, or, at best, a crypto–fifth column rebellion against the regime. Johnston Pettigrew's encounter with a perennially out-of-step European country provides its own unique insight into the Southern mind on the brink of a struggle for independence.

Notes

1. Maury to Mary Pettigrew Browne, May 6, 1870, Pettigrew Family Papers, Southern Historical Collection, University of North Carolina at Chapel Hill (hereafter SHC).

2. Pettigrew to James C. Johnston, March 15, 1851, SHC.

3. Pettigrew to Ann Pettigrew, June 10, 1852, SHC.

4. *Russell's Magazine* 6 (March 1860): 529–40.

5. Pettigrew to Gov. Zebulon B. Vance, May 22, 1863, Governors Letterbooks 50.1, 255–56, North Carolina Department of Archives and History (hereafter NCDAH); Pettigrew to Jane Petigru North, May 19, 1863, SHC.

6. Collett Leventhorpe to Mary Pettigrew, May 14, 1867, Pettigrew Family Papers, NCDAH.

7. Pettigrew to William S. Pettigrew, June 18, 1861, SHC. Copies have been identified that were given by the author to Trescot, a South Carolinian and pioneer diplomatic historian; his sister Mary Blount Pettigrew; his maternal "Grandma" Mary Blount Shepherd; a cousin, Louise Petigru Porcher; Ellison Capers, a Charleston intellectual colleague, later a Confederate brigadier general and an Episcopal bishop; and Louis G. Young, Pettigrew's aide during the war. There also exists one unbound copy on which someone, not Pettigrew, has made numerous inexplicable corrections.

8. Minnie North Alston to Caroline North Pettigrew, July 17, 1861, and James Louis Petigru to Pettigrew, June 24, 1861, SHC.

9. William Henry Trescot, *Memorial of the Life of J. Johnston Pettigrew . . .* (Charleston, S.C.: John Russell, 1870), 42–43.

10. Theodore Bryant Kingsbury, *Our Living and Our Dead* 3 (December 1875): 784–85.

11. Cornelia Phillips Spencer, "General Pettigrew's Book," *University of North Carolina Magazine* 6 (March 1887): 267–68.

12. Ludwig Lewisohn, "A History of Literature in South Carolina, Chapter 11: Pettigrew and Trescot," *Charleston News,* August 30, 1903.

13. Nathan W. Walker, "James Johston Pettigrew," in *Library of Southern Literature,* ed. Edwin Anderson Alderman and Joel Chandler Harris (Atlanta: Martin & Hoyt, 1909), 9:3984.

EDITORIAL NOTE: The new contents pages preserve the spellings of the original, which do in a few cases vary from the spellings in the chapter openers or the text.

PREFACE TO THE FIRST EDITION

Another book! Yes, but a small one, and mostly about Spain.

Every person thus assaulting the Public should be prepared to excuse himself, by stating the provocation, the purpose, and his capacity for executing that purpose.

For provocation, I can pretend little beyond the itching which tempts everyone to commune with others about what has profoundly interested himself. The book will show that the offence has not been committed with malice aforethought. Nothing was further from my intention on crossing the Pyrenees than to become an author. I went to Spain actuated by the purest motives of selfishness—to gratify myself. On my return, I was strongly impressed with the erroneous ideas prevalent among my acquaintances upon this subject; ideas transmitted to us generally by the oftentimes clever, but always partial writings of English travellers and historians (whom we should have learnt by painful experience sufficiently well to appreciate), and fostered by political troubles of our own. The conception we still retain of the Spaniard, notwithstanding the many excellent productions for which the world is indebted to our countrymen, would represent him enveloped in a huge cloak, shaded by a still huger *sombrero*, and rejoicing in a half-drawn stiletto, his country devastated by the Inquisition, and the abode of ignorance, idleness and prejudice. Such I have not found it.

The purpose, therefore, is to portray the country in the plain, unadorned light of truth, so far as I am able, without exaggerating its beauties or its defects; sometimes narrating the incidents of travel with, perhaps, unjustifiable minuteness, at others indulging in generalization, seeking an excuse for its want of method, its mixture of personal and public concerns, of fact and reflection, in the title which the volume bears. I have not the vanity of expecting or hoping to instruct such as have been there already, and are better acquainted with the Peninsula than myself. My whole ambition has been to present it as it appeared to me—a faithful reflex of the journey. If upon some favored spot, I have felt the spirit of the Past upon me, it has not been banished from the narrative, however incongruous the mosaic might seem, for the Past of Spain is perpetually recurring to the traveller, and he who regards only the Present renounces half the pleasure of his opportunity. It has seemed to me, therefore, most in keeping to adopt the epistolary style, in substance if not in appearance, and so I have done.

For qualification, I may say that, some years ago, when more youthful and impressible, I travelled there extensively under certain advantages; that my thoughts since have often been directed thither, and that though the present journey embraced a comparatively small extent of country, it served to correct previous misconceptions, and to give me confidence in the opinions I have formed. Upon one point I have been inexorable—in refraining from any allusion, however remote, to such as have extended to me the courtesies of hospitality or acquaintance, though rendered aware, by the example of Europeans in America, how much such breaches of propriety add to the piquancy of mere books of adventure. I conclude by vouching that the following pages contain, in my belief, the truth and nothing but the truth, and as such I have ventured to give them to the public.

June, 1860.

Notes on Spain and the Spaniards,

in the Summer of 1859, with a Glance at Sardinia

Quid dignum memorare tuis, Hispania, terris
Vox humana valet?

CHAPTER I.

THE ITALIAN WAR.

Mount Cenis—Entrance into Italy—A Prisoner of War—Feeling in Turin—Announcement of the Armistice—Of the Peace—Sketch of Sardinian Politics—Position of France—Of Germany—Austrian Tyranny—Events of the War—French and Austrian Armies—Peace of Villafranca—Conduct of Russia—Effect of the War—Ultimate Aims of Napoleon.

It was on the night of the 4th of July, 1859, that I crossed Mount Cenis, on the way to Turin. Though the precise date was a matter of accident, its associations were in happy unison with the object of the journey and the sentiments which prompted me. It was my birthday; but far more, it was the day that ushered into life my native land—a day ever memorable in the history of the world—not so much because it had added another to the family of nations, as because it had announced, amid the crack of rifles and the groans of expiring patriots, the great principle, that every people has an inalienable right of self-government, without responsibility to aught on earth, save such as may be imposed by a due respect for the opinions of mankind. Once more this great battle was to be fought, no longer in the wilds of the American forest, but on land renowned through all ages, and rendered sacred by recollections of intellect, art and religion. Now, as then, a tyrant empire had, with vain boastings, poured her legions upon a devoted land; now, as then, the oppressed few, forgetting their dissensions, had risen to burst their chains asunder; and now, too, as then, a great nation, the generous French, were rushing with disciplined battalions to aid struggling, expiring humanity. It was certainly humiliating that so large a portion of Europe should have remained unsympathizing spectators of the contest. On the part of an American, acquiescence in such neutrality would have been treason against nature. Inspired by these sentiments, I was hurrying with what speed I might to offer my

2

services to the Sardinian Government, and to ask the privilege of serving as a volunteer in her armies—perhaps a foolish errand, if measured by the ideas of this unromantic century. No emotion of my life was ever so pure, so free from every shade of conscientious doubt or selfish consideration. At the distance of four thousand miles, we were happily ignorant of the underhand intrigues, if any there were, which so frequently disgust one in the turmoil of politics. I saw but the spectacle of an injured people struggling, as America had done, to throw off the yoke of a foreign and, comparatively, barbarous oppressor, and as we passed battalion after battalion of brave French, slowly ascending the mountain, I felt toward them all the fervor of youth, fired by the grateful traditions of eighty years ago.

The rays of the western sun beat with their utmost intensity upon the troops, many of whom, particularly the younger ones, appeared utterly exhausted. The effect of the heat in rendering them deaf was remarkable. They would frequently be first made aware of our approach by feeling the horses' breath upon their necks. We aided them as much as lay in our power by taking their knapsacks, which were hung about on the diligence, giving it the appearance of a huge pedlar's wagon. There were several battalions of the line, one of chasseurs de Vincennes, and some squadrons of cavalry scattered along, the men by no means large, but of well-developed muscles and prepossessing countenances. As night came on they halted to camp, and we continued our journey alone. The snow still lingered on the summit of the Pass, but descending about three o'clock, we suddenly turned to the east, and the hot air smote us as from an oven's mouth. We were in Italy. Soon the gorgeous vegetation of the southern slopes of the Alps appeared to delight our eyes, the morning breeze springing up saluted us with the refreshing odors of the tropics, and amid vineyards and well-cultivated lands we wound our way down the mountain to the railroad station at Susa, where I was charmed to get rid of a fat, vulgar, French commis, who had been very brave and warlike until we commenced the descent; it then became necessary for him and the conductor to exchange words as to the proper speed of the diligence, such was the creature's fears of being precipitated over the parapet. A few hours more brought us to Turin. On entering the station I saw a new sight, which made a strange impression upon me at the time—a prisoner of war. I can scarcely describe the painful effect it produced. A dead man is simply a man dead—nothing uncommon. All men are mortal, and a few years more or less matter little, but here was a train filled with beings who had deserved well of their country, and perhaps even acquired the respect of their conquerors, who were yet deprived of that dearest of all liberties— the liberty of locomotion. It furnished food for reflection : for of all the misfortunes of war, this seemed to me the most direful, involving the loss of honor and liberty alike. On our train was a party of conscripts from Savoy, who had been in high glee all the way, singing and rejoicing at the prospect of encountering the enemy. The meeting between them and the Austrians was amusing. The latter, as far as I could see, appeared quite contented with their lot, and received the goodhumored raillery of their victors with smiles. The sight was refreshing to humanity—this separation of the Government from the individual; but there was something unnatural in it, and I would have been far better pleased to see them scowling from the windows of their prison, as though they had felt a conviction of the justice of their cause, and a personal interest in its success. But such can only be in Republics, where those who declare the war fight the battles. Leaving the prisoners to their fate, I entered a little omnibus—one of the blessings which the last ten years have conferred upon Turin—and in a few minutes was comfortably lodged in an old palace, now converted into a hotel, the apparently inevitable fate of such structures in Italy.

As it was still early, I sallied forth into the streets. The city presented, in one respect, a striking aspect—the total absence of young men : all were gone to the wars. The better class of ladies, too, had disappeared from the promenade—for they had either lost or were in daily apprehension of losing some dear friend. The war news was, of course, the absorbing topic of conversation among the men; who collected under the Arcades and in the Cafés, discussing the chances with anxious countenances. They felt confident of ultimate success. Enthusiasm pervaded all classes; nor was it the enthusiasm which delights in loud boasts and empty professions, but that much more valuable quality which, having counted the necessary sacrifices, devotes itself to the accomplishment of a great work. Mere

social intercourse could, therefore, be scarcely said to exist.
Over the city reigned the breathless calm which precedes a
convulsion—for any moment might bring news of another and,
perhaps, final struggle under the walls of Verona. In the midst
of this state of suspense, the public ear was suddenly startled
by the rumor of an armistice to be granted at the urgent request
of the Emperor of the French. Words cannot express the astonishment of the community upon learning that the Generalissimo
of the allied armies had paused in the height of success to crave
a delay which could only operate in favor of the weaker party,
by affording them an opportunity of recovering from their demoralization. As Napoleon had never yet acted without some
adequate motive, there was a general disposition to suspend
judgment upon the armistice until the press should communicate the reasons. None were given, and the world was left to
conjecture what advantage could accrue to the Allies which,
by any possibility, might compensate for the injustice of leaving
Venetia exposed to the forced loan lately decreed. A large
majority still felt unabated confidence in the ultimate accomplishment of the famous programme, " From the Alps to the
Adriatic." The cold, unimpassioned nature of Napoleon, the
calculating prudence with which he had hitherto conceived,
the tenacity with which he had maintained, the skill with
which he had executed every political plan, rendered them sure
of the fulfilment of the late promises. In this belief they were
confirmed by the vigorous preparations made for continuing
the contest. A few far-seeing politicians began already to suspect that the armistice was preliminary to some arrangement,
whereby France and Austria might be united against any
power that should prove disagreeable in the future settlement
of Europe, but they were in a small minority. These doubts
were soon solved by the announcement of the Peace of Villafranca. Its announcement fell like a thunderbolt. The first
impression was a stupefaction. Men stared at each other in
gaping wonder, as though their senses were unable to comprehend the intelligence. To this succeeded a furious outburst of
indignation against the Emperor Napoleon. Execrations were
poured upon his name and race. The late idol had been transformed into a hideous demon. His portrait was withdrawn
from the shop windows, and it is said that Orsini's appeared.
This may be true, though I did not see it myself, but it must

not be forgotten that Orsini is regarded by very respectable persons in Italy as a Brutus, nobly sacrificing himself for the good of his country, rather than a fanatical assassin, which is his position in America. Bitter comparisons were instituted between the glorious proclamations with which the French army had crossed the Alps and their impotent conclusion. Every wild and impracticable scheme was suggested; some even proposed to continue the war alone. But the rage of indignant Italy was fruitless—for it was worse than folly to suppose that Sardinia could contend single-handed with Austria, aided, perhaps, by France. The war, for the present, was ended. In the midst of all this excitement, there was one feature highly creditable to the Sardinians—the generous, unselfish manner in which the news was received. Their own country, Lombardy, Tuscany, Romagna, were forgotten in universal commiseration for the condition of Venice, so cruelly abandoned to the oppressions of the common tyrant, thrust back, as it were, into the vindictive jaws of the monster. The sentiment was expressed in every way known to the heart. Among the poetical effusions, was one peculiarly beautiful upon the separation of the two sisters, Lombardy and Venitia, which I regret not having preserved. A profound gloom shrouded the city as though it had been overwhelmed by some terrible disaster. The Bourse fell, not from want of confidence, but because the purchasers were in mourning; it was not a time to buy and sell. There was no marrying or giving in marriage that day in Turin.

The war, so far as it involved external enemies was, in my opinion, hopelessly over, for the fifty thousand French soldiers that were to be left in Parma, Modena and Tuscany would repress any attempt at a popular movement in those Provinces, and the accumulation of Austrian troops in Venetia rendered idle all thought of insurrection there. Nor was it probable that France and Austria would re-commence hostilities immediately. A civil war between the Bolognese and the Papal troops was much more within the range of possibilities. But for a foreigner to interfere in any such contest would not only be impertinent but unwise, as in these conflicts it is very difficult to find out the truth, much less to strike the balance of right, so I concluded to spend the summer in some agreeable country, within call in case of a renewal of hostilities, when

the opportunity would be renewed of which the armistice or
rather the peace had deprived me.   It would, however, be
scarcely admissible to leave Italy without a word upon the
events of the summer.

The ill-advised campaign of 1849, which ended with the battle of Novarra, placed Sardinia at the feet of Radetsky, and
had not France, aided by England, interposed to arrest the
progress of the Austrian arms, it is more than probable that
their domination would have extended from Turin to Messina.
Mouthing demagogues, useless there as elsewhere for practical
good, had, against the opinion of every sensible patriot, precipitated their country to the brink of the abyss.   The ambassadors of France and England protested against the movement
in advance upon Lombardy.   The reply was: "Will you guaranty the existence of the monarchy? for further resistance to
this agitation will cost us the throne, and we will be as far
as ever from the object of your wishes—the preservation of
peace."   As such a guaranty was impossible, under the circumstances, the drama was played out to its catastrophe.   Fortunately, the independence of this corner of Italy was saved
from the general wreck, and from it Italy is destined to be
regenerated, gradually, perhaps, but as surely as Spain was
from the mountains of the Asturias.   The demagogues having
been fairly tried, and found wanting, gave way to honester
men, and the work of regeneration commenced.   Upon the
abdication of Charles Albert, Victor Emanuel ascended the
throne, fresh from the bloody field where the Italian cause had
gone down.   Never for a moment has he swerved from the
rôle which his good fortune cast upon him.   Conscientiously
has he maintained his coronation oath as a constitutional king,
and with equal firmness has he fulfilled the duty, to which he
was bound by no written oath, of inspiriting a new life into
his whole country.   The particular line of policy, pursued
with consistent and masterly statesmanship, is probably due to
Count Cavour, and was a happy combination of passive and
active warfare.   The former consisted in offering to Italy and
entire Europe the spectacle of an Italian nation enjoying the
advantages of self-government, alike removed from the violence and anarchy of Democracy and the tyranny of military
dictatorship.   The latter in sustaining the spirit of the Italian
patriots by every means which diplomacy could suggest or

excuse, and allowing no new outrage on the part of Austria to pass without, at least, a protest. The last, and not the least, precaution consisted in enlisting the moral support of France and England, previous to every important step. The contingent furnished to the Crimean war was thus a skilfully conceived idea, as, besides gratifying the Allies, it necessarily procured the admission of the Sardinian plenipotentiaries into the Paris Congress, and gave France, England and Russia an opportunity of protesting against the Austrian-Italian system, though from widely different motives. The world knows how admirably the whole plan succeeded. The eyes of all Italian patriots were turned incessantly towards Sardinia, which represented throughout Europe the Italian idea, the heart; to Austria were left only the manacle and the bayonet.

The interest of France in the Italian question, to a certain extent, is patent. The rivalry which, in ages past, caused such bloody wars upon these very fields still exists, and will continue to exist, so long as Austria maintains a footing south of the Alps. Nor can any French Government look with indifference upon the extension of either the influence or territory of its hereditary enemy towards the south-eastern frontier. It is a feeling, therefore, which partakes both of the past and present, and the warnings of history upon this subject cannot be safely disregarded by the statesmen of St. Cloud. But I am disposed to give Napoleon himself more credit for sentiment in the matter than is generally done. It is only natural that he should desire to be the benefactor of the land whence his family derive their origin. He is too experienced not to see that, after the brilliant career of the first Emperor, something more than mere military glory must be his distinguishing merit with posterity. He has manifested a determination to batter, undermine, destroy, by every means in his power the treaties of 1815, which were directed principally against his family and country. But I believe he is really ambitious of advancing humanity, so far as that can be done consistently with the maintenance of Bonapartist ideas. The Italian war, moreover, coincided with his avowed policy of uniting the so-called Latin nations under the lead of France— constituting a moral, if not a geographical, empire. Of course, most persons having control of half a million soldiers would like to make a trial of their skill; but he is too politic to stake

much upon so uncertain a venture, merely for the pleasure of
playing at the game of war.   It soon became apparent to both
France and Italy, that a collision was possible, if not inevitable, and that jealousy of the former power might perhaps
enlist a certain portion of Europe in behalf of Austria.   Napoleon, following the example of the wise steward, sought to
make friends against that contingency.   The Tory administration of England having scouted the idea of an alliance, secret
application was made to Russia, who, to avenge herself upon
Austria, most willingly accepted the office of "keeping the
crowd off," as they say in the backwoods, and letting the parties fight it out fairly.   I do not think that the Emperor of the
French expected war, certainly not so soon; but he had made
every possible preparation.   Herein did he show consummate
skill as a ruler; forming a striking contrast to those imbecile
fatuities, who are ever ready to plunge in without first count-
ing the cost, or taking the slightest precaution against defeat.

The conduct of Austria in taking the initiative can hardly
be pronounced impolitic, as the ultimate choice lay between
war and a Congress, and the latter would certainly have been
fatal to her influence.   It is true, that by placing herself in
the aggressive, she gave lukewarm friends an excuse for declining to step forth in her behalf; but upon whom could she rely?
Many persons in England did, and do still, doubt the capacity
of the Italians for self-government; but the English people
never would have tolerated a war simply for the purpose of
upholding Austrian usurpations, and after the reiterated de-
nials by the French Government of any intention of acquiring
an increase of territory for France, there would have remained
no other excuse for interference.   Germany, headed by Prussia,
played apparently a hesitating and very undignified part, but
such was unavoidable.   The Germans had a just want of confidence in and an apprehension of Napoleon, and were, therefore,
not disposed to see Austria defeated and cowed by him; but
they felt an equal detestation of Austria, and would have been
delighted to see her driven out of Italy by the Italians.   The
more clear-sighted, moreover, believed that even for the purpose of resisting French aggression, she would be much more
available after her unsound Italian members had been lopped
off than before.   It was impossible for Prussia to take any
decided part until the war reached the frontier of Germany,

more particularly since Russia was prepared to pour an army corps across the Polish border at the first movement. The loud school-boy cries uttered by Austria after the peace, that her friends had not helped her, were, therefore, not only undignified, but unjust, as she was in a position which precluded any honest sympathy. In view of all these circumstances, I must think that her policy of sudden invasion, before the Allies could finish their preparations, was bold, perhaps desperate, but well conceived, as it offered the additional advantage of relieving her from the immense cost of constant expectation, which her exhausted credit could ill sustain.

The question has been mooted whether Sardinia were justifiable in provoking the war, but of this I cannot entertain the shadow of a doubt. I consider the presence of an Austrian soldier in Italy as a constant cause of resistance—a standing grievance. The nature of the Austrian tyranny is not perfectly understood in America. Up to the period of the reaction which followed the downfall of Napoleon, the Austrian Government truly merited the name of patriarchal. The mildness, the unaffected simplicity of its rule, its respect for vested right were universally acknowledged. Then the new ideas began to ferment. Progress is the child of education and intelligence. It was, therefore, only among the educated intelligent classes that these ideas took root. In an unfortunate hour for the Government, it adopted the system of Metternich, which he had borrowed from Napoleon, and which consisted in the repression by armed force of all liberty of intellect. Fouché re-appeared with his legion of spies. After the Revolution of 1848, this detestable scheme became a mania. The laborer who contented himself with the plough or last, cannot be said to have been oppressed. Rather the contrary, for the effort was to break down the influence and authority of the better classes over this very population. But let any one, high or low, aspire to the impertinent liberty of thinking for himself, and he became at once an object of suspicion to the police. The fundamental laws of the empire were rudely broken, with the hope of reducing all to a hopeless, savourless, abject equality of servitude. The same policy, with twofold stringency, was extended to Italy. The peasant, who tilled his land and ate his grapes, and sang and danced in the cool evening, was a favorite, and, in many respects, fared better than under the

effete nobility, who enjoyed a monopoly of the soil. But woe
to him who thought that man was endowed with intelligence
for other and higher ends! For such there was no mercy :
every species of obloquy and insult was heaped upon them,
and, unfortunately, they comprised the most influential portion
of a population whose lively imaginations, excited by the continual contemplation of the memorials of past freedom, would
not permit them to remain content with the lot of mere hewers
of wood and drawers of water. Surely the patriots who attempted to procure for their country a nobler future, need no
apology to an American public. It will thus appear why the
Austrians, not entirely without reason, counted upon a party
among the peasantry, though the doors of every respectable
house in Milan and Venice were closed against them, and ladies
refrained from appearing on the public promenades, lest they
should be insulted by courtesies from their hated oppressors.
The dearest luxuries of life were resigned merely for the purpose of making a demonstration. On one occasion, the whole
population gave up the use of tobacco, to prove their unconquerable determination of embarrassing the Government by
every means in their power, while, by way of counter-demon-
stration, soldiers and police agents were required to smoke in
public on all occasions. Many found a melancholy pleasure in
subscribing to the monument on the Citadel square at Turin,
or the armament of Alessandria, both of which produced violent recrimination on the part of Austria. Such was the situation of affairs when the cloud of war burst.

The energy displayed by Austria in commencing hostilities
was short-lived. Some obstacles prevented the entire success
of the plan, but there was scarcely a sufficient military reason
for not throwing ahead at least a strong advanced guard,
which might have done infinite mischief, and perhaps have
taken Turin, for the Allies were evidently surprised, and once
at Turin, it might have lain like a huge armadillo, and drawn
in the French contingents as they successively arrived. The
inaction which ensued at Austrian headquarters, had the appearance of paralysis. The whole advantage of the forward
movement was lost, and time was afforded for the concentration
of a respectable force advancing simultaneously by way of
Susa and Genoa upon their left flanks. Then came the battle
of Montebello, fought, as Gen. Giulay said in his despatch, to

make the enemy develope his force. If that were his object, it must be confessed he succeeded admirably. This was followed by Palestro, where Victor Emanuel proved himself to be the first in war, as he had been in peace. Then came the beautiful turning of the Austrian right flank, and the battle of Magenta, in which the gallant MacMahon, manœuvring principally for the safety of his own corps, had the good luck to cause the utter defeat of the enemy, and was rewarded with the Baton of Marshal and the title of Duke. The great battle of Solferino crowned the whole. In a military point of view, the campaign was most remarkable. The Austrians fought well and bravely, and with the energy of despair, for their officers had strangely enough inoculated them with the idea, that if taken prisoners they would either be murdered in cold blood and devoured by the Turcos, or poisoned. Days after the battle of Palestro, many were dragged half-starved from places of concealment, who refused to drink wine or other colored fluid from the hands of their captors. Their being so completely out-witted in strategy is partly owing to the fact, that they with difficulty procured any information of the enemy's movements, while they could scarcely parade without its being as well known at the Allied headquarters as at their own; and subsequent developments have shown that even some of their Generals were in French pay. Another great cause was the want of unity in the command, for, as Napoleon says, "in war men are nothing: one man is everything." In this respect the state of affairs in the Austrian camp was lamentable, and Gen. Giulay received great blame for a vacillation, which, in all probability, was attributable to the Council of War at Vienna, rather than to him.

But still the difficulty remains of explaining how, in a succession of pitched battles, they were invariably defeated. According to the Napoleonists, it was due to the rifled cannon, but in many of the encounters they were not used. Others attribute their success to the innate superiority of the French. *Quien sabe.* The fact is incontestable that the Austrians were most outrageously beaten. In one respect, the experience of the war was very different from what had been anticipated. The invention of the Minié ball and the rifled cannon would, it was thought, abolish cavalry and reduce infantry charges within a small compass. Yet the proclamation of the Emperor,

warning the army that, notwithstanding the improvements in
fire-arms, the bayonette still continued the Frenchman's weapon, was fully justified by subsequent events. Never before
had it been brought into such terrific play. The Zouaves,
indeed, had the dangerous habit of throwing away their cart-
ridges in order to force a charge with the favorite weapon.
The Sardinians have not received their full share of praise for
the part they performed. The battle of San Martino, though
nominally a part of Solferino, was almost a distinct engagement, even more warmly contested than the other, and if the
palm of bravery can be awarded where all are equally brave, it
should rather be to the Italians, the most of whom had never
before seen service. Four times were they driven from the
plateau, and four times did they steadily regain it against
superior numbers and with immense loss. But, as usual, the
larger nation has carried off the lion's share of the glory. The
French army is certainly a magnificent engine. The conscription, though it bears heavily upon the country, gives a much
higher tone to the rank and file than the recruiting system,
and the plan of reserving a certain number of promotions for
the bravery that is without the aids of fortune or rank, offers a
stimulus of which we can form little conception. The French
cavalry, somewhat unexpectedly, also beat the Austrians; but
I think an American will be struck with the abominable horsemanship of all Western Europeans, except the Spaniards, who
are really *caballeros.* No Mexican would ever have made the
mistake of supposing French, Germans or Italians to form one
animal with their steeds. They flop about in a most terrific
manner, and seem, if one may judge by the great precautions
taken in the way of bits, to regard the horse as an enemy, a
sort of wild beast. The English have written themselves into
an equestrian reputation, but those who come to America are
certainly neither graceful riders, nor masters of the animal.
Bad as they are, however, they are better than some of their
neighbors.

One portion of the French army—the light corps, such as
Zouaves and Chasseurs à pied—is beyond criticism. They
seem to unite every requisite of a soldier. As skirmishers, in
the advance or retreat, they are naturally without superiors.
Yet it is in line with the bayonette, that their principal glory
has been acquired. Easily subsisted, always cheerful, having

the courage of desperadoes without their lawlessness, the voice of the officer never fails to meet a response in the deeds of his men. At the battle of Palestro, where the third regiment fought with the fury of demons, they were seen one moment thrusting the Austrians over the bridge, and the next extending the butts of their rifles down to save them from drowning. Such is the French soldier.

At the signing of the peace of Villafranca, the Austrian army was still strong in numbers, but utterly demoralized, without confidence in their Emperor, their Generals or themselves. Peschiera would have fallen in ten days; Mantua was blockaded; the impregnability of Verona laughed at; Venice awaited but the first bomb to rise, and the machinations of Kossuth and Klapka had reduced the Empire to the brink of internal dissolution. The feeble remnant of its credit was gone, and the abyss of bankruptcy had already began to yawn at its feet. No wonder Europe was astounded when Napoleon commanded the troubled elements to be still, and sued the prostrate Hapsburg for peace. He had told the Italians that Italy was to be free from the Alps to the Adriatic; that their own wishes would be consulted as to their future destiny; he had called upon them to be soldiers to-day, in order that they might be free citizens of a great country to-morrow. Yet, in the face of all this, a peace was concluded, in which Lombardy was bandied about between the two Emperors as though it had been a mere piece of land; Venice was left, practically, in its original condition. The Dukes, who with unprecedented unanimity had been driven from their thrones for complicity with the common enemy, and who had even drawn the sword at Solferino, were to be restored again upon an extorted promise not to do so a third time. Yet it was coolly announced that the "mission" had been fulfilled, because forsooth Italy was to become a Confederacy, that is, Sardinia was to be crowded into a council chamber, with one powerful and bitter foe—Austria—two other scarcely less decided opponents—Rome and Naples, and three satellites of Austria. This latter proposition was received with cries of derision, and fell still-born. The French Provincial Press, les Journax des Préfèts, which are without independence and utterly undeserving of respect, abused the Italians in round terms for their ingratitude, pretending that the programme had been carried out fully, as though the war had been undertaken for the purpose of liberating Lombardy, whereas its object was to drive the Austrians out altogether— Italy for the *Italians*—in a word, a principle not a fact. I by no means say that every one was willing to go the length of an *entêté* Frenchman opposite to me at the table d'hôte, who exclaimed with great emphasis, " *c'est le principe, Messieurs ! et moi, je tuerais mon père et ma mère pour un principe,*" but it was, nevertheless, the idea that they were fighting for a great principle which aroused the Italian nation. The Emperor, who is a far honester man than his supporters, in his manly speech to the Corps Législatif, at St. Cloud, admitted that he had been compelled to leave his programme incomplete, assigning as a reason therefor that he found himself on the verge of being involved in a war with the Germanic Confederation, and asserting that his course had been dictated solely by the interests of France. Had he added " the interests of his dynasty," the whole truth might have been told. This speech had the effect of opening the eyes of the Italians to the real motives for the powerful assistance they had received. It was not purely for an idea, nor from any quixotic generosity that so much French blood had been poured out upon the plains of Lombardy, but merely to lessen Austrian influence in Italy, so far, and so far only, as might keep her dependent upon the ruler of France, not to make her united, independent, self-subsisting, and, least of all, to place her under a constitutional Government, which is as abhorrent to the House of Bonaparte as to the House of Hapsburg. But let us bless the giver, and not look the gift-horse in the mouth. In truth, too much had been expected, and the Emperor himself for once forgot his caution in specifying too distinctly the goal of his ambition. No doubt the attitude of Germany was calculated to startle him, but so long as Russia remained firm, there was little danger to be apprehended from that quarter. Hitherto nothing could be more satisfactory than the manner in which Russia had performed her part, not only in drawing the sword, but in impressing upon Prussia that the Germanic Confederation was a purely defensive, not an offensive, organization. The idea was certainly preposterous, that the League, not content with guarantying to each member its Germanic territory, should extend its protection over the non-Germanic provinces of Austria, though it had not the correlative power of enforcing a compliance, the just demands of Foreign Powers, thus in effect turning a nation loose upon the world with full authority to do wrong, yet shielded from all responsibility. In 1850, Austria had nearly effected her cherished purpose of forcing all her possessions into the Confederation, and Europe stood quietly by saying nothing. The circulars of Prince Gortschakoff, in 1859, opportunely restored matters to their proper footing. It was whispered about, however, that the visit of the Russian aid-de-camp, after Solferino, was to announce that the punishment of the delinquent had gone far enough. The truth of this report has never transpired. If well founded, then Napoleon was amply justified by necessity in the step he took, as the democratic element he had aroused behind him was calculated to cause as much apprehension as the enemy in front. He certainly came back to Paris in a very bad humor. Among his several speeches, I preferred his reply to the diplomatic corps. Its causticity showed him to be still a human being, and not entirely a machine of Government. That body, with a sycophancy worthy of the days of the first Napoleon, had humbly begged to be permitted to return thanks to him for having granted peace to Europe. The request was vouchsafed. His response was contained in two sentences, in substance as follows : " Gentlemen, your Governments manifested such jealousy and impertinent suspicion, that I thought it proper to make peace. I thank you, as formally as I can for the honor, and the door is open for you to go." The confusion of *les oiseaux dorés* may be imagined.

The peace of Villafranca may be safely set down as the most complete diplomatic failure on record. Not a single provision has been, or could have been, carried out, except the cession of Lombardy, and that was a *fait accompli* already, quite independent of the treaty. The notion of a Confederacy was soon given up as impracticable. The Dukes were not restored; though for that mercy the Italians have to thank the Lord and their own determined military opposition, not the benevolent intentions of the high contracting powers. Neither has Venice received those ameliorating institutions so loudly promised. But, though the effect of the peace was thus naught, that of the war was tremendous. It destroyed the prestige of the Austrian military organization, shook every tyrant in Italy, revived the patriotism of the whole land. It summoned again into active life those who have the greatest interest in the stability of society, and whose participation in public affairs is the best preservative against disorder. Few people have given to the world a nobler example of moderation and wisdom than the Italians since the flight of their Dukes. Mazzini, and his wretched crew of assassins, were unhesitatingly and ignominiously driven out. With the exception of the murder of Anviti, scarcely an act of violence has been committed by a populace, to whom self-constituted apostles of liberty have been preaching that the stiletto was the only key to freedom. The provisional Governments maintained order and protection to life and property as vigorously at Florence as Napoleon did at Paris; and a considerable part of Europe was not only astonished, but disappointed, and, if the truth must be told, scandalized, to find law in the place of confusion, and liberty where they had fondly expected anarchy. The drama is not yet played out, nor can the most far-seeing predict the ultimate result of the contest. It has placed France at the head of Europe, so that, in the language of Frederic the Great, not a gun can be fired without her permission. The Emperor, by the management of the reserve at Solferino, has added to his civic crown the laurel leaves of the conqueror. Despot as he is, he has rendered service to the cause of humanity, is crushing the embryo Robespierres and Murats of the Revolution of 1848, and the infamous school of light literature which debauched the world under Louis Philippe. The fall of the temple, unfortunately, along with these false gods, destroyed some true believers; but the art of preserving liberty is a mystery as yet unrevealed to Europe, and detestable though the present Government be, it is by no means certain that it is not the best for the French. The Italians are content with independence; the French need something more. No Government can retain their respect, which is not surrounded by the halo of military glory. "*L'Empire c'est la paix*" was a deceitful dream, *L'Empire est la gloire et la guerre*. Every party to the treaty of Vienna must be made to bow in humble atonement. Russia was the first to feel the wrath of the avenger. Austria came next. Prussia will soon be made to surrender her transrhenane possessions; and, to crown the glory of all, the French tri-color will float over the Tower of London. Every impartial observer in Europe feels that such is the inevitable decree of fate. Its fulfilment may be deferred, but come it must and will.

Chapter II.

TURIN, BY GENOA TO LUCHON.

Off for Spain—Situation of Turin—Novarra—Rice Plantation—Beauty of the Country of Italy—French Officers—Approach to the Mediterranean—Genoa—The Young Poictevine—The Palaces—Reception of the News of the Peace—Voyage to Marseilles—French Manœuvring Squadron—Marseilles—The Provençeaux—Journey to Toulouse—Cette—The Hungarians—Languedoc—Capt. Ingraham and Coszta—Bascassonere—Toulouse—French Centralization—Arrive at Luchon.

The proclamation of peace, entirely frustrating the object of my journey, was doubly provoking, since a great battle was imminent under the walls of Verona, such as Europe had probably not beheld for centuries. It would have been a hand to hand encounter, of unexampled bitterness. To have witnessed in cold blood this scene, from motives of mere curiosity, could gratify a prize-fighter only, but to have borne a part in the excitement and dangers of a contest, pregnant, perhaps, with the fate of self-government and national independence in Europe, would be a glorious recollection, a theme of endless discourse in after-years. The war, however, was over for the present. At least such was the general opinion, and I saw no reason to dissent, though there was every prospect of its breaking out afresh when the time came for carrying the Treaty of Villafranca into execution. In the meantime I was at liberty to spend the summer according to my preference, about which I had little hesitation. For an American what country possesses such attractions as Spain? To Spain does our continent owe its birth. The romance of its earlier history, followed by a military and civil empire, whose extent had never before been equalled, and united with the charms of its present life, have amply justified the partiality which Americans display for the land of the orange and the olive. Death on the battle field is doubtless very pleasant, but next to that is certainly life in Andalusia. Some years ago, returning home from the usual

3

course of German education, I had passed the winter in that enchanted garden, and a remembrance of its delights had haunted me ever since. Was it imagination? Was it the transitory effect produced by contrast with the cheerless regions of the North, where my previous years had been passed? Was it reality? Elsewhere in Europe there was little to compensate for the moss-draped oaks, the sweet-smelling magnolias, the flowering vines of my own home: for the sensitive honor running at times into extremes, which is yet the main-spring to the character of a gentleman: for the enthusiasm, sincerity, and gentle nature of our own beautiful women. All these had a place in my recollections of Spain, and it was impossible to resist the attraction, even at the risk of being disillusioned. I, therefore, decided upon an immediate departure, delaying only long enough to embrace the opportunity offered me of visiting a rice plantation.

Turin is much inferior to other Italian cities in treasures of art. The Gallery of Paintings and the Egyptian Museum are said to contain objects worthy of a visit, and I visited them, but, in truth, the public mind was too much occupied with other matters to allow one to appreciate these. The old citadel, however, surprised me, as it proves that all the essential principles of fortification, as applied to modern warfare, were well known long before the day of Vauban and Coehorn, and that the progress since made by the science has been much more gradual than is supposed, consisting simply in the development and application of these principles with increased accuracy. The new part of the city is built up with elegant mansions, and its general appearance is the best evidence that can be desired of the blessings of good government. Situated as it is at the junction of the Po and the Dora, and in the centre of the ample valley of Piedmont, which includes the head-waters of these streams, and is bounded on three sides by the Alps, its environs, and the views from the elevations in the neighborhood, cannot but be fine. Switzerland and Italy here melt into each other. The Collina di Torino, a long hill running parallel to the Po on its eastern bank, and covered with villas and groves, would charm a Neapolitan, while the panoramic view from the terrace of the little church on its summit, including the semi-circular range of the Alps, from Monte Rosa to the heights above Genoa, reminds one of Berne. But its

political importance, and the extension of railroads, have made ·
Turin too familiar to our countrymen to need a description; so
a sweltering morning in July found me coursing down the left
bank of the Po. The train soon reached Novarra, where the
station was already filled with the returning baggage of the
Imperial suite.

I delivered my note of introduction, and after an appetizing
breakfast, we started for the country. The heat was sickening; no July on the Pee Dee could have surpassed it, nor was
there any sea-breeze to temper its violence. But this heat
continues only for a few hours in the mid-day; as night comes
on the cool air, descending from the neighboring peaks of
Monte Rosa, makes ample amends for the sufferings of the
day. The summers, moreover, are comparatively short, and
do not encourage that luxuriant tropical growth which renders the tender grass plots of the North so rare in our country.
All travellers, who can make up their minds to endure the dis-
agreeabilities of the season, bear testimony to the beauty of
the country of Italy during the summer. Indeed, if one wishes
really to see Italy, the summer is the only time to travel
there as elsewhere. It is peculiarly unfortunate for us of the
South, that we should be exposed to foreign criticism in the
nakedness of our winter garb, while the contrary rule is applied to the North; for the beauty of every country must be
judged by its aspect when presented under the most favorable
point of view, and it should be seen, too, not only from the
ramparts of great cities, but in the midst of the country itself.
For that purpose, I could not have selected a more propitious
time to visit Sardinia than the present. The valley of the
Ticino is almost wholly devoted to the rice culture. The plan
of operations differs somewhat from ours, as the water is kept
on till a few weeks before the harvest, and thus, to a certain
extent, the deleterious consequences of periodical irrigation
avoided. This system adds very much to the beauty of the
landscape, and gives to the fields the appearance of meadows;
but it destroys the grand views offered by our plantations, and
the prominent feature of such scenery with us, the majestic
river, is entirely wanting. The product is not so great, nor
does the grain equal the American in size and whiteness.
Whether it be as agreeable to the taste is more than I can
tell, as it was always brought upon the table in combination

with some substance which disguised its flavor. The machinery for reaping, threshing, pounding and cleansing is better than I expected to find, but is still far behind what is in common use among us. There is, however, a disposition for improvement, which is fostered by the Government as far as lies in its power. I have little doubt but that the cultivation of rice will eventually disappear from Europe. No .Circassian constitution can withstand the malarious diseases which seem its inseparable concomitants at present, and unless chemistry or medicine come to the rescue by revealing some anti-miasmatic specific, it must, in the course of time, be surrendered to Africans and Asiatics.

In this part of Italy, the dairy seems to be considered more profitable than any other department of agriculture. The perpetual snows in the neighborhood furnish them with a never failing supply of pure water, which nourishes their meadows all the year round. The cattle were handsome and in good plight, but the poetry of the operation disappeared with the sight of the dairy-maid—a healthy, red-skinned fellow, clothed in a pair of short breeches, and having a one-legged stool strapped on behind, with which he went whisking about from cow to cow, filling his piggin with great alacrity. The idea of officering such a department with a man was shockingly unpicturesque. I was surprised to learn that an American-patented invention for milking was not unknown. But if the dairy-maid was not picturesque, the hay-makers certainly were. It was the mowing season. Peasants, men, women and children, in full Alpine costume, with broad straw hats and fluttering ribands, had come down to the work. Heavily laden hay-carts, drawn by fawn-colored, plaintive-eyed oxen, were returning from the fields. On every side extended a wilderness of green, interspersed with hedges and trees, upon which hang in soft marriage the clustering vine. In the distance, rose the snowy Alps, delicately illumined by the rosy rays of the evening. It was a scene of perfect rural felicity. How strange it seemed, too, that I should from the bank of a rice-field gaze upon the regions of eternal ice. The alacrity and respectful deportment of the employés struck me most agreeably and elicited remark; but I was informed, what is, indeed, true almost everywhere, that this was more apparent than real, and ceased with the business relation. The

Italians should be a happy people. The beautiful country, fine climate, the cheapness of necessaries, and even luxuries, when compared with American prices, ought to satisfy the most exigent. They have a greater taste for rural life than the nations to the north, which is not to be wondered at. The style of cultivation frees the country from the aspect of solitude which reigns in the foggy climes. Nor are they cursed with that class-character of disposition which erects such a barrier between the great landlord and all around, and which necessarily makes him lonely in his grandeur. But all this is nothing, so long as Austria sits at the gates of Verona. Italy needs, and must have, a Government which can secure to every one the fruits of labor, by protecting him against the eternal wars, revolutions, coups d'Etat, and states of siege, which seem chronic in some portions of Europe. If the late contest have secured this end, it will prove the most profitable investment of treasure that was ever yet made.

The City of Novarra is situate upon an eminence on the western border of the valley of the Ticino. It is a well-built place, surrounded by beautiful walks, which have been laid out on the dismantled walls, offering a fine view of Monte Rosa and the neighboring chain. The only prominent historical association, is the painful one of the great battle of 1849, which prostrated the Sardinian monarchy; at present, it was the theatre of very different emotions. During the whole night crowds perambulated the streets, singing patriotic songs and giving vent to their joy in other less appropriate manifestations. From this place it had been my purpose to visit the battle-fields, but there is very little to be seen at such places. The dead are soon interred, the peasants return, plough up the land, sow it afresh; and the only evidences of the late struggle are a few shot-torn farm-houses, and the increased fertility of the soil. The Governments in Europe, moreover, have a very unpleasant way of seizing the railroad trains, which they intended to do here for the purpose of transporting the French army back to France, so it might have been difficult to return. I, therefore, thought it better to proceed the next day immediately to Genoa. The train was filled with French officers returning from the war, in high spirits and well bronzed. One of them, a captain, had received a curious wound in the side at Magenta, a bayonette having passed between his spine

and his intestines without doing serious injury to either. He
was almost entirely restored. There seemed to be but one
opinion among them—regret and astonishment at the conclusion of the peace. It was evident that they felt themselves
compromised in the public estimation by the events of the
last few days, though without reason, as the Italians never
ceased to feel grateful to the French army which had so nobly
poured out its blood in their cause, whatever might be the
opinion entertained of the Emperor. Once, a friend came to
the window and asked them why they were returning: " *Eh !
ma foi ! la mission est faite,*" they exclaimed, but such was not
their real belief. Our journey was of a wholly military character. The bridge over the Po, near Valenza, was still lined
with gabions, placed there to defend the passage, while the
Austrians were west of the Ticino. At Alessandria, the Government seized our train, thereby affording us an unwelcome
opportunity of walking through the town, which offered nothing to our admiration, except soldiers and cannon and muni-
tions of war. I succeeded in getting on the next train, which,
threading the Maritime Alps by a magnificently engineered
road, at length issued from the great tunnel, and Genova la
Superba, surrounded by fortress-crowned summits, with the
deep blue Mediterranean extending to the southern horizon, lay
at our feet.

What can equal these mountain approaches to the Mediterranean, whether in Italy or Spain ? They seem gates into
Nature's Paradise. This favored sea has been, and ever will
be, the seat of beauty and civilization. That it witnessed the
triumphs of Greece and Rome, has added to, but did not origi-
nate its charms. In vain many other nations of Europe erect
splendid monuments, and surround themselves with all the
luxury of boundless wealth. The shores of the Mediterranean,
even in their desolation, possess a hidden and irresistible attraction, which will outweigh all their magnificence. No traveller
forgets his first entry upon its magic territory; I may be pardoned for recurring to my own. It was in the month of March,
before the completion of the railway to the Adriatic. We had
slowly, in the Eilwagen from Vienna, climbed the Semmering
Alp, and traversed a dreary, crumbling country in the midst
of snow and mist. The Grotto of Adelsberg had but served
to deepen the gloomy impression of the journey. Early the

next morning our little carriage reached the mountain pass, above Trieste. The coachman (honored be his memory!) with humane anticipation of our delight, halted the vehicle and awakened us. What a prospect saluted our wondering gaze! The North with its fogs and brawling blasts was gone; the lovely South smiled upon us. Underneath lay the city, surrounded by a vegetation that seemed tropical by comparison with the stunted shrubbery of Carniola and Styria. The hillside sparkled with villas just emerging from the shadows of the night. Far beyond stretched the Adriatic, its blue waters covered with sails, which the sun was beginning to tip with rosy light. Enveloping all, floated around us the pure air of Italy. Shall I be ashamed to confess that we spent the day seated upon the sea-wall, our legs dangling over the side, and our whole selves revelling in the *dolce far niente?* Now that I have seen Andalusia and Valencia, Naples and Genoa, I fear the view over Trieste would be common-place, but it was the first love, never to be forgotten.

One may travel through the world, and yet be astonished at the beautiful situation of Genoa, and the magnificence of its palaces. As to the former, it has been ranked with Naples, Lisbon, Constantinople, Algiers and Cadiz, as pre-eminent; and, whether seen from the sea or the land, is considered little inferior to its rivals. From every elevation a magnificent view is unrolled, uniting the elements in such a combination as is rarely to be found away from the Mediterranean. The city was filled with French, the wives and daughters of officers, and it was pleasant to witness their delighted surprise at scenes so far surpassing even *la belle France.* I remember strolling up one evening with a mixed party of French and Italians, on a grand fraternization to the Castelletto. As we reached the terrace, and the prospect burst upon us, one of the girls, a young Poitevine, daughter or niece of a Captain in the Guard, started as though she had lost her breath, and was so overpowered that for sometime she could only articulate " *Mon Dieu! comme c'est beau!*" until her companions became alarmed. At first I thought it mere Gallic affectation; but no, it was real emotion, I never before beheld such sensibility to the beauty of scenery as was manifested by this child. If that of Genoa needed commendation, the narration of this incident would be the most delicate compliment I could offer. Of course, the

young heroine is destined by nature for a poetess. We sat for
a long time listening to the hum of the busy city, the echoes
of the evening guns answering each other's reverberations,
the rolling of the drums, as the patrols passed along the narrow streets, and watching the ever-changing hues of the dying
day. Yet, with all its beauty, there is a want of sufficient
expansion in the prospect. It embraces only mountains and
sea, while Naples and Cadiz relieve the too sharp contrast by
undulating plains.

The Palaces of Genoa degrade most others, by comparison,
into mere dwellings. The grandeur of their dimensions is surpassed by the elegance of the architecture. It would be a useless task to describe what is familiar to all the world: if I am
to give a preference, it would be for the Palazzo della Scala,
than which I know nothing of its kind more exquisite. I visited it in the morning, when the light fell full upon the marble
staircase and rendered it almost dazzling. The cicerone says
that the occupant is a young bachelor. What a charming time
he must have, and what damsel so hard-hearted as to refuse the
owner of such a house! They are filled, too, with the works
of the best masters, among which, I confess, none pleased me
more than the portraits of a Marquis and Marchioness of the
Brignole Sale family in the Palazzo Rosso, executed in the best
style of Vandyke, and probably surpassed by none, unless it be
those of Charles I. I thought, too, that the distribution of the
pictures among the several collections, rendered the visits more
agreeable. Each contains about enough to please, without
wearying the mind and the body, as too often happens in the
enormous galleries of the capitals. Viewed simply from an
æsthetic point, these Genoese Palaces are beyond criticism;
from the historico-social, it is somewhat otherwise. The Pyramids of Egypt were at first objects of mere wonder, then of admiration, as proofs of the wealth and resources of a kingdom,
which could afford such magnificent mausoleums for its sovereigns. But subsequent philosophers have discovered in them
evidences of a frightful inequality, which could thus absorb the
labor of millions in gratifying the caprice or whim of a ruler.
The history of the Middle Ages, too, is yet to be written.
What more striking testimony to the utter insignificance of
the mass of contemporaneous mankind than the great feudal
fortresses with which Europe is studded. And so these palaces

are painful evidence of preponderance of a few, commanding the services of thousands to minister to their luxury—a state of things scarcely possible where the profits of industry were fairly divided between labor and capital. This system is perpetuated throughout Europe. I was told by a merchant—a prosperous one, it is true—that he paid a larger tax to the Government than capitalists whose income amounted to $60,000 a year.

The streets of Genoa, as of most southern cities, are narrow, scarcely more than ten feet in width, and the houses tall, so that not only heat, but light is excluded. No traveller in the month of July will complain of them for these peculiarities, but they are far from complete success, for the heat was suffocating. My great delight, and the only escape, was to go out three times a day beyond the mole and float about, without fear of shark or stinging-nettle. There is one pretty promenade upon the old rampart, which in the evening is thronged with ladies in a handsome summer costume, the chapeau being replaced by a white lace or muslin veil pinned to the hair and falling over the neck and shoulders somewhat after the manner of a Spanish mantilla. Yet, even with this advantage, there were few whom one would venture to call beautiful, nor did I think them particularly distinguished for grace. The fraternization between the inhabitants and the French was thorough; the sole subject of conversation was the peace, and but one opinion was expressed there, as elsewhere, without, however, disturbing the harmony of intercourse between the two nations. The annexation of Lombardy to Sardinia will redound more to the advantage of Genoa than any other city in Italy— for, since the invention of railroads, it has become the natural outlet of the whole sub-Alpine region, at least as far as the Mincio. The same builders up and pullers down of nations— railroads—have caused Trieste to absorb the trade of Venice, so that the three cities of Trieste, Genoa and Marseilles are engaged in the same struggle for the commerce of the Levant and prospectively of the East, which animates the Atlantic cities of our country in extending their connections with the West. Marseilles is backed by the powerful Empire of France, Trieste by Austria under the shield of the Germanic Confederation, to which, though an Italian town, it was most improperly annexed. Genoa must rely upon the valley of the

Po, the railroad over Mount Cenis, and, perhaps, over the St. Gothard, and, best of all, upon its free Government, securing to industry protection alike against the tyranny of Governments and the tyranny of mobs. It was natural, therefore, that the Genoese should desire a further increase of territory. The place was, moreover, converted into a vast magazine, and the military bureaus were daily distributing thousands of francs among the inhabitants. Sacks and barrels of provisions of every sort were piled upon the wharf, all useless now. A disagreeable circumstance for Governments, but a fortunate one for their people, that this amusement is so costly. Genoa is admirably fortified, all the heights being occupied, with the intention of rendering the place impregnable against their northern foe, should he penetrate thus far. So that, in the last resort, the monarchy might find a safe retreat, and, if necessary, revive the glories of Massena's defence. The land rises so abruptly from the water's edge that the place might be commanded from numerous points; but all the old castles have been dismantled to relieve the apprehensions of the citizens, as the Sardinian Government professes to rule by the voluntary submission of the people, not by virtue of ball and sword. The Genoese at heart are Republicans, and still sigh for their former independence, whose loss in 1815 they attribute to the English influence at the Congress of Vienna, and thank them accordingly. Their republican tendencies are excusable. Every allusion to their great countryman, Christopher Columbus, must bring to their minds the former greatness of their country and the happy continent beyond the water. The memorials of the discoverer are cherished here with veneration. There are three autograph letters in the Palace of the Municipality, which, somewhat out of season, were shown to me on the strength of my nativity, for we are considered his children. The intelligent young gentleman in charge of them seemed quite as enthusiastic as myself over the flourishing old Spanish hieroglyphics. Genoa may well be proud of her son. The character of few heroes will bear inspection; their epitaph is, too often, " the greatest, wisest and meanest of mankind;" but Columbus is worthy to stand beside Washington—peers in virtue as in renown, freemen and children of freemen.

When the time came for our departure, we found ourselves again incommoded by the superior necessities of State. The

regular steamer from Leghorn had been chartered by the
French Government to transport the victorious army to Marseilles, and we were placed aboard a miserable little affair,
which occupied four and twenty mortal hours in the passage.
The stewing heat of Italy rendered the sea breeze delicious,
and the fair weather enabled us to. enjoy it to the utmost by
spending the night on deck, thus cheating the ravenous herd
that awaited us in the cabin berths. No voyage can be more
agreeable than coasting thus along the magnificent shore of
Liguria. The lofty range of the Appenine and Maritime Alps
continued in sight the whole evening, and the effect of the
light upon their summits after the sun had disappeared below
the horizon and left their base in darkness, is not to be described to those who have never seen Italy.

Notwithstanding the smooth sea, most of the passengers,
particularly the women, were deadly sick; one lady of apparently a sound constitution, screamed vehemently, not to use a
stronger expression. The unfeeling nature of man was displayed in the vigor with which we supped, breakfasted and
dined in the midst of these unromantic sufferers. A poor
woman among the second-class passengers lay upon the deck
the whole time, a picture of misery. A little child of four
years of age, tearfully attempted to arouse her, until convinced
by a kind-hearted sailor that it was not death, when the confiding innocent, seemingly relieved, lay beside her and slept.
At dinner a lady feminine (I know not of what nation) sitting
at the table, which was on deck, on the side next to the bul-
warks, whenever overtaken, (an accident of triple occurrence,)
cooly turned her head, without leaving her seat, paid the penalty of those who go down to the sea in ships, and checked, but
not defeated, returned, smiling, again to the contest. The
person beside me incontinently left, handkerchief in mouth. I
had no idea of being thus cheated out of my meal, but it required a considerable effort of will. Her husband and the rest
of the company complimented her undying courage, and to
that, at least, she was entitled.

Our company was of the usual mixed description that throngs
the Mediterranean, a social *olla podrida*. Among others there
was an old Scotchman who had lived a long time in Texas,
while it was an independent State, and was thoroughly imbued
with our local prejudices. Quite unaffected and very sharp,

canny as canny could be, the old fellow narrated to me some occurrence in Leghorn, in a dramatic style, making each character speak for himself with national peculiarities. Among his *dramatis personæ* was an American, the peculiarity of whose conversation seemed to consist in the fact that it was entirely nasal and one-third of it oaths. I am sorry to say that both of these are considered characteristic of us in Europe. The latter, at least, is unfortunately too true. A practice which the English have almost given up, seems to have become more and more popular in America, with certainly little advantage to our eloquence. An Arab, two Commis, one decent enough, the other selfish, forward, boastful in the worst style of his class, an English merchant from Leghorn, his wife and maid, whom I made the usual and awkward error of mistaking for the mistress, and a French family roaringly sick, completed the list. The steamers in sight successively passed us; but the next morning we overtook near Les Isles de Hyere, a French fleet of four line-of-battle ships, and one frigate, exercising squadron manœuvres, and, as it was calm, we had the satisfaction of running them down. This is a regular manœuvring ground for the ships on the Toulon station, where the French marine is as carefully drilled as the army, and, if an opportunity were offered, would doubtless bear aloft the national standard upon the sea with as much credit as their countrymen have done on land. The French navy has entirely recovered from the demoralization of the revolution, and is officered by the best blood in France, for the army is too democratic to suit the relics of the old regime. Every one who has had an opportunity of comparing, can vouch for the difference.

Shortly after passing this squadron, the morning breeze died away, the sun became more radiant, the sick women howled louder than ever, the light-haired Commis still favored us with accounts of his heroism on various occasions, the mate and myself discussed radishes, until about noon, we were all delighted to see the Chateau d'If, and to glide into the enormous and odoriferous docks of Marseilles. With what sickening fury did the sun pour down his rays, and with what woful stenches did he surround the custom-house, where we were detained an hour in the enjoyment of these luxuries.

The progress of Marseilles in the last ten years, reminds one of our American cities. Its connection by railroad with Lyons on the one hand, and Bordeaux on the other, has opened to it the whole of France, while the extension of its commerce with Algiers and the Levant, has made it the mistress of the Mediterranean. Should the Isthmus of Suez be canaled, no bounds can be set to its greatness, though Trieste may prove a formidable rival. Our passports underwent a rigid inspection, and as a natural consequence, all honest men were delayed, while the rogues, if there were any, escaped free. It is strange that Europeans cannot be convinced of the folly of this system of obstructions. Inconvenient as it is to strangers, it must be infinitely more galling to natives, who, if out of their district, are liable to be arrested by any impertinent gens d'arme, and asked all sorts of questions, if nothing more. One must travel in Europe to appreciate the unspeakable blessings of American liberty. Being somewhat in a hurry, I took the night train, not, however, without seeing between the hackmen and the porter of the hotel, a specimen of the quarrelsome nature for which the lower class of Provençaux are distinguished in France. I was the unfortunate cause of the difficulty. The effect of the Revolution of 1789, in putting the bottom of society upon the top, is more apparent here than anywhere else in the country, though probably Lyons is a more dangerous place to the Government, as there the outbreaks are systematic. The cafés in Marseilles are magnificent, the handsomest in France, but they are filled with rowdyish looking blouses, as are all the thoroughfares. The better class of the population seem to withdraw from public, or at least disguise themselves when they appear. Certainly, they are not visible to a mere stranger. There is here none of that bonhommie to be found in the gatherings of Bordeaux, Strasbourg, or Rouen. Judging the Marseillais by those I have met in travelling, and at watering places, I should form a good opinion of them; judging them by the population in the streets, it is doubtful which way the balance would incline. However, I did not investigate them very closely upon the present occasion, as I left in the night train for the west, and they may not be as black as they paint themselves. I was much indebted to one of them for undertaking to wake me up at the junction, as travelling in vehicles at night has an overpowering somnolent effect upon me, and I should otherwise have found myself coursing up the Rhone.

Dawn broke upon us at Nismes, with its famous amphitheatre, the first specimen of its kind in Europe, except, perhaps, that of Verona. It has one great and not usual advantage, viz: that it can be seen. Montpellier, renowned in the annals of exile, whether by persecution or disease, next appeared. A few miles farther on we made a long halt at Cette, upon the Mediterranean. The station is some distance from the town, close to the shore. Gloomy clouds hung over the sea, and its waves beat sullenly upon the sandy beach. It made upon one the impression of being at the uttermost end of the earth, Cimmerian darkness beyond. We here took on a number of prisoners of war belonging to the regiment of Wasa, which was utterly destroyed at Solferino, the largest portion having been left dead or wounded upon the field, and the remainder, some six hundred, with the colonel and standard, taken prisoners in a church under peculiar circumstances. They were rather under the medium size of our people, and by no means so contented with their condition, as I had expected to find them. One of the non-commissioned officers spoke German, and we had a long conversation, winding up with a present of a handful of cigars (European), which is their great want. They were very kindly treated, and had no complaint to make of their captors. Now that the war was over, I wondered that they were not discharged. No such thought seemed to disturb them, as they made their purchases of provisions. From Cette we took the great road connecting the Mediterranean and the Atlantic, passing through the former province of Languedoc, dear to the French Protestants of the Carolinas, as the home whence many of them were driven by the stupid tyranny of Louis XIV. It is a pleasant, gently rolling country, resembling some portions of Spain, particularly in the absence of trees, an evil which the inhabitants have seen great reason to regret, but take no pains to remedy. The population is evidently a different race from the French of the North. They are more fiery in their appearance, but have that graceful courtesy which is characteristic of the South of Europe. Vineyards and olives covered the face of the earth. At one of the stations a gentleman entered who seemed to have more general information than is usual away from the great capitals. He expressed profound admiration for the Koszta affair, which he thought worthy of a great nation, and was sure that Captain Ingraham must be a hero.

I informed him that the gallant captain was a townsman of my own, no braggart, and one who would have done exactly what he threatened, had not the matter been satisfactorily arranged. What interested me particularly about this gentleman was, his knowledge of the literature of the Troubadours, and of the efforts made to preserve the few remnants of the customs of his province, which are rapidly disappearing under the centralism of Paris. He took it for granted that I was a poet, because, forsooth, I had read some of that literature, and was not unfamiliar with its distinguished names. Europeans, with their one-sided education, have no idea of the universal smattering which most Americans acquire, and are eternally mistaking us *at first* for *savans*. Even young Englishmen from the colleges know very little of the past, except the ancient classics and the wars of this century. My acquaintance once thought of emigrating to America, after the Revolution of 1830 had overthrown the Legitimists, and regretted not having done so. I suggested that it was never too late to do a good thing; but he said he had planted his beets and his vines, and they could not now be transplanted.

Nothing on the route interested me more than the distant view of Carcasonne. The new town on the western side of the river is built in the usual style, but the older portion, so far as outside appearance went, is a gem of the middle ages, and seems to have stepped out of a picture. Its lofty walls, machicoulis towers, and massive keep, were as well preserved as though the Saracen had retired yesterday from the siege. Most of the middle age fortresses are so hemmed in by modern buildings, and so much altered, that the isolated portions alone remind one of those old times. But this is left just as it was built, and I doubt whether there is a finer specimen in Europe.

The face of the country began to change somewhat as we approached Toulouse, and to show signs of a temperate climate. The city is interesting for its historical associations, rather than for any present beauty. It has one or two fine squares in the modern style, and a grand esplanade, but there was much more pleasure to be derived from wandering about the irregular, pebble-paved streets, which recalled the times of Raymond and his confreres, than gazing upon the glaring common places of later days. The number of fine old cities in France is great, and inhabited by pleasant people, but the concentration of every-

thing into the hands of the Government, and the location of
that at the capital, has taken the life out of them. The ambition of every Frenchman, noble or roturier, is to live at
Paris. The gradation of all employments culminates there.
Toulouse formerly was the seat of a fine university, rendered
illustrious by the name of Cujas, whose memory still lives in his
native place. It has been absorbed by Paris. Thither young
men of every occupation flock, ostensibly for the purpose of
studying, and return with the latest vices of the Quartier Latin,
to complain of the fate which has not furnished them with the
means of residing at the metropolis. I have frequently been
asked why I did not live in Washington. Charming idea, certainly! One day while I was at Seville, a party of French
engineers at the table d'hote were discoursing of the delights
of Paris. " But," said a Spaniard, " every Frenchman cannot
be born at Paris." " True, but every Frenchman can move to
Paris. I love my province, yet nothing could induce me to pass
fifteen days there. There is no place like Paris; it is the only
place in the world." " Yes," says another, "and the only place
in Paris is the Boulevard des Italiens." " Yes," says a third,
" and the only place in the Boulevard des Italiens is the Café
Tortoni." " And," maliciously, adds a fourth, " the only place
in the Café Tortoni is table No. 7." The metropolis, like the
loadstone mountain of the Arabian Nights, has drawn the bolts
from the trembling fabric of the provinces. I happened to be
at Bordeaux the fourth day of the *Coup d'Etat* in 1851. The
universal exclamation was, what can *we* do? We must await
the result of the contest in Paris. In 1814, the surrender of
Paris sealed the fate of Napoleon. Had the allied army, in
1793, marched upon Paris, the French Revolution would have
been strangled without difficulty. It is almost impossible to
estimate all the evil effects of such a system, which enlightened
Frenchmen are beginning to perceive, as it makes the happiness of millions a football between the garrison and the seething population of one or two faubourgs. " *Cette belle centralisa-
tion que toute l'Europe nous envie*," is by no means so common a
phrase as it was a few years ago. If the landed gentry would
copy the English in their attachment for a country life, as they
do in many less worthy respects, the evil might be somewhat
remedied; but the efforts of Louis XIV, aided by the Revolu-
of 1793, have effectually demoralized the French noblesse, who

have lost the last vestige of their local influence. The titles themselves are falling into disuse. Both the Napoleons endeavored to resuscitate the aristocratic idea by creating dukes who did not respect even their own appellations. As Duke de Magenta, McMahon is nothing, as Marechal de France, he is a great man. The example of the nobility in quitting their lands has been followed by the people, until the emigration into the cities has become a serious injury to the agriculture of the nation. The fathers of our Constitution showed their profound wisdom in requiring that every member of Congress should be an actual inhabitant of the State which he represents, and it is a pity that the provision could not be extended to every officer under the Government.

The present Emperor has not openly evinced any desire to decentralize France; and even if he wished so to do, it would be too great a venture at present. Indeed, his glory and strength consist in a brilliant government. As for attachment to his dynasty or to that of the Orleans family from any feeling of loyalty, even he must know that there is not a suspicion. The notion is laughable. The various revolutions have utterly eradicated any such sentiment, except here and there among the Legitimists. His influence is, therefore, individual, and the power must be jealously retained in his own hands. But the injustice and danger of the present system have not escaped his perception, and he has effected great reforms in some respects. The Government of Louis Philippe, and the efforts of those affiliated with him in political sentiments, were directed towards the establishment of a Bourgeoisie in its broad sense. That is to say, to the concentrating all the powers of Government into the cities, forgetting that by means of their superior knowledge of the art of party organization, and through the press, which is substantially confined to Paris, the cities already exercised far more influence over the country than they were entitled to either by their stake in the community or by their political integrity. Napoleon was elected by the rural population against the wish of the cities, though many of the bourgeoisie did vote for him from apprehension of the Socialists. He has in some measure restored the balance between them, and in so far has acted as a patriot. The great lines of railway have been completed, the provinces have received a share of the appropriations for internal improve-

4

ment, and the life blood has commenced flowing back to the
extremities. All this is entirely contrary to the Socialist
Government established in 1848. The sole idea then was to
squander the public treasure, drawn from the whole country, in
erecting National workshops where the idle of Paris might be
rewarded for lounging while the honest peasant toiled to pay
the taxes, which were to support the iniquitous system.
Maréchal Bugeaud, on his first entry into the Assembly immediately after the Revolution of 1830, exposed this abomination,
and was most unmercifully abused therefor. The experience of
our own country has shown that the great cities, with all their
enlightenment, are very unsound depositories of political power.
The complete decentralization of France is perhaps impossible
so long as it remains surrounded by jealous and powerful neighbors; but a great step might be safely made in that direction.
The blow given by the Emperor in 1859 to the aristocracy of
finance, was happily conceived, happily timed, and most happy
in its results. It had always been the habit hitherto to nego-
tiate the great Government loans through one or two bankers,
such as the Rothschilds, who made by the operation a certain
per cent., frequently without incurring risk. At least it has
always happened that the big suckers escape through the net
of national bankruptcy; the minnows only are caught. Nothing
could be more unjust than that the Kings of Change should
thus levy a tax upon the nation's necessities merely because of
the advantage given them by their overgrown fortunes and
central positions. We have seen something of the same kind
in our Mexican loans. Napoleon put an end to this abuse by
simply reversing the glass. The rate of interest was fixed, and
investments invited, the least amount having the preference.
The result so far as the treasury was concerned, is well known.
Treble the required amount was subscribed, and the speculators
were deprived of their toll. It was the egg of Columbus, and
hereafter the example will probably be followed on all ordinary
occasions.

The great encouragement which he gives to the commercial
interest reacts in the same direction, as it tends to counterbalance the social and financial preponderance of the metropolis.
But all this will avail little or nothing so long as the political
centralization continues, and that, in the present state of
affairs, seems unavoidable.

Sights at Toulouse are rare. Among them is a queer bass-relief at the Cathedral, representing Calvin in the shape of a hog, preaching. Underneath is written: " *Calvin, le porc prêchant,*" — a relic of the good old times not yet gone out of vogue in the South of France, when neighboring villages of different faith met midway to discuss their differences of belief by a few "apostolic blows and knocks." There is also a fine hospital, and a law school. But five or six hours suffice to see the wonders, and about sunset I took my place on the banquette of the Luchon diligence, fortunate to get even that amidst the throng of passengers for the Springs.

The country from Toulouse is very different from that we passed through in the morning, which had been treeless and verdureless. This was Piedmont, and the early light of the next morning disclosed the velvety turf of the Pyrenean valley, through which coursed the arrowy Garonne. A mist hung over the land, broken by occasional showers, but gradually cleared away, giving a fine view of the mountain wall that rose before us. The road followed the sinuosities of the river, ascending rapidly. At length we entered the stately avenue which leads to the village of Luchon, and, amid the recommendations of hotel valets and lodging-house keepers, and the friendly salutations of beggars, were deposited at the Bureau on the Alle d'Etigney. Fortunately the hotel to which I had been recommended was full, and I was transferred to an apartment upon the square in front of the bathing house, which commanded a beautiful view of the mountains and the valley of the river, with an obliging landlord, and a couple of brisk Luchonaises, his daughters, who charged themselves with the care of the outer man.

CHAPTER III.

BAGNÈRRES DE LUCHON.

The situation of Bagnèrres de Luchon was a surprise. After
Baden Baden and the other Rhine spas, I was far from expecting that any spot could be found to rival them; but I must
candidly give my preference to this pride of the Pyrenees. The
mountain chain here attains in the Maladetta its greatest
elevation, some twelve or thirteen thousand Spanish feet, and
presents those indispensable requisites of grand mountain scenery in this climate—glaciers and perpetual snow. The valley of the Garonne enters the range almost perpendicularly,
with enough variation in direction, to diversify the ride. Bagnèrres de Luchon is some two thousand feet above the sea (the
same elevation of the village of Asheville, in Buncombe.) Just
below the town the valley divides; the left or southern leads
to the Port de Benasque, and by another branch to the Val
d'Aran, the right to the Valley d'Arboust and the Lac d'Oo.
What had been lofty hills now become mountains, and close in
upon the river which is transformed into a torrent. Cultivation of the cereals ceases, except here and there a patch upon
the slopes. Numerous subordinate valleys branch in from the
principal one, leading to meadows and cascades, glistening
amid the luxurious foliage until the bare and bleak summit is
attained, offering savage views over Aragon to the south, and
beautiful landscapes on the side of France. The Pyrenees are
certainly not so grand as the Alps. They offer nothing to rival
the view from the Col de Baume over the Valley of Chamouni
and Mont Blanc. Indeed, what country can? Many years
have elapsed since, after a long morning's walk from Martig-
ny, I crossed the crest and stood overwhelmed by the majesty

of that scene. But it is as vivid in its recollection as of yesterday. Except the Rock of Gibraltar, nothing so deeply im-
presses one with the consciousness of the utter insignificance of
man. The green valley of Chamounix almost lost in the distance; the bare rocks lifting themselves out of endless glaciers,
that had existed and moved before man disturbed the harmony
of the universe; Mount Blanc, monarch of all in its spotless
robe, placidly towering far above, unruffled by the commotions
of man or nature, wrapped in the dead silence peculiar to that
elevated atmosphere, and so necessary to the enjoyment of
sublime emotions. It was a place to bow down and worship in
sincere abasement, the Creator who made them and us alike.
There is nothing equal to it here. Nor can the Pyrenian chain
offer lakes such as Lucerne or Como, Geneva or Maggiore.
But then it has visions of pastoral beauty to which Switzerland
in turn has no counterpart; valleys that would satisfy the
dreams of an Arcadian poet; gentle landscapes or rather pan-
oramas rolling out over the fair plains of Languedoc, and
scenes of wild gradeur over the mountains of Aragon and
Catalonia, which, if not so sublime as the Alps, are far more
impressive. The valleys, too, offer more variety, and a never
ending change of light and shade is produced by ascending or
descending a few hundred feet, offering under a different play
of light a different view. From any given spot, too, there is a
far greater choice of excursions, than in the Alps, owing partly
to the opposite physical character of the two sides of the
Pyrenees. But it would be better to say, first, a word upon the
town itself:

Bagnèrres de Luchon must always have been a mountain
outpost of considerable importance, at least in the middle
ages, when the rule among mountaineers was universal that—

> Those get who have the power,
> And those keep who can.

During the eighth and ninth centuries, the country on both
sides of the mountain was from time to time in possession of
the Spanish Arabs of the Empire of Cordova, and for many
years after its downfall, the Mohammedan rule was perpetuated
in the country of Saragossa by the family of Beni Hud. The
mountains themselves were probably in the possession of the
Spanish aboriginal inhabitants who, accustomed to the endur-

ance of every privation, and without the sentiment of fear,
always preserved an actual independence, until a late date,
when they have succombed to the enticement of civilization and
luxury. Travellers with well stuffed purses have conquered
those whom no armies could subdue. This is universal history, and many have wisely thought that the Florida Indians
might have been driven out without shedding a drop of blood,
and at one-tenth of the expense, by simply cutting off their
intercourse with civilization, and subjecting them to the privation of whisky and gunpowder. I fear the Luchonais would
be equally incapable of resistance. The village was evidently
considered in those days a military outpost for the defence of
the fertile country below. It commands one of the finest
entrances for a foraging party into France. The situation of
the Castel Viel, about which there have been so many disputes,
would demonstrate its purpose, and nothing could be better
calculated for defending the entrance from the Port de Benasque or Val d'Aran, occupying as it does a rock at their junction
and entirely commanding the approach. Frequently as I sat
upon its summit, enjoying the beautiful evening view, and saw
the Aragonese peasants coursing down the path, have I fancied
myself transported back to the time when the watchman kept
his guard, and would have sent winged warning of the approach of danger, and I have felt called upon to admire the
admirable judgment which the Middle Age warriors displayed
in the selection of such posts. The entrance down the valley
of Arboust is similarly defended. These towers are supposed to
be of Moorish origin. There are no other relics left of that dominion. The Romans, however, seem to have been fully aware
of the excellence of the water of Luchon, and a great many
votive offerings, made in gratitude for a renewed lease of life
and health, are preserved in the Museum at Toulouse. One
is still shown at the bathing house here, bearing inscriptions of
gratitude from T. Claudius Rufus and Fabia Festa, the former
to the nymphs, the latter to the God Lixon, from whom the
place derives its name. But the barbarians who succeeded to
the empire of the Romans, did not inherit their cleanliness or
perhaps their maladies, and the virtues of its water remained
comparatively forgotten, until about the middle of the last century. For a long time it was forbidden to search in the hill
for new springs, lest the existing ones should be injured; but

of late, excavations have been scientifically conducted with unexampled success, greatly increasing the amount and sometimes the strength of the water. At present there are sixty-four different sources, all of which, except eight, are due to these skillful investigations, and the daily yield is more than eight hundred thousand litres. Though the principal ingredient is sulphur, the combination is different in them all, and the temperature varies from 80° to 150° or more degrees, so that the advice of a physician is necessary to invalids, otherwise great injury might result from their use. The bathing facilities are superb—plunge baths, sitting baths, tubs, douches, inhalation, aspiration, and every other variety, all under one grand establishment, which is regulated by the Government of the Commune, so that there is never confusion as to time or person. The alternating douch is very pleasant to those who are not sick. The performer, in an oil cloth suit, stands at one side of a room, with a muzzle of gutta percha, or some such substance in each hand, and plays upon you first with the warm, then the cold, then the warm again, then both together, until the epidermis is most effectually scoured, and the vigor of existence elevated to the highest point. The water is also taken internally, but in much more moderate quantities than our physicians in America are in the habit of prescribing. It is strenuously advised by the attendants to cease the use of the water for a few days in the middle of the cure, and leave the locality entirely. Experience has shown that the efficacy of the treatment is thereby doubled. The valley abounds also in springs of a chalybeate nature; of the invigorating effects of the one at the Castel Viel, I can speak from experience. They say at Luchon that the temperature and strength of the mineral waters increase in proportion to the height of the range, at whose base they are situate, but as Luchon is just where the Pyrenees attain their greatest elevation, this statement may not be the result of strictly impartial deduction.

In consequence of the spread of its reputation, Luchon has become transformed into a regular watering place. The old town no longer suffices for the accommodation of its numerous visitors, and a new one, in modern style, has been erected. Commodious hotels and lodging houses line the Allée d'Etigny on both sides, up to and beyond the bathing house, and all the comforts of life abound. The neighboring forests are filled

with game, small and large, including still a few bears and
wolves: The Museum contains specimens of the bouquetin,
which must be glorious sport. The bears, to judge by one that
was brought in during my visit, differ little in size or appearance from those of our swamps, but have a more ferocious
aspect. Very few visitors hunt them, and the natives do not
seem to know much about the scientific way of doing the thing.
They are not sufficiently cultivated to regard Bruin in any
other light than that of a thief and a robber, for sporting generally enters very little into the amusements of the French.

The situation of Luchon is admirable, whether for health or
recreation. The valley spreads out to a considerable width,
forming rather a basin, which is speckled over with hamlets,
and thronged with the most pestilential brood of beggar children to be found in Europe. The adult population is entirely
given up to the entertainment of the visitors—not that they
are without the expectation of a recompense: but they have,
at least, the good taste to prevent this object from appearing
too openly on the surface, and there is room left for the flattering doubt whether your personality do not enter for something
into the politeness with which you are received. The local
costume is not pretty, nor are the neighboring villages distinguished for cleanliness, but the new portion of Luchon is quite
satisfactory even to a critical invalid. The bathing establishment is unrivalled for its conveniences, which are peculiarly
necessary at sulphur baths, owing to the liability to take cold
in these damp valleys, on the north of the chain. The attendants are courteous and capable. Take it all in all, I know no
place of the kind so well conducted.

Immediately behind the bathing establishment rises a spur
of the mountain, called Supra-Bagnèrres, whence there is a fine
view over the village and the valley. Few more animated and
variegated scenes can be found than that presented by the
Allée d'Etigny at noon. There are the white hotels lining the
street on each side, between them the dark foliage of the four
rows of trees arching above, and beneath this perpetual shade
a sauntering, ever-moving throng of all nations—the inhabitants in the provincial costume; guides with close-fitting jack-
ets, a slender, active, jaunty-looking set; Aragonese traders,
beautifully and powerfully formed, with flashing Spanish eyes,
dark hair and striped mantas. Every now and then a fierce,

half wild Catalonian peasant offers the wares of his province.
Anon comes an Englishman, with a tall, strapping lady on each
arm, in the manner irreverently styled *à la chandelle* or *en
sandwich;* here a Parisienne with the latest fashion, mouse
colored boot, and little hat, all worn with inimitable grace;
and sometimes, but rarely, glides by one of those matchless
forms of beauty, one of those pensive faces, with deep, expressive eyes which Spain alone can produce. Every now and then
the crowd opens, to make way for some city gentleman from
Marseilles or Bordeaux, who is venturing his first essay at
horsemanship, with feelings depicted on his countenance which
all may interpret, but none envy. As the shades of evening
begin to fall, the scene is shifted to the little square and before
the bathing establishment, when the crowd is increased by
numerous nurses and children, the latter playing with distress-
ing propriety and regard for *les convenances.* There is one
great want at Bagnèrres, that is, a conversation-house or Kur-
saal, as it is called at the German spas, in some central place,
where balls could be given and promenades made in bad
weather. The old frequenters complained much of the change
which has come over the sociability of the place. In former
times, several of the more distinguished guests were in the
habit of holding conversazioni, to which entrance was easily
obtained, and the intercourse continued, if agreeable to both
parties. Now, all is formal and ceremonious. The fact is probably true, but it is in the nature of our modern civilization.
We have the same yearly complaints nearer home. Formerly
wealth and its advantages were inherited and had been enjoyed
by their possessor in the formation of his manners. Now they
are most frequently acquired, and are no evidence of elegant
deportment or correct morals; indeed, rather the contrary.
But there is yet a much greater appearance of good breeding
here than at most watering places. The whole race of fancy
gents is wanting; no 2:40 trotters, or long 9's. The orthodox
way of passing the day is to rise at or before dawn and take a
bath, as it is said to be much more efficacious when the pores
are relaxed by sleep. Invalids then return to bed until the
bath fever is over. The sound in body and mind take a short
walk and breakfast. Universal activity immediately ensues.
Every species of locomotive apparatus is pressed into service,
from the donkey up to the four-horse calêche, and to the sound

of cracking whips, echoed around the valley, the universal population is off for some excursion. Those who get back in time
repeat the bathing and drinking process; then dine, and then
the ball, if there be one, which was rare during my sojourn.
These excursions are under the charge of the guides, whose
leadership, however, is interfered with sometimes by powerful
divinities. That ubiquitous rascal, Cupid, is frequently about;
Diana, too, and, at times, Mercury. Be that as it may, if one
has pleasant acquaintances, the day does slip by with astounding rapidity. ·

It is in excursions that Luchon is peculiarly rich, and they
are in regular gradations from a half-hour's walk to a journey
on horseback of twelve or fourteen hours, or of two or three
days to the summit of the Maladetta. Walking, however, is
not a favorite means of progression on the continent. For a
gentle evening stroll, there is nothing more delightful than the
avenue on the bank of the river along the *Allée des Veuves*. A
promenade by the villages of Mamet and Montauban in addition offers a water-fall, rather puny, but a very slight variation
to the monotony becomes interesting at such places. A visit to
the Castel Viel requires more time. The other excursions are
generally made on horseback.

The first requisite is a guide, about which there is no difficulty, as the excursions are rarely attended with risk. The
whole system of guides, as every thing else, is under the
Government organization, prices both of men and horses being
regulated according to a tariff, and a previous examination
being required to test their capacity. It is very seldom that
one is dissatisfied with his choice, as they unite every requisite
for their profession. Small, and not so physically powerful as
the Swiss, they are lithe, active, and graceful. Indeed, as they
are always on horseback, and have especial charge of the
ladies, they may be said to be even elegant in their manners.
They are ever ready to draw with invariable good humor upon
an inexhaustible fund of small talk, some of it quite instructive
to those who have any curiosity to penetrate beneath the surface of society. They have a proper pride in their country,
and are always prepared to defend it against the assumed superiority of Switzerland. Nor are they wholly given up to the
skinning of the traveller. They are the perfection of guide for
this place — talkative if you wish to talk; silent if you wish to

meditate; and having enough of the *savoir faire* to be agreeable companions. The habit of galloping thirty or forty times a year over the country renders them familiar with every inch of the ground, and acquainted with the effect of light and shade, so necessary to the selection of the proper hour of the day for each visit. Of course, their knowledge is superficial. But what do you expect? The guide is not a schoolmaster.

The first excursion that we undertook was to the Lac d'Oo. It is necessary to start at an early hour, as the effect of the scenery is greatest some hours either before or after the meridian, so that daylight found us in the saddle. The Luchon horses are small, active, long-winded, and exceedingly sure footed, resembling our marsh tackies: They do not make much speed, but they seem to, and the pleasure is pretty much the same. Our two guides kept up a great cracking with their whips as we walked down the Allée d'Etigny, according to the regulation, which forbids even trotting through this street. The cracking of the whips seems to be an indispensable part of the performance, and it is necessary to submit to it. The magic word to increase the speed of mules and donkeys is "arri," which is said to be Provençal. In Spain it is pronounced "arré," whence the word "arriero," a driver of mules or donkeys. But both are from the same Arabic expression, used for the same purposes, and its presence in Provence is a lingering remnant of the Moorish domination. Our horses needed no encouragement, however, and bounded along the highroad as much inspirited by the morning air as ourselves. The country of Arboust as far as the village of Oo was well cultivated, and for a mountain region thickly settled, in the old style, the hamlets being perched where they might be defended against a sudden assault. At Oo we took the country road, and soon reaching the head of the valley, commenced a steep ascent of zig-zags, which occupied considerable time. As yet, though the ride had been very agreeable, the scenery presented nothing striking; but we suddenly attained the level of the lake, and the view well repaid the journey. The stream, as most others in these mountains, descending from the summit of the chain, forms deposits of water in basins at successive heights. There seems to be no doubt that both sides of the Pyrenees were once covered with snow and glaciers far down in the valleys. The disappearance of these evidences of former

cold, both here and in the Alps, would seem to militate against
the theory which maintains that the world has been gradually
cooling. But that subject must be left to philosophers, though
we discussed it at the time with vast gravity. There are at
present no signs of lakes below the region of vegetation, and
the few that remain are doomed to disappear in the course of
events. The Lac d'Oo is filling slowly by the double effect
of the cascade from the Lac d'Espingo, in wearing away the
precipice and in precipitating its debris into the water. As yet,
it has not suffered much, and is about large enough to suit the
scenery around. The mountain cliffs, denuded of all vegetation, rise nearly perpendicularly from its western edge. On the
east there is room for the path which leads up to the summit of
the chain, so that it is completely walled in except on the north,
by which we entered. Our arrival was well-timed, the lake of
dark blue being still in the morning shade, but the light
reflected from the western cliff penetrated its waters to the
very bottom. It is scarcely more than a half mile in length up
to the cascade that empties the surplus of the lakes above, the
roaring of whose waters was the only sound heard in this solitude; nor was there any sign of life except the *chalet* and the
little boat which plies across to the cascade. Without entering
more into detail, it may be safely affirmed that the scene
deserves its reputation. The horse path ceases here, but foot
passengers can continue to mount by a cow trail to the Lac
d'Espingo, which I did alone with one of the guides, for the rest
of the party remained below. The Lac d'Oo is between four
and five thousand feet high; that of Espingo some one thousand
feet higher, but greatly inferior in beauty. The waters have
receded considerably, owing to the gradual wearing away of
the ledge over which the stream pours. The margin thus left
is covered with luxuriant herbage, and is the pasturage-ground
of the Commune, whose cattle pass the summer here. At a
rough guess, the surface of the lake must have once been five
hundred feet higher than at present. The path, if path it can
be called, continues to scale the mountain leading to the Port
d'Oo. None but smugglers and hunters, and they very rarely,
ever pass this way. There are three other small lakes. At the
second, we turned off to the left, towards the Lac Glacé. Here
there was no sign of a path, and, though the horizontal distance
is scarcely a mile and a half, it was one of the toughest walks I

ever undertook, and I count myself a good pedestrian. It was very much like ascending the pyramids. Perhaps the rarity of the atmosphere was partly to blame, for it is eight thousand feet above the level of the sea. All who desire to enjoy wild scenery should not fail to make this excursion. Its wildness does not consist simply in the absence of animal and vegetable life, but desolation seems to have become aggressively positive. The guide said it was a fine place to hunt bears, but the inducements that could prevail upon even a bear to haunt such a spot were certainly not visible, as the prospect on all sides is over naked rocks. The descent was scarcely less fatiguing than the ascent, and it was long past noon when we rejoined our party at the chalet d'Oo. A lunch well earned, and well paid for also, restored my spirits, and we cantered back to the village. The excursion to the first lake is a favorite one with visitors. Few venture to attempt the Lac Glacé, nor would it be advisable for any who are not willing to make considerable physical exertion. But for such it is the first of all.

Up the Valley of Lys is much easier, and, so far as beauty goes, more attractive. The road ascends gently through pasturages and by cascades up to the head of the valley. For some distance in advance can be seen the Cascade d'Enfer, embosomed in the dark green of the firs. I effected a rough measurement by dropping stones, which succeeded very well, to judge by the agreement between the times. Above the Cascade d'Enfer is another—the Cascade du Cœur. The headwaters of the stream forming these cascades are separated from the Lac Glacé by the Glacier of Crabioules, but the scenery of the two valleys is totally different. Yesterday the face of nature was stern and rigid; to-day it was covered with smiles. This is really the place for a hunter. The little bridge above the second cascade, the only connection between the banks of the cleft for a long distance, has been the death spot of many a bear; and as they cannot transmit their experience from one to another, it will probably continue fatal to the doomed race. This excursion being of easy accomplishment is very popular. The valley is surpassed by few in the Alps for its pastoral beauty, and every thing connected with it is in unison.

For panoramic views, it is necessary to ascend the Boucanère, situated to the north-east of Luchon, and to some extent isolated from the Pyrenees. The journey requires a whole day and fair weather, but it is worth the trouble. We were not fortunate in the weather, for the plain to the north was overspread with a haze. To the south, however, we enjoyed a glorious view of the Maladetta, and the whole chain extending a considerable distance east and west. Below us were the valleys of Luchon and Aran, with their tributaries, their green fields in beautiful contrast with the snowy peaks above. It was truly magnificent.

The etymology of the word "Pyrenees," has puzzled the learned. The Greeks derived it from the fire continually burning upon it in the forests. The inhabitants still insist upon the *Pics Nérés*—Black Peaks. The Celtic scholars say *Birrennou*, the plural of *Bir*—a peak. The peaks certainly are not black, nor is there any account of fires raging on their sides, and the view from Boucanère would prove, at least, the applicability of the last derivation. The word which, by common consent; has been adopted to signify a "pass," (*Port* in French, *Puerto* in Spanish,) is certainly from the Latin, though it was not the common word used by the Romans. No other modern nations use it, and no other ancient, so far as I know, except the Greeks, though it would seem the most appropriate.

One day while the rest of the party were reposing after their fatigue, I strolled over to the Val d'Aran. A mule path leads up to the Port du Portillon, which is scarcely more than five thousand feet high, and offers nothing remarkable. The ascent is quite rapid as far as a valley half way up, level and well cultivated; thence it traverses a thick wood, and, at the summit of the pass, we enter Spanish territory according to the treaty, but not by natural boundaries, for the Val d'Aran is upon the head-waters of the Garonne, and the natural boundary would give the whole of it to France. The French claim even more, for the waters of the eastern slope of the Maladetta disappear in the earth at the Trou du Taureau, and penetrating under the Sierra, rise again near Viella. But their southern neighbors will scarcely consent to part with any portion of the Maladetta, which is essentially Spanish in appearance and character. The Val d'Aran is by no means so, yet such is the influence of government and association, that the inhabitants of Canejan and those of Fos, both upon the Garonne, and within cannon shot of each other, are said to differ as much as Calais and Dover.

A half hour's walk brought me to the Spanish custom-house, where I fraternized upon a mug of milk and a good segar, and exchanged a few words of Castillian. The common language of the people is a harsh Catalonian patois, quite unintelligible to a Spaniard. A half hour more brought me to the Chapelle St. Antoine, situate on the edge of the wall that lines the valley. Whether this view be celebrated or not is more than I can say, but it deserves to be, for I have seen but one in the same style which merits a comparison. In the summer of 1851, a young friend, who has since attained enviable distinction in the world of letters, and myself, stopped for dinner at the village of Nauders, in the valley of the Inn, on the borders of Tyrol. After finishing the meal, the damsel of the house, in her grenadier hat, put us on the way to the Engadine, in Switzerland. Guide book in hand, we crossed the meadow, threaded the little copse, ascended the mountain side, turned the edge of a wood, and gazed down into what seemed a miniature Paradise, where the serpent had never entered—the beautiful Swiss valley of the Engadine. Those who have done the same, will need no description. It was the perfection of Alpine scenery, and though I have visited many renowned valleys since, its impression has never been weakened. The prospect from the Chapel of San Antonio recalled it instantly, and yields to no other rival. Seen, as I saw it, it is the gem of the excursions from Luchon. The valley is quite broad, and chequered over with variegated fields of grain, in different stages of maturity, extending to Castel Leon, in the direction of Biella. Towards the north, the prospect embraced the gorge at the Pont du Roi, which forms the boundary between France and Spain. Down the valley placidly flowed the Garonne, washing the suburbs of numerous villages, the principal being Bosost, and perched upon the cliffs were others, whose white walls glistened in undefiled purity. No animate thing appeared to disturb the harmony of the prospect, as though eternal serenity had chosen here a resting-place. I feared to continue the descent, lest the sight of dirty streets and idle beggars should disturb the illusion, and would have willingly spent the day upon the rock, watching the shadows of the clouds as they floated slowly over the landscape. A couple of boys broke in upon my revery with a request for coppers, consenting, in return, to dance the Jota. The performance was not very distinguished, though given with a hearty good will, but it broke the charm and I returned. Descending from the Portillon, I encountered a custom-house officer, a French Basque, on the look out for Spanish segars, which form the principal object of contraband in this locality. We returned together to his post. He had little fancy for the Aragonese and Catalonians, whom he represented as very much given to using the stick upon each other, and occasionally upon a *Douanier*, wherefore he always carried a gun, unloaded for fear of accidents. He was quite familiar with the adjoining provinces of Spain, and strongly recommended a friend of his as my guide, which recommendation I followed, little to my subsequent satisfaction. On rejoining our party at dinner, I was loud in my praises of the Chapel of San Antonio, and we repeated the excursion next day with increased gratification, abstaining from a farther descent into the valley, as I sincerely counsel all tourists to do. With this precaution, they can scarcely fail to be satisfied with the Val d'Aran.

There were many other excursions around Luchon worth an effort, and the season still continued at its height, the number of visitors daily increasing. French and Belgians there were in abundance, and a few Russians, with a scattering of English; one family lodging in my own house, with whom I struck up an acquaintance. Two good-looking young ladies, with long flaxen curls, questionable ornaments to my taste, and a mama, whose "*bullion pour le petty gerson.*" afforded great amusement to the lively Luchonaise that waited upon me. There was also an American family in Luchon, at least I one day heard some persons at the spring talking in a nasal tone, and saying "nawthin'" for nothing, which is an unerring indication of a certain locality. But we were about to separate, with a rendezvous in Andalusia, and under such circumstances, a longer sojourn at Luchon would have been devoid of most of its interest. So that I sent for the friend of the Douanier, who agreed, at ten francs a day for himself and each horse, to escort me to Barbastro in Aragon. The rest of the party proceeded to Marseilles, to take the steamer for the South.

CHAPTER IV.

LUCHON, BY BARBASTRO, TO ZARAGOZA.

The Port de Venasque—The Maladetta—Entrance into Spain—Scenery—Venasque—The Castillian—Change Guides—Le Peña de Ventinella—Campo—The Bota—Sta. Liestra—The Young Student—Graus—Scenery of Aragon—Barbastro—Company to Huesca—Sertorious—Arrive at Zaragoza.

The sun shone brightly over the eastern mountains, one of the latter days in July, as we mounted our horses for the journey, myself on one, the guide on another, and a third loose with the baggage. The rapid rising of the mist foreboded rain, but the guide stood security for good weather, and we sped up the valley at a brisk trot. The Castel Viel was still in the shade as we halted a moment at the chalybeate springs, to take a last draught of its precious water. After an hour's ride, the road branched off to the left towards the hospitalet, and we pursued our way up the ascent through the most beautiful mountain wood imaginable. Covering the steep side above and below down to the foaming torrent, extended slender beech trees, whose height recalled our own forests. From time to time little streams bounded down over the road, adding their refreshing murmurs to the shade, which we found agreeable enough after the scorching sun of the valley, for Jean was already in a profuse perspiration. These forests are under the protection of the Commune, which accounts for their preservation. Continuing our journey, we gradually ascended above the region of trees, then the bushes vanished. At last, about noon, we reached the hospitalet on the mountain bosom, where every species of vegetation disappeared, except the short, vigorous grass of the pasturages. We here called a halt of a half hour to refresh the animals and ourselves. The black-eyed damsel, who served the wine, informed me that upon the setting in of the winter season, they all migrated to

5

the village, leaving, as they were compelled by law to do, some provision and a list of charges, and that a theft of the articles so left was unknown. This sounded very much like a *canard*, but such was formerly the case in Switzerland to the extent of leaving the shops unprotected. The progress of civilization is rapidly doing away with these antiquated barbarisms. A few years more, and such vestiges of primeval ignorance will have disappeared even from the recesses of the Pyrenees.

The view around the hospitalet commences to be interesting. Its situation is sufficiently elevated to afford glimpses of the distant horizon, and is yet within the region of life. The tinkling of bells floating down the mountain side revealed the flocks that were peacefully browsing above. A long train of goats were slowly winding up the track to the Pic de l'Anticade, which seemed of immense height. On the left ran the path to the Port de la Picade, and in front towered the Port de Benasque, which we were to scale—a naked, forbidding aspect, relieved only by the tents of a few road-workers, who were repairing the injuries of the last storm. We recommenced the journey by a path which my unpracticed eyes could not detect from the hospitalet, though looking back from above, its windings could be easily followed. The ascent was very steep. For a couple of hours we really toiled, mounting zig-zags scarcely fifty feet in length. We finally entered one of the basins so common in the Pyrenees, once the bed of a lake. Then came the four pools, at different heights, filled with almost black water—lonely jewels in a setting of adamant. After that, was another basin surrounded by lofty perpendicular walls, from which I saw no outlet. It was the dwelling-place of desolation. Vast masses of distorted rock lay heaped around, as though the place had been blasted by the curse of an avenging Deity. In all the shady spots were collections of snow, slowly distilling the head-waters of the Garonne. Overhead hung the ink-blue sky of these altitudes. The view towards France over the plains of Languedoc and Gascony was boundless. Luchon had disappeared; its valley had become a thread, l'Anticade a mere mole-hill. No sound disturbed the death-like silence, nor was aught of life visible, except the white speck far, far below, representing the hospitalet. We mounted on the left by a break-neck path, suspended between heaven and earth, such as makes the traveller feel himself entirely at the mercy of his horse. Suddenly turning, I saw above me the Port de Benasque—a simple split in the rocky wall, just wide enough for a loaded mule to pass, and not more than ten feet in length. We ascended a staircase of ziz-zags, some fifteen feet each, entered the pass, and beheld one of the grandest views in the world. It was Spain! noble, romantic Spain! Adieu pretty landscapes! meandering brooks and verdant prairies! luxurious couches and artistic meals! Adieu to the circean enticements of Europe! Adieu to a civilization which reduces men to machines, which sacrifices half that is stalwart and individual in humanity to the false glitter of centralization, and to the luxurious enjoyments of a manufacturing, money age! Welcome, *dura tellus Iberiæ!* Welcome to your sunny plains, your naked mountains, your hardy sons and your beautiful daughters! your honored cities, sacred by the memorials of a dozen rival civilizations, and your fields watered by the chivalric blood of as many contending races! As an American, thrice welcome to the land of Isabella, of Columbus, of Las Casas! Yes, it was Spain. I reined in my horse, and gazed silently upon the scene. Directly in front rose the savage, craggy mass of the Maladetta, the monarch of the Pyrenees, draped in robes of eternal white. No Eastern sovereign ever sat in more solitary grandeur. Unconnected even by a spur, it stands alone as though scorning companionship with humble satellites. A deep valley lay between us, so that the view embraced its steep sides from the summit to the base. Unlike Mount Blanc, it does not rise to a well-defined peak, but is somewhat elongated, presenting several points of rival height. To the north it is covered by enormous glaciers, from which the disengaged rocks go thundering down. The pine forest had been prostrated by numerous avalanches, and the bleaching trees lay regularly arranged as though the triumphing storm-giant had thus placed the trophies of his victory. The Maladetta is so called from its terrific aspect, and from its interposing a dangerous, and in certain seasons, insurmountable obstacle to the inter-communication between the valleys of Benasque, Aran and Viella. For a long time its ascent was deemed one of the irresolvable problems, until successfully accomplished by a Russian engineer, whose experience in the Ural mountains gave him superior

knowledge of the means of overcoming the difficulties presented by its treacherous glaciers. The excursion is now safe,
and of comparatively easy performance, under the charge of
guides expressly designated for the purpose. From its snows,
spring the head-waters of the Esera, and, strange to say, of
the Garonne also, which disappear under ground, and rise
again on the northern side of the dividing ridge in the Val
d'Aran. A party was up on the Maladetta to-day, and their
horses and attendants were visible in the valley below, where
they had bivouacked the previous night.

The Port de Benasque being, as said, a narrow slit in the
perpendicular mountain wall, is a famous place for the wind,
which almost blew me off my horse. Jean informed me that
when the winter winds really do blow, the common adage holds
true, that the father does not wait for the son; and I think
myself, that whatever might be the strength of paternal affection, it would be very difficult to withstand such a current. An
advance of a few feet from the pass caused the view to open to
the right and left, the latter toward the Port de la Picade, the
former down the Valley of Benasque. The force of the sun
now became very great; it was the glorious sun of Spain, and
its genial rays inspired us with renewed energy. Nor was
this the only proof that we were out of France; the pathway
immediately offered such an appearance as would have thrown
McAdam into an epileptic fit. No doubt the Gauls and Iberians saw it just as we did. We found it more convenient to
dismount and pick our way, leaving the road to the horses. A
descent of a half hour brought us to the Spanish hospitalet at
the head of the valley, a vile concern into which I did not
enter, being quite content with the odor and the sight of the
woman preparing tripe in a neighboring rivulet. I preferred
strolling off to the Esera, and taking an icy bath in the shade
of the Maladetta. A bath is certainly not romantic, but there
are spots, the grandeur of whose impression cannot be impaired, and this is one of them. It is impossible to avoid being
penetrated by the poetry of the nature around. The last
hour's journey had unmistakably transported us into a different land, morally, physically and geologically. Nature wore a
different aspect. The merely beautiful had given place to the
serious, earnest, perhaps stern, but grand—fit emblem of the
inhabitants. A dead silence, the silence of the eternal snow

reigned undisturbed, save by the roaring of the water, or anon
the discharge of some rock from the glacier. On my return to
the hospitalet, I found a collection of Aragonese *arrieros*, who
had been carrying wine to Luchon, and were returning by my
route. They were very anxious that I should dismiss my guide
and accompany them, which proposal I declined, as Jean had
the recommendation of chattering continually about one thing
if not another, principally himself and the dangers he had *not*
passed through, whereas the arrieros wore an air of meditation altogether too philosophic for companionship. The animals having eaten their luncheon, (Luchon horses are always
lunching,) we commenced descending the valley to Venasque.

By this time the clouds had collected, and two or three times
during the afternoon we were thoroughly drenched by passing
showers, the only set-off being the pleasure of convincing Jean
that I was a better weather-witch than he. The scenery of
the Valley of Venasque gains in grandeur what it loses in
beauty, though not deficient in the latter. Numerous streams
leap down the mountain, tossing and foaming over the rocks,
but the vegetation, as is usual in Spain, extends only a short
distance from the water's edge. After an hour or so, we came in
sight of the Baths of Venasque, perched far up the mountain
on the left, (El Ventuoso,) whose steep slope is broken at the
spot just enough to make space for the hotel. A less inviting
prospect could scarcely be imagined. Not a tree or shrub
above, or for hundreds of feet below it. The solemn stone
building presented the appearance rather of a place of punishment, and the waters must indeed deserve their reputation to
induce an invalid to spend the summer in so forbidding a locality. Farther on, we passed the ruined wall of defence which
was extended across the valley to guard against the inroads of
the French. The country now became thoroughly Spanish—
stone houses, narrow, high-arched Moorish bridges, stern mountains, and sky of deepest blue. The most interesting sight on
the route is the Moraine, said to be the finest in the Pyrenees.
The rocks are enormous, and symmetrically arranged as if by a
geologist. They resemble lines of fortification, and their size
is evidence of the gigantic force of the glacier, which centuries
ago deposited them in their present position. We were several
minutes in threading our way through. The valley gave marks
of fertility, and as it was harvest time, the fields were filled

with peasants in a costume partaking both of the Aragonese
and Catalonian. Various indications announced the proximity
of a town of importance, and about an hour by sun we descried
the dismantled fort of Venasque.

Avoiding the regular Posada, we went through the dirtiest
of streets (Venasque is a great cattle town) to a private house,
where we were received by the smiling hostess with rejoicing.
As became an old traveller, my first efforts were devoted to
preparations for getting away on the morrow, which involved
certain ceremonies : my passports were to be viséd, the horses
entered at the custom-house, and security given for their
return. The message from the mayor's house, in reply to a
request for an interview, was to the effect that his Honor was
out in the fields gathering in his crop. Two or three visits, in
person, had no better result, so I concluded to dispense with
his Honor's services, and, under the guidance of the landlady's
little daughter, started out to "do up" the town Consistently
with the truth, it is difficult to praise the ancient town of Venasque, though the antiquarian may find among the houses and
walls numerous relics of the olden time, when the Moors gar-
risoned it against the irruptions of Charlemagne and other less
distinguished fillibusters. The trade consists, for the most
part, in the export of wine and the import of horses from
France, which is quite an extensive business, but the few narrow streets are thereby kept in an astonishing state of mud, in
nowise aided by the rivulet flowing down the centre. We
made directly for the parish church, which was opened by
an old woman, jingling a large bunch of keys, and I found
myself, in the most approved style of tourist, surrounded by a
group of respectfully-admiring children. Its great boast is a
recumbent effigy of some saint, placed there by Don Fulano
Tal, a rich citizen, and resplendent with gold and silver. My
admiration was quite equal to the occasion for it. A well-
dressed gentleman, a relative of the hostess, as he informed
me, was here kind enough to introduce himself and take the
place of my young conductress. He was a Castillano Viejo,
an old Castillian, and had the characteristics of the race—a
certain formality, coupled with the utmost courtesy of manner,
and not only of manner, but of feeling; a reserved dignity,
founded upon the possession of those advantages which he, at
least, valued above all others—pure blood, elevated character,

and a reasonable degree of education. After visiting the jail, a formidable dungeon-looking antiquity, which, to the credit of Venasque, was empty, we took a stroll on the Paseo. The outside of Venasque redeems the inside. An elevation of three thousand feet, (for the southern slope of the Pyrenees is much less abrupt than the northern,) gives to the atmosphere an elastic purity, and the almost rainless plains of Aragon, below, prevent its being surcharged with mountain damp, while the neighboring peaks attract sufficient clouds for its vegetation. The valley here widens out and is covered with luxuriant crops, through which course the waters of the Esera, foaming over their rocky bed. As this is the age of material progress in Spain, somewhat resembling the fermentation which took place among us ten years ago, the universal talk is of railroads. Among the favorite projects is one to pierce the Pyrenees. Venasque thinks itself pointed out, by the peculiar advantages of its situation, as the proper place for a tunnel, connecting it with the valley of Luchon. Other valleys indulge in the same fond expectations, and as no money has yet been voted, an amicable war of opinion rages. My companion felt great interest in the question, and was possessed of considerable information. Like all Spaniards, he was jealous of his locality, and dwelt upon its peculiar beauties and excellencies — an amiable failing which is always agreeable to me, for I have never found one worth knowing who did not think his native land, all things considered, the first in the world. Local attachments are pronounced, by the modern school of social philosophers, to be relics of barbarism, ignorance and prejudice, forgetting that prejudices are given us by the all-wise Deity, as well as reasoning faculties, and equally for some beneficent purpose. The time may come when prejudices will disappear, when one's country will have no greater claim upon him than China or Hindostan, and the sufferings of the Bushmen will arouse as lively a feeling of sympathy as those of his fellow-citizens. But this millenium has not yet reached Spain. Patriotism, an attachment to, a preference for one's home, is still a virtue prolific of measureless good, and for its foundation rests upon enlightened prejudice. Of all nations, Spaniards have this sentiment most strongly developed. Every Spaniard believes that Spain, with all her faults, is, or can be made, the centre of the earth, and

his own province the centre of Spain. Nor is this sincere conviction on their part distasteful to strangers, being founded
upon a good opinion of their own country, not a depreciation
of others, the contrary of which renders Englishmen so odious
throughout the world. I should have a poor estimation of one
who was above this *prejudice*, for it is the main spring to the
exertions which they are making for the improvement and
regeneration of their country. The varied necessities of life
frequently cause them to seek their fortunes in far distant
lands, but they cherish in their hearts the same feeling of
attachment to their romantic birth-place. And, surely, we
Americans, who have such ungovernable national pride, will
not blame them for the sentiment.

After a dinner in the regular style, with abundance of garlic,
I happened, between the puffs of my cigar on the balcony, to
express a desire of hearing, once more, a genuine Spanish air.
A decently-dressed person in the balcony opposite, about ten
feet off, immediately produced his guitar, and performed several pieces quite creditably, which gave rise to a flying conversation. Do not suppose that my vanity was aroused, for I
knew enough of Spanish manners to comprehend that I was
indebted for the pleasure to Spanish courtesy, rather than my
own excellence, or, to use the favorite expression of the German Professors, that it was subjective, not objective. That
over, Jean made his appearance, with the suggestion that,
if I preferred it, he would return in the morning to Luchon,
and the son of the hostess, a competent person, would accompany me as far as Barbastro. She, herself, followed with the
assurance that her son was a most excellent individual, eminently a *mozo de confianza*, and, by way of further recommendation, he could lodge me at private houses, where there were
neither fleas nor bugs, *ni pulgas ni chinches*, (fond delusion!)
Jean expressed great doubt about his being able to proceed
without the mayor's permit, but this, evidently, was not the
sole reason. So, after hearing argument, I delivered judgment
to the effect that little stress was to be laid upon the mayor's
permission, as office-holders are the servants of the sovereign
people, and it was his duty to have sought us out; and, secondly, that I never changed any settled purpose without some
sufficient reason, and none such had been given : he must, consequently, continue. They retired, convinced against their

will, and left me to my meditations and slumbers, and anything else that might be prowling about. I had several battles during the night, but the repose induced by the gentle murmuring of the river quickly healed the wounds, and I was up and had taken chocolate by the break of day, truly refreshed. Another visit from Jean : a small oration, with many gestures, giving a variety of reasons why the proposition of the preceding night should be accepted, the whole winding up with the alarming announcement that the baggage-horse limped. I immediately descended to the stable, which, according to custom, was immediately under the parlor. The animal was brought out, and, sure enough, he did limp most decidedly. Quite a collection of the neighbors had assembled, with faces of exceeding length. The few who knew a little French re-echoed in sympathizing tones, *" il boite! il boite!"*

By this time I had perceived other reasons for changing the guide. Jean, though a fine fellow in some respects, had evidently miscalculated his familiarity with the road to Zaragoza, and his knowledge of the Spanish tongue, but Gascon-like, never confessed it, so that I in all probability would have acted the part of his interpreter, which " unluckee conthratong" had happened to me once before in going from Switzerland into Italy, and was an experience not to be repeated. So I enquired as to the chances of a remount. All around assured me that they were magnificent; a superb horse for the baggage, a mule beyond reproach for myself. I objected to riding a mule, and expressed a preference for the horse. They protested, dwelling much upon the mule's long stride, his *pas allongé*, but I was allowed to indulge my fancy. The cattle were then paraded, the horse was scarcely worthy of the eulogium pronounced upon him, but the mule was magnificent. His color was of the most delicate mouse, black mane and tail, black cross on his withers and quarters, larger, too, than ordinary horses, and with a benign expression of countenance. I acknowledged myself wrong, and decided for the mule. He was then saddled, and a halter put on him. Upon this point, however, I was inexorable. In vain did they assure me that he had never had a bridle in his mouth, and that mules went much better with halters. I replied that I had consented to waive my dignity in mounting him at all, solely because I reflected that bishops, and even the patriarch of the Indies, rode

such animals, and that an humble believer might safely follow
their good example, but that it was utterly out of the question
for an American grandee and colonel in the militia to use a
halter. With infinite reluctance a bridle was produced, and I
mounted. By the united efforts of Jean and the neighbors
operating before and behind, *el macho* who, like his master, evidently had strong local attachments, was persuaded to leave
the village, at the outskirts of which Marcial presented himself
in all the glories of a clean shirt and a collar of excruciating
dimensions. Marcial was a sturdy young Aragonese, girded for
the walk. A pair of *alpargatas* or hempen sandals, which are
preferred to leather during the dry season, protected his feet.
Out of them rose long, blue stockings; then came breeches of
a darker hue; an immense sky-blue sash encircled his waist;
and his whole man was surmounted by a gay handkerchief
wound in bandeaux around his head. Upon the whole, the
exchange of guides was fortunate. Every traveller will learn,
sooner or later, by experience, never to take a French or an
English guide, if a reasonably competent Spanish one can be
procured. Their performance invariably beggars their promises. Occasionally they may be necessary, but rarely, as no
intelligent traveller should be dependent on his guide for any
thing beyond the functions of a conductor. With them, too,
the connection is measured by money alone; whereas your
Spanish servant is insensibly drawn towards you by a sort of
sympathy, proceeding partly from the fact that he does not
recognize any inferiority in his position, and discharges his
duty to you rather because he is your guide, and you are under
his guidance, than because he expects to be paid for his services. I have never parted from one without receiving a
hearty shake of the hand, indicative of real good feeling, very
different from the way of the world leave-taking of your cos-
mopolite, who, with heartfelt sincerity, cries out, "*Le Roi est
mort ! vive le Roi !*".

After a half hour's vehement exertion, it became painfully
apparent that *el macho*, indeed, knew not the mysteries of the
bridle, which I despairingly threw over his neck, supplying its
place with a good stick, that answered the purpose of a tiller
admirably. We pursued our way to the south down this
lovely valley, amid harvest fields and meadows, where the
whole population was engaged in gathering in the grain.

After an hour's ride the road ascended from the river bank and passed behind an Eremita, (as a country church apart from a village is called,) between it and the mountain on the right. A few hundred yards farther on it turned at right angles to the east, and offered to our eyes a most beautiful landscape. On our left extended the valley in an almost straight line to the Puerto de Venasque, down which glittered the river, both sides bordered by verdant fields, like a thread of silver lying upon a velvet carpet. Behind us was the Eremita, situate upon a craggy bluff some hundred feet perpendicular from the water's edge, the whole face of the rock covered with ivy and climbing vines up to the terrace. The valley was walled in on both sides by naked mountain chains extending to the foot of the Maladetta, and the view was closed by the Pyrenees themselves. How grandly they appeared through that clear atmosphere! The heavens, indeed, seemed to repose on their summits. The prospect to the right was not so grand, but quite as beautiful, for the valley here widens out, and the mountain slope, from the bank of the stream half way up to the summit, was covered with fields of golden corn, among which sparkled numerous villages in the morning light. After pursuing its new direction for a mile or so, the river turns again to the south, but we cut off this detour by crossing the spur. From the dividing crest the view embraced a wider range, though its snug beauty was proportionably diminished. *The path was superlatively execrable. We frequently met regular bandits, so far as appearance went, dressed in the approved style of picture-book-robbers, but they were harmless and polite, and to your "*buenos dias*" never failed to return "*qué los tenga vm. muy buenos,*" literally " may your worship have them (days) very good." Highway robbery during the nineteenth century has, for the most part, been confined to uncentralized countries, such as Italy and Spain, and as a natural consequence, the majority of robbers are of a southern cast of features, with dark hair, bright eyes, and an olive tinge of complexion, all of which are faithfully reproduced in illustrated works. By a natural confusion, a certain very usual style of Spanish dress and countenance has come to be considered evidence of cut-throat propensities, and sensation travellers return heartfelt thanks at safely passing some harmless individual, whose worst emotion, probably, was amusement at their outlandish costume. Such is the origin of half the thrilling narratives of robbers which have almost past, so far as actual experience is concerned, into the same gulf as the long, low, black schooners with raking masts, that formerly played so conspicuous a part in our sea-tales. At least it has never been my good fortune to be robbed, though I have been in many strange and wild places, and among wild-looking men. Descending through the wheat fields, we halted at Chia, a hamlet, where we breakfasted upon what happened to turn up—not very luxurious fare—seasoned by a little conversation with the natives, the principal item of which, according to my recollection, was a desperate complaint on the part of the grand-dame about the diminutive size of the chickens in her country. By way of increasing her dissatisfaction, I gave her a glowing description of our Shanghais, their enormous legs and sonorous voices, which filled her with amazement not unmixed with incredulity. The male population of the hamlet was busily engaged in threshing. Machines there were none. The method consisted in striking the sheaf against a smooth, flat stone, which succeeded wonderfully well. The operator regretted the necessity of using *maquinas de sangre,* " machines of blood," as he styled himself, but he was no capitalist, and the land owner resided in some city, and thus the country remained without improvement.

Beyond Chia the road got worse than ever, until toward noon we descended again to the river, which was about to enter the magnificent gorge called, I believe, La peña de Ventimilla. The parallel chains between which we had been travelling close in here to about two hundred yards. It was, perhaps, the most striking scenery on the route. The road ran along an elevated ledge or step some fifty feet above the level of water. Above that, on the right, rose the western ridge of crumbling rock, entirely devoid of vegetation except a few struggling pines. The eastern slope was densely wooded. Toward the south the view was closed by the ridge's making a sharp turn athwart the valley, while behind it was visible an immense horizontal mountain of bare rock, with sides apparently perpendicular, which seem to be a great distance off, and fairly quivered in the merciless heat of midsummer. Behind me, far, far up the valley, reposed the sleeping Pyrenees. After proceeding half a mile or so along the shady bank, the path led

over a true devil's bridge to the opposite side. Soon it turned
sharp to the east, and the gorge became so narrow that there
was barely room for the stream and the road, which frequently
mounted midway in the air ere a sufficient variation from the
perpendicular could be found to yield it space. The river, now
a mountain torrent, chafed and roared below like an imprisoned demon. For an hour the scenery continued of the grandest and wildest description, as though the foot of man had
never before wandered thither. In the midst of all, I could
not resist the temptation of scrambling down the bank with no
little difficulty and plunging in. What a delicious bath! The
pale green water, of almost icy temperature, flew by with the
velocity of the wind and required all my strength to keep from
being swept toward the cascade, which was thundering a few
score yards below. But the trouble was well repaid, for I
emerged the color of a rosebud, and with the strength and activity of a professed gymnast. The desolation of the gorge
now became greater still, for a crumbling stone appeared
which offered no hold for the trees and shrubs, and rendered
the path itself insecure. At a very narrow place we unexpectedly encountered an exceedingly corpulent padre. Neither
of us could turn round, and his reverence could not even dismount. It looked as though we should have to enact captain
Riley over again. As the padre was down-hill, Marcial took
his animal by the tail and I by the head, and we thus succeeded
in backing him to a more convenient spot, where he gave us
his benediction. His face was anything but tranquil during
the operation, and with reason, for any restiveness might have
sent us all over the precipice. At length, mounting a lofty
height that overhung the valley into which that of the Esera
was about to merge, and turning a corner, we beheld the plain
of Campo. It was very pretty, but I fear more by comparison
with what we had just passed through than from any intrinsic
beauty of its own. The mountains retire, leaving a semi-circular valley of a couple of miles in diameter, well-cultivated
with cereals; and the river, repenting the boisterous days of
its youth, widens into a gentle pastoral stream, cows standing
in its water and sheep wandering on its banks. The town,
miserable indeed, yet of some pretension, having no neighbor
better than itself, formed a central point in the view, and that
was enough for a passing traveller. At the edge of the plain,

on all sides, rise bare, forbidding hills. This was the last of the Pyrenees: henceforth it was Aragon, a roasting sun, barren mountains, and a dryness of atmosphere most grateful to my own feelings, but sadly deleterious to agriculture and to the beauty of the landscape. After passing Campo, the hills closed in again upon the river, and the heat became intense. Fortunately, Marcial met among the arrieros a friend, and that friend had a *bota*. By way of parenthesis, a *bota* is a skin, generally a pig's or goat's dressed with the hair on and pitched. It is then turned wrong side out, sewed up all except one foot, and filled with wine. The open foot is tied with a leather string, and thus arranged, the *bota* is the ordinary means of transporting that article on horse or donkey-back. It may seem strange that this custom should be retained; but in some parts of Spain skins are almost cheaper than wood, and are frequently used in its stead, even for military bridges. After the customary salutations on the present occasion, the *bota* was produced. First I took a draught, a deep one, out of the open leg; then Marcial, then the friend. Being pressed, I wiped the edge of the leg and repeated, Marcial ditto, friend ditto. The odor of the skin was too strong for my disaccustomed olfactories, so I "passed" on the third round. The rest played their hands out, and we separated rejoicing. The crumbling stone continued to present all manner of fantastic appearances, misleading me as to castles, for which I was as hungry as the renowned knight of La Mancha. One rock, some two hundred feet perpendicular and five hundred in length, with a round tower at its right angle, presented the exact appearance of an immense feudal fortress. As following the river, we wound around its base, it required little play of the imagination to fancy one's self transported back to the days of Charlemagne and Bernardo del Carpio, and to people the valley with helmeted knights thronging to avenge the dolorous rout of Roncesvalles. Later in the afternoon, vines and olives appeared, and at sunset we drew up in the village of Sta. Liestra, our halting-place for the night.

Leaving the horses below I walked up, and after the usual ablutions took my seat in the balcony to view the world. On the wall was sculptured a huge coat of arms, some eight feet in length, with a knight's crest; the house opposite was similarly ornamented. I enquired after the families to whom they had belonged; no one could answer me. Their very memories had died out, yet centuries ago these devices had been borne aloft by gallant warriors, who had, doubtless, struck many a blow for Aragon and our mother church, and caused many a turbaned infidel to bite the bitter dust. The very hall in which I sat had perhaps been the theatre of knightly feastings, the scene of gaiety and luxury. Then, the gentleman resided on his estate, and led his neighbors both in peace and war, setting before them for imitation his own light, feeble though it were. Now, he has abandoned the manly simplicity of this life for the luxury of cities, and his virtues and influence wilt beneath the baneful shade of idleness. The parish priest alone remains to sustain the cause of religion and education. It seems to me that this is the growing evil of our civilization. Not only in Europe, but in America, all who look beneath the surface detect the progress of this continually spreading cancer—the substitution of a few overgrown capitals, with a fermenting mass of discontented paupers, for the healthy, vigorous, honest population of the country. The facility of railroad communication will do much to relieve the ennui and monotony of a country life, and secure to its inhabitants the advantages of the city, without imposing upon them its burthens. This, however, would be only a partial remedy. The welfare of the agricultural laborer imperatively demands the substitution of steam machinery on the plantation as well as in the manufactory. Yet this might end in establishing there, also, the regime of the capitalist, sympathizing with the proletariat only through wages grudgingly paid and thanklessly received. Sta. Liestra had suffered much from the cause I have specified, but there was some good left. While I was at supper in a cool place by myself, a handsome young gentleman of engaging phisiognomy presented himself with the usual compliments. I found out that he was of some sixteen summers, just returned from school at Barcelona, a relative and the pride of the family, and also of the whole village; modest without being bashful, which, indeed, is not a Spanish failing or virtue, even the children having an ease of manner, an absence of mauvaise honte, remarkable, to say the least. The conversation was very pleasant by contrast with the world outside of Spain, where the education is of the cramming order, and boys are so dreadfully wide awake. My young friend had no inconsiderable stock of Spanish prejudices and knew little of things beyond the borders of his own country, but then his thoughts were fresh and buoyant, and he possessed a really poetic imagination. He disliked both English and French, knew that America was a republic, but did not exactly comprehend the practical working of a republic, nor how there could be a country without a king. The feast of his village saint, was to be celebrated shortly, and he and the curate were going to Graüs to-morrow to make some arrangements connected therewith. I suggested that he should write a poem for the occasion. With a slight confusion of manner he confessed that he had written something—*una cosita*—a *saynete* (a dramatic composition ranking between a comedy and a farce). He was anxious to know if we had any picture galleries in America. I replied in the negative, but that they would come in time, as we were a young people, having only a population of thirty millions. At this the hostess, who had come to call him to supper with the family, uttered an exclamation of amazement, crossed herself devoutly, calling for help upon San Francisco de Asis, and took him off, not however before he had given me a lesson in the art of making cigarettes and presented me with a paper book. Antonio reminded me forcibly of the student in Don Quixote. While I was preparing to retire, he returned to get his guitar and some papers, for it seems I had been installed in his room. Seeing a package neatly folded, I suggested that it might be the *saynete*. He informed me that it was, and opened it. A mortal terror seized my soul; my knees quaked beneath me, for I thought he was about to read it, and thirteen hours in the saddle, followed by a refreshing supper, had disposed me for the "balmy," so that I would not have relished the best "Capa y Espada" of Lope. (Little did I then think that I would shortly become a torturer of the public, a *hostis humani generis*, an author.) The cloud passed by, however, and I turned in, anticipating rosy dreams in which I was to be wafted upon the waters of Paradise, under a canopy of mantillas, and lulled into obliviousness by the sweet music of fans. But oh! horrible recollections! Oh! night, blacker than the depths of Ethiopia! I had been attacked at Venasque, but that was only Magenta; this was Solferino. All branches of the service were engaged; "*toute l'armée a donné.*" Their rifled cannon battered my reserves, and their Zouaves gave me no mercy at close quarters. It was always *à la baïonette* and *tête baissée.* For two hours did I sustain the unequal contest with direful deeds and oaths infernal. In vain did I fall back to a stronger position on the brick floor, enveloped in a sheet—my winding-sheet it might have been. Defeat was inevitable, and before one o'clock I had left the field and taken my seat by the window, waiting for day. At the first peep I summoned Marcial, and reproachfully imparted my misfortunes, the relation of which brought a look of innocent astonishment into his face as he assured me that he had not been "grazed."

We took chocolate, saddled in hot haste, mounted, and were about to be off, when hearing myself addressed as "Caballero," I looked up and saw Antonio and the cura on the balcony, taking their breakfast previous to departure. They overtook us shortly afterwards, while watering our animals in the stream, Antonio on a gaily-caparisoned mule, the cura on a demure pony, preceded by an active, good-humored peasant, bearing the *saynete* aloft in his hand as though it were a banner. The sun rose magnificently, causing the lofty hill-range on our left to resemble a fire-tipped wall, and the little church on its crest to sparkle as a diamond. The cura was a coarse young person, with a sensual look, and poor company; but Antonio and myself kept up a brisk talk during the three hours that we passed, threading villages and olive groves, until we reached Graus. The view from the bridge over the Esera in the morning light, extending far up the valley, amid plantations and luxuriant gardens, was very pretty. At the town gate I bade farewell to Antonio, and, I hope, at some future day, to hear that the young student of Sta. Liestra, has become one of the ornaments of his country.

Mine host of the Posada de la Cruz, at Graus, gave me a capital breakfast, though I disgusted him greatly by mixing water with his good wine, which Spaniards never do, though models of temperance. We then discoursed the relative advantages and disadvantages of beards in warm weather, one of which manly ornaments grew upon my face; then the ancient glory and present prosperity of Graus; then the heat, which was terrific. He counseled night traveling, but as it was, at least, a seven hours' journey to Barbastro, I concluded to go through in the day. Indeed, powerful though the sun be in Spain, I find that its effect is counteracted by the universal dryness of the atmosphere and the breezes which sweep over its plains, so that there is no perspiration, and after the longest day's ride

6

a glass of cool water restores me completely. The whole population of Graus were seated at work on the shady side of the street, or under awnings, as we passed out the southern gate. I cannot say that they impressed me much one way or another. After a few hundred yards, we bade farewell to the Esera. I really felt a sort of regret as we turned away to mount the table-land on our right. It had been our only companion on the journey. We had seen it spring from the glaciers of the Maladetta, playfully disporting as it were in the nurse's arms. Hour by hour had we witnessed its growth and perilous voyage amid the rocks and shoals of infancy, the joy of neighbors and the admiration of strangers. We now left it a placid, stately stream, hurrying on to unite its waters with the Cinca and the Ebro, then to be merged in the boundless ocean, and we were never to see it more. Such is too often the traveller's fate with animate and inanimate creation alike. Yet beneficent provision of Nature! that as we advance in age, the wide-spreading landscapes, and the dear faces we gazed upon so fondly in our youth, rise the more vividly to memory, while the fainter outline of subsequent events serves but as a foreground to the picture. For a couple of hours we continued to ascend the elevation which separates the two rivers, until about half an hour beyond Puebla we reached a little chapel on the highest point, whence we enjoyed an immense prospect over the broad valley of the Cinca, and the arid, endless mountains and table-lands of Aragon. It was one of those striking views that the horseback traveller in central Spain so often finds, cheerless but magnificently impressive, and though offering no one point of beauty, yet enchaining you by an admiration of its grandeur. A long descent among oak and olive plantations, brought us to the rocky bed of the river, of which in summer the water occupies but an insignificant portion. We crossed on a flying bridge, and I had out my towels ready to offer the customary sacrifice to the nymphs who presided over the pellucid waters, when I found, to my surprise, that it was postively hot, even at a depth of three feet, such is the enormous body of heat that becomes accumulated in the whole body of Spain during the long summer droughts.

We mounted the hills again, pursuing the general course of the river, the bed of which becomes very broad—a couple of miles or so, and is covered with large white stones, so that at a

distance in the glittering sun-light it resembled a vast lake.
Numerous hamlets, surmounted by towers, were strewed along
the eminences that overhung its banks. It at length broke
away to the left, straight for a long distance, finally disappearing
between two lofty bluffs, while beyond in the wavy blue haze
seemed the great ocean itself. Just at this point I met my
first Spanish beauty, a young girl riding on a donkey. Her
face was closely veiled from the glare, but female curiosity,
perhaps coquetry, exposed regular features, a transparent, rosy,
brunette complexion, raven hair and dark dreamy eyes; a delicate foot peeped out from the stirrup. Judging by the appearance of the father, they doubtless belonged to the class of
substantial yeomen. After this I felt myself really in Spain,
and my spirits rose in proportion. The road hitherto, though
much thronged, had been a mere path; it here widened into a
carriage-way. We were evidently approaching a place of some
trade. Numbers of donkeys and mules, with their owners,
were returning empty, and the road was bordered with well-
tended groves of olive and oak. The oak was called *carrasca*.
I asked Marcial for the difference between this and the oak
called *encina*. He replied that they were the same, only the
latter term was used in Castile, the former in Aragon. I subsequently put the question to half a dozen others in different
parts of Spain, receiving different answers, so that I hardly
know to this day whether they be the same or no. Such is the
difficulty of extracting the truth in Spain by mere interroga-
tion. The reason for my curiosity was this: I had read that
the word *encina* is derived from one of the few Berber roots
which have passed over into the Spanish language, viz.: "zen,"
meaning "an oak," whence the French word *chêne* with the
same signification. Now, the Moorish kingdom of Zaragoza
was principally settled by the Berber tribes, and it seemed to
me strange that this term of Berber origin should have been
rejected here, yet adopted in the Castiles. The generic term
encina, is generally applied to all evergreen oaks, except the
cork, which are called *alcornoques*. The name for the deciduous is *roble*. Meditating upon oaks and Berbers, we crossed a
lofty ridge, and descended over exhausted streams into the
ancient city of Barbastro, where I was very nicely lodged in a
large high-pitched room, with a balcony and two alcoves, in
which this time there were neither fleas nor chinches. Marcial

had made the whole journey on foot in the broiling sun and
dust, and I would not have stood in his shoes for his stockings,
though these were of the largest sort. He, however, did not
seem to mind it, and took his departure immediately on the
road home. El macho, too, performed his duty faithfully, only
he was a little too scientific in the matter of zig-zaging, which
operation he persisted in going through when there was no
manner of necessity for it, and when there were really zig-zags,
he approached so near the precipice as to engender a suspicion
that he intended slyly to commit suicide; but having arrived
safely, I refrain from criticising the bridge that carried me
over.

The jaunt I have described is one rarely made by pleasure
travellers, nor could it be recommended to young gentlemen,
wedded to champaigne *frappé*, and an evening stroll on the
Boulevards. But for those who desire to see Spain and Spaniards as they are, this is the only way to travel. In these two
days I was brought into contact with more genuine natives than
I would have met in a six months' sojourn in Madrid. Moreover,
the scenery on a part of the route is very fine. The country,
too, has yet the bloom of virgin freshness upon it, so different
from the opposite slope of the Pyrenees. In consideration of
these recommendations, I forgive and almost forget the wounds
inflicted upon my feelings by the inhospitable denizens of Sta.
Liestra.

The scene from my balcony was characteristic. As the evening came on, the young Barbastrians thronged out to enjoy
the atmosphere. One party was engaged in a rampant game
of miniature bull-fight. Another collection of six-year olds
had a quiet game of cards; the wonder was how they managed to recognize the figures under the accumulated grease of
ages. Here came a boy with a tambourine, leading two blind
old guitar-players; there a lady with mantilla and fan, gliding
along from vespers. After supping on a delightful partridge,
(partridges are always good in Spain, though cooked too dry,)
served up by the black-eyed, soft-voiced Angélica, the landlady's niece, I proceeded to the Alameda. The Alameda is
elevated, and was swept by a delicious breeze from the mountains; but the population did not add to the beauty of the
scene, so after cooling off, I retraced my steps. Across the
narrow street, some fifteen feet wide, was one of the principal

houses in the place, whose occupants chatted away in the balcony till past midnight, varying their conversation with a little
music, to the memory-awakening notes of which I was lulled
into sleep. The next day Barbastro was soon seen. The
Bishop's Palace, the Çathedral, the Barrack, complete the list.
Nor is its history more interesting; the only event of any
importance being the famous siege by the Christians, during
which, some stones having fallen into and choked the aqueduct,
the Moorish garrison was forced to surrender, and the historians of both nations agree that unheard of atrocities were
perpetrated. The Mohammedans narrate the common events
of a sack as something unknown, and the Christians excuse
them by rage at the death of one of their leaders. That such
occurrences should require especial execration from the one, or
an apology from the other, speaks well for the comparatively
humane manner in which their warfare was conducted.

There being no inducement for delay at Barbastro, I took
passage in a nondescript sort of vehicle, which was to set out
that afternoon across the country to Huesca. It was neither a
diligence, nor a tartana, nor a galera, but united the disagree-
ble peculiarities of all. My companions were an elderly gentleman, his wife and daughter, from Santander, good-hearted,
but not handsome. I pardoned them, however, in consideration
of the pretty girl they embraced at parting, who had beauty
enough to save a city. They had been spending the summer
with a friend near Barbastro, and were returning home. A
Basque servant-maid accompanied them. The corner of the
vehicle was occupied by a commercial traveller from Zaragoza,
a jovial, impertinent, middle-aged man, who had an eye out to
windward, and travelled with a cork ice-house, the contents of
which we found very refreshing. After getting rid of the proprietor of the concern, who persisted in addressing me in such
execrable French that I was compelled to summon a Spaniard
to interpret it back into Spanish, we started, accompanied by
the yells of the Mayoral, Zagal, Mozo de Mulas, and the bystanders in general. The magnificent highway which is in
process of construction, not being finished, we took the common road. Clouds of dust, and such jolting! Once when we
were compelled to dismount in descending a ravine, I found
that the dust had accumulated to the depth of a foot. There
was no danger of robbers, however, for the Guardia Civil, two

and two, were perpetually patrolling the road. Not far from Barbastro, we passed on our right a long, lofty hill or loma, gradually increasing in height until it ended in a huge rock, extending into the plain like a promontory. On the verge was a building, a fortress in the middle ages, now an Eremita, and from which it is said half the province of Huesca can be seen, as might well be. Except this, the route was uninteresting enough. The servant-maid and the Mozo de Mulas—a fellow Basque—tore the country to pieces with their tongues; they could not make up their minds which deserved deeper damnation, Barbastro or its inhabitants. I subsequently drew out the mayoral, who was a native, upon the same subject. He was loud in his praises; it was a very fine country, the best in all Spain; here you could grow everything. *Pais muy bueno ; el mejor pais de España ; aquí se coge todo.* They then argued the point at length. At Siétamo, the birth-place of the great statesman, Aranda, we halted for a few minutes. The landlord gave us some mugs of his best wine, while his two daughters, beautiful as a pair of startled gazelles, stood at the gate. My fellow-travellers mistook me for an artist, whether from my admiration of these beauties, my poverty or general outlandish appearance, I cannot say, but it is always agreeable to be mistaken for an artist. Your artist has no evil-wishers save his rivals, for his aspiration is not after the things of this earth, but some ideal, abstract conception which never has existed and never can. The very character of his occupation brings him into sympathy with the whole race, and his only enemy is the imperfection of his nature, which is perpetually striving to grasp the ideal, and as perpetually failing in the attempt. The error, however, did not save me from banging about in the machine, and we all exchanged most unartistic congratulations when, about eleven, P. M., we reached the venerable city of Huesca, and reposed our battered and bruised limbs in the very respectable Parador de las Diligencias.

The principle personage in the inn was the French *maître de cuisine*, who welcomed me with unfeigned pleasure. He had lived there many years with little satisfaction, but it was now too late to return to his former home—the old tree would not bear a second transplanting. He had married a wife, also—in short, the landlady—yet could not help feeling that he was a stranger in a strange land, and his soul was glad at the rare opportunity of speaking his native tongue. I think he exerted his utmost skill to delight my palate, and succeeded, so that we became bosom friends during the few hours of my sojourn.

Huesca is a fine specimen of an old Aragonese city, though the hand of decay seems to be upon it. The country around is exceedingly fertile, and the water furnished by the Isuela raises its productive capacity to the highest point; but this of itself is not enough to maintain its former position. Being the capital of a province, the Courts and Government give it some little appearance of life and elegance, which is wanting to its rival, Barbastro. The principal street is a fine one, clean, and lined with regular buildings, and the cathedral is a beautiful gothic edifice. The view from it over the *Vega*, and the numerous villages in sight—twenty they say—is very pretty. Yet, notwithstanding, it is painful to compare the present with the past of this venerable place. One of its noblest distinctions is still perpetuated, at least in name. Sertorius, whose fertility of genius, grand talents, and marvellous deeds in resisting so long the various Generals of Rome, recall the Italian campaigns of Napoleon, or the equally celebrated one of 1814, made Huesca, together with Evora, in Portugal, the joint capitals of his Government. Few conquerors have evinced a desire to benefit the human race apart from the advancement of their own renown. Sertorius was a grand exception. In the midst of the most intoxicating successes, the half-subdued melancholy, even romance, of his disposition, caused him to recognise and to seek some higher gratification than that arising from worldly fame. Among other noble deeds was the founding here of a school or university, to which Spaniards of distinction were encouraged to send their children. After years of warfare, the Romans, despairing of victory in the open field, were saved by the faithless Perpenna, who caused the hero to be assassinated at a feast. On opening his will, the vile traitor was found to be the chief object of his bounty. With him perished the institutions he had planted, but many centuries after, the university was reestablished, and in memory of its first founder, received the appropriate name of La Sertoriana. Its glories, however, have decayed with the decaying fortunes of the city. It is a high-school rather than a university, and of its former grandeur retains only the name.

I made a desperate effort to enjoy Huesca, but one morning

exhausted its wonders, and for a stranger, its agreeabilities. The diligence to Zaragoza, in which I had secured a place, passed over a fine road, but through a parched, wind-blown country, until it reached the valley of the Ebro, and then nature put on her fairest robes. The water of the river, drawn off through a hundred canals, converted its *Vega* into a garden groaning beneath crops of every description, both tropical and temperate. Threading these evidences of exuberant fertility, we crossed a magnificent bridge, and entered the world-renowned capital of Aragon.

CHAPTER V.

ZARAGOZA—JOURNEY TO MADRID.

"Roughing it is very pleasant, but I confess it was refresh-ing once more to see an iron bedstead, a footbath, and the other appliances of a first-rate hotel. Drawing the bed out of the alcove, which, though ornamental, is an abominable place to spend the night in, I slept soundly, being disturbed only by dreaming that the French were bombarding the city, and awakening to find the Barcelona diligence rushing at half-speed beneath the window, through the Coso, as the principal street is called. Sunrise found me pacing around the walls—not so difficult a task as one would suppose, and at that hour of the day, under the shady avenues, rather a pleasant prom-enade. This accomplished, and a general notion of the city obtained, I at once proceeded in search of el Portillo, the gate where Agostina, the famous Maid of Zaragoza, snatched the torch from the dying artilleryman and sent fiery death into the ranks of her country's foes. A cicerone had been procured for me at the hotel, and, it seems, had been on the steps waiting as I passed, but, in truth, he had such a José Maria air that no one would have thought him engaged in so peaceful an occupa-tion, and he turned out, in fact, to know less of the place than I did myself. While I was, therefore, engaged in making enquiries among the loiterers around the Portillo, a person passed, who, fortunately, could point out the very spot where the heroine stood, about a hundred yards inside of the present gate. His father was a prisoner at the time, but his mother had witnessed the occurrence, and often described it to him. I

stood reverently upon the hallowed ground, for if there is anything in history worthy of admiration, it is the conduct of the
women of Zaragoza, both peasant and noble, in their resistance to the most unjust of aggressions, and against a mighty
conqueror, at the sound of whose footsteps all Europe trem-
bled. The heroine of this incident is most conspicuously known
to fame, but there were hundreds of others who, like the
Countess of Bureta, amid the roar of artillery and the crash of
their homes, faithfully and fearlessly discharged their duty to
the living and the dying—objects of sacred imitation. The
resistance offered is surprising, when we reflect that Zaragoza
is without walls capable of withstanding artillery, and that up
to this period the French had scarcely found any in Europe
who dared to oppose them longer than a few months, and then
only after great preparation.   But the physical and material is
a small part of the siege of Zaragoza : it is the moral that
redounds so much to the credit of its defenders, and shows in
such striking and peculiar colors the character of the inhabitants of Aragon.   A comparative handful of troops, with no
hope of aid from without, and no definite end in view, actuated
simply by a hatred of submission to the invader, braved the
hitherto unconquered terror of the world, and with such success that it seemed as though the personal attention of the
great war god himself would be necessary for its reduction.
After the breach of the outer wall had been effected, the contest
was continued from house to house with bayonet and knife.
The passage of the streets was as dangerous as crossing the
ditch of a fortress.   Even when the French reached the Coso,
every effort to seize the houses on the opposite side was for a
long time baffled.   The defence of Zaragoza may have been
an isolated effort leading to no tangible result, and an error in
a mere strategical point of view, but its moral effect is not
thus to be measured, as it furnished a model for the resistance
of the Spaniards during the whole war.   The siege of Gerona,
during the same mighty contest, that of Barcelona in 1823, and
of Saguntum and Numantia in ancient history, are parallel
instances of the same spirit.   From time immemorial, the Aragonese have been noted for obstinacy of character and fixed-
ness of purpose. Less fortunate in external polish than perhaps
other portions of their countrymen, they amply compensate for
its absence by the more solid virtues. Industrious, energetic,

possessing in an eminent degree what the French call *droiture*, they have always enjoyed more of practical liberty than was the usual lot of the Peninsula, though their province produced few of the exalted geniuses which bore so proudly aloft the flag of old Spain. Even down to the time of Philip II, during the age of Charles V, of Henry VIII, and Elizabeth, they maintained their independence of the royal authority. It is true, this attachment to liberty sometimes runs into extremes, and the common people are much given to be *camorrista,* or headbreaking; but when there is occasion for it, they are never backward in giving a fair share to the enemies of their country, which makes amends for little faults at home.

Zaragoza boasts two cathedrals, which appear conspicuously on approaching the city. The most ancient is styled the Seo, the old Limousin word for cathedral, a grand, venerable structure, though blocked up, as such edifices too frequently are, by all sorts of inferior buildings. It would be scarcely possible to enter into a minute description of its treasures, without copying confidingly from Ponz and other books, as the faint light scarcely affords the traveller an opportunity of seeing, much less of criticising them. The general effect in the morning was exceedingly impressive. Badly lighted at best, the interior, at that early hour, was shrouded in gloom—a few rays only struggled down from the dome; the whole producing the soft influence which such edifices should. The chapels contain many magnificent funeral monuments, the grandest of which, according to the usual fate, honors the least worthy—the inquisitor, Pedro Arbuez, whose cruelties and oppressions drove the population to madness. One of the great patrons of the Seo was the Cardinal Pedro de Luna, a schismatic Pope, under the title of Benedict XIII, who is here commemorated. With true Aragonese obstinacy, he resisted all attempts to procure his resignation. It is narrated that on the introduction of a delegation of black friars from the Council of Constance upon some such errand, he exclaimed: "here come the crows." "Where the carcase is, thither come the crows," wittily replied one of the brethren. But wit was as ineffectual as violence; he died at the age of ninety, defying his enemies to the last, like a true Iberian.

From the Seo I proceeded immediately to the Cathedral of Nuestra Señora del Pilar. Near the steps a beggar held out his hand, in which I placed a copper. Another, who appeared equally meritorious, came forward; it would seem partiality to refuse him. Two women now advanced with like recommendations. Unfortunately, this last act of beneficence took place at the entrance, and half a dozen rushed forward to the Samaritan, so unexpectedly dropped from Heaven, crying "Señorito! una limosna para el amor de Dios!" This was too much, and I took refuge incontinently behind the fount of holy water, which they could not pass. They were the only ones I encountered from Venasque to Madrid, and that, too, in a country where, if you believe travellers, beggars compose half of the population.

The Cathedral of our Lady of the Pillar, an enormous structure some five hundred feet in length, was as full of light as the Seo had been of darkness, and for this reason the first impression was an unpleasant one. It was impossible to avoid seeing what was going on, and everybody and everything within the walls, so that the congregation must have continually felt that they were in the world and of it. The very magnificence of the choir and the high altar was disagreeable, as the mind was filled with what you saw, and existence was an existence of the eyes. Nor during my stay in Zaragoza was I able to overcome the first impression; whereas, a visit to the Seo was always productive of pleasure. The original cathedral was erected to commemorate the descent of the Virgin upon a certain pillar, since held in great veneration, and enclosed in a chapel especially dedicated to the purpose, which, by way of exception, is built in the body of the church. It is an oval, of the Corinthian order, and of a richness of decoration unbounded. According to the tradition, St. James had been instructed by her to erect a temple upon the spot where the new religion should be most favorably received. In compliance with her request, he had wandered through many lands, and was finally engaged in baptising the faithful in the waters of the Ebro, when a bright effulgence displayed the Queen of Heaven upon this pillar, pointing out the chosen spot. A mass was celebrating as I entered. It was, of course, numerously attended, and, apparently, by persons deeply imbued with feelings of devotion. My attention was particularly attracted to a beggar in the depths of poverty and misery, if his outward man corresponded with his real circumstances. Dirty, shrivelled, and resting upon two crutches, he limped up to the grating in front of the altar and threw in, one by one, coppers to an amount that, by a reasonable calculation, might have supported him a whole week. It would be useless to question the sincerity of his belief. The rest of the worshippers, though not so demonstrative, were, doubtless, equally in earnest, as their countenance, plainly evinced.

I took my place among them on bended knees. True, I did not believe that the Virgin had descended upon the pillar, any more than a great many good Catholics. Yet, there was a certain pleasure in participating in the worship. Was it religion? was it poetry? was it sympathy with the by-standers? or was it a mere revery? I cannot answer satisfactorily even to myself; but it was a pure, placid emotion, that I have often felt upon such occasions, and which, if not religion, is very nearly allied to it. Some Protestants regard such ceremonies and those who participate in them with a species of aggressive contempt. I cannot sympathise with them. Every revealed system must rest for its foundation upon either reason or faith. The former decides upon evidence, scrutinised by the light of a critical intellect; the latter seeks its "evidence of things unseen" only in the heart. How many of us have intelligence, learning, or leisure to investigate the grounds of our belief in even the simplest article of faith? What immense erudition is requisite to decide whether the gospels containing a narrative of the Saviour's life be forgeries, revelations or mere histories? How often do sects split upon the mere literal rendering of a Greek sentence? And if the learned, who have devoted their whole lives to this alone, be so feeble, how shall we expect strength of wisdom from the mass of mankind, who have not the first element of critical science? We believe in the existence of a Saviour, and denounce as infidels and horrible monsters all who refuse assent to our faith. And why do we thus believe? Because we have been told so in our youth by persons of learning and probity, in whom we have confidence, and whose better judgment in this matter we substitute for our own. The Aragonese believes in the Madonna del Pilar for identically the same reasons. The Protestant points to St. Domenic, Torquemada and Alexander VI; the Aragonese to Calvin, Luther and Henry VIII. The only satisfactory arguments, after all, to the common mind, being those drawn *a pos-*

teriori from the effects produced by each religion. And even here the danger of confusion is great, by mixing up mere church polity with religion itself, for the temporal power of Spanish bishops is no more an essential part of the Catholic religion, than that of the English bishops is of the Protestant. The character of the priests, too, varies with locality and surrounding influences. Many in the humbler ranks of the Spanish clergy are unfit for their place, and have followed the profession for a living. Can more be said for the English? Read Thackeray and Charlotte Brontë, and if they fail to convince, consult the living exemplars. At all events, the higher walks of the Spanish clergy are filled with the noblest and purest of men, and no one of them in our day has enriched his family with £100,000, hoarded from a salary which was granted to him for the support of the poor and necessitous. Nor does morality seem to be merely a question of religion. The lower order of Scotch are moral, industrious and Protestant; the lower order of Irish are moral, indolent (in Ireland) and Catholic; the lower order of English are immoral in the last degree, industrious and Protestant. The Protestant idea is, perhaps, better fitted for the affairs of this world, as it dwells more upon the fulfilment of our duties towards our fellow-man. In a word, it is a fine support for those who, in the consciousness of strength, need no assistance. But for the broken in spirit, for those who, disappointed in their hopes, and crushed beneath an unrelenting fate, would fain turn from the world and forget its pleasures and sorrows alike, I fear it offers little consolation. Even for the earth we need something more than morality, something apart from and higher than humanity or its virtues, as is proven by the small number of Protestant churches in which the Protestant idea is carried out to its legitimate deductions. It is, therefore, the height of an absurd vanity for us, with upcast eyes, to thank the Creator for not having made us like those publicans. Be all this as it may, I feel a profound respect for sincere devotion, wherever and however manifested. Not only so, but I have ever considered it consistent both with courtesy and principle to honor religious ceremonies even when they might not meet with my personal approbation. I have knelt before the Elevation of the Host and bowed my head on the Paseo at the solemn peal of the Angelus, without feeling myself the worse therefor, and some of the pleasantest recollections of my life are these Spanish cathedrals, where the sombre grandeur of the architecture and the devotion of the congregation harmonized in elevating me above the mere materiality of existence.

Between the cathedrals, and near the Seo, are the remains of the Casa de la Diputacion, where the old Parliament held its sittings. The Aragonese are justly proud of the liberty which their ancestors enjoyed. Of course, it was not a democratic liberty, such as we now think indispensable, for in the middle ages no such idea was recognized, except, perhaps, in a few commercial cities, and even there in a very modified form. But in Aragon, Government was acknowledged to be a contract, which required obedience from sovereign and subject alike—a sort of Constitution, which was carefully impressed upon each succeeding monarch by the formula of coronation, "We, who as good as you, and together more than you, make you our King and Lord, upon condition that you respect our privileges and liberties; and if not, not." Nor could the sovereign enter upon the exercise of his powers, until mutual oaths had been taken in Zaragoza, Barcelona and Valencia. The rights of the subject were not considered franchises extorted from the monarch's hands by successful rebellion, but were regarded as inalienable, even though in abeyance. Not content with this, they established a grand Court, composed of the Justicia, who held by life tenure, and who was especially charged with the preservation of the constitutional guarantees. He could draw to his jurisdiction all complaints of illegality, even against the king; could discharge, by a species of *habeas corpus*, all persons unjustly confined, and protect them for a day afterwards. He was thus enabled to save the monarchy against the danger of popular revolutions by restraining its head from the commission of those acts of tyranny which generally give rise to such commotions. A sort of Council of Associates was nominated by the king out of a list presented by the Cortes as a check upon his power, and a Committee of four Inquisitors drawn by lot—one from each branch of the Cortes—met on the 1st of April and sat for eight days, to hear all complaints that might be made against him or his associates by any except the king. If presented by them, he was tried by seventeen Judges, taken likewise by lot from the whole Cortes, and punished at discretion. This was really our system of Government in its essentials—a fundamental law, *above* the Government, and an independent Judiciary, to prevent infractions of that fundamental law, the difference being that our Constitution embraces and protects all; their's, as a general rule, only the privileged classes. Aragon and the United States are the only countries in the world that have ever embodied the true conception of a free Government, viz : a machine which shall preserve order and protect the nation, while guarantying the rights of the minority against the power of the mere majority. The English, to this day, though comparatively a free people, live, so far as their Constitution is concerned, under the absolute control of a majority. One vote in the House of Commons (itself representing a twentieth of the nation) may change the ministry, fill the House of Lords with its creatures, and pass any laws, however preposterous, which the Courts have frequently declared that they have no power to arrest. The nineteenth century furnishes examples of the way in which this may be accomplished. The House of Austria found the Constitution of Aragon very inconvenient. Philip II swept away the last trace of its liberties, and the French battered down the Parliament House.

Among the sights of Zaragoza is the princely mansion of the great merchant, Zaporta, and one or two others of like reputation. Their glories are departed. Half the columns of the arcades are destroyed, and the courts lumbered up with every unsuitable thing. Zaragoza is no longer the capital of a great kingdom, with monarch and nobles and the attendant luxuries of a court; Madrid has absorbed all that class of the population, and, until revived by the railroads now in progress, she must be content to see her ancient palaces crumble. I confess, too, that, fresh from the palaces of Genoa, I was not filled with the orthodox degree of admiration in visiting these.

The panorama from the Torre Nueva is fine. Of course, you are expected to admire the clock, and to read the numerous sentences on the wall, in a very old handwriting, warning the visitor to prepare for death : not altogether inappropriate, as the tower leans considerably from the perpendicular. On every side are visible the ravages of the French artillery. The façade of the Sta. Engracia still remains upright, a lonely witness to its horrors, the monastery and the body of the church having been utterly destroyed. This monastery was founded by Ferdinand and Isabella, and was famous for its relics and for the tombs of the great historians, Blancas and Zurita, who have so nobly preserved the records of departed liberty. The main attack of the French, at the second siege, was in this quarter, and the breach was effected, if I mistake not, by a mine under this very church. Many of the half-ruined and deserted convents are turned into granaries and sometimes stables. Monks and nuns have been swept away by the progress of events, and throughout Spain their habitations are desolate. The Casa de Misericordia, for the aged poor, a fine building, and a most praiseworthy institution, makes a grand show from this tower. The view extends beyond the city over the valley, for a long distance up the hills on either side. The position of the French batteries is easily recognized. Modern improvements in artillery have now rendered such a defence as that of Zaragoza more difficult, and it is easy for us to see how feeble the guns of that day must have been; but their effect is painfully apparent in the Faubourg, beyond the Ebro, which has never recovered from the devastation.

The principal and only fine street in Zaragoza is *El Coso*, which cannot rival the Calle de Alealá, but the walks outside the city walls may challenge comparison with the best. An Alameda, not yet finished, and which will be very handsome some day, leads out of the gate of Sta. Engracia, by the statue of Pignatelli, lately erected, to a beautiful avenue, where you may stroll the hottest day with pleasure, to the Casa Blanca on the grand canal—a shady spot dedicated to dancing the jota, and other Aragonese amusements. To the north-west, likewise, without the walls, is one of the few remains of the Moorish dominion in Aragon—the Aljaferia—a castle-palace of the Beni Hud, who do not appear generally to have emulated the taste of their Andalusian rivals for the fine arts. The Aljaferia is a fine old pile, and, after passing through the hands of the Inquisition, has been appropriated to the use of the garrison, who, though by profession men of blood, are by practice gentle lambs, compared with their predecessors. It was here that occurred the first abortive attempt at revolution against the Sertorius Government. Its gallant leader paid the penalty of his life, but his memory was avenged by the Vicalvarists. Mr. Ford mentions the Aljaferia as the birth-place of Sta. Isabel

7

of Hungary. I think he is mistaken; this was a different person, and died in Portugal, of which country she was queen.

Among my casual acquaintances at Zaragoza was a French
exile, a lawyer, whom I met at the *tertulia* of my banker's
wife. He was heartily tired of it; complained dreadfully of
the hatred which the inhabitants bore to the French and English; that they called his countrymen *gabachos*, (a word whose
precise signification is uncertain;) that he kept on good terms
with every one, because he never entered into an argument;
assassinations were frequent; the women, though handsome,
took no exercise; the people of property entertained very little; the priests were all Carlists at heart, praying a restoration
of the feudal Government and the Inquisition. The only
thing he praised was the climate, and he had lived here seven
years without knowing what it was to have a pain or an ache.
All this must be taken with many grains of allowance, and I
was far from adopting his conclusions. The fate of an exile is
a hard one, and few can bear it with equanimity. The expression of his countenance was sad, indeed, and I doubt not that
he embraced the opportunity, shortly afterwards afforded, of
returning to his native land. Next me at the table d'hôte of
the hotel sat a navy officer and his wife, who were equally
decided in their praises. The golden mean probably lies
between the two.

Having spent as much time as was desirable in Zaragoza, I
took my seat one night, at eleven, P. M., in the *berliña* of the
diligence for Madrid. We had just been favored with a magnificent tropical storm. The rain had descended in torrents,
and the thunder echoed around the city as though the last
trump had sounded. A subdued muttering among the hills,
and piles of black clouds, seemed to threaten a renewal of its
terrors, though the air had become so cool as to make us but-
ton our coats and raise the windows of the coach. But public
conveyances in Spain wait for neither time nor tide. The
Spanish diligence is doomed shortly to go the way of all flesh.
For a progressive traveller, who "does up" western Europe in
six months, (as a fellow-countryman, on his way to the East,
once told me of his own exploits,) the railroad is a great con-
venience; but such as wish to see not only the configuration of
the country, but the people, and those of all ranks, will regret
this means of meeting agreeable, at least interesting, company,

and sometimes of making lasting acquaintances, which seldom happens in a railroad train.   The machine, itself, is constructed upon the same plan as the French, but more commodious.   The first copartment, the *berliña*, next the team, has places for three, with windows in front and on the side, giving a view of the whole country.   Next comes the *interior*, for six, sitting face to face; and last of all, the *rotonda*, the inmates of which can scarcely be recognized after a dusty ride.   On the top is the *coupé*.   This vehicle, cumbrous as it seems, must not be confounded in its rate of speed with the German *lucus-a-non-lucendo*, Eilwagens and Schnellposts.   The rapidity with which they are whirled along is startling; for the Spaniards are Jehus in their driving, and a person ignorant of the seven-fold hide that covers a Spanish mule's body, would think it high time for the anti-cruelty-to-animal society to interfere, but one cut with the lash inflicts more pain upon one of our thin-skinned beasts than half an hour's beating upon them.   The general director is styled the *mayoral*, an appellation common to most superintendents in Spain.   Second in command under him is the *zagal*, who is changed at every relay, and sits in his seat on top, or anywhere else he can.   His principal occupation or amusement is, to descend at unexpected moments, and, running around the team, to administer a sound beating with rigid impartiality. Sometimes he fills his pockets with pebbles, and, with unerring accuracy of aim, communicates his wishes to the various animals.   His legs are of the most approved pattern and unquestioned excellence.   The last functionary is the postilion, the *delantero*, who generally rides the whole way through, if not more than forty hours, or so, though against the regulations. Nothing has aroused my admiration more than the endurance displayed by these boys.   They seem absolutely made of steel, and freed from the necessity of sleep.   Formerly, no diligence was considered complete without an *escopetero*, armed with a formidable-*looking* carbine; but the improvement of the *guardia civil*, or country police, has rendered such a precaution unnecessary, though he is still, occasionally, retained, from artistic considerations.   The team consists of seven, or more, mules, and one postilion horse.   The female mules are gallantly provided with names, Capitana, Generala, Negra, which they recognize perfectly; the males generally receive the generic designation of *macho*.   One or another of these words is eter-

nally in the mouth of the zagal, and a free passenger is
expected to work his passage by aiding in the vociferation.
One such, the next day, seated just in front of berliña, continued, for three hours, without intermission, to cry out, *andá !
andá! andá! andá! ànda! ànda! ànda! ànda!* until we were
driven to desperation.

Our postilion was named Manuelito, a well-made, lithe, little
fellow, of about fifteen.   He wore a pair of blue pants, a gaily
ornamented velveteen jacket, with a segar case stuck into one
pocket, and a yellow handkerchief fluttering from the other.
Around his waist was wound a bright red sash.   The trumpet
swung over his left shoulder, and one of his fingers boasted a
silver ring.   A leopard-skin cap, jauntily worn on one side,
completed his costume.   Manuelito was evidently proud of his
post.   As the weather looked threatening, he donned his little
cloak, mounted, and, amid frantic yells, we flew through the
gate, over the fortress ditch, and commenced our journey.

There was nothing to see, and no light to see it with, so I
composed myself to sleep, and slept soundly until the vehicle
suddenly stopped, and it seemed as if Babel had been destroyed
again.   We were descending a mountain side, a precipice on
our left, the diligence slewed nearly at right-angles across the
road, and the nine mules kicking for life.   The three extra
passengers, friends of the mayoral, were darting off from the
ledge in front of the *berliña*, like frightened birds.   But far, far
above all rose the multitudinous sound of oaths, every man
swearing for three and crying out " *Para el coche! que va á
matarse el macho!*" The tongue had broken, and as the forward animals are attached, not to the tongue, but to the body
of the vehicle itself, it had continued to proceed, the broken
end lacerating the side of one of the wheelers considerably
before the motion could be arrested.   With some difficulty the
animals were unhitched.   Then, again, rose the sound of many
voices : who had first perceived the trouble ; who had not ; who
first cried out ; the mule was much hurt ; the mule was not
much hurt, &c., &c.   Then every one took out his tobacco
pouch and coolly made a cigarette.   I began to think we were
in for the night, but after ten minutes the cigarettes were
smoked out, and the mayoral commenced mending the tongue
in a really workmanlike manner, so that it lasted till we
reached Madrid.   When I next awoke it was daylight, and we

were threading the mountain country that leads into the province of Almunia. The bleak slopes were covered with flocks
of sheep and herds of donkeys, who gleaned a meagre support
under the charge of dogs and wild-looking men, clothed in
sheep-skins. One little girl, tending a single sheep, had quite
a romantic appearance in this savage wilderness. Descending
out of the gorge, we entered the valley which leads to the town
of Almunia, with its loop-holed wall and ditch, suited to the
warfare of the olden time.

While we were waiting for chocolate, I took a stroll down
the long straight street that runs through the centre, saw nothing remarkable except some fine shoats, and was quite willing
to proceed on the journey. The fertile vega of Almunia, with
its vines, and olives, and fruit trees, is very pleasant to the
sight after so much aridity, but the scenery soon relapsed into
its former condttion, and the road continued to ascend and
descend the hills until we entered the enchanting vega of
Calatayud, by whose walls flow the Jalon and the Giloca. Here
sun and water have done their utmost, and have produced a
fertility without bounds. The temperate and south temperate
zones unite in emptying the horn of plenty into its lap.
Among other productions it is famous for its hemp, which is
considered much superior to that of Northern climates, and is
preferred in Spanish dock yards. Calatayud, as its name
(Kalat Ayub, the Castle of Job) indicates, was founded by the
Moors. The materials were taken from the ruins of the Roman
city Bilbilis, renowned as the birth-place of Martial, who, after
leading the life of a brilliant rake in Rome, returned to pass
the remainder of his days in contented seclusion at home.
Bilbilis is another of the many ancient and important cities in
Spain which have utterly disappeared. The diligence stopped
at a posada without the walls, fronting the promenade which
skirts the river. I embraced the opportunity afforded by the
delay of breakfast, to stroll through the principal street, as it
was probably the only occasion I should ever have. The outside of things was prepossessing; streets scrupulously neat,
and a general air of well-being characterizing the population.
Churches are numerous, to judge by the spires. I entered one,
that of the Holy Sepulchre, which was quite handsome and in
good taste. Calatayud is the second city in the old province
of Aragon, and is said to be the seat of much wealth. The

situation and the fertility of the surrounding country yield to none in the north of Spain, and the climate is pleasant, except when the north-west wind blows over the Sierra of Moncayo, which elicits bitter complaints on the part of the natives. In ancient times its waters were supposed to possess the same virtue in tempering steel, which has since rendered Toledo so famous. I am not aware, however, of any manufactory at present existing. Calatayud has a unique peculiarity in Spain that no adjective has been formed to designate its inhabitants. Those of Madrid are styled *madrileños*, of Malaga, *malagueños*, of Cadiz, *gaditaños*, but some years ago a member of the Cortes having occasion to speak of the inhabitants of Calatayud, found himself at a loss. Calatayudeños was too harsh, so the extinct Bilbilis furnished the classical epithet of Bilbilitano, or some such word. At least I was so told.

A delightful breeze blew down the valley as we lost sight of Calatayud and continued our journey toward the mountain chains, separating Aragon from the plains of New Castile. Ateca offered its modest beauties. On the left, beyond the valley, were several fine ruins and one massive monastery or convent of apparently ancient date. My two companions in the *berliña* were returning from the baths of Panticosa, in the Pyrenees, a celebrated resort, though somewhat difficult of access. One was a Madrileño, the other an Estremeño, (Estremeduran,) both gentlemen, and agreeable people. They had taken me for a soldier, but our intercourse was peaceful, and, to me, instructive, as the society of intelligent Spaniards generally is, because they preserve the freshness of their thoughts, and have some opinions beyond those contained in the newspapers. Of incidents the journey was barren, except a famous stall in the team. The side of the road had been covered with stones, lately placed there for the purpose of macadamising. Manuelito conceived the idea of passing a string of wagons by galloping over these stones, but the ascent was steep and we stuck hopelessly fast, without being able to return to the beaten track. The animals were beaten singly and collectively until I felt called on to protest against such cruelty, and remembering my boyish experience, when passengers were expected to carry rails to make corduroy for the stage coach, proposed that we should dismount and put our shoulders to the wheel, as that appeared to be the only chance. This seemingly

novel expedient was adopted. The stones were scraped away
in front of the wheels; we took our position behind. At the
given signal a general yell was raised. The zagal whipped the
mules in front: we pushed in the rear, until our efforts were
crowned with success, but Manuelito, who used to look around
so smilingly, was now quite crest-fallen and did not recover his
spirits during the whole stage.

As evening approached, we commenced the ascent of the
mountain range which bounds the great central plateau of
Spain. The road followed a bounding stream, that leaped from
ledge to ledge of rock, and covered the valley with herbage of
softest texture, receiving frequent rills, that coursed down the
mountain side. Venerable *nogales* and other deciduous trees,
extended their foliage over us. The scene was diversified by
scattering farm-houses and occasional castle ruins which de-
monstrated the importance of the pass in the wars before the
union of the two Crowns. Half way up was a noble monastery, grandly situate upon an immense mass of rock. As night
closed in, we reached the summit of the ridge, where we took
our mounted guard, and proceeded along the table-land called
Llanura de las Serranias, which separates the province of Soria
from that of Guadalajara, and is almost above the limit of cultivation. About ten o'clock, a halt was called for supper at
Alcolea del Pinar, which lies upon the brow of the ridge, where
it begins to sink to the south-west.

It was a short meal with me, and I descended from the
Posada to enjoy the bracing atmosphere. The little town is
on one of the most elevated situations in the peninsula, and
exposed to the winds which swept over the plains of New Castile, and whistled gently around the streets. The temperature
was delicious—elasticity itself—with the freshness of our November, just cool enough to render desirable a light cloak
thrown over the shoulders. All around was bathed in the mellow light of the moon. On approaching the diligence, I beheld
one of those visions which oftentimes make the stranger in
Spain regret that he was born. It was a young lady, cast in
the fairest mould of her sex; a transparent, rich, blonde complexion (not the peach and apple of Northern climes), exquisitely chiselled mouth and chin, mild but expressive blue eyes,
glossy raven locks, and a grace of person betrayed in every
attitude—truly an apple of gold in a net-work of silver. She

seemed an Ionic column, draped for an artist's pencil. I embraced the first opportunity of offering some courtesy, and of
evincing a respectful admiration. Her voice was a fit accompaniment to the expression of such beauty. She had only come
to see a friend off, and as the signal for departure sounded, I
entered the diligence, sorrowful to think that this brilliant,
pure as the breeze that floated by, would probably be thrown
by fate to some creature incapable of appreciating its excellence. Her name is unknown to me, as her friends dismounted
during the night, and I had no informant save my dreams, yet
I am sure it was Inez.

I awoke as the first streak of dawn began to purple the East.
Ahead and behind, and on both hands, extended the plains of
Castile, covered with the stubble of the wheat—the best in
Europe, which had just been harvested. Donkeys and sheep
were gleaning the remains. We reached Torrijo, with its ancient walls and towers, and fine old ruined castle commanding
the valley, down which we whirled along the bank of the river,
enveloped in a choking dust, apparently six inches deep. The
Aragonese costume had disappeared; the hat and sombre brown
cloak of *paño pardo* of Castile were now universal. In the
due course of events, we arrived at the City of Guadalajara
(Wady al Hajar—the River of Rocks), where we had to wait
some time for the departure of the train, which I spent in
reviving my recollection of the place. In the middle ages, it
was renowned for the deeds of the Cid and his family, and was
one of the outposts of Christendom against the kingdoms of
Valencia and Murcia. It was subsequently made the residence
of the great family of the Mendozas, one of the noblest names
in Europe, fulfilling for centuries every requisite of nobility.
Like most other of its compeers, its origin is lost in the band of
sturdy warriors who, in the eighth century, rallied around Pe-
laijo and his successors in the mountain fastnesses of Asturia.
In the fifteenth century, the Marquisate of Santillana, the
second created in Spain, was conferred upon Don Iñigo Lopez
de Mendoza, so famous for his statesmanship and his literary
accomplishments. His little ballad, commencing

> Moza tan fermosa,
> Non ví en la frontera,

continues to be admired in our day. Of his sons, the elder,

Don Diego Hurtado, was created Duke del Infantado. The territory composed of the cities of Alcocer, Salmeron, Valde Olivas, and others depending upon them, was called the Infantazgo or Infantado, because it had been possessed by various Infantas. Henry the IV bestowed it upon Don Diego Hurtado, and, in 1475, it was erected into a Dutchy in reward of his services. Proud of the literary reputation of his father, the great Marquis, he had entailed the library, and directed that it should be preserved in the palace at Guadalajara. Whether it has escaped the ravages of war, I do not know. The younger son was made Count of Tendilla, who was succeeded in his honors and titles by Iñigo Lopez, second Count of Tendilla, and first Marquis of Mondejar, one of the most celebrated of the Generals who aided in the conquest of Granada. He was the father of five sons, all of them attaining great distinction in their several occupations, particularly Don Diego Hurtado, the author of the classic Guerra de Granada, who, in war, statesmanship and literature, worthily sustained the reputation of his family. The famous Cardinal Mendoza, who raised the standard of the cross upon the Torre de la Vela, in the Alhambra, and was styled the third King of Spain, is familiarly known to all Americans. One of the last of the race unhesitatingly placed his immense fortune at risk in the War of Independence against the French, who, in revenge, sacked the palace at Guadalajara, and even desecrated the tombs of his ancestors, while Napoleon excepted him from the general amnesty. This is an aristocracy indeed. Within the few past years the title has become extinct, or rather has lost its separate existence, by merging in the ducal family of Ossuna.

The Mendoza palace is still the great attraction of Guadalajara, though sadly fallen from its historic grandeur. Its size is immense, and its first court magnificent. Some of the vast suites of rooms yet retain remnants of former beauty, and here and there is a rusty relic of ancient days. The church of the Franciscans is more interesting, for here are the tombs of those proud warriors and statesmen whose fame once filled the earth. Besides this, there is little of interest at Guadalajara, though the town is clean, and comparatively well built, and it is the seat of the excellent engineer school of the army.

At length the diligence was placed on a car, and we started.

Manuelito collected his *peseta*, from the company, which I paid willingly. With the exception of one stage, when the leader was a little unwell, he had been in the saddle for thirty-one hours, and had made a distance of forty-five leagues, all the time at a hard trot or gallop. Instead of going to sleep, as I should have done, he made up a segar which I gave him, into a dozen cigarettes, and commenced enjoying himself. The country to Madrid was, as usual in the Castiles, a table-land or mountain plain. Innumerable threshing-floors were in operation. Machines of the rudest description, such as described in the Old Testament. As the summer is generally a continuance of fair weather, the sheaves are not housed, but placed on a level spot—the era—and threshed by means of a sort of sled—a *trillo*—driven over them, the *trillador* standing upon the *trillo*. In winnowing, instead of using fans, the operatives throw the grain with shovels to windward, which causes the chaff to be blown back upon themselves, so that I wonder there should be any eyes left in Castile after the harvest. The ancient city of Alcalá de Henares, so renowned for the University of Cardinal Ximenes, since removed to Madrid, and for the Complutensian Bible, looked as it did formerly. One of the villages on the road has attained a celebrity since my first visit—Vicálvaro, the scene of the battle between the troops of the Sartorius Government and O'Donnel and Dulce—who have consequently been called the Vicalvarists, or, as they call themselves, the "heroes of Vicálvaro." Winding around the observatory hill, we entered the station of Madrid, and, hitching on five grays, drove up the Prado and down the magnificent street of Alcalá to the hotel.

CHAPTER VI.

MADRID.

As my stay in Madrid depended upon circumstances beyond
my control, I went immediately into lodgings, where I found
myself very comfortable. My hostess being an Andaluza from
Seville, was, of course, graceful and talkative, and retained considerable traces of a blonde beauty, that must have increased
her attractions—a great many years ago. The rooms were as
elegant, in a different style, as could have been furnished· in
Paris. The parlor to the front was provided with two balconied windows, which afforded a view of "over the way," and
also up and down the well-thronged street. The sleeping
apartment was of modest dimensions, but sufficiently large, and
provided with mirrors and tables of modern make; a fine
Valencia matting, made of the *esparto*, which grows in that
province, covered the floor. In fact, I was somewhat surprised
at the progress which had been made since my last visit, for
lodgers then had to content themselves with pieces of furniture, that in aspect and position resembled a broken down
quadrille. Everything was scrupulously neat. Of the two
female domestics, one was a Valencian, the other a Castillian,
and each duly impressed with the superior merits of her province. During my sojourn, they took frequent occasions of
discoursing to me upon the subject, all of which I heard with
interest and a certain profit. Nothing gratifies any Spaniard
more than a patient listener to such dissertations. The hostess was particularly glowing in her eulogies upon Seville, fair

Seville, and insisted on my laying the bachelor crown of martyrdom at the feet of some Andaluza. In the spirit of contra-
diction, I suggested a Valenciana. She scouted the idea,
protesting that *las Valencianas son muy guapas, pero no tienen
gracia! no tienen gracia!* Whereas, the Andalusians united
beauty, grace, wit and sincerity. In my inmost heart I could
not gainsay its truth. The only other occupant was a young
lawyer from Valencia, of an exceedingly mercurial temperament. At times very lively and entertaining; then again don-
ning a face for a grievance. In these latter moods he supplied
me with enough scandal and complaints to have kept the whole
profession occupied for a month.

The plan of living in Madrid is almost exclusively that of
floors, very few families occupying an entire house. To this
there are naturally some objections, the principal of which is
that the occupants have no settled home; but as none except
the wealthiest can afford to purchase a large mansion, and of
such is the city at present composed, the great majority are
compelled to choose between this, which at all events secures
the privacy of a portion, or the abominable system of hotel
boarding, so prevalent in certain parts of America, and which
is, perhaps, the most ruinous plan ever contrived for breaking down the sentiment of family—that corner-stone of a
republic. For single gentlemen there are boarding houses,
(casa de huespedes,) which are agreeable to strangers without
acquaintance, as they frequently contain very pleasant company, and are good schools for learning the language. Some
of the nobility have enormous palaces, far more remarkable for
their size than elegance. The residence of the banker—Sala-
manca, beyond the Prado, formerly belonging to the Queen
mother, is a beautiful building. But the proprietors of ordinary wealth frequently content themselves with the first floor,
leasing the others out in the usual manner. The house may
thus be filled with all classes of society. On the ground floor
will be a shop; in the *entre-suelo* a family, or perhaps a barber
or a modista; on the first floor the proprietor, and so on gradually descending in worldly means, though not necessarily in
respectability, until the explorer attains the poets and painters
in the attic. As most Spaniards have very little ambition to
make a display in society, their habitations are sufficiently
large, and they would have good reason to rejoice with Socrates

if they could fill even the smallest closet in Madrid with true friends.

However much a traveller may read, he still, in spite of himself, expects to find Madrid embowered in orange groves and harmonious with the song of nightingales. Such is far from being the reality. It has always been a puzzle to antiquaries to conjecture what possible reason could have induced the Spanish sovereigns to select Madrid as the site of their capitol. Except its lofty elevation above the Manzanares and its central position, it possesses not a single recommendation. They deserted the ancient cities which had occupied that pre-eminence —Seville, Cordova, Toledo, Valladolid, Burgos, Lisbon, for a miserable village, devoid alike of external beauty and historical reminiscences. It has grown to be a grand and magnificent city, but at a fearful cost both of money and life. The country for miles around is little better than a desert, producing scarcely any of the comforts which its society demands. Not a tree or shrub enlivens its dreary plains, and even wood, (a few olive roots,) in a place where winter rages with unwonted severity, has to be transported from the Guadarrama. At its great elevation of twenty-five hundred feet, the summer's heat is intense, and in winter, when the wind blows from the Guadarrama, I have known the sentinels to freeze in their boxes at the Palace. Individually, I have no fault to find with the climate. The air is exceedingly dry, and I found both heat and cold invigorating. But the almost universal opinion is that there is no more detestable climate in the world, and the majority is probably right. In the summer, the thermometer was generally quoted at two, P. M., as varying in cool spots from twenty-eight to thirty degrees Reaumur, and at daylight from fifteen to seventeen, and about ninety-five to one hundred, and sixty to sixty-five of Fahrenheit, so great is the radiation from this bare hill during the night. Crossing the Prado at noon to the Museo, does give one a premonitory idea of the lower regions, for the glare is so intense, that you scarcely dare open your eyes. In the winter, the temperature depends entirely upon the locality. On the sunny side of the street it is quite pleasant; cross to the shade, and you are transported to Iceland. Notwithstanding the bitter cold, certain semi-tropical plants survive, owing, I suppose, to the excessive dryness of the atmosphere, which renders a frost very rare, simply benumbing

them without inflicting farther injury. In addition to the mere
discomforts of the climate, there is the little mountain breeze,
which steals gently over the plain, freighted with death, and as
they repeat,

> Mata á un hombre,
> Y no apaga una luz.

The principal effect of an incautious exposure to this air is
the *pulmonia*, which attacks man and beast alike, and is as sudden and violent in its course as yellow fever. It is the great
terror of the Madrileños, and, probably, a third of the deaths
among the robust part of the population during the winter
can be traced to this source. The best evidence of the unfa-
vorable climate is to be found in the appearance of the families
that have resided there continuously two or three generations.
Very few exist after a hundred years, and the stranger is surprised to find how few among the inhabitants are city-born.
They are hardly considered fit to nurse children, all who can
afford it, employing for that purpose Pasiegas, natives of the
Valley of the Pas in the north-west, who bring a stock of exuberant health from their country. So far as physical health is
concerned, it would be better for the nobility to adopt the old
French plan of sending the children away until they have
attained size and strength.

In spite of all these disadvantages, added to the high price
of the commonest necessaries of life, Madrid is the great Mecca
in the eyes of most Spaniards. It is the Court—it alone is the
Court. For a hundred different reasons they flock hither, some
because they have received a little office, some because they
have received a promise of one, some because they hope to
receive a promise of one; and, once here, nothing but the
direst necessity can drive them away. A change of ministry
may cost the *empleado* his place, but he does not, therefore,
return to the rank of citizen. He becomes a *cesante*, or, as it is
more politely expressed, *sin empleo*, and lives on the hope of
regaining his position. He enters the over-filled ranks of the
" discontented," and is ready for treasons, stratagems and spoils.
The *empleo-mania*, or rage for office, has been characteristic of
Spain ever since the commencement of its decline. To attain
this end they will go any lengths, suffer any privations, adopt
any expedients. Strange that they never thought of the very
simple one of organizing a party to proscribe the " wild hunt

after office." They might even yet learn something from our side of the water. This state of things in Spain can easily be accounted for. Under the reign of Charles V and Philip II, the class of *pretendientes* was scarcely known, because of the continued external activity of the monarchy, which offered to every energetic person an avenue to wealth and distinction. Under their successors, the whole policy of the Government was changed. The nation, wearied with a world-sovereignty of a hundred years' duration, determined to be content with its present condition. From that moment, industry declined and finally died out, and there was no honest means left of gaining a livelihood. The poor gentlemen who had been accustomed to live by the sword, first pressed their claim upon the Government for a support. The example once set was universally followed, and thousands, who without being gentlemen, were poor as any poor gentleman ever was, rushed forward. Crowds of gaunt figures beset the doors of the ministers, demanding, frequently, in no very humble tone, that their wishes should be complied with. Bad as things are, still they have changed much for the better; and, as industry revives, there is every reason to suppose that this ulcer of Madrid will disappear. At present, Madrid has all of the vices and few of the virtues of a great capital. Its bankers are speculators, or mere money-changers, and its merchants shop-keepers. No one can point out the office it performs in the body politic, for it cannot even aspire to the position of the luxurious stomach, which, at all events, serves some good purpose. The spleen would suit it better, as the functions of that organ have not yet been satis-factorily ascertained. We do ample justice to Madrid, if we rank it as the fly-wheel of the monarchy.

The famous Puerta del Sol, or Gate of the Sun, is the great square of Madrid. No longer a gate, it is in the very centre of the city. In the last seven years, the mania for improvement has reached even this hallowed precinct, and a semi-circular space of buildings at the north has been demolished, in order to enlarge and to give it some regularity of shape. One of the first buildings destroyed was the little church of *Nuestra Señora del Buen Suceso*, with its illuminated clock, that stood to the east between the *Calle de Alcalá* and the *Calle de San Jeronymo*. This is one of the few churches I ever entered in Madrid, as, for the most part, they possessed no attractions.

Not so with the Buen Suceso, which was the resort of the fashionable world, owing partly to its situation and partly to its privileges. As Madrid hours are very late, many a fair dame used, on her way home in the morning, to repent here the indiscretions of the evening's entertainment, and its privilege of celebrating mass as late as two, P. M., drew the slothful to its altars. It was, moreover, an exceedingly convenient place for the loungers on the Plaza, and its clock is poorly replaced by the one over the *Casa de Correos*. Readers of the old comedies will particularly regret its loss. Strangers from a distance, judging by the world-wide renown of the Puerta del Sol, expect to find a park of many acres, laid out in grass-plats and fountains. On the contrary, it is scarcely wider than some of our great avenues, and is paved with glaring stones. But it is the heart of the Spanish monarchy. All the principal streets of the city empty into it. Everybody going from one quarter to another, and all the diligences cross it; every one who has no fire at home, and nothing to do, (about ninety-nine per cent.,) goes to the Puerta del Sol, to enjoy its sunshine; every one who has a picayune's worth to buy or sell, passes by the Puerta del Sol; every one who desires to tell, or to hear a falsehood, goes to the Puerta del Sol, so that about guard-mounting, the place is crowded with a motley assemblage of all ages and costumes. Le Sage certainly knew nothing about Madrid, or he never would have taken the trouble to call up the Devil-upon-two-sticks, *El Diablo Cojuelo,* to retail scandal. Los Diablos Cojuelos, that saunter about this square, without the external cloven hoof, would willingly have saved his real majesty the trouble of appearing. The middle-class of the population are, for the most part, idlers, whether *empleados* or *cesantes;* the lower is composed of the very dregs of the populace from every city in Spain; the former always ready to excite, the latter always ready to carry out a revolution. Imagine them collected together, and solely occupied with each other's defects, and form an idea if you can of the conversation. If I believed one fortieth part of what I heard there, I would have thought there was not one honest man, woman or child above ten years of age, in the city ; that the judges were corrupt, the ministers traitors, the priests atheists, the lawyers rogues, the doctors murderers, and the editors and telegraph agents a fraternity of liars. There is some truth in what they

whisper about, but the superstructure of scandal is so enormous as to make one despair of finding the little layer of
veracity below. In this place no reputation is sacred, and no
slander too surprising not to find some believers. I was told
the most abominable things about the president of the ministry, with a circumstantiality of narrative calculated to carry
conviction. My informant was a *cesante*. All the rest were
handled in the same manner, and neither sex spared. The
demolition of the church del Buen Suceso will be severely felt
in the next world, for instant confession and absolution would
be necessary to save some of these offenders.

The affair of the one hundred and thirty thousand loads of
stone was at this time making a great commotion. Without
entering into the matter minutely, it is sufficient to state that
a member of the ministry of Sartorius was charged with being
privy to a corrupt contract with the Government for the delivery of stone. He had been impeached, but the Senate had
failed to convict. Since then, a person behind the scenes had
come out with an exposé of an exceedingly damaging nature
to the offender, who had replied from London. This brought
forth a renewed attack. The Puerta del Sol was in its glory,
the defenders of the Sartorius ministry carrying the war into
Africa, by attacking O'Donnel, whose character could ill afford
to lose anything. Unfortunately, the sun left but a small strip
of shade in front of the Casa de Correos, so that the crowd was
rather compact. Peace was maintained, however, for no one
objected to the abuse of his friends, provided his own liberty of
speech were not restricted. The correspondents of the foreign
newspapers wrote that the O'Donnel ministry would scarcely
survive the shock caused by the failure to convict, or, perhaps,
the attempt to shield the peccant minister, and that a revolution was not improbable. Of this I saw no signs whatever,
and Spaniards make no secret of such things, so that the rumor
is apt to reach your ear long before the event, and is half forgotten ere the result is actually accomplished; but the ferment
might have assumed larger proportions had not the Morocco
difficulty intervened. The Puerta has naturally been a focus
of insurrections, as it commands the circulation of the city, and
a few barricades thrown up at each street would be inconvenient. For the same reason, a strong guard is placed there to
suppress the first outbreak. A regiment of determined men,

8

with artillery, could easily put down any insurrection; but, unfortunately, Spanish insurrections generally commence with the military itself, and, as I once heard an old legitimist say, after the coup d'etat of the Garde Nationale: "Ma foi, il faut bien une armée pour la garder."

Notwithstanding all these defects, the Puerta del Sol has great attractions for a native, and also for a traveller. A certain phase of life is seen to perfection, and, in a social point of view, it is one of the liveliest spots in the world. The ever-moving crowd and gay shops of the Boulevards, are wanting; nor is their any resemblance to the crush of Fleet street and the Strand; but, by way of compensation, it offers the costumes of every province in Spain. The gay majo of Andalusia, the soberer colors of Aragon, the working dress of the Gallican brush against the last foppery from Paris. Thousands cross it in a thousand directions, and for a thousand purposes. Now the crowd makes way for a battalion of infantry with flying colors, not large, but fine-looking fellows, well formed, and of active march; or an escort of cavalry, with trumpets sounding the marcha real, announces the approach of royalty. The tinkling of little bells, followed by a priest with the eucharist, on its way to cheer some departing soul, hushes the confusion into respectful silence, and causes the more devout to fall upon their knees before the mystical elements. These are temporary interruptions; the great business of slandering is immediately renewed.

Among the circulating population of Madrid, none oftener cross the stranger's path than the Gallegos, or inhabitants of Gallicia, the north-west province, situate upon the ocean and the Bay of Biscay, considered the Beotia of Spain. Leaving their rainy mountains, these hardy sons of toil are found wherever an honest penny is to be turned, and in Madrid enjoy a monopoly of the carrying of water, which, in an elevated city and almost rainless climate, is an extensive business. The place of Portador de Aqua is regularly bought and sold as that of an agent at the Paris Bourse, involving the obligation of attending fires. They scorn the aid of donkeys, and with cask upon shoulder, stagger along, not particularly mindful of whose head runs against it. They are as honest as the day is long, and as proud, for the Gallicians and the Asturians claim nobility as their birthright, and yield to none of the artificial distinctions of rank which have been created since the time of Pelayo. If one of them by chance receives an accession of fortune, or a title, instead of being elated, he merely considers that his original position is at last acknowledged. This little conceit, far from rendering them idle, has the effect of preserving them from the commission of many petty meannesses.

The lower classes of Madrid furnish the Manolos and Manolas, whose favorite haunt is the quarter toward the Manzanares, between the palace and the gate of Atocha, particularly around the Plaza de Cebada, or Barley Square, where public executions take place. They are the male and female counterparts of that portion of the American population which is called, in slang language, " B'hoys," not that there is, after all, any very close resemblance between them. Notwithstanding their reputation, they have little of the wit which redeems the similar classes in other Spanish cities. They have, or rather had, for the race is fast disappearing, a peculiar costume, and the women were distinguished for carrying a dagger in the right garter, which was not unfrequently appealed to, so that the act of stooping by a Manola was generally followed by a rapid widening of the circle around, as a stroke from her experienced hand was apt to be painful in its consequences. This class furnishes sweethearts for bull-fighters, and wives for the barricade heroes. Beyond that, there is no useful purpose to society which they are known to subserve. The men are always ready for any deed of violence which may enure to their advantage. Yet they have a sort of celebrity, and figure largely on public occasions, while the costume is frequently seen at fancy balls to grace the delicate figures of the aristocracy.

Owing to the variety of strangers collected from the different provinces and from abroad, society in Madrid is much more gay than in most other portions of Spain. In the winter, if there be no cause of mourning at the palace, there is a round of balls and parties from the first of January until Ash Wednesday. There are numerous *Tertulias* besides. The presence of a diplomatic corps from the dining countries of Europe, has introduced this habit also, and with it the drinking of wine, for the pleasure of drinking, which is quite unknown to Spaniards. The last two enjoyments are still confined to foreigners, and even they soon get out of the habit. After spending some time among these sober people, it is really a relief to see a gentleman lolling about with purple face and staggering legs, pronouncing the scenery too-ral loo-ral, or avowing a readiness " to whip his weight in wild-cats," according to idiosyncrasy.   It looks so cheerful and home-like, as though the good old Anglo-Saxon civilization had not entirely disappeared from the face of the earth.

The opera in Madrid is very fine, and the taste of the Madrileños for scientific music is better than usual, though they have never produced a great composer.   Theatres there are in abundance, the principal of which are the Principe and La Cruz, where it is possible occasionally to hear a piece from the classic drama.   The French vaudevilles have routed the national comedy in Spain, Germany and Italy, and if there is any useless occupation in the world, it is listening to a Parisian vaudeville; well enough, when it is a secondary means of accomplishing some other end, but its attractions, in a foreign country, translated into a foreign idiom, and performed by people whose national peculiarities prevent their entering into its spirit, would scarcely overcome that offered by the Paseo and a segar.   The saynete is really Spanish, and performed admirably by Spanish actors.   Here they are at home, rehearsing their daily life.   If an actor forgets the words of his part, it is very easy for him to supply them *ex tempore*.   When they pass from the vaudeville to the saynete, it is as when an Andalusian in Paris quits his tight-fitting Boulevard dress-coat, and slips on his majo costume, to go to a fancy ball.   Where everyone else is constrained, he is at ease.   Quite the reverse happens with the vaudeville, the easy frivolity and gay emptiness of which the tragic Spaniards never really appreciate.

Spanish theatres are pleasantly arranged for paying visits, as the boxes are frequently owned, or hired for the season, and the occupants expect to receive company between the acts. The entrance tickets are sold at the door, which give admittance to any part of the house, but no right to a seat, so that one may enjoy the society of his friends without being bored by the play.   There is one curious arrangement about Spanish theatres worthy of remark.   A little gallery is set apart, where none but women are admitted, and such a chattering is kept up!   Such a waving of fans, and arranging of mantillas! The place is called by various names.   *Tertulia de las mujeres* is proper; but by the irreverent it is not unfrequently

styled *el gallinero*, or "hen-house," from the eternal fluttering
and cackling. A sentinel has especial guard over the fair pul-
lets that enter therein, but should, perchance, any adventurous
rooster evade the watchfulness of this Argus, the ancient, but
still formidable hens, would speedily eject him.

The hours at Madrid, in winter, are ridiculously late. In
summer, it is well enough to turn night into day, because night
is the pleasantest part of the twenty-four hours, but such a
course in the winter is sheer folly. Eleven to one, generally
the latter, is the time for going to an evening entertainment,
and daylight the time for leaving. So that some of the population seldom see the sun in the months of December and
January. This has, doubtless, much to do with the unhealthy
pallor that characterizes the ladies, in contrast with the robust
health so universal elsewhere in the Peninsula. Even State
business is frequently transacted at night. In truth, fashions
here are a strong Paris graft upon a Spanish stock, in some
respects very pleasant, in others involving puzzling contradictions. Unfortunately, the gravity of the Castillian does not
cloak here his proverbial sincerity or probity, and complaints
are long and loud about the faithlessness of the Madrileños.
Part of this is true; part of it, however, is due simply to its
misfortune of being a capital, where forms and ceremonies frequently usurp the place of real emotions. Nor would it be
just to enter this sweeping denunciation against the whole of
Madrid, for it should rather be confined to the Court and Government circles. An apparently insignificant evidence of the
domestic feeling, in a certain class of the population, is the
manner in which Christmas is celebrated. For days before,
droves of turkeys can, or could, be seen wending their way to
the city—for every family must have its turkey. The streets,
on the Christmas when I was there, were, after an early hour,
deserted, except by ourselves, i. e., myself and another American, and one beggar, on horseback, who pursued us with
unconquerable pertinacity. The old maxim of "a beggar on
horseback," was familiar to us; and I supposed that this was
not an unusual custom, but it struck us as absurd to give charity to horsemen, so we obstinately refused, though the ground
was covered with snow. I afterwards learned that it was the
universal custom to give to beggars at Christmas, so much so,
that they regard it a right, and those who cannot walk borrow

horses for the purpose. So that, after all, the poor fellow was
not to blame, and we had failed in the greatest of Christian
duties upon the anniversary of the day that brought our
Saviour into the world. This little circumstance has remained
in my memory ever since, accompanied by no few regrets.

Christmas Eve, or *noche buena*, (the good night,) as it is
called in Spanish, we went to a puppet show, a *nacimiento*, one
of the few relics that have come down from the ages when it
was not considered disrespectful to represent sacred personages upon the stage. The first-class seats were at the moderate price of a *peseta*, or twenty cents. The room was not
large, and was filled with children, generally under the guar-
dianship of their fathers. It was delightful to see the relation
of confidence and friendship existing between them. The
curtain rose upon a church scene, an old sacristan and an
altar-boy lighting the long candles. The latter did not give
satisfaction to the former, for the old fellow dealt him a tremendous whack upon the head, which was returned in good
earnest, amid the roars of the audience, and the two went skirmishing off. The subject of the representation was suitable to
the occasion—the Flight into Egypt—and the principal characters, naturally, Joseph and Mary. Their adventures were
numerous, as may be supposed. Once they experienced great
difficulty in finding lodging. It was already late at night;
various people were knocked up and made their appearance at
the windows, but refused to admit the wayfarers, some of them
hinting strongly that they were no better than they should be,
strolling about in this manner, and that the ass had been
stolen. On another occasion they were assaulted, but Joseph
made such good use of his staff that the robbers were soon put
to flight. This part elicited great applause from the children,
and brought down the house. But, do not suppose that they
left the hall with the slightest irreverent feeling. It is one of
those strange contradictions, handed down from a remote date,
that no one would believe if not instructed by history or experience. The small children were certainly none the worse for
the exhibition, and the large ones slept quite as soundly.

Foreigners complain that the Madrileños are fond of eating
at the expense of others, but are not given to reciprocity, and
various reasons are offered in justification, all of which have
their influence. It is partly habit, partly poverty, for very

many families of high descent and respectability are greatly restricted in money matters, and are compelled to resort to many shifts in order to keep up appearances of decency. Indeed, it is a wonder how many of them live through. Many persons upon receiving an office remove hither with their families. They die or lose their office, but the family never returns; and as there is no means of gaining a livelihood, they remain, if they marry, for generations, in straitened circumstances, stealing forth at dawn or dusk to church, in order to avoid a display of their misery. Natives and foreigners agree that Madrid is the least Spanish city in Spain. Its inhabitants take a pride in adopting the customs of other countries and rejecting their own, without discrimination between what is worthy of preservation and what not. Madrid, therefore, is essentially imitative, and, as a natural consequence, it produces nothing great. Spanish ideas, Spanish manners, Spanish men, Spanish women, must be sought in the provinces, at Seville, Valencia, Saragoza, or Burgos. Yet the Madrileños are excessively proud of their home, and think that a residence here compensates for a multitude of misfortunes.

The Puerta del Sol is by no means the only gathering place for the Madrileños. The city has an unusual number. Most distinguished among them is the famous Prado, a magnificent promenade, with numerous avenues, extending a couple of miles toward the gate of the Atocha. From the Puerta del Sol two fine streets lead thither, the Carrera de San Geronymo and the Calle de Alcalá, the latter one of the noblest in Europe. Of ordinary width at the beginning, it widens rapidly, curving gently to the west. As the Prado is in a sort of valley, the Calle de Alcalá offers a noble prospect, and when filled with the gay throng of fantastically decorated vehicles and mules, on their way to the bull-fight, it is, perhaps, the most striking scene in Spain. About sunset in the summer, one endless procession covers its walks to enjoy the moonlight and evening air upon their favorite promenade. The Prado itself has undergone many changes, and in its present shape would scarcely be recognized by the old travellers, who a century ago described its wonders. At first it was, doubtless, a meadow, as its name indicates, but there must have been much more water then than now. During the residence of the Austrian sovereigns in the Palace of the Buen Retiro, on the opposite side, it became

the greater theatre for assassinations, and a general rendezvous
for all who had reasons for concealing their deeds from the
light.   Charles III—to whom, with his enlightened ministers, the Counts of Aranda and of Florida Blanca, Spain is
indebted for so many benefits—transformed it into an elegant
promenade, upon which Castillian grandeur displayed its virtues and vices.   He even attempted, in imitation of the Czar's
attack upon the Russian beards, to abolish the cloaks and
broad hats so admirably calculated for intrigue, but without
the same success.   Time and the convulsions of the War of
Independence have silently accomplished these changes, and
hats, poignards, antedeluvian coaches, and even cloaks have
disappeared from the more fashionable portions.   Certain portions have become gradually dedicated to certain purposes and
certain classes of society.   The favorite walk for the gay world
in summer is the salon between the Calle de Alcalá and of
San Geronymo, an open space of some two or three hundred
feet in width, with rows of stone benches and neat iron chairs
on each side, and a place for carriages and equestrians separating it from another walk under the trees.   Here from eight to
eleven in summer, and from three to five in winter, are assembled the rank and fashion of the metropolis, and a beautiful
sight it is.   Two files of elegant equipages pass continually in
stately review, resplendent with the "*flor y nata de la Aristo-
cracia.*"   Representatives from every province in Spain, and
from various nations of Europe, meet to form or renew acquaintances.   Languishing eyes flash beneath dark mantillas ;
a gentle wave of the fan is responded to by the removal of
polished beavers ; flirtations are commenced, and courtships
concluded ; politeness, cordiality, nay friendship, seem to unite
the whole population in one elastic band of a common brother-
hood.   It is whispered that these appearances are not always
borne out by the reality, and that when the minister of yesterday bows with winning grace to the minister of to-day, he
does not the less for all that wish his excellency at the bottom
of the Manzanares.   But let us leave those investigations to
the travelling Heraclitus, or the evil genius of the Puerta del
Sol, and enjoy the world not as it is, but as it seems to be.   The
Prado in summer does not offer the same throng, nor as great
variety as in winter, but the pure moonlight of an August
evening throws an indescribable charm of romance over the

scene, and it is worth the trouble of roasting through the day, for the sake of enjoying the night. Notwithstanding the invasion of French milliners, the costume of the ladies who promenade on foot is generally Spanish, but of the men, what shall I say? In place of the grand old style of former days, they have substituted dress coats, narrow brim felt hats and sticks; so that with all due respect it must be said, that the bucks of Madrid recalled in personal attire, the gentry known in America as "Bowery swells." What strange infatuation could have induced them to select such a dress is inconceivable, more particularly since, when suitably clad, the majority of Spaniards are remarkably well shaped and elegant. On horseback they appear much better, and galloping on prancing Andalusian coursers, beside the carriage door of some fair beauty, recall the gallant cavaliers of a past age.

Beyond the Prado lie the beautiful gardens of El Buen Retiro, a delightful resort at all seasons of the year. Below them is the Botanical Garden, which, in the beginning of the century, bid fair to be the most extensive in Europe. It was intended to collect specimens from the whole of the Spanish dominions, comprising, at that time, a respectable part of Europe and Asia, and half the continent of America. But the wars of Napoleon involved the destruction of this as of many other munificent projects. There used to be here a great manufactory of porcelain, called La China, which the English, on their retreat from Madrid, blew up; the Spanish say from commercial jealousy; the English say to prevent the French from converting it into a fortification. Between the two, Spain fared like the cats who called on the monkey to divide their cheese. The one nibbles off Toledo, the other Granada, then again Madrid, and so justice proceeds. Passing outside the city walls by the gate of *Recoletos*, the promenade is continued still a considerable distance. Crossing the Prado by the Calle de Alcalá, the street ascends to the gate of the same name on the road to Valencia, one of the finest structures in the kingdom. Just outside is the *Plaza de Toros*, or Bull ring. During the extreme heat of the summer the *funciones* are suspended, and its only attraction at this time was an animal whose performances had been remarkable. Eight horses had already fallen when the progress of the drama was interrupted by a storm, if I do not forget, and the hero was reserved for the

breed. He looked sufficiently miserable, quite thin, having lost
two-thirds of his weight, his neck covered with wounds, and
the sole companion of his sorrows being a brindled ox, with a
bell around his neck. To the west, again, beyond the Buen
Retiro, is the Museo, and still farther on, the Calle de Atocha,
another fine street, which, after crossing the Prado, leads to the
Church of Atocha and the observatory. On the side towards
the city there are no buildings fronting upon the Prado itself,
which has always struck me as something strange. But the
trees shut out the view from all that is insignificant. As the
sun declines, the scene is enlivened by the play of fountains,
some of which, as those of Neptune, of Apollo, and of Cybele,
produce a fine effect, though they may be criticised, if one be
so disposed. But the most striking monument is that of *El
Dos de Mayo*, or the second of May, erected in honor of those
who, on the 2d of May, 1808, refused to surrender their cannon
to the French troops, and thus commenced the War of Independence, which undermined the power of Napoleon, and was
the original, though not the immediate cause of the downfall
of that arch-tyrant. Well may Spaniards be proud when remembering that three officers, with a half battery of cannon,
in downright disobedience of orders, braved the despot of the
age and certain death in defence of the honor of their country.
The anniversary of this event is celebrated with almost as much
enthusiasm as the Fourth of July with us. All true patriots
must wish that it may long continue to remind them of
the danger to which they are exposed from their ambitious
neighbor.

Following the *Calle Magor*, which leads from the *Puerta del
Sol*, in the opposite direction, we reach the *Plaza del Oriente*, in
front of the Palace, forming a semi-circle, with a beautiful
garden in the centre, which is ornamented by an equestrian statue of Philip IV. It represents him on a prancing
charger, mane and tail streaming in the breeze. By moonlight, it is one of the most elegant productions of art in the
world, and seems really to live. The Plaza del Oriente is frequented rather by nurses and the bourgeoisie than those who
aspire to be reckoned among the beau monde of nobles and
Manolos. All the children in Madrid seem to have given one
another rendezvous, and your toes are continually crushed by
trundling hoops or the wheels of goat carts and similar infan-

tile abominations. The amount of talk was astonishing. The Palace itself may compare favorably with any in Europe. By day its whiteness is dazzling, but in an August night it appeared a mass of virgin snow, recalling the Ice Palace of Russia. The site was formerly occupied by the Moorish Aleazar, subsequently by a royal residence, which was destroyed by fire. The present edifice was built by Philip V, of a stone from Colmenar, which, in the pure air of Madrid, preserves its pristine appearance, as though quarried yesterday. Vast as it is, it is by no means equal to the plan first proposed, which startled the sovereign by its immensity. The inside contains many grand saloons, with gorgeous furniture and beautiful frescoes, but they are tiresome things to describe, and are, after all, much like similar arrangements in other capitals. The stables, however, are well worth a visit for all who delight in fine horses, from the graceful Cordovese barb to the thorough-bred English courser. Owing to the absence of the Court, they were at present comparatively empty, but on the previous visit they contained, in my opinion, the handsomest, I will not say the best, stud in Europe. I have remarked that Spanish horses belonging to the better classes, frequently present rather a pot-bellied appearance; some persons have told me that it is caused by the habit of stuffing them with quantities of unnutritious food, and the little violent exercise they take. Those that are engaged in constant occupation certainly have no such defect. *Quièn sabe.* The great ambition seems to be to get them fat. The adjoining coach house contains a most curious collection of those ancient-looking vehicles which bruised the bones of deceased grandees, and have been happily replaced by *coupés* and *landaus.*

The view from the terrace of the Palace over the Valley of the Manzanares, and the country intervening to the Guadarama, is sternly grand; and some winter morning when the wind blows from the snow-capped peaks, those who wish to know the sensation of cold in its greatest degree, can have their curiosity fully gratified. It is in these sentry boxes that soldiers are so frequently found dead. No wonder that former sovereigns preferred the sunny exposure of El Buen Retiro. The palace gardens extend to the little river, far below, from whose banks the white palace, towering on the hill above, presents a magnificent appearance. The Manzanaus has some-

how managed to attain celebrity, though none can exactly tell
why.   Victor Hugo, and other poets who never saw it, speak
of Seville and its Guadalquivir, Madrid and its Manzanares.
Could they only see this puny brook, this

Duque de arroyos
Y vizconde de los rios

of Gongora, struggling to escape the attacks of the direful
washerwomen that line its banks, how disappointed they
would be !   The feast of San Isidro or the Entierro de la Sar-
dina, makes its banks re-echo with the clicking of castagnettes
and the sound of merriment, but its muddy waters add little
to the entertainment.   Farther on, there is a very pleasant
walk in winter, Las Delicias.   I strolled down one August
afternoon and found the effluvia, difference of size considered,
equal to that of the Thames at London bridge, which, towards
the end of June last, was the most abominable stench that ever
saluted my nostrils.   Fortunately, the Manzanares is too far
removed from the city to extend its influence thither.   Though
so insignificant a thing, it has the honor of being spanned by
bridges of which the Mississippi might be proud.   The magnificence of these structures is in amusing contrast with the
general scarcity of water, and has greatly provoked the satire
of poets and travellers.

Madrid possesses two galleries of paintings, which are unrivalled except by the Vatican.   The first of these is the Academy of San Fernando, small in numbers, but priceless in value.
The gems of the collection are three paintings by Murillo,
which were taken to Paris from Seville by Soult, whose net
caught everything from church plate to works of art.   One
represents St. Isabel dressing a sore upon a beggar boy's head;
an incongruous subject for a fine picture, you exclaim, and it
does seem so in its present position; but had it been restored
to the hospital for which it was originally painted, the selection of the subject would have struck one as exceedingly happy.
All the excellencies of the art are here united.   The invention
is good, as nothing could have more forcibly impressed the idea
of .charity in a public hospital, than a beautiful woman of
the highest rank performing so loathsome a part as the healing of a beggar's sores.   The composition is still better.   The
little beggar himself is bent over a basin, his hands resting

upon his knees. A bare-legged man seated upon the floor, a
hard-skinned old woman, and another boy occupy the foreground to the right. In the centre of the picture, beside the
beggar, is the Saint, while the background is filled with her
noble assistants, in the finest style of Andalusian beauty. The
contrast between these groups is visible even in their hair and
the minutest portion of their dress, and reminds one of Titian's
" Tribute Money " at Dresden. The effect produced by this
contrast of the highest style of beauty with unkempt beggary
is most agreeable, for the beggars are by no means portrayed
in a revolting manner. The drawing and coloring leave nothing to be desired. The other room contains two large pictures
representing the Dream of the Roman Patrician, about *Sta.
Maria Maggiore* and its Fulfilment. In the former, the Patrician is discovered dozing at the table, while the Virgin floating
in the clouds, points out the site of the future church. Perhaps
it would not be venturing too far to say that this is the finest
portraiture of womanly beauty I have ever seen. Goddess she
is not, but a woman, a lovely, pure, angelic woman, such as the
artist himself might become enamored of. Both figures are
true Spaniards. The Patrician is a real Castillian Cavalier,
and the Virgin, no one but an Andalusian could have painted.
The Fulfilment is not so striking. The Patrician and his wife
kneel to the Pope, explaining the revelation that had been
made. The artist could not refrain from taking a sly cut at
the clergy, by representing an old Priest or Cardinal anxiously
fitting his glasses to take a look at the lady. These three Murillos are worth most of the galleries in Europe, and the Directors have done well to separate them from the Museo.

The two rooms contain half a dozen other paintings of merit.
An " Ascencion," by Murillo ; a fine " Crucifixion," by Alonzo
Cano, and a " San Antonio," by Ribera ; but they have been
overshadowed by the others, and do not receive the notice to
which they are entitled.

The other gallery is at the Museo, a collection as remarkable
for the excellence as for the number of its paintings. It contains more good pictures than can be found in any capital in
Europe, except always Rome. At the time of the greatest
glory of modern art in Italy and Germany, and the Low Countries, the Spanish dominion extended over those countries, and
its throne was filled by monarchs who were imbued with a

genuine taste for the beautiful in paintings. The relations of Charles V with Titian, of Philip IV with Rubens and Velasquez, were rather those of friendship than command. The execution of Charles I of England, almost the only person in that country who seems to have had a taste for art, afforded an opportunity, eagerly embraced, of procuring some fine works that had wandered thither. The natural relations of empire caused a legitimate flow of the master pieces of artists toward the centre of influence, and thus were collected in the various Spanish palaces the choicest treasures of Europe. The greater portion have found their way to the Museo. The number, according to the official catalogue, was two thousand and one, including, of the Italian schools—ten Rafaelles, one Buonarottis, three Leonardo da Vincis, forty-three Tizians, ten Annibal Caraccis, sixteen Guidos, seven Andreas del Sartos, four Correggios, two Domenichinos, thirty-four Tintonettos, twenty-five Paolo Veroneses, nineteen Poussins, ten Claude Lorraines. Of the German, two Cranachs, nine Albrecht Dürers, two Holbeins. Of the Low Countries, sixty-two Rubens, twenty-two Van Dyckes, a Rembrandt, fifty-three Teniers, fifty-four Johann Brughels, five Van Eycks, twenty-three Snyders. Of the Spanish, forty-six Murillos, sixty-four Velasquez, eight Alonso Canos, eighteen Juanes, six Morales, fifty-eight Riberas, fourteen Zurbarans, &c., &c., numbers which will serve to show the vast range embraced by the gallery. Many of them are among the best works of the authors. The Rafaelles are not surpassed out of Rome, except by the Dresden Madonna, and the same with regard to Venice may be affirmed of the Tizians. " Lo Spasimo di Sicilia " has been awarded a place, perhaps *the* place of honor. Of course, the verdict of the artistic world must be right, but I have never been able to reconcile myself to it. I have failed to perceive a trace of divinity in the Saviour; He presents to me rather the appearance of a person, crushed by physical suffering, falling under the grievous weight of a heavy burthen. The attention is withdrawn irresistibly, as from something disagreeable, to the bystanders, the weeping women and the soldiers. No accuracy of drawing, no excellence of portraiture of the subordinate characters can compensate for such a deficiency. How different the Transfiguration! There the divinity in the Saviour's face, enchaining the attention, causes all defect of detail, all incongruity of composition to be forgotten. The history of this painting, ("Lo Spasimo,") and of its hair-breadth escapes by flood and field, is like a tale of adventure. But whatever may be said of "Lo Spasimo," the five Rafaelles in a row—the "Agnus Dei," "La Perla," "La Madonna del Pesce," "La Rosa," and "The Visitation," are unequalled this side the Alps. "La Perla" and the "Madonna del Pesce," in particular, may justly claim a place after the "Madonna di San Sisto," for the beauty and purity of the Virgin, as Rafaelle chose to delineate them, and the artlessness of childhood, the sentiment of affectionate respect have never been more exquisitely portrayed.

By far the finest among the numerous Titians is the equestrian painting of the Emperor Charles at the battle of Mühlberg, in which the Protestant cause was so nearly ruined. The execution, as to drawing and coloring, is what one might expect from the great master in those departments, but the attitude of the Emperor is stiff, uneasy, constrained, positively awkward, compared with the boundary freedom of the Velasquez opposite, and I turned away in disappointment. But in the appendix to the catalogue are given extracts from the contemporary historians, which show that during the whole campaign he had been martyrized by the gout, and, in the battle itself, resembled an embalmed corpse or a spectre rather than a man. If such were the model of Titian, his success has been perfect. Every movement, every position, every feature betrays the warrior Emperor struggling against physical disease and exhaustion—the triumph of unconquerable will over the weakness of the body. It would not only be the best portrait, but the best painting of the artist, and, in its sphere, inimitable. Amid the number of others by Titian, two are worthy of especial remark: "La Gloria," representing the apotheosis of Charles and Philip, and "La Bacanal," in the Salon. This latter is exquisite. Ariadne, exhausted with grief, lies sleeping upon the grass. The vessel of the faithless Theseus is seen ploughing the waves in the distance. But the dawn of joy is breaking; innumerable bacchantes and nymphs are celebrating with dance and merriment the approach of Bacchus, who is to console the weeping fair one, and to inaugurate the reign of pleasure upon the earth. All this with the richness peculiar to Titian and Correggio.

The Guidos are numerous and much praised, but all of that

sentimental, lack-lustre, lifeless aspect, which characterizes his paintings, with a few rare exceptions. The specimens of the vigorous, healthy brushes of the Caracci and Demeniguino, are far superior, particularly the sacrifice of Isaac by the latter, which is worthy of all commendation. But of the foreign schools, there is nothing more beautiful than four landscapes by Claude, all of the same size, which are placed in the circular room at the end of the gallery. At each succeeding visit, I remained more firmly convinced that no artist had ever equalled, and none would ever surpass, these divine productions.

The Dutch and Flemish schools have contributed more than their quota, and are pronounced to include many *chefs d'œuvre*, but it is almost impossible for a Southerner, unless a professional artist, to appreciate at their proper value the coarseness of their o'er true copies of nature in all her corpulency, when contrasted with the ideal of the Italian and Spanish schools, and as my admiration was not aroused by them, I shall leave them to others who have been more fortunate. Indeed, rich as the gallery is in works of foreign artists, its peculiar excellence is in the home department, in which it is unique, not only out of but in Spain. The best works of Murillo are at Seville, but Velasquez can be seen in Madrid alone. The few that have wandered beyond the Pyrenees are very inferior specimens. Each of these sons of Seville has claims to stand at the head of Spanish art. The latter is more manly, vigorous, a better master of men, possessing in an unequalled degree the power of transferring to canvass the life of his subjects, but entirely devoid of imagination, invention, and the higher style of ideality. To the latter was granted a transcendent perception of the beautiful in humanity, of that loveliness of the soul which borders upon divinity, of a purity soaring above the earth, and a felicity of embodying his conceptions, that has rarely been approached. It is very difficult to judge between two such opposite characters, each being perfect in his sphere, and every critic will probably decide according to his preferences for the school at the head of which they respectively stand.

The Murillos at Madrid differ much in merit. Some are in the very best style, others appear to me far less successful, if the subject be properly indicated. Certainly the Holy Family resembles a home evening in a cottage rather than an assem-

blage of saints, though in other respects it be ever so fine. But
there are others worthy a trip across the ocean. Can there be
a grander figure than the St. Francis de Paula? Was ever
holy meditation more nobly portrayed? And did ever human
revery imagine a more exquisite idea than the Concepcion in
the Salon? The Magdalen is very different from what one
would expect; it has none of the beauty which seems unavoidable, when Murillo paints woman, but represents a real sinner
doing real penance. Indeed, the one which is marked as belonging to the school of Murillo, is much more like what one
might have anticipated. All the children are exquisite: the
St. John, the Virgin taught by St. Anna, the Infant Saviour
and St. John are among the most satisfactory pictures in the
gallery. I like the Crucifixion, too. It is a gloomy subject,
and should be so treated, with a dark back ground, and no
other figures to distract the attention. The Crucifixions of
most artists, introducing a large collection of persons with all
the accessories, generally shock one. They sink the moral
in the physical, and convert this tremendous event—which
rent the vail of the temple in twain, and shook the earth to
its centre—into a mere worldly scene of suffering and punishment. By the same reasoning I think it, therefore, a radical
error ever to paint the Descent from the Cross. Our God is
a living God, not a dead body. Such representations arouse
nothing but admiration, whereas those of the Spanish school
give rise to very different reflections and emotions.

Velasquez is the true hero of the Museo. He cannot be seen
elsewhere at all. Here he is in his glory. His want of ideality
and sublimity has been too frequently pointed out to need repetition, but he unites all the other requisites of a great artist. If
faultless drawing, strong coloring, a vigorous hand, and an
unequalled power of making his creations live and move are
sufficient to entitle an artist to the first rank, his claim to the
position must be assured. But Velasquez is a painter of life,
of positive existence and action. Contemplation, meditation,
passive, negative being, were either above his capacity or
beneath his attention. Compare Titian's Charles V with
his equestrian paintings of the Count Duke of Olivarez, of
Philip III and Philip IV. The latter are real, existing men
and horses. Don Balthasar, galloping over the plain, is faultless, inimitable. I attempted to discover some particular

9

in which the reality would have appeared differently (and nothing is easier for those who are not painters, than to point out the errors of those who are), but in vain; boy, horse, sky, the arid Castillian earth, were reflected from nature as in a mirror. His portraits have the same characteristics. The lofty intellects of Rafaelle's Pope Julius, and the brilliant coloring of Titian are wanting; but who else ever painted such a truculent, determined old Turk as his Barbarossa, or such a Govern. ment applicant as his Pretendiente, or such soldiers as his Surrender of Breda? His portrait of Don Balthazar leaning upon an arm-chair, is equal to his counterpart of the same person on horseback. Few young princes have been so favorably transmitted to posterity. I confess to a particular weakness for this picture. It is one of those that eternally look down from the recesses of memory. The imaginative pieces are not so happy. If the Forge of Vulcan was really so intended, it is a great failure, notwithstanding the felicity of execution. They are good looking, strongly-characterized blacksmiths, but neither gods, demi-gods, nor devils. And the Coronation of the Virgin is positively woful. Nor are his landscapes more to my taste, although they rank high. In Spain, where the sun is seldom obscured, and an ocean of light rolls over the face of Nature, it is difficult to conceive why Velasquez should have made her so sombre. In these alone has he failed to truth.

The Prometheus, by Ribera, is a grand picture, not beautiful; disgusting, perhaps, in the fidelity of its details, and eminently practical; but, for all that, it is not the less the work of a master hand, as much distinguished for strength as that of Titian is for elegance. In representing saints such as San Pablo, he is naturally in his element. They are fine, determined, venerable old men, but mortals; and, in thus portraying them, he has probably come nearer to historic truth than such as present them to us in the garb of semi-angels. Passing over many paintings by artists of greater renown, I would mention two which certainly made upon me a decided impression. The one is La Divina Pastora, by Alonzo Miguel de Tobar, a pupil and imitator of Murillo; the other is Saint Agueda dying in prison. This latter is by no means a pleasant subject, yet I invariably found myself glancing toward it on entering the principal gallery.

Mr. Ford seems to have had a personal cause of quarrel with Madrazzo, the director, for three or four pages of the guide book are devoted to abuse of him and his management; and, as English and Americans generally derive their opinions from this source, the directors deemed it necessary to reply, which they have done in a stinging note to the preface. His whole-sale accusation of repainting, his complaint that the catalogue gives only the subjects and size of the pictures, (as if a cata- logue was intended to do more!) his bad Spanish, and worse criticism, they handle easily. But one paragraph puzzled them. They could not decide whether the author were jesting or in earnest, when he coolly asserts that the varied coloring of the different Spanish schools was derived from and varied according to their respective food. Thus, the Andalusian *olla* is the richest in Spain; hence Murillo and Velasquez, Sevil- lians, used brown. Estremadura is famous for its red-peppered sausages; hence Morales adopted brighter colors. The Valen- cians like mulberries; hence they use purple. "Localism is the essence of the Spaniards." Such a criticism would puzzle wiser doctors than the Academicians. By way of reply, they pursue the strain: The English are great eaters of roast-beef; hence the partiality of the English artists for red. The Flemings and Dutch, of butter; hence the predominant yellow. The Bo- lognese, of sausage; hence the coloring of Carracci and Guido, &c., &c. Thus, Brillat Savarin would seem to have touched bottom in philosophy when he exclaimed: "*Dis-moi ce que tu manges, et je te dirai ce que tu es.*" The subsequent editions of Murray have corrected the Spanish and the personal accusation of repainting; but this obnoxious paragraph, and the other criticisms, are retained as choice tit-bits, giving the author very much the appearance of a bull in a china-shop.

The Armeria Real is as eminent among armories as the Museo is among galleries; that of Dresden being the only col- lection in Europe to boast a comparison in the beauty of work- manship, while in historic interest, it is much inferior. There are relics from the remotest ages of modern Spain, when the nation was confined to a small corner of the present kingdom, and every subsequent period is likewise fitly represented by swords and shields in more or less abundance. Their former owners were, for the most part, personages of world-wide renown; whereas, the collections of Dresden and the Tower at

London are of mere local importance, few English warriors except Marlborough, Wellington, and Nelson, being known out of the Islands, or the United States. The arrangement is happy. The smaller articles are enclosed in cases against the wall, while the centre is occupied by a double row, faced by the flank of knights on horseback, with a few pieces of beautifully ornamented artillery interspersed among them, and numerous banners hanging from the ceiling above, so that the appearance of reality is well sustained. The full suits of armor date mostly from the period when Spain controlled the artists of Italy and Germany, for few of them bear the impress of native workmen; but the collection of swords is thoroughly Spanish, and of course unrivalled in the world. Most of the great artists are represented, particularly Julian del Rey, the armorer of Boabdil, and a converted Moor, the most famous of them all, whose brand of the Perillo, or Little Dog, is well known, though few have ever seen it except here. There are also specimens of Miguel Cantero, of Sahagun, Ruiz, Martinez, many of whom belonged to families that transmitted their skill from father to son, and others of almost equal celebrity. When the War of Independence commenced in 1808, the patriots broke into the armory for weapons to use against the French, and many a Toledo of the first temper did renewed service in defending the soil of the Peninsula against invasion; but the collection was thereby despoiled of a considerable portion of its treasures. What remains has been placed in excellent order, and is well preserved. It is one of the best places in Spain to study or refresh one's biographical history.

The oldest piece is a rusty short sword, covered with venerable petrifaction, which was found in the Tagus. It was supposed to have been dropped there in a battle between Hannibal and the Carpentarii—rather a far-fetched conclusion, when the slight foundation for this opinion is considered. Then comes a bridle-bit picked up on an old field of battle in Andalusia, and said to have belonged to Wamba, the Gothic king. Perhaps, it would be better to remain content with the assurance that it is of the Gothic age, which is confidently asserted by those in authority. About the next there is more certainty—the sword of Don Pelayo, whose authenticity is proven as well as such ancient relics can be proven. It is simple and Gothic in form, and was preserved down to the middle of the last century in the sanctuary of Cavadonga, as his sword. In antiquity and historic interest, it surpasses anything of the kind in Europe, for with the strokes of this blade were laid the foundations of the great Spanish monarchy, which, for good or evil, has exercised such an immense influence upon the world. Next in chronological order are the Durindana of Orlando, the Paladin of Charlemagne, and the sword of his conqueror at the battle of Roncesvalles—Bernardo del Carpio—who occupies so large a space in the old ballads. As the existence of the two heroes themselves has been doubted, the authenticity of their swords will scarcely be admitted. The former is supposed to be as old as the twelth century. Of the latter it is affirmed that the Emperor Charles took it away from the convent of Sta. María de Aguilar, where it had been preserved as a relic of its master. Then come the war saddle and the famous sword—La Colada— of the Cid, which there is no good reasoning for questioning, except the general one of a want of belief. Like the sword of Pelayo, they were carefully preserved at a time when the rage for mere antiquities had not commenced, and when nothing was deemed worthy of such care, unless there was connected therewith an idea of reverence. In those times, therefore, the fact of such preservation with and on account of the accompanying tradition, is reasonably good proof of the authenticity of the object.

Leaving the heroic age, there are the weapons of St. Ferdinand and Jaime el Conquistador, both as true heroes as ever drew a sword. Then the armor of Don Alonzo V; the partisan of Don Pedro, the cruel; the swords of Suero de Quiñones, the hero of the Paso Henroso, so famous in the history of chivalry; of the Haros; of the Marquis of Santillana; the armor of Iñigo Fernandez de Velasco, the constable of Castile; and numerous others down to the reign of Ferdinand and Isabella, at the commencement of modern history. The swords of the Catholic sovereigns are preserved, the latter bearing quite a belligerent motto, " *Deseo siempre gera.*" With them are the swords and armor of their great chieftains, of Luis Hurtado de Mendoza, second Marquis of Mondejar, and third Count of Tendilla, who was made Governor and Captain General of Granada, one of their most distinguished Generals; of the Count of Altamira; of the proud Benavente; of Garcilaso de la Vega, " he who slew the Moor;" and, lastly, of the great captain, Gonsalvo de Cordova. The last, from the inscription upon it, was a sword of honor, and is used still on occasions of state—such as taking the oath at the commencement of a new reign, when it is borne by the head of the Velasco family, as inheritors of the Countship of Oropesa. It is also worthily used in the ceremony of conferring knighthood.

The succeeding age of Charles and Philip includes a much greater number, and the workmanship of the suits of armor is more elegant, as they proceeded from the first artists of Italy, Germany and the Low Countries. Of Charles, himself, they are numerous; two of them being particularly fine. There are two other relics which give us an insight into his campaigning life—the one his iron campaigning service, the other his litter for being transported about when afflicted with the gout, which did not justify him in neglecting the affairs of war and politics. They were evidently intended for practical use, and are of the simplest description. The armor of Philip, if anything, surpasses that of Charles in elegance of finish. Most of the great men who illustrated their reigns are also represented. Juan Arias de Avila, Count of Puñon-rostro, and Juan de Padilla, the two opposing leaders on opposite sides of the war of the Communeros; Pedro Arias de Avila, brother of the Count of Puñon-rostro, and himself a great warrior; the Constable of Bourbon; the Duke of Escalona, whose noble refusal to receive the traitor into his house, has made him the historical representative of Castillian loyalty; Garcilaso de la Vega, the poet; the learned and accomplished Andres Rey de Artieda, who was wounded at the battle of Lepanto, a worthy companion of Cervantes in letters and in arms; Alonzo de Cespedes, a warrior distinguished for his strength as well as skill. He, with Rey de Artieda and eight others, swam the Elbe with their swords in their mouths, to capture some boats belonging to the enemy. His feat of taking the gate of Toledo off its hinges, when refused admittance, recalls Sampson of old, while his gallantry, in handing the Cathedral fount of holy water to a lady, who, owing to the press, was not able to approach, surpassed, as well in strength as courtesy, the conduct of Augustus, the strong, of Saxony. Diego Garcia de Paredes, the Sampson of Estremadura, was renowned for a similar feat. The full weight of their arms fell repeatedly upon the enemies of Spain. The famous Marquis of Pescara and his nephew, Alfonso de Avalos,

are here; Pedro Fernandez de Cordova, Marquis of Priego;
Diego Hurtado de Mendoza, the historian; Juan de Urbina;
Alvaro de Sande; the fighting Bishop of Acuña; Sancho Dà-
vila, the thunderbolt of war, one of those who swam the Elbe,
sword in mouth; Antonio de Leiva, the hero of the battle of
Pavia, who, from humble origin, rose to be the first General of
his age, and to count on his muster roll the name of Charles
of Ghent; Juan de Aldana, who received the sword of Francis I
at Pavia; the incorruptible Hernando de Alarcon, who led the
vanguard in the battle of Pavia, who saved Charles at Tunis,
and to whom were successively confided the custody of Francis
and Pope Clement; Alejandro Farnese, Duke of Parma; the
Duke of Alva, the Elector of Saxony, whose defeat at Mühlberg, seemed to seal the fate of the Reformation; Don Juan de
Austria, the hero of Lepanto; the great Admiral Alvaro de
Bazan, Marquis of Sta. Cruz, who projected and was preparing
the invincible Armada at the time of his death; and Pedro
Mendez de Avilés, the conqueror of Florida. It seemed as
though Philip had been truly contending against the heavens.
The best Admirals of Spain, the Marquis of Santa Cruz, Mendez de Avilés, the Duke of Poliano, Davila, who had all enjoyed
a long experience upon the ocean, died in succession, and the
command fell into the incompetent hands of the Duke of Medina Sidonia. Had Sta. Cruz survived, the result of the expedition might have been different, and Elizabeth, reeking with
the blood of Mary of Scots, and hosts of innocent sufferers of
every faith, martyrs to her vanity or fear, might have fallen,
with but little regret, so far as she was individually concerned.
The armor of Columbus, and the swords of Cortes and Pizarro
carry us back to the early days of our own continent. The
latter was lent to Downie, during the War of Independence, by
the Marques de la Conquista, the representative of the Conqueror, in whose hands it was not disgraced, though, during his
lifetime, he eluded every attempt of the owner to recover possession of it.

The Armeria contains likewise trophies of the conquered.
The original sword of Francis I was removed by the French,
but an exact copy supplies its place. Boabdil, Ali Pacha, the
Turkish commander at Lepanto, his son, and various others
have contributed. There are also many most elegant shields
unconnected with historical events, and worthy of the skill of

Cellini, particularly one representing Hercules in the act of removing his Pillars to a boat in which is the Emperor Charles, standard in hand, and crowned by Victory. At the prow stands Fame, with the motto, "Plus Ultra." Another shield represents the Rape of the Sabines. Another, Petrarch's Triumph of Love. Another, the Shield of Minerva. Another, a Battle Scene near Carthage — all of exquisite workmanship. The collection of implements of war of modern times, and from the middle ages, is very fine—as Spain produced eminent gunsmiths, and her iron was peculiarly suited for that purpose. The display of Moorish weapons is unique. In addition, there is a capital index to these numerous treasures in the catalogue, so that the Armeria Real is one of the satisfactory exhibitions of Europe, and affords as much pleasure to the student as to the mere sight-seer. Spain was formerly as celebrated for its artillery, particularly its brass pieces, as for its swords. The foundry at Seville stood deservedly among the first in the world. This is still the favorite branch of the service, and ranks very high—but the guns themselves no longer enjoy their pre-eminence, nor is there any collection in Madrid to equal that of Paris.

The galleries, the Armeria, the Prado, and the Puerta del Sol, are the principal attractions in Madrid for a stranger. But there is some pleasure to be derived from merely sauntering about and catching the living manners as they rise. For my own part, I took great interest in witnessing the departure of the diligences. One started from the hotel where I was in the habit of dining. Though the rage for locomotion has much increased in Spain, it has not yet become an off-hand business as with us. They no longer think it necessary to make their wills, and bid an eternal adieu to all relatives and friends when starting on a journey to Soria or Burgos; but an expedition of the kind continues to make a sensation, and it is a point in Spanish courtesy to meet a friend some distance without the walls on his arrival, and to accompany him a few miles on parting. The leave-taking now occurs at the diligence office. Such benedictions and recommendations! Such kissings on both cheeks! And what a fine opportunity of investigating the nature of this electrifying operation, and arranging the various species and genera into a science! There is the stage kiss, a mutual placing of the head of the one over the shoulder of the other, as melancholy horses hang theirs over a fence. Then there is the formal kiss of friendship, a very respectable and well regulated performance. Then comes the edifying kiss of relationship to elderly aunts and cousins; then the kiss of affection, more to the point; and, last of all, the dearest boon vouchsafed by Heaven to man, the kiss of love! This alone escaped the wreck of primeval bliss, and, ye gods! how exquisite must have been the garden whose every tree produced such fruit! I have noticed one peculiarity about these scenes; that after the departure of the diligence, the prettiest one of the circle of abandoned and desolate friends was always kissed over again by the rest, until an inflammable bystander would be disposed to cry out, "No more of that, an' thou lovest me!" What could have been the reason of so strange a proceeding? Are they always the ones that stand most in need of consolation? or does this belong to the class of gentle mercies doubly blessed, blessing the giver as much as the taker? The more experienced must answer the question. Then, too, the society of the strangers collected in Madrid is varied and agreeable. You get used to the eternal defamation that exudes through the pores of the body social. The clubs and reading-rooms have increased in number and respectability. There is some relief from the dreadful ennui which used to fall upon the visitor after exhausting the novelty of the scene, so that upon the whole, I can imagine how a person, who had never seen Andalusia, or who could forget its proximity, might pass his time quite agreeably in Madrid, the pride of Spain and the joy of the human race.

Chapter VII.

TOLEDO.

Approach to the City—Moorish Aspect—Sta. Cruz and the Alcazar—The Cathedral
— The Muzarabs—The Fonda—Padilla, and the Comuneros—Escalona—The
.Synagogues—Jews in Spain—San Juan de los Reyes—Don Julian and la Cava
—Manufactory of Arms—Beautiful View of the City—General.

It would never do to leave Madrid without revisiting the
Fortress-city of Toledo. So, one hot morning, an acquaintance
and myself took our places in the cars, which have now rendered the journey of easy accomplishment. The oasis of Aranjuez, with its dense foliage and shady walks, tempted us sorely
after the arid, seething, roasting country through which we
had passed. But we made no halt, and continued on our way
down the river. The cars were very commodious, and were
furnished with a double roof that aided materially in keeping
off the heat of the sun's rays. Nor were we inconvenienced by
dust or smoke. An indistinct mass, blocking up the valley of
the Tagus, soon announced the proximity of the capital of the
Goths. We coursed down the pretty Vega, closely hemmed in
on either side by the naked hills, for a half hour longer, and
landed at the station outside of the walls. The appearance of
Toledo is noble. The river, making a semi-circular curve to the
left in order to pass the hill, or rather immense rock upon
which it is situate, bursts through the Sierra with the fury of a
fretted and impatient giant; while, upon the Madrid side, the
summit is crowned by the huge Alcazar, frowning perpendicularly down upon the roaring Tagus, and presenting a grand
point of view for miles distant. The gaily dressed zagal, who,
in response to our hints, vowed that he never had been and
never expected to be in love, but had arrayed himself so stun-
ningly merely for general effect, drove us at half speed along
the Paseo, past the statue of Wamba, over the bridge of Alcan-

tara, one of those structures which drive the artist wild, and up by zig-zags into the city, making the most wonderful turnings of sharp. corners in streets scarcely wider than the diligence, and deposited us safely at the Posada.

Breakfast despatched, the guide was summoned — Cabeza (a head) by name. He was a spare personage, fifty-one years of age, somewhat battered, and the worse for wear. Had been a Carlist soldier; on the downfall of that party, an exile in France. Six wounds in the head, two balls in the leg, and one arm shattered, were the sole rewards of his long service,—quite enough for one man. On our way to the Santa Cruz, under his guidance, we passed through the City Square, an irregular, open space, still called the Zocodover, as Moorish in appearance as in name. It was the time of the *Feria*, and but for our own costume, we might almost have fancied ourselves in the age of one of the Abd-er-Rahmans. To visit the Santa Cruz and the Alcazar, it was necessary to call upon the Colonel, as this was not the regular day, so we first proceeded to headquarters. He was very courteous, but had one of those severe, unsympathizing military faces which would cause any one indicted for treason to challenge him incontinently. The staff in the ante-chamber were a much more jovial set. The hospital of Santa Cruz, built by one of the Mendozas, is, notwithstanding the neglect of centuries, still a remarkably beautiful structure. The entrance and the first Patio are in the finest style. One may travel far and near, and see little to surpass this court. I know nothing north of Andalusia equal to it. It has been brushed up of late for the purposes of the Military School, and the process was still going on with manifest advantage. The second Patio, though large, is much more simple. Workmen were engaged in cutting up the church, one arm of the cross being quite sufficient for the necessities of this irreligious age. Situate upon the edge of the precipice, the prospect must be fine, and particularly the view from windows of the comedor or dining-room, down into the valley of the Tagus, and over the country beyond, which is indeed superb. The chief-cook insisted upon our visiting his department, also, and looking into the huge pots in which his dinner was boiling. Faithful to my duty as a traveller, I report that the pots were of good size, and the odor of the dinner agreeable at a distance. No extra charge was made for this enjoyment.

The Alcazar is situate upon the very summit of the Toledo rock, overtopping the whole city. It is an immense fortress palace, or, rather, the remains of one, in the solid style of the old Spanish architecture, the greater part dating from the time of Charles and Philip, though the foundations were laid figuratively, and perhaps actually, in the reign of King Wamba. At present, little survives except the naked shell, which frowns desolately over the walls of rock that hem in the foaming river. The interior was blown up by the English or Portuguese, or, perhaps, both, fired by the French, and desecrated by a thousand impious hands. From its parapet you see the situation of Toledo. The Sierra here crosses the valley of the Tagus, which winds around the city on your right hand as you look up the stream, making for itself a precipitous passage through the ridge. The rock on which the city stands seems to be an independent hill, being thus separated by the river on the right, and a depression nearly to the level of the plain on the left. But, in truth, it is a part of the Sierra itself, and, owing to its magnificent position—commanding the communication between the centre and the west of Spain—was always a post of the first rank of importance. The Goths made Toledo their capital, and it is full of recollections of the age previous to the conquest by the Saracens. With them, in turn, it was a place of influence; and its history during this period is of the greater interest, because of the number of Christians who remained under the Mohammedan rule, enjoying a liberty of conscience that puts contemporaneous Europe to the blush. Under Alfonso VI, it again became of importance; but, since the days of the Emperor Charles, Toledo has remained in a state of petrifaction, as if preserved for the benefit of travellers. You see a finished city precisely as it was three centuries ago, a mediæval Pompeii; for I doubt much whether a single building has been pulled down or built up in all that time. The prospect to the south-west is quite equal to that toward the north. The immense Cathedral stands nobly in the foreground, its spire piercing the heavens, and all its ornaments glittering in the blaze of a Castile sun. Beyond and around lay the city, and through the fertile Vega flowed the golden Tagus, hastening to the orange groves of Lisbon. After taking a glance at the extensive stables, which, as usual, are under ground, we descended into the town on our way to the Cathedral. The streets were narrow and steep, made for a horseback people; the houses small, and without windows on the outside,—a regular *Morería*. In a great many were yet visible the wooden lintels, placed over the entrance by the Moors, as the carved inscriptions testify. They have survived the vicissitudes of perhaps a thousand years; for the air of Spain is so pure that some kinds of wood last almost forever. Everything was ancient. A little *café*, a trapezoidal court with an awning drawn over it, into which we stepped to refresh, seemed to have been just disinterred; though I doubt whether the Moors had so cooling a drink as *agraz* wherewith to lower the temperature of their parched bodies.

We soon entered the Cathedral, which, in every point of view, is a magnificent edifice. The richness of ornament is astonishing, and not inappropriate, with the exception of the immense, confused, involuted, and intricate marble work behind the *retablo* or the *tras-altar*. The general effect even of this is good when seen in a certain light. It is needless to say that most of the valuables were secreted during the War of Independence, otherwise modern travellers would have faint opportunity of admiring them. The chapels are full of curiosities and interesting historical tombs, but I pass them by, as once commencing one could scarcely know where to stop. One of them, however, the Muzarabic, deserves more particular mention.

The history of the Spanish Church, if impartially written, would be the most interesting of Christendom, because from its commencement, the prelates, owing to their superior enlightenment, enjoyed a respect and an influence in political and social affairs which were by no means yielded to them elsewhere. Under the Goths, they were the depositaries of civilization. Hallam turns away from the history of the Goths with a contemptuous sneer, simply saying that the annals of barbarians are unworthy of investigation. But this is an astonishing misconception, for of all the northern nations, the Goths became the soonest civilized, and partly for the very reason that they did adopt, to a certain extent, the civil and canon law. Being the first of the barbarian tribes that overran the Roman Empire, their name and that of the Vandals were perpetuated as synonymous with barbarity and desecration. When their successors appeared upon the stage, the world had grown used

to such excesses, and they no longer provoked those fierce
denunciations. They had the further misfortune of incurring
the anathemas of the faithful by their obstinate adherence to
the doctrines of the Arian heresy. Yet, historians have vied
with each other in repeating these maledictions, without stopping to institute a comparison or to investigate the propriety
of this odious pre-eminence. Certainly they were far superior
to the contemporaneous Franks and Anglo-Saxons. The Spanish prelates seem to have been always influenced, both under
the Goths, and, subsequently, by the prevailing trait in the
national character—an unwillingness to submit to foreign domination, and refused to yield more than a nominal supremacy
to the Pope. Under the dominion of the Saracens, the bond
uniting them with Rome became weaker still. The Caliphs of
Cordoba even presented the bishops. Upon the conquest of
Toledo, the Mohammedans, who were strangers to the Christian doctrine of religious intolerance, granted the usual terms
to the vanquished, that is, a certain number of churches (six
in this case: St. Luke, St. Sebastian, St. Mark, St. Torcad, Sta.
Olalla, and Stas. Justa and Rufina) were set apart for their
worship. In addition, they were granted an Alcalde, who dis-
pensed justice among them according to the old Gothic Fuero
Juzgo. The same sort of polity is still preserved among
Oriental nations, particularly with regard to foreign consuls.
These subject Christians were styled by the conquerors Muzarabs, which was strangely enough derived by philologists, from
mixti arabes, a derivation that no Arabic scholar would have
made, for the Arabs were as ignorant of Latin as the Latins of
Arabic. The inhabitants of Arabia have always been distinguished by their pride of descent and taste for genealogy, not
only of horses but of men, and their over copious language
lends itself to the expression of minute shades of difference.
The original inhabitants of the desert, the descendants of Kah-
tan, the Arab al Arabi, never admitted an equality with even
the descendants of Ishmael, who were distinguished by some
modification of the word Arab, applicable to such as became
Arabs subsequently. It is much more reasonable, therefore, to
suppose the word Muzarab to be a corruption of Mostarab,
meaning an imitator of the Arabs. Mr. Ford attributes this
correction to Gyangos, but Gyangos makes no such claim, and
Casiri had pointed out the true derivation long before. After

the reconquest, the Alcalde of the Muzarabs continued to judge the citizens of Toledo according to the Fuero Juzgo; the other Christians were ruled by the Alcalde de los Castellanos, according to the laws of old Castile, which, of itself, would prove who the Muzarabs were. They retained also the Gothic Liturgy of San Isidore in its integrity. After the reconquest, the French wife of Alfonso and the Archbishop, likewise a Frenchman, persuaded him to conform to the general practice of Christendom, and to abolish, in Toledo, as he had done elsewhere in Castile, this relic of ancient days, but the Toledans rose in arms, and it was agreed, in accordance with the spirit of the age, to refer the question to the arbitrament of the duel. Unfortunately, Juan Ruiz de las Matanzas, the champion of the Muzarabic ritual, was victorious. The trial by fire was then appealed to with like success. The obnoxious work of the Goths came out unscathed. The exultation of the Spaniards was boundless, but the ultimate success of the persevering monarch is said to have given rise to the proverb, so common since,

> Allá van leyes
> Do quieren Reyes.

A one-sided compromise was finally effected, and in spite of the movement made by Cardinal Jimenez, the Muzarabic Ritual has, I believe, entirely disappeared, except in the service of this chapel. It differs in some points from the common Missal, though I am not sufficiently skilled in theology to say whether these differences be vital.

It has been supposed, at least it was so charged, that the subject Christians introduced into their belief many corruptions from Mohammedan sources. But universal experience has shown that a vigorous faith is preserved in greater purity under oppression than when uplifted by worldly prosperity. It is probable, however, that the exterior observances were somewhat modified by the various points of agreement which the two religions presented. The Mohammedans respected Jesus as a great prophet, inferior only to him of Mecca, and so were many of the Jewish patriarchs and prophets held in equal reverence by the three great creeds which divide the children of Abraham, the common father of them all.

Vanse días, vienen dias,
    Venido era el de San Juin,
    Donde Cristianos y Moros,
    Hacen gran solemnidad,
    Los Cristianos echan juncia,
    Y los Moros arrayan.
Los Judios echan encas
    Por la fiesta mas honrar.

That the essential doctrines of belief suffered any alteration or corruption is scarcely to be supposed. If any such there were, the terror of the Inquisition has effectually rooted them out.

The Cathedral of Toledo, among other precious relics, boasts also a marble slab, upon which the Virgin descended to place the *Casulla* upon the shoulders of St. Ildefonso. Cabeza reverently thrust his two fingers into the holes which devotion has made, and kissed the tips of them. May he derive all the benefit he anticipated. He assured us we were fortunate in the time of our visit, being the fair, as the image of the Virgin would be clothed in her jewels. To describe all the treasures contained in a Cathedral that has received and merited the appellation of "La Rica," would be a task as tedious as unprofitable. The great mediæval Cathedrals are said to resume in themselves the history of their times. This is eminently true of that of Toledo, which is a repository of ancient art and history. I liked nothing about it better than the beautiful appearance of the towers from the Alcazar. The sonorous peal, too, of the bell is grand. But whatever may have been the effect of the Cathedral, it was surpassed by that of the cloister, which seemed to us, coming out of the narrow glaring streets, the most beautiful sight we had ever beheld. The elegant colonnade and luxurious green of the Patio might well reconcile one to an abnegation of the exterior pleasures of the world.

After loitering about awhile, we returned to dinner at the Posada, and enjoyed the meal, thoroughly, under the awning. It was a foretaste of Andalusia. Hitherto on the journey through Aragon and Castile, I had seen little to recall the Spain of the Poets. The style of domestic architecture, the dress and habits of the people, had savored somewhat of the chilly north. Here we felt once more at home. Seated on a rickety chair in the *Patio*, surrounded by dogs, cats, women

sewing, and arrieros with *fajás* and *calañes* hats, and the thermometer standing at 140° in the street outside, we admitted
that mere existence was beginning to be agreeable.

The manufactory of arms being some little distance beyond
the walls, the host offered us, after dinner, a carriage at three
dollars. We proposed one and a half, the full value, which he
refused. We started to walk. He came down to two. Our
pride declined meeting the offer of compromise, and fortunately, as we would thereby have missed a very pleasant stroll,
and, in all probability, have been jolted nearly to death. So
off we went under the reluctant leadership of Cabeza.

There were two spots in Toledo, very interesting in their
historical associations, which I had overlooked on the former
visit. We proceeded to them at once. The one was the site of
the residence of Padilla, the leader of the rebellion of the Comuneros against the Emperor Charles, the last vigorous stand
made for the old Spanish liberties. Contemporaneous historians, writing under the influence of the monarch, have dwelt
upon the frailties of the rebels. Yet, making due allowance, it
was a noble effort to save their country from the ever increasing
preponderance of the royal prerogative. But the struggle
was in vain. The united power of the Sovereign of Spain, of
Germany, of Italy, and of America, was too great. The rod
of the anointed swallowed up the smaller rods, and Padilla
atoned for his temerity by the forfeit of his life. His noble
wife, Maria de Pacheco, refused to surrender, and when forced
to yield the suburbs of the city, retired to the Alcazar, where
she, for a long time, continued to resist, until, all hope gone,
she succeeded in effecting her escape to Portugal. Every trace
of the rebellion was obliterated and the very dwelling of its
chief razed to the ground, so that one stone should not stand
upon another. The Court was removed to punish the city,
which had sympathized with this attempt, and the pall of absolutism remained four long centuries, stifling every aspiration for
freedom. Had the prayer of the Comuneros been granted,
Charles might not the less have been the great Emperor, and
Spain would have been free. In more fortunate times a returning sense of justice caused the spot to be marked by a small
tablet, commemorative of the event.

The other was even more interesting—the ruins of the palace
of the Duke of Escalona, the head of the Pacheco family.

10

When the Constable of Bourbon, who had fought against his native country, and was branded throughout Europe with the name of traitor, came to the Spanish Court, after the battle of Pavia, its lofty cavaliers were unable to conceal their horror of a crime which shocked all those ideas of honor and loyalty that formed the foundation of their knightly character. Charles requested the Duke of Escalona to receive him into his palace. The subject professed his readiness to comply with the commands of the sovereign, but the proud grandee vowed the destruction of the mansion so soon as his unwelcome guest should have departed, considering that the house which had sheltered a traitor was unworthy to continue the residence of a Castillian gentleman. The ruins yet remain, the noblest monument that any mortal ever erected to himself. Cabeza fitly remarked, that the times had changed, and that treachery was now the shortest road to preferment and to fame.

Our route lay by the two Synagogues, quite unique in Christian Europe, for nowhere else did the Jews enjoy sufficient security to justify them in making a public display of their wealth. Notwithstanding their present bigotry, there was a time when Spaniards were as distinguished for their liberality in tolerating difference of religious belief, as they have since been for its opposite. The Toledan Jews boasted a very ancient origin, and asserted that, when consulted by their brethren of Jerusalem as to the crucifixion of our Saviour, they returned a strenuous remonstrance, of which a copy exists in the library of the Vatican, arguing, hence, that they were not to be included in the just hatred of Christians. The Vatican, doubtless, contains many strange documents, which, if brought to light, would require the history of modern times to be re-written. Whether this be included among them, is a more doubtful matter. Credat Judæus. The position occupied by the Spanish Jews, between the Christians and the Mohammedans, capable of benefiting or injuring either party, would have been much more efficacious in securing them a respectable position than any such remonstrance of their ancestors, however well authenticated. Be the reason what it may, the fact is beyond dispute, that, in the Peninsula, this people, the oppressed of all nations, enjoyed an immunity to be found nowhere else. Partaking of the peculiarities of the nation, from whose midst the edict of the Inquisition banished them,

they have, even in exile, been characterized by an uncompromising haughtiness and pride of birth, denying equality with
their brethren of the faith from less favored lands. These two
Synagogues were built in the pride of their power. The
smaller of them, now Santa María la Blanca, was built as far
back as the ninth century, the century after the conquest by
the Arabs. The other—El Transito—was erected by Samuel
Levi, the famous treasurer of Don Pedro, who enjoyed, perhaps, greater influence in the kingdom than any of his faith
had ever done before or has ever done since. In the earlier
days of the Spanish monarchies, the struggle for national
existence was too engrossing to permit of attention to aught
but the science of war. The light of knowledge was kept
burning only at Constantinople, Bagdad and Cordova. To
the latter the Jews had full access, and hence in the nascent
Christian kingdoms they are found in exclusive possession of
certain occupations, such as medicine and finance. From time
immemorial, they were conspicuously engaged in the treasury
department, which was a source at once of power and unpopularity, and had much to do with their final expulsion. From
whatever cause, their privileges were far greater in the Peninsula than in any other part of Europe; among them, the
capacity to hold land, which was not conceded to them elsewhere, so far as I can remember. Their subsequent expulsion
was an utterly unnecessary and indefensible act of intolerance,
but it was effectually accomplished. The race disappeared
from the soil of Spain, and the accounts, renewed from time to
time, of Hebrews still secretly professing their faith, though
filling high offices, even in the hierarchy, are mere idle tales to
gratify the credulity of untravelled readers. The two Synagogues are both of simple rectangular shape, and in outside
beauty rival the glories of fire-engine house architecture, but
within are the splendor and minute elegance of the East.
Costly woods, which Solomon was so fond of using, slender
columns, fairy latticed galleries for the women, who were thus
concealed lest the eyes and thoughts of men should halt between heaven and earth, all illuminated by the rays of the
western sun, streaming in rosy waves from above, produce a
complete illusion. But the *désillusion* is at hand in the tawdry
modern ornaments of the one, and the vile collection of old
rubbish deposited in the other. Some guide-book or traveller

complains of the surliness of the custodian. He either has not
been changed, or has left a worthy successor.

In the same neighborhood is the Church of San Juan de los
Reyes, erected by Ferdinand and Isabella in gratitude to their
tutelar saint. The noble façade is still ornamented with the
chains placed there by the Christian captives whom the success of the Moorish war had freed from slavery, but the body
of the edifice, and particularly the exquisite cloister adjoining,
are in a sad state of dilapidation. The former still contains
some fine works, among them a magnificent wooden statue of
some saint, by Alonso Cano: the pensive head is uncommonly
good. Cabeza remarked, "that head is better than mine"—a
fact we did not dispute, as his must have been somewhat dam-
aged by its six wounds. The pulpits, too, are gems in their
way. Among the decorations were scattered plentifully the
arms of the Catholic kings, with the yoke and the arrows.
There is also a gallery of paintings, which we looked at from
politeness. The court of the cloister was grown up with broad-
leaved tropical plants, forcing their vigorous life amid the ruins
of fountains and broken statues. Part of the upper corridor
had fallen, and fragments of sculpture lay scattered around.
The whole was a melancholy sight. Its cowled inhabitants
were gone forever. The stillness of death reigned around, and
the sound of our footsteps, echoing in these deserted halls, was
painfully audible. Progress is certainly desirable everywhere,
but its triumphal procession is too often like that of Jugger-
naut, marked with the mangled remains of what is most beautiful, and the sacrifices which this deity demands are frequently
so revolting as to cause its divinity to be questioned.

Opposite to the Church are the ruins of the Palaces of Jimenez, of Wamba and of Roderic, as at least of what are so
called. From the last is a view down into the gorge in the
river upon the Moorish mills, and the tower where La Cava is
said to have been bathing when seen by Don Roderic. Much,
perhaps all of this, is apocryphal, but why destroy these romantic fables? We cannot live by bread alone. The connection of Don Julian and his daughter La Cava with the invasion
of Spain by the Moors, was received without question, until
the rise of the historico-critical school, when it came to be regarded as a fable and the pure invention of Monkish chroniclers. This was the other extreme. Subsequent investigations

have shown that the truth lies in the middle ground, and this romantic incident will probably resume its place in serious history. As told by the old historians it is substantially as follows :

In the days of the Gothic kings, it was the custom that the daughters of the nobles should be educated in the Royal Palace at Toledo, and form a portion of the Queen's Court until the period of their marriage. At the accession of Don Roderic, one of the principal magnates of the realm was Count Julian, descended from the blood royal, and related to the rebellious sons of Wittiza, and the traitor Bishop Oppas. He was entrusted with the Castle of Ceuta, in Africa, then the bulwark of Christianity against the advancing tide of Mohammedan conquest. In accordance with the custom of the kingdom, his daughter, La Cava, was in attendance upon the Queen. One day, when the young ladies were diverting themselves by bathing in the golden waters of the Tagus, Don Roderic, in an evil hour for Spain, looked from his window, and spell-bound by the extraordinary beauty of the fair Cava, forgot himself, his kingdom and his religion,

> Ay de España !
> Perdida por un gusto y por La Cava.

Beside herself with grief at the affront, La Cava wrote a pathetic and touching letter to her father, who hastened to Toledo, his heart overflowing with revenge. Roderic, surprised at his sudden appearance, inquired if he had procured certain hawks for hunting, which he had been desirous of obtaining from Africa. "I have," replied the incensed parent. "They will accompany me on my next visit, and they are such hawks as you have never seen before in your life." Pretending that his wife lay mortally sick at Ceuta, and that nothing could assuage the pangs of her malady except the sight of the beloved Cava, he succeeded in returning with his daughter to Africa, where he entered into the negotiations which led to the landing of the Mohammedan army and the battle of Guadalete. This event must therefore have happened a year or so previous to A. D., 711, and the little tower on the bank of the river has been pointed out by tradition as the scene of its occurrence. As before stated, the history of La Cava received implicit faith, until a critic remarked that the name of neither was mentioned in any writing previous to the chronicle of the Monk of Silos, who lived in the twelfth century. The two contemporary chronicles, and that of Dulcidio, of Don Alfonso, and the Emil-. ian, do not even acknowledge their existence. This silence was considered conclusive, and the famous history of Don Julian was banished to the misty reigns of fable.

Since then, however, the attention of Spanish literati has been turned toward the Moorish authors, and they have enjoyed the peculiar advantage of seeing the picture of their history from two exactly opposite points of view. Many difficulties have thus been cleared away. The researches of Gyangos, in particular, have thrown great light upon the present matter, and established conclusively that so far as Don Julian is concerned, his existence at least is not a fabrication of the Monk of Silos, for he quotes Arabic authors of an early date, who, however much they may differ in the spelling of his name, and his position under the Gothic monarchy, agree in calling him Lord of Ceuta, and in assigning him. a prominent place in the preparations for invasion. The silence of the early Christian authors can be easily explained, when we reflect that a treason of this sort would naturally be better known to the Moors, and moreover that Don Julian (or Ilyan as they call him) was probably a half independent chief, paying only a nominal allegiance to the Gothic monarchs, and choosing his side in war, without thereby attracting much attention to the motives by which he might have been prompted. Apostacy seems to have cost very little at that day. Munuza, subsequently the Moorish commander of the northern frontier, and the hero of another romance, which has been ornamented by poetry and the drama, was, from his name, evidently a Basque renegade, Muñoz or Muñez, playing a similar part with Don Julian. As for the two contemporaneous authors, one of them, Isider Pacensis, describes the invasion in less than twenty, and the other the continuator of the Biclarense, in less than ten lines, without mentioning the names of Bishop Oppas, or the sons of Wittiza, about whose intrigues there can be no doubt. If their silence were sufficient negative proof, the history of that era in Spain would be reduced to meagre proportions. The succeeding chronicles were written in the recesses of Gallicia, Leon and the Asturias, far away from the local tradition, which was probably known only to Don Roderic and the courtiers, and it is natural, that the few survivors, if any there were, should not perpetuate the memory of an occurrence redounding so little to their honor, and whose connection with the subsequent invasion was probably unknown to them. Moreover, the Monk of Silos merely says that the insult to his daughter increased the disaffection of Don Julian, who was already leagued by family ties with the rebellious sons of Wittiza, and that they were all alike engaged in the negotiations with the Moors. The peculiar prominence assigned to him was an embellishment of subsequent historians.

In all this, however, there is nothing said about La Cava, and historians and guide books give her up for the same reason that they formerly gave up Don Julian, because she is not mentioned in the early chronicles. That La Cava is not the invention of any Christian, is evident from her name, which is pure Arabic and rather an appellation. What her real Gothic or Roman name was, is unknown. She is sometimes called Florinda. The Spanish chroniclers drew the tale, therefore, either from an early Arabic author, whose work is lost, or from some tradition current among the Moors. The thing in itself was not improbable. It is well known that the Gothic Counts or *Comites*, were the companions of the sovereign, and that their children were educated at the Court, a custom perpetuated to a very late day in Spain, not only by the sovereigns themselves, but by the great magnates. That the daughter of Don Julian should have been sent to Toledo, or to Seville as others have it, is natural. The act attributed to Don Roderic is possible, if we believe the general accounts given of his dissolute morals, though a great part of the crimes laid to his door were pious fictions to explain the heavy judgment of Providence upon him. On the other hand, it is not probable that the Moors invented this tale, because there would be no motive for their so doing, and because it contains references to customs of the Gothic Court with which they would scarcely have been acquainted, and which were altogether different from their own. The eloquent letter that Mariana attributes to her, is, of course, a subsequent composition, for if the confiding Cava knew even the alphabet, she was far in advance of contemporary beauties, and of some of her fair countrywomen a great many hundred years afterwards. The bath itself, is probably equally apochryphal. Popular traditions are poor

reliance in mere matters of detail, but they are seldom without
some foundation in general fact, and unless contradicted by, or
inconsistent with ascertained events or unreasonable in themselves, are not wholly to be rejected, because not reduced to
writing till some ages have elapsed.   So, in spite of the almost
unanimous opposition of critics, I was determined not to be
cheated out of the existence of the young lady, and gazed over
the parapet with as much interest as though Don Julian's
daughter were present in reality as well as in tradition.

Leaving the city by the beautiful Gate of Cambron, we
descended to the river bank, and pursuing our way through
luxuriant gardens, irrigated by water wheels of the most
Oriental type, the veritable Moorish *norias*, and giving and
receiving *abur* from the peasants, we reached the manufactory
of arms.   It is strange that some favored spots seem peculiarly fitted for the production of cutlery, without its being
possible to assign any satisfactory reason therefor.   Some
attribute the virtues of this locality to the atmosphere, others
to the water.   Whatever be the cause, Toledo has always been
famous for its weapons.   Owing to neglect, they once well
nigh lost their well deserved reputation, but are now fast
rising again into repute, and bid fair to equal those of the
sixteenth century.   The white arms of the Spanish service are
made here, and already compare favorably with any in the
world.   The building itself offers nothing extraordinary—a
large court surrounded by workshops.   Nor did the process
seem to be materially different from that pursued at Chateau-
rault and other places.   In old times, a great many demi-
cabalistic expedients were resorted to, but they have been
long since abandoned.   The weapons are tested in the most
effectual manner, both as to strength and temper.   The blades
are thrust against a wall, and bent nearly double.   They are
then struck violently on the flat side upon some hard substance, and the edge is finally tried on one of the softer metals.
The daggers are driven by some strong-armed person through
a copper or silver coin.   After passing through such tests, they
may laugh at bone or cuirass.   Those famous blades that were
packed in a circular box, can still be made, but more sturdiness
is required at present.   In truth, it is not easy to understand
how such flexibility was consistent with the necessities of
actual service.

I embraced the opportunity of selecting four poignards of approved quality, as they were tested before my eyes, and have no doubt they will prove equal to any emergency. I only hope there will be no necessity for trying them. One of the workmen from Cadiz maintained that the locality was of no importance, and that their excellence depended entirely upon the skill of the artizan. Cabeza, who was a native of Toledo, fired up warmly in behalf of the steel-tempering waters of the Tagus. As they were evidently partial witnesses, I rejected the opinions of both,—but it is certain, that though other localities have been tried, this, by unanimous consent, has been selected as producing the best.

Between the Fabrica de Armas and the city lie the ruins of the old Christian Basilika and the Roman Circus. It is supposed that the Roman city extended over this plain, as the modern one must do, if it extend at all, just as has occurred at Granada. Built upon a lofty rock, Toledo suffers, as it has always done, for want of water. In old times, the business of supplying it with this indispensable fluid was in the hands of the Gabachos, who came for that purpose from the French Pyrenees, whither they returned after accumulating a small fortune. As I have before remarked, the word "Gabacho" is of very uncertain origin and meaning. It is now applied almost exclusively to the French as a malediction. They were called here *Azacanes*, from the Arabic word, signifying "Waterer."

On the way back we enjoyed a magnificent view. The whole heavens in front were covered with a black mass of thunder cloud, such as tropical climates alone can show. The wind was coursing furiously down the upper valley, sweeping and tossing high into the air vast clouds of dust on both sides of the city, charged with the earthy odor of freshly fallen rain. Projected upon the cloud, and struggling between its gloom and the rays of the setting sun behind us, was the white line of the city from the gate of Bisagra, by the Casa de Locos, to the ruins that crown the banks of the Tagus; palaces peeped over palaces, and, reaching far above all, was the glittering Cathedral upon the summit of the rock, with the ponderous Alcazar in the back ground. This view, alone, would have repaid us for the visit. As the storm was some distance off, we proceeded leisurely, stopping to look at the outlines and scanty remains of the Roman ruins. After that we challenged

Cabeza to a race up the hill, and, thanks to his many wounds, distanced him; had he been thirty years younger, the victory might not have been so easy. He evidently thought us "originals," perhaps madmen, though the exact part of the world which honored us with a home puzzled him. He was kind enough to congratulate us upon our grammatical Spanish and fine pronunciation, which, from a Toledano, was very satisfactory, though he reluctantly admitted, when hard pressed, that our fluency was not so great as that of the natives.

We re-entered by the gate of Bisagra, and, leaning over the parapet, enjoyed the prospect which extended on three sides. On the plain below stood the vast convent of Afuera; and, beyond that, were the ruins of the castle, to which the romancers say that Don Julian retired with his daughter. On the right, the view embraced the valley of the Tagus, the Paseo, and the castle of Cervantes on the eminence beyond the bridge of Alcantara; to the left, was the road we had just left, behind us rose the city, tier after tier of ancient houses mounting above each other, until the whole culminated in the rosy towers of the Cathedral. As the sun disappeared, we wound down the eastern slope, crossed the bridge, and took our seats in the train. A few miles out, we met and traversed the storm, and ten o'clock found us seated before a cold fowl and a flask of Val de Peñas at the Fonda in Madrid, pleased with ourselves and the whole world.

There are few more interesting excursions than the one I have just described. It was a visit to the past, the yet living past, without vigor, but still existing.   Toledo is fortunate above most cities in preserving relics of the various phases of civilization which have existed in the Peninsula—the Roman, the Gothic, the Moorish, the Spanish up to the age of Philip II— and it has always been the favorite abode of the Christian hierarchy. Whoso has not seen Toledo, has not seen Spain. Nor are the reveries of the past disturbed by the advancing tread of the present. In former days, when the treasures of America found their only exit through the Spanish galleons, and prelates were powers in the State, the Archbishop of Toledo and Patriarch of the Indies enjoyed a salary estimated at $600,000, a fearful sum at that time, though very little of it went to the gratification of his personal wants. The number of priests, monks and nuns was limitless. They have all passed away, but the tenantless convents and monasteries attest their former opulence. This world-renowned city, the home of Wamba, the favorite seat of councils, the bulwark of the Moors, the last asserter of Spanish liberty, has dwindled to a fifth-rate town, whose scanty population scarce suffices to protect its crumbling walls. Even the railroad seems to have entered the conspiracy, by drawing off its population to the superior attractions of Madrid. The primacy, the manufactory of arms and the military school alone give the semblance of life. Everything beyond the merest necessaries is sought at the capital. Even bull-fights have ceased; those of Madrid being so accessible on great occasions. When the communication with Lisbon is opened, a change may take place, though in the present age of peace and ease, it is difficult for a city built upon a hill to maintain its importance.

CHAPTER VIII.

MADRID TO SEVILLE.

The reasons which detained me in Madrid having ceased to exist, I made all speed to embark for Andalusia, and a bright August morning found me in the Seville diligence. I occupied the berliña alone. A young Catalan and his bride, an intellectual-looking Italian, were in the interior. They fraternized with me immediately as a fellow-countryman, at which I knew not whether to be pleased or mortified, for, though it is generally flattering to be mistaken for one of that handsome race, yet it was provoking to be told in Italy that you had a Spanish accent, and in Spain an Italian accent. However, as they were very agreeable people, the offence was venial. The rotunda received a bull-fighter, a stout, well-made fellow, a little Sevillana, who said "Si Señor" so prettily, and a young man on his way to the Havana. There was the usual collection of friends to see us off, but the young man in the rotunda was most to be envied. He bade farewell, with commendable serenity, to several elderly persons, and, finally, to a handsome young lady, who must have occupied a much dearer place in his affections. She struggled in vain to suppress the tears that fell from her cheeks. How exquisitely beautiful she looked! Oh! ye dreamers who doat upon the Madonnas of Rafaelle and the Magdalens of Correggio! reserve your admiration for a Spaniard in tears, not the tears of real affliction, but those which reflect the image of love, and which, alas! absence dries too speedily. And if those tears, perchance, are shed for you, fortunate mortal, inscribe your name among the ever happy, and pray to be

removed to the mansion of the blessed, for you have experienced all that earth can offer of felicity. Yet, who would
believe it, this faithless swain was laughing at breakfast, two
hours later, as though the aching heart in Madrid had no
longer a place in his memory.

As the dreary nature of to-day's ride was familiar by experience, I begged the mayoral to give me some company; any
would be better than none. A few miles out, my request was
granted in the shape of a long weazened, good-humored antiquity, who descended from the coupé until some one more
worthy than he should appear. He was ushered in by the
mayoral, with profuse commendations, and though he was
innocent of many things, and probably did not know whether
George Washington was born in Kamschatka or Patagonia, or
that the British lion had bit the dust at New Orleans, yet he
knew all about La Mancha, which was much more to the
present occasion. We whirled on the railroad by Aranjuez to
the station at Tembleque, where we took our mules and em-
barked, for it seems like undertaking a long sea voyage. The
ancient looking square of Tembleque, with its slender colonnade, was familiar, but for many weary hours the road remained
utterly devoid of all interest, save that conferred by the immortal Cervantes, who, with rare success, has rendered one of the
most unattractive countries in Europe a centre of interest to
the whole literary world, for he enjoys with Homer the felicity
of being read and admired in all countries, and his fame seems
destined to survive through all ages. To do La Mancha justice, it must be said that the dullness of the country is by no
means a characteristic of the people, who are as good-humored
and lively a set as exist in Spain. Hard-working in the day,
but work once over, devoted to dancing *manchegas* and singing
Seguidillas until the morning. And then they produce the
Val de Peñas wine, which is the especial growth of the triangle
between Manzanares, Val de Peñas and Cuidad Real. There are
said to be two kinds, white and red, though I have never seen
the former. The red is full and rich, of more body than most
French wines, except perhaps some of the Côte d'or, and is a
great favorite in Spain, when it can be procured, for the means
of communication from one province to another are still such
as to require the pig-skin and the mule. A considerable portion of the best is consequently consumed on the spot. In

some parts of La Mancha good water is so scarce that the juice
of the grape, in its various forms, is the ordinary drink of the
inhabitants.

As for points of interest on this road, there are scarcely any,
save, as I have said, those which recall the gallant knight.
Near the City of Ocaña, on the left, Areizaga underwent a
disastrous defeat, resembling in causes and consequences that
of Gates at Camden. A few leagues farther on we passed a
villainous-looking gang of prisoners—galley slaves—" creeping
like snail unwillingly to" work on the road. I do not remember, in my whole life, ever to have seen people make such an
interval between the setting down of one foot and the lifting of
the other. The thing had evidently been reduced to a science.
At the Pass of Puerto Lapiche, Don Quixote encountered the
wind-mills, whose descendants are still flourishing, and defeated
the Biscayan after nearly driving him crazy by asserting that
he was not a "gentleman." Farther on is a Venta, said to be
built upon the spot where the Don was knighted, which may
or may not be so. His second *salida* was near our road into
the Sierra Morena to the Venta de Cardenas, whence he was
taken home in a cage. Toboso, the cave of Montesinos, and
other localities mentioned in the third *salida*, all lie to the left.
Many foreign editors and illustrators of Don Quixote have
been far from comprehending the various assemblage of good
and bad traits which are combined in the character of the two
principal personages in the history. The famous illustrations
of Tony Johannot will, I am sure, give little pleasure to any
one who has resided in Spain long enough to appreciate its
inhabitants. He makes Sancho a sort of Dutch boor, and the
knight ridiculous and absurd. Both are erroneous. Don Quixote is a monomaniac, but a true and loyal gentleman, whose
hands were never soiled by anything unworthy of the exalted
ideal which, in his madness, he adopted as a model. The spirit
that prompted him has always existed in Spain. It elevated
her to the throne of the world. Something beyond the mere
practical, some little ideality is necessary to greatness. The
veneration and enthusiasm of a soldier for a strip of soiled,
shot-torn bunting, fluttering from an old staff, is purely imaginative; yet, what noble deeds has it not prompted! In our day,
devotion to an idea is stamped as Quixotism, fanaticism, and
considered fair subject for ridicule. Even chivalry has become

a term of reproach. The next generation will probably be convinced of its error, and confess that happiness is not confined to the gratification of bodily or even intellectual desires.

A long causeway led over the now dry *ojos de Guadiana.* The same treeless, brown, dusty landscape, bounded by blue mountains, and covered with blue sky, continued until, at length, toward sunset we approached Manzanares, a considerable town, which, with its gardens and irrigated fields, seemed a very oasis. It was almost the first green I had beheld since leaving Aranjuez. Manzanares ransacked the highways and byways of beggardom to give us a suitable welcome. One of the applicants—a good-looking, tidy-clad matron—had some peculiar claim upon the purses of travellers. She was blind for one thing, and had received a good education in her youth, sufficiently evidenced by the correctness of her speech. I was too glad to escape by paying the required tax. Here my venerable companion was forced temporarily to give place to three brisk manchegas—just one too many, as there were only three seats—though the mayoral said, that as I had in the morning complained of want of company, I should not complain now of too much, lest it might be supposed I was hard to please. We had a lively time to Val de Peñas, where they dismounted, and the ancient resumed his place. He was very apprehensive of being upset in crossing the Sierra, and was continually saying: " *Pienso que hemos de volcar ; el ganā-o no vale nā-a.*" (I think we are going to upset; the cattle are perfectly worthless.) I gave him all the consolation in my power, which was to the effect that I could not prevent the upsetting. It is strange how people of a certain age dislike the idea of being killed! and how loth they are to follow the doctrines of predestination into practice ! Not that I was particularly desirous of dying upon the threshold of Andalusia; in fact, I never felt less in the humor of receiving extreme unction than at that moment. We sympathized on one point, at least. Contrary to good manners, but very consistent with nature, I forgot the perils of the road and slept soundly. An unworthy envy of my superior powers of repose prompted him to awaken me frequently under pretext of offering water and other courtesies of the road, until I hinted that all men were not endowed alike in this respect, and that opening my eyes would not necessarily close his, whereupon he unburthened his heart and vowed that

it was a shame to sleep so, while he was condemned to hopeless
watchfulness.   We made an amicable truce, however, and I
awoke in Andalusia, as we were thundering down the rocky
street of La Carolina.   To my surprise, all sorts of accidents
had happened during the night; the tongue had broke, the
mules had got loose, &c., &c., but we were all sound in body
and in mind, and exchanged congratulations at finding ourselves once more in the land of the cloudless climes and starry
skies.

If, in crossing the Pyrenees, the traveller feels himself in a
different land, equally strong is that conviction in passing from
La Mancha to Andalusia.   The sun was just rising above the
hills, yet the little *posada* had the hot, still temperature of a
tropical country.   Its well-swept tiled floor would have been
worthy of Holland.   Plants of various descriptions, neatly arranged in pots, adorned the irregular court, and the dining
room, ornamented with rude prints of the Virgin and of the
romantic exploits of some of the conquerors of Peru, evinced,
at least, an humble taste for the beautiful.   On the outskirts of
the town was the *Paseo*, with its immense oaks and walnut
trees.   Hedges of aloes and cactus skirted the roads, and olive
groves covered the hill sides, while far in the distance were the
lofty Sierras of Jaen and Granada quivering in the heated
atmosphere.   With what rapture did I find myself once more
in fair Andalusia! and how unutterably sweet to the soul was
the music of joys that were passed, but yet survived in memory!   My first passage over this road had been in midwinter.
Leaving the chilly, freezing winds that howled over New
Castile, I had crossed the Sierra Morena about noon, and
descended the valley of the Guadalquivir on the evening of a
warm day in January.   "Behold Andalusia!" exclaimed my
companion, himself a Sevillano, pointing to the land that
unrolled itself before us.   The ravines widened out into luxuriant valleys, concealed in whose bosom flowed the head-
waters of the Guadalquivir, pouring their silver tribute on.
White farm houses relieved the green of the olive and the
orange.   The city of Baeza, the pastures of Ubeda, celebrated
for the best of Andalusian steeds, and even the Cathedral of
Jaen, it was supposed, with the golden-tipped Alpujarras beyond, were visible to a practiced eye in the rays of the evening
sun, whose mellow warmth diffused light and health to the

animate world. As the balmy breezes floated by, laden with odors from a thousand fields, it seemed to me then, and it seems to me now, though long, long years have intervened, a fairy scene, whose harmony would have been marred by the most dulcet tones that ever issued from mortal. The natural charms of the country, infinitely heightened by the strong contrast of the morning, threw me into one of those undefined, dreamy states of bliss so dear to the Oriental imagination, which find no adequate description except in the experience of the Hasheesh. Upon the present occasion, hesitating anticipation had yielded to the certainty of experience. Then it was a dream of doubtful fulfillment, now it was a reality. The approaching month was to compensate for an age of tedium and strife.

Andalusia is the poetry of Spain. It is the Spain of which we read and dream. What glories can compare with its glories? What other land in Europe thus combines the remains of Roman, Moorish and Spanish grandeur? What thus unites every product of the earth, from the orange and olive to the tender flowers which bloom at the verge of perpetual snow, all in one beautiful harmony? What can boast such treasures of mineral wealth? What such noble specimens of animate creation? What so cloudless a sky? Truly has it been styled the mansion of the blessed.

La Carolina is the fruit of an effort made in the last century to re-people the wastes of the Sierra Morena with a new population drawn from Germany. Olavides, the mover of it, fell under the ban of the accursed Inquisition before his work was completed; but the foundation of the colony was laid. Many travellers have thought that they perceived, in the fair complexion of the inhabitants, traces of their Teutonic origin. The children are lighter colored than those of most southern nations, but the adults seemed to me real Spaniards in everything except the contour of the face. Indeed, complexion is entirely an affair of climate, though not necessarily of latitude; the features and the shape of the head are more enduring evidences of race. This attempt at colonization was not very successful. The emigrant did not coalesce with the native population. Nor have such attempts ever been successful except under ancient Rome and in the United States. The remedy for a declining population should have been sought, not in the importation of human beings, but in the reform of those political evils

11

which chained the energy of her people and forbade their increase. Under enlightened Governments, such as now rule Spain, there is and can be no deficiency of men.

One of the pleasures of travelling in Andalusia is that every valley and every plain have been the scene of some romantic conflict during the long contest which raged between the Christians and Mohammedans for the possession of this favored region. A few leagues from La Carolina, near the Sierra, lies Las Navas de Tolosa, a name ever to be honored in Spanish annals. After the empire of the Beni Omeyah had fallen to pieces, the Spanish Arabs found it necessary, from time to time, to appeal to the Berbers of North Africa for support against the ever advancing wave of the Christian conquest. The Berbers, indeed, did not always wait for an invitation. Andalusia was famous throughout all the Mohammedan dominion as the earthly paradise; and the leader who could cross the Straits of Gibraltar, and successfully establish himself in its possession, was envied of the human race. The Almoravides, having conquered the Empire of Morocco, pursuant to the invitation extended to them, entered Spain under Joseph or Yusef ben Taxfin, and, in 1086, gained a signal victory at Zalaca over Alfonso VI. The Almoravides, in turn, made way for the Almohades, a sect of Unitarian reformers, who, under Jacob or Yacoub al Mansour, with equal glory and fame, overthrew Alonzo VIII at Alarcos, near Almagro, in the year 1195. Still, the Christians, notwithstanding these defeats, pursued their steady course of aggression until Mohammed Nasser eddin Allah (defender of the faith of God), son of Al Mansour, determined, by one great effort, to restore the Moorish Empire to its pristine glory, and crush forever the aspiring Christian nations.

The religious war was proclaimed throughout Andalusia and Al Magreb, and the Emir crossed the Straits at the head of an immense army, threatening to stable his horses in the portico of St. Peter's. While making his final preparations at Seville, he received an embassy from King John of England, which besought his aid against the Pope and the rebellious Barons. But the noble Mohammedan, having informed himself as to the true character of that worthless monarch, rejected his prayer with disdain, expressing equal disgust for the meanness of the sovereign and the cowardice of the subjects who could submit to such a master. The approach of so formidable an opponent threw Europe into terror. Innocent III issued a bull arousing Christendom to a sense of its danger, and proclaiming remission of sins to such as should join the Holy Crusade. The rival banners of Castile and Aragon, followed by all their chivalry, floated in conjunction over the walls of Toledo. The Archbishops of Narbonne and of Bordeaux, the Bishop of Nantes, two thousand knights, ten thousand horsemen, and fifty thousand foot from beyond the Pyrenees, joined the allied forces; some in the true spirit of Crusaders, some influenced by an expectation of the tangible rewards of this earth, others under the fascination which dangerous emprise possesses for the generous youth of every age. The clergy bore their part not only spiritually, but temporally. Processions and a fast of bread and water were ordered at Rome, while many a Spanish bishop exchanged his crozier for a battle-axe. Long centuries had elapsed since such discordant elements were united, and the army set forth with the prayers of Christendom for their continued harmony. But dissensions soon destroyed the good accord which had been anticipated. The foreigners thought it best to begin their pious work by a general slaughter of the Jews, and forthwith commenced upon those in Toledo. The Spaniards were too civilized for such religion, and defended their countrymen, sword in hand. With great difficulty, this first commotion was appeased. Don Diego de Haro, Lord of Biscay, the hero of the ballad commencing—

En Burgos está el buen Rey—

was then sent out at the head of the foreigners as an advance guard, and stormed the town of Malagon. And now, says Archbishop Roderic, the devil, envious of such good fortune, turned the hearts of the ultramontanes from the holy cause. By dint of earnest persuasion, they were prevailed upon to continue as far as Calatrava, two leagues distant, whose garrison made a desperate defence, and were permitted to retire with their lives. This put the finishing stroke to the disgust of the ultramontanes. They had been debarred the pleasure of murdering the Jews, they had clamored in vain for the sack of Calatrava, and were determined to retire to their homes. Deaf to the entreaties and reproaches of their allies, they replied that the heat was too great; thus anticipating the soldiers of one of our regiments at Buena Vista, who refused to

drink from the canteens of the Mississippians because the water
of Saltillo, some miles to the rear, was so much cooler! The
booty was generously divided between the foreigners and the
Aragonese; and they departed, in the language of an eye
witness, "without honor or glory." True to themselves, they
attempted, on the way, to take Toledo by treachery; but the
inhabitants closed the gates, and bade them defiance. As
the captive Moors had been sent off under the escort of Don
Diego de Haro, in order to preserve the honor of the Spaniards, at least, the ultramontanes reached their homes in
sufficiently bad humor. Yet Mr. Ford seems to think that the
English and French were entitled to the glory of the campaign,
and were cheated out of it by the Spanish historians, just as
the inevitable "Duke" was centuries later! The truth being,
that, with the exception of the Archbishop of Narbonne and
Theobald de Blazcon, a knight of Poiton, but of Castillian
descent, with some one hundred and fifty others, all told, not
one of the whole herd remained.

El Nassr, who had been quietly waiting at Jean, in expectation of some such event, now advanced towards the Sierra Morena, and ordered its passes to be occupied. The Christians
presented themselves at that of Al Muradal, which was strongly defended, but Don Diego de Haro, who, like Bosquet, in the
Crimea, seems to have been present whenever needed, sent his
son with a detachment to seize the neighboring heights, and
thus forced the Moors to fall back for a short distance, but to a
much stronger position, which in fact proved to be impregnable. The Christians were now reduced to great distress and
perplexities. To retire for the purpose of seeking another pass
would have the appearance, and might induce the necessity of
a retreat, which, under the circumstances, would have been a
rout. At this moment a shepherd (or San Isidro, in the guise
of one) offered to lead them up by a goat path. Don Diego
de Haro and Don Garcia Romero, volunteered to follow, and
on Saturday, the 14th July, 1212, the astonished Musselmen
beheld the whole Christian encamped on Las Navas (the
plains) de Tolosa. Battle was immediately offered to the
Christians, who, however, declined the challenge. That and
the following day were spent in resting from their fatigues
But on Sunday, at midnight, "the voice of joy was heard in
the tents of the just." The heralds sounded the note of pre-

paration. The Mass of the Cross was celebrated. Every soldier confessed his sins, received absolution, and took his place in the ranks. The King of Navarre commanded the right wing; the King of Aragon the left; in the centre were the Castillians, in four grand corps, commanded by Diego de Haro, Gonzalo Nuñez de Lara, Roderic Diaz, and the King. Not far in front, on an elevation, was visible the Emir's Red Tent of Battle, and the sacred camel that carried the Koran of Othman. The Emir himself was surrounded by a circle of chains, and his guard of forty thousand men formed, with their pikes, an impenetrable wall. At the rising of the sun, the trumpets ordered the charge. As the volunteers, forming the first line of the Mohammedans, advanced, the Christian centre either retreated or was driven back, but the two wings closed in upon the flanks of the enemy. The issue was doubtful. More than once did Alfonso exclaim to Roderic: "Archbishop, let us die here!" But the stout-hearted prelate replied: "Nay, noble King, let us conquer here." At length, when all but honor seemed lost, the cross of the Archbishop and the standard of the Holy Virgin were advanced, and the tide of victory changed. The volunteers, to the number of one hundred and sixty thousand, were utterly routed. Not content with this success, the Christians charged the second line, composed of Almohades and Arabs. When the battle was at the highest, the Andalusian Moors, to revenge the various affronts they had received from the Hajib Ibn Djamea, rode off the field. Confusion immediately ensued. The followers of the Prophet every where took to flight, with the exception of the Sultan's guard, whose circle of spears defied the efforts of the Christians, until backing their mail-clad horses upon the points, they forced an entrance, burst the iron chains, and El Nassr himself was compelled to seek safety in flight. Night alone checked the bloody pursuit. The number reported to have been slain is scarcely credible. Archbishop Roderic puts that of the Moors at two hundred thousand, and that of the Christians at twenty-five, which one of the best modern historians of Spain has interpreted twenty-five thousand. But the other eye witnesses give similarly marvellous numbers. Alfonso says that by the confession of the Moors themselves, one hundred thousand fell, while scarcely twenty-five or thirty Christians were missing. The Archbishop of Narbonne estimates them respectively at

sixty thousand, and fifty. It really seems as though St. Jago
were present. The Moorish writers too, say that of the hundreds of thousands who entered the battle, scarcely a thousand
escaped, while famine created as great ravages among the
fugitives as the sword. In these days of gunpowder and
tactics, such slaughters are scarcely possible; but it was far
otherwise when every man met his enemy face to face, and the
battle became a series of individual encounters. The plunder
was of course boundless. For the two days that the army
remained encamped upon the field, they used no fuel except
the spears and arrows of the Moors. Even the silken tent of
the Emir, and his gold embroidered standard fell into the hands
of the conquerors, and were presented by Alonzo to his Holiness.

Great was the rejoicing throughout Christendom at the news.
Te Deums were chanted, and the lineaments of the shepherd
sculptured in the choir of the Cathedral at Toledo, where they
are still dimly visible. The King of Navarre placed the chains
upon his shield in memory of his prowess in bursting through
the defence of the Emir's camp. Many private families also,
the Zuñigas, Peraltas, Abarcas, hence derive the same emblem, while others bear the Cross, emblematical of the heavenly
signal which appeared to cheer the Christians on. It was one
of those overwhelming defeats that seal the fate of races and
religions. The western Moslems never recovered from its
effects, and for centuries afterwards did their poets and historians continue to bewail the dark day of Alakâb. This campaign is instructive as affording an opportunity of comparing
the Spaniards and Moors with their contemporaries, bringing
into strong contrast the cowardice, brutality and bigotry of the
one, and the chivalric gallantry and humanity of the other.
No better evidence could be desired of the superior civilization
enjoyed by the two races, which divided the Peninsula, over
that of the Europeans to the north of the Pyrenees.

A few miles farther on is Bailen, the scene of another victory
over an invading foe, not less distinguished in its day, and of
consequences even more momentous. In the year 1808, Europe
was physically overwhelmed by the armies of Napoleon, and
morally crushed beneath a belief in the invincibility of his
eagles. Austerlitz, Jena and Friedland, had successively reduced the three continental nations to the silence of despair.

Spain and Portugal had been apparently conquered. Every English army that landed, whether in Holland, Italy or France, had been driven with ignominy into the sea, and universal empire, like a paralyzing death-pall, hung over the eastern hemisphere. As the daylight succeeds the darkest hour of night, so did the victory of Bailen startle the ear of expiring Europe. It was stealthily whispered about, even in Paris, that an army of eighteen thousand Frenchmen, under one of the best Imperial generals, had laid down its arms before Castaños and his collection of half armed Spaniards. Foy describes the effect upon Napoleon. He cried with rage, not at the material loss, for what were twenty thousand men to him, who disposed at his whim of the lives of millions? But the charm of invincibility was gone. "Is your Majesty unwell?" "No." "Has Austria declared war?" "Would to God that were all!" exclaimed the Emperor. Bailen was to Europe what the battle of King's Mountain had been to the Southern States in the American Revolution. To appreciate its effect, one must have heard old people tell of the prostration of our own country when in the hands of two worthy patriots, but incompetent generals, sent us by Congress; the good cause had gone down, and no Whig dared avow his principles. It was then that the beacon light, kindled by our hands upon our rugged mountain-top, sent forth beams of joy and hope throughout the land. And so did the Spaniards, trusting to no foreign aid, arouse Europe to a renewed struggle for her independence, a struggle which was not to cease, till from the South and the East, the conquering generals met in Paris itself. English writers have endeavored to depreciate the value of Bailen, wishing, as usual, to monopolize for their island the credit of the Peninsula resistance, but all dispassionate men will ascribe to this glorious victory the regeneration of prostrate nationalities, and, in its ultimate consequences, the salvation of Europe itself.

As a military operation, the campaign was, in some respects, curious enough. One half of the French army under Vedel was at Carolina. Bailen was occupied by a portion of the Spanish. On the road to Andújar, was the main body of the French under Dupont, and beyond them the Spaniards under Castaños, so that the advantages of position were almost exactly equal. The diligence road runs at right angles through

the battle field. Both sides have been freely criticised for having placed themselves respectively between the mill stones.
Fortune decided for Spain, and in a few weeks, scarcely a
French soldier remained south of the Ebro, except the Portuguese army of poor Junot, who, after vainly attempting with
inferior numbers to force the British position at Vimeiro—cut
off from communication with France, and menaced by a nation
in rebellion—concluded the Convention of Cintra. The panic
of Dupont can be explained but not excused. Nothing could
excuse a General for surrendering with eighteen thousand disciplined troops. Surrounded with a hostile peasantry, whose
activity isolated him even from his own advanced guard,
crisped by the rays of an Andalusian midsummer sun, parched
by thirst amid these burning hills and exhausted river-beds,
embarrassed by loads of treasure, the plunders of many a cathedral and convent, it is not altogether wonderful that he should
have become confused, have vacillated and despaired. More
than this cannot be said. Napoleon regarded him with horror,
and never called him into service again. But the general opinion in the French army has always been that he was too
severely punished, and that the necessity of making a terrible
example influenced the Emperor's conduct as much as justice.
It was a universal and not unfounded complaint with his officers, that he demanded from them in Spain, with young conscripts, results which would have done honor to veterans.

At Bailen, the high road to Granada branches off, and we
received a reinforcement of passengers, two of whom, very
pleasant gentlemen, entered the berliña. They were going to
visit some relative residing near Carpio. Mistaking me as
usual for an Italian, the conversation turned immediately to
the war. It afforded a good example of the astonishing
ignorance of many well born and educated Spaniards upon
external affairs. It was with some difficulty I convinced them
that Victor Emanuel was not a republican at heart, leagued
with Garibaldi in a secret alliance against monarchy and religion throughout the world ! We had a severe argument upon
the Italian question in general. It is to be hoped that they
learned something more upon the subject than they knew
before. From Bailen the road continued to descend rapidly,
crossing several streams—mountain torrents in winter, but
nearly dry at present—one of them bearing the appropriate

name of Rio Seco—a very common appellation of rivers in
Spain, and not unfrequently well deserved. At length we
reached the far famed Guadalquivir, and about noon halted for
breakfast in the ancient city of Andujar.

The great, and so far as I could see, the only manufacture of
Andujar, is that of porous earthen jars for cooling water,
which are indispensable to Andalusian comfort, and are found
in every house. It is one of the inventions that are well
worthy of being introduced into our country. Filled in the
night, the contents are found in the morning of exactly the
desired temperature, and to my taste more agreeable than ice
water, besides being much more cleanly. As the effect is produced by evaporation of the fluid that oozes through the jar, a
low dew point is requisite, which is the case in nearly every
part of Spain. Suitable clay can be found all over Andalusia,
and, if I do not forget, in Cuba also, but that of Andujar either
is or is thought to be better adapted to the purpose, communi-
cating, moreover, no earthy taste to the water, and is consequently preferred. It is surprising to see how much will exude
from a pitcher even during dinner, and the greatest luxury
of a hot climate is thus placed within reach of the poorest
family.

A nice young Norman had joined us at Bailen, on his way to
Seville. The diligence being full and he the last comer, it was
necessary to displace the mayoral from his seat; he, in turn,
displaced the zagal, who sat where he could, which, generally
speaking, was nowhere. All this had to be paid for *extra* by
way of a *gratificacion* to these functionaries. The Frenchman
paid it with many protests, complaining that it was a mere
cheat and an imposition upon him as a stranger. My companions took the accusation very much to heart, as they thought
the honor of their country involved, and made great efforts to
explain, but neither party understood the language of the other
sufficiently well, so they prayed me to clear away the stigma
from Andalusia, which I was able to do satisfactorily at the
next stopping place. I mention this because it is an example
of another of the thousand traits of Spanish character that find
a counterpart in the United States, or at least in the Southern
portion of them—that sensitive, even thin-skinned national
pride, which feels that the conduct of every individual reflects
either for good or evil upon the general character, and regards

the public as inseparable from the individual reputation of its members; whereas the general disposition of Europe is to consider the government òr the public and the individual as distinct beings.

Leaving Andujar and its Moorish tower, we ascended slowly from the left bank of the Guadalquivir. Every step developed, with increasing beauty, the characteristic charms of the South. From the top of the first little *cuesta* we looked down into a delicious green valley with a stream and antique Moorish bridge, that caused us all to exclaim aloud with admiration. Even the mayoral caught the contagion. From that time forward the road ascended and descended lofty hills with table lands, through immense olive groves, extending far as the eye could reach. Interspersed among the pale green could be seen numerous farm houses, surrounded by white walls, and occasionally a Moorish tower, that had done good service in the olden time, would rear its head to the light of the evening sun. To our right, at some distance, flowed the river in a broad fertile valley, and beyond stood the Sierra Morena with its groves and sparkling villas up the mountain side. Peasants, in the graceful Andalusian costume, were everywhere at work. Sometimes a horseman would pass us with his rifle slung over the saddle, then a long string of mules laden with merchandize, and more rarely an equipage of the better sort came flying by. The scene was lively compared with the Castiles, in which you seldom see any one out òf the towns.

At sunset we descended the hill side into the valley of a stream that here enters the river. We passed through a village, crossed the stream a little above its mouth, and beheld one of the most lovely landscapes I remember ever to have seen. None but a painter could adequately represent it. The road skirting the river bank ran for a half mile directly west; on our right was a grove of Spanish oaks interspersed with olives, and protecting from the fury of the mid-day heat a green, worthy of Scotland. At some little distance in front stood the intensely Moorish looking town of Carpio, rising to a point steep on the left, with its castle and church projecting against the ruddy sky, while directly along our path was the smooth bosom of Guadalquivir, bathed in the golden light of the sunset. The Sierra Morena bounded the view beyond. A different play of light might, perhaps, deprive it of its charms; but as we saw it, I retain few more beautiful visions.

Leaving the town, we were quickly plunged into darkness. Andreas, our one-eyed postilion, had a narrow escape. His horse fell and was run over by the rest, but Andreas alighted on his feet on the right hand side of the road. How he got there no one could tell. The mayoral accused him of being asleep; a pardonable offence, considering that he had been in the saddle thirty-six hours—all the way from Madrid. About midnight we passed around the walls and entered Cordova, our mules striking fire from the precipitous street, and took lodgings in the Fonda Rizzi.

The architecture of the Fonda was thoroughly Andalusian. A considerable part of the building consisted of the Court or Patio, exposed to the air, and floored with marble, with tables and chairs arranged around the fountain. This Patio is bordered by a colonnade, upon which open the various rooms. I recognized the place immediately, but it appeared to me that the Patio formerly was in the second story. The mystery was soon solved by learning that the original entry had been from another street on a different level. At that time I had thought it a beautiful place, and had been fully impressed with all sorts of poetical feelings. But I had not then seen Seville, which spoils one's taste for most else. Indeed, such was the attraction it possessed for me, that I could not refrain from starting the next morning on the railroad at early dawn. In 1852, we were still confined to the diligence across the hills, at an expense of twenty-four hours' additional travelling; but were rewarded, first, by the famous view of Cordova from the opposite hill; then by the City of Ecija, on the banks of the beautiful Genil, which, rising near Granada, passes here to its union with the Guadalquivir; and, lastly, by the truly magnificent morning view from the City of Carmona, which embraces not only the Vega of Seville, but even the mountains of Ronda, and, as they say, the Alpujarras. Ecija, situate in a valley, surrounded by high table lands, is supposed to be the hottest place in Spain, and is called "*La ciudad del Sol*," or "*La Sartenilla*," "the frying-pan." The city is famous for its antiquity, its fine promenade, and the blue blood of the inhabitants of its Calle de los Caballeros.

The railroad now passes directly down the broad valley of
the Guadalquivir, most of the way upon its right bank. As
may be supposed, the soil is of exuberant fertility, and produces
everything that can be desired, except, perhaps, the temperate
fruits. The Sierra Morena skirts it on the north-west, its steep
side is ornamented, near Cordova, with numerous villas, whose
white walls, glittering in the rays of the rising sun, could be
seen from a great distance. The deserted Convent of San
Jeronimo is well worthy of a visit in the winter, when the
green crops cover the earth. The view from its terrace is
superb, as it is, indeed, from any part of the path; but, at
present, the heat of the dog-days had already parched up the
vegetation. This valley was said by Cardonne to have contained, in the time of the Beni Omeyah, twelve thousand
villages; and subsequent writers for a long time received this
statement with wonder, but respect, until our countryman,
Prescott, suggested that there was not actual space upon the
river banks for so great a number, much to the amusement of
certain Europeans, who quoted this example of what they considered American practicality, but they adopted the result. It
seems that Cardonne's error arose from a mistranslation, and
not from a disposition to invent. Whatever might have been
the case formerly, at present the towns are not very numerous,
and the population is reduced to the number requisite for the
cultivation of the soil.

The breezy morn was delicious, and the life around unbroken
by a single discordant feature. It was Andalusia, and nothing
but Andalusia. Every village had its place in history as the
scene of some knightly encounter. Castles and antique Moorish mills adorned the river bank, while the heights on the right
were studded with watch towers. Beautiful Andalusians with
fans, crowded every station. The fine weather and unclouded
skies of summer had seduced the neighboring population into
the fields, and we frequently passed little thatched huts or
tents, the habitations of the family since the end of the rainy
season, father, mother, and children within, the pig and the
donkey without, leading a harmonious existence together.
Lower down the valley roamed those herds of bulls which furnish combatants for the ring. The river approaches the Sierra
at the town of Almodovar (the round castle) del Rio, winding
around a beetling crag, which overhangs the bank with its

ruined fortress. My solitude was here relieved by the entrance
of a gentleman from Lora, dressed in the Andalusian costume,
somewhat modified to suit .the better class. The modification
consists in substituting pantaloons for the breeches and gaiters.
He wore a nicely fitting, embroidered jacket, a neck handkerchief, the ends passed through a ring, a calañes hat, round, with
the border turned stiffly up two or three inches. A red sash
surrounded his waist, and a gun completed the whole. This
latter is an almost invariable accompaniment of an Andalusian
when journeying off from the immediate highway. I am afraid
to say how many we had on the diligence. The gun and the
fan went together. My companion, like all Spaniards, was
very proud of his immediate locality, his *pais* and his *pueblo*.
Being in a state of exhilaration, and thoroughly *tête montée* with
the near approach to Seville, I agreed with him to the full, and
suggested some points which he had overlooked. This laid the
foundation of much good feeling. At Lora he dismounted, and
I was just regretting my return to solitude, when the opposite
door opened, and a party entered. First, a gentleman of some
fifty summers, very subdued in look, as if pressed down beneath
the weight of responsibility. He was emphatically *seco* (dried
up) *muy seco*, but not disagreeably so. Then came a good
humored mamá. Then four young ladies, in great spirits,
" with eyebrows like the new moon of Ramadan, and mouth
like the seal of Solomon," each handsomer than her predecessor. Another mamá, of the sub-acid character, " qualis de-
cet esse duennarum," brought up the rear, and filled the coach.
The best looking took the seat by me; another, opposite; by
her side, a mamá. They were going to Seville to spend a day
and shop a little; were full of joyous anticipations, and dressed
out to kill. Flashing eyes, black lace veils, a rose peeping out
from the glossy folds of their tresses, and a fan, were unmistakable evidences of their country. Every click of the latter
was like the crack of an electric battery. The gentleman and
myself could just see each other's heads over the piles of
muslin. (I suppose it was muslin, for I am not skilled in this
department.) As soon as we were well settled, and I had
recovered from the first overwhelment, my former companion
came to the window, and, presenting me to them in a general
way, added: "Caballero, all these were brought up in my
pueblo." I made my acknowledgments, and vowed that, though

Lora had appeared fair in my eyes before, it must now be considered the choice garden of the earth. But the opportunity afforded by the introduction was not neglected. The young ladies were full of fun, elegant in person, graceful in manner, and innocent in soul. Everything interested them, and they were interesting about everything. When some more decided hilarity broke forth, the mamá would look at me with a sympathizing smile, and exclaim : " Ah, las niñas !" whereupon " las niñas " would take a fresh start. And so the time passed until, crossing the Guadalquivir, the town of Carmona, upon its lofty hill, became a landmark, as we sped along the now open country, amid a vegetation that rioted in tropical luxuriance. At length the far famed Giralda appeared above the trees. The sight of it, after so so many years of absence, recalled the lines of the " Ancient Mariner " when he approaches his native town :

> Oh, dream of joy ! Is this, indeed,
>   The light-house top I see ?
> Is this the hill ? is this the kirk ?
>   Is this my own countree ?

It is, perhaps, not easy to say why I hailed Seville with such joyous welcome. Localities exercise a strange, oftentimes inexplicable influence, and when our train entered the station, I really felt as though the object of a long journey had at length been attained.

CHAPTER IX.

SEVILLE.

I was not sorry to part from the company at the station, for four young Andaluzas, *vestidas de gala,* with four mantillas and four fans, all crowded into one railway carriage, were rather trying to the nerves, so placing myself at their feet, I proceeded to a new hotel erected since my last visit. It was a great improvement over the old *Posada.* Do not expect, however, one of our Broadway caravansaries, full of people, and baggage, and rich furniture, and huge chimney places, and noisy bar rooms, with other comforts of a cold climate. Brussels carpets and gilded decorations there were none; but then there were marble courts and splashing fountains, cane bottom chairs and mats, camp bedsteads and balconies, with a genuine good humor on the part of the employés, which made you feel yourself a part owner of the establishment.

The first business was, of course, to see old acquaintances, at least such as one could venture to visit at that hour of the day. Returning, I passed by my former quarters in the Plaza Sto. Tomas, where I had resided a winter, selecting the house partly on account of its proximity to the Cathedral, the Alcazar and the Patio, partly because of the Barber of Seville, whose shop was on the opposite side of the square, for there is nothing like living directly under the influence of the *genius loci.* You smile at such stress being laid upon the barber. But he is not in Andalusia a mere chin-scraper; he is the factotum. His acquaintance is indispensable, and you may live a thousand years in Spain and yet learn nothing of the Spaniards unless

you know the barber. Spaniards, even when bearded, which
is very rare, leave a little vacant spot somewhere for the
express purpose, I have thought, of giving an excuse for visiting that functionary. If they shave themselves, still his
services are required, half a dozen times in the course of the
week, to trim their hair. In places too poor to support a
whole barber regularly, he makes periodical visits on his mule,
with his apparatus and the helmet of Mambrino slung over
his shoulders. On out-of-the-way roads you may meet him
exactly as he is described by Cervantes, and his approach is
welcomed with all the delight which the dispenser of gossip is
known to awaken. He there retains the importance which
the march of improvement in cities has curtailed. He is the
confidant of both sexes, and consequently knows the secrets of
the whole community. In his capacity of barber-surgeon he
heals the diseases of the body as well as the mind, and the
heart has been, from time immemorial, under his especial
superintendence. In general, he shares the esteem of the community with the priest, and, on the frontier, with the contra-
bandista. He is an established wit, too, and his feeblest jokes
cause hilarity to wrinkle the soap-suds upon the faces of admiring patients. Nor are his functions confined to mere gossip.
He can get up a fandango or bolero, if desired, and fill any
chance vacancy by bearing a part himself. The guitar is a
portion of his being. *No hay barbero sin guitarra?* What's a
barber without a guitar? No class in society can dispense with
his services. The French imitate the Spanish in appointing
one for each company or battalion of soldiers. In the day of
queues, it was the fashion, in the Spanish army, for the soldiers
to sit in a circle, each upon the knees of his neighbor behind,
while combing the hair of his neighbor in front, to the great
saving of time and barbers. But the disappearance of queues
and beards has restored the lithe fraternity to their former
pre-eminence, for it is found no easy task to shave and be
shaved simultaneously.

There was little, however, left in the Plaza Sto. Tomas to
hang this barber episode upon, for the old shop was shut up to
undergo repairs, and I was compelled to transfer my patronage
to another in the Calle de las Sierpes. The lodging-house was
occupied, too, so I hied to a friend of a friend of my Madrid
hostess—a Cadiz lady—who, upon her recommendation, would

doubtless consent to accommodate a *caballero tan fino como vm.* as she was pleased to add. It is never advisable to criticise a compliment, nor did I stop to inquire whether the epithet *"gastador"* might not have been appropriately inserted in the recommendation, for Spaniards respect an open hand. A pull at the bell-rope was followed by a *"quien es?"* (who is it?) from above, uttered in a musical voice, with an Andalusian accent. Good sign : the house began to feel comfortable at once. The reply of *" amiga!"* (friend) caused the door to be opened by a string from above, and I entered a modest *Patio.* The old pass-word, to obtain admittance, used to be *" Ave Maria purisima!"* to which the reply was, *" sin pecado concebida"* (conceived without sin). The common answer is, *"gente de paz,"* or *" España,"* but in the cities these are seldom heard. *"Amigo,"* or if it be your own house, a ferocious *"yo"* answers every purpose of a night key. Doña Carmen soon made her appearance. When the object of my visit was announced, we were joined by two young ladies, one, apparently twenty-five, very talkative and lively; the other, the owner of the voice, about eighteen years of age, and I cannot say that my expectations were disappointed. We mutually inspected each other. I was more than content, for I dislike to live in a house with ugly or disagreeable women. Doña Carmen impressed upon me that she was not in the habit of taking lodgers, but that mine was an exceptional case. I hinted, in reply, that I seldom went into lodgings, except in exceptional cases. Terms were soon arranged, and I found myself installed upon the ground floor, to avoid the heat, though I was almost persuaded, by my hostess and her daughters, to believe that the temperature, notwithstanding the evidence of the thermometer, would be freezing, for when a handsome Andaluza makes an assertion, however improbable, you find yourself yielding an unhesitating assent, as though it were sheer folly to question its accuracy.

As the evening closed in, I wended my way to the Cathedral Tower—La Giralda—to enjoy the panorama, and to see what changes seven years had wrought in the capital of Andalusia. This wondrous tower, the admiration of all who behold it, is the work of the Moorish architect Geber or Guever, who undertook its erection, probably, by the command of Yacoub al Mansour, in gratitude for the signal victory of Alarcos. In those days it served the double purpose of astronomy and religion. Such

12

was the affection felt for it, that when the city was conquered by San Fernando, the Moors intended its destruction, and were deterred only by the direful threats of the Christians. Subsequently, at the pulling down of the old Mosque, this was retained by the chapter on account of its extraordinary beauty, and their decision has been sustained by the unanimous approval of travellers. It stands on the outside of the Cathedral, at the north-east corner, in the angle made by the wall of the Patio de los Naranjos. The original tower, as erected by the Moors, is simply a square of some fifty feet, and rises to the height of two hundred and fifty, up to the gallery where the bells are hung. Above this is a smaller continuation of a hundred feet, added by a Spanish architect, Fernan Ruiz, and, unlike most continuations, worthy of the original. It contains the famous clock. The whole is surmounted by a bronze figure of *La Fé* (Faith), fourteen feet in height, and weighing twenty-eight hundred pounds, which yet turns with the slightest breeze, and, by a palm leaf in one hand, indicates its direction, while the other displays the *Lábaro*, the banner of Constantine. The elevation of the whole is more than three hundred and fifty feet. The lower or Moorish portion is charmingly decorated with balconied windows, sustained by double marble columns, and, after attaining a certain height, with arabesque work. The Spanish addition is more elaborately ornamented, but the two harmonize beautifully, and, at a distance, appear of a delicate, rosy hue.

It had been my habit, on the former visit, to mount the Giralda every evening at sunset for the prospect, so that it was prominently connected in my mind with the charms of the place. Even the tones of the principal bells were familiar, and I have often, before retiring, listened, in my house, on the Plaza, near by, for the sonorous peal of Sta. María, as it boomed over the city, announcing the hour of midnight. Ascending the ramp, which is so broad and gently inclined that two horsemen have ridden up abreast, I reached my old friends. There they were, just as they had been when I last saw them. All the world has acknowledged the peculiar influence of the sound of bells in awakening the associations of memory—more powerful than even regular music. The well-known instance in the life of Napoleon, who, after an existence spent in war and the selfish strife of politics, was momentarily overcome on hearing the sound of the bells of Brienne, stealing up from the valley, is an illustrious example. What a moment was that! How reproachfully beautiful must have appeared those days of childhood's innocence, when seen across thirty years of ambition and blood! Who, in our humbler lives, has not acknowledged their effect, when returning to a spot hallowed by recollections of former happiness? I am sure I never felt it more strongly than in Seville. The church bells in Spain are regularly dedicated, and have baptismal names, as though they were individuals. My favorite of these was the large one to the east, within the outer wall of the tower, called Sta. María or La Gorda, weighing some sixteen thousand pounds, the work of Juan de Balabarca, and presented by the Archbishop Gonzalo de Mena. Corresponding, on the western side and nearly equal in weight, is San Miguel. At the four corners are Sta. Catalina, Omnium Sanctorum, Sta. Cruz and St. Jago. These are all large, and struck by moving the clappers—*de golpe*. In the embrazures of the outer wall, commencing on the right of Sta. María, are San Juan Bautista, Sta. Lucía, San José, San Pedro, Sta. Ines, Sta. Barbara, San Isidro, San Pablo, Sta. Cecilia, San Cristóbal, San Fernando, and Sta. Justa—all *de vuelta*. Sunday morning, at nine, A. M., is a fine time for the latter. Sta. Lucía, in particular, is a great sufferer. Every bell has its boy, and they are made to turn over frantically by winding the rope around the axle and then causing it to revolve. Every now and then one of the ringers goes flying up into the air twenty feet, as though he were about to plunge out upon the Cathedral; it is only to stand astride the axle and get a better purchase, but it makes one hold his breath to see the performance. Last spring a poor fellow did get his feet entangled in the rope, and was, consequently, dashed into a thousand pieces upon the pavement, three hundred feet below. One day I determined to find out from the guardian the exact hours of striking the Sta. María. "A very simple matter," you will say; "only ask." No such thing. To get reliable information about the smallest matter in Spain requires a regular system of cross-examination, for Spaniards are not teachers by nature. So offering him my *petaca*, we took a seat on the upper gallery, near the clock, and commenced. To the first direct interrogatory he answered, "High Mass, and at no other time." By dint, however, of hard work and much reiteration, I at last made out that it occurred four times in the twenty-four hours : first, at *Madrugada* or early Mass ; secondly, at High Mass, about half-past nine o'clock ; thirdly, at *Oraciones;* and, fourthly, at midnight.

But, in talking about the bells, I have forgotten the prospect, and the sun is getting low. Even those who do not admire Seville, admit that the panorama, from the Giralda, is something superb. From this great height, the city and the surrounding country are laid out like a map at your feet. The narrow, Moorish streets seem little lanes, winding about among the white houses and the domed temples, dwarfed beside the immense Cathedral, which reposes directly underneath, with its thousand pinnacles pointing to the world above. Then comes the Lonja or Exchange, with its beautiful court and colonnade. Beyond that, to the south-west, the enormous tobacco manufactory, the palace of the Dukes of Montpensier, and the flowery Salon de Christina. Farther still, the delicious Paseo, with its orange and lemon groves, and the golden Guadalquivir coursing at its feet. To the north-west, the Plaza de Toros is conspicuous. On the opposite side of the river, extends the gipsy faubourg, La Triana, the home of the fancy of all kinds. A little beyond, across the fields, rises the Chaboya, a steep spur of the Sierra Morena, with the old Convent of San Juan de Alfarache, whence there is such a magnificent view. Farther to the north, lies the old town of Castilleja de la Cuesta, where the conqueror of Mexico lived and died. The plain itself is spotted over with villages—Alcalá, Algaba, Santi Ponce—built from the ruins of the ancient Italica, the birthplace of the Roman Emperors. The back-ground is filled with the Sierra Morena, whose bare summits are bathed in an ocean of light. The horizon, on the opposite side, is bounded by the hills of Carmona and Alcalá, and the mountain chain of Ronda. Seen from the Giralda, Seville looks as though it had never known a spot of dirt, owing, doubtless, to the purity of the atmosphere, rather than to any extraordinary care that is taken of it. Two changes of importance were visible—the grand Plaza de Isabel, which makes a fine show from this point, and the iron bridge over the river, replacing the former one of boats—which, together with the Mosque and the reparation of the aqueduct of Carmona, are attributed to Yusef, of the dynasty of the Almohades, in the latter half of the twelfth

century. As the sun neared the horizon, its purple light transformed the whole into a fairy scene, to which all the colors of
the rainbow contributed. It was difficult to realize that these
localities, intimately connected, many of them, with events
which influenced, more or less remotely, the discovery and
fortunes of our hemisphere, and are, consequently, familiar to
American youth in the pages of our most gifted authors, were
truly around me. This city was the favorite of Columbus, and
the subsequent residence of his children; and here are still
deposited the records which contain the early history of our
continent. Yon village is honored by the sepulchre of his
family. From this river sailed the great fleets which were to
renovate the Old World by pouring into its lap the riches of
the New. Here were born the chivalric warriors who lent
such romance to our early history, and the dialect of the Spanish Americas attests, to the present day, the influence of this
province over their destinies.

The Giralda is generally represented, as in the celebrated
paintings of Murillo, standing between the two Saints, Justa
and Rufina, who have preserved it against many a storm, and
are its especial guardian, though their protecting care extends
over the whole city. These young ladies were daughters of an
humble maker of earthenware, who lived near the gate of La
Triana, poor in worldly goods, but abounding in wealth of
piety and faith. It seems that one of the Pagan ceremonies in
Seville was the procession of Venus Salambo, a Phœnician goddess, whose image, representing her in lamentation for the death
of Adonis, was carried about on the shoulders of women, while
the crowd ahead demanded contribution from all they met.
On one occasion the procession halted in front of the sisters'
shop, with the usual request, which they indignantly refused,
protesting that they worshipped one God, maker of heaven and
earth, and not a senseless idol. The bearers of the precious
image, horrified at such impiety, let it fall, so as to slily break
the earthen pots, right and left; at least that was the result.
The two Saints, not to revenge the loss of the pots (as the
historian carefully assures us), but to destroy a heathen mon-
strosity, retorted upon the idol, which was considerably dam-
aged in the conflict. They were immediately thrown into
prison, and tortured in every way to make them acknowledge
their error. The Roman Judge once forced them to follow

him barefoot to the Sierra Morena. Finally, Sta. Justa died, and her body was ignominiously cast into a well, whence it was rescued by the Bishop, and decently interred. Sta. Rufina was delivered over to a lion, but he, as usual, refusing to perform his part, she was killed by the executioner, and her body burnt. They died in the true spirit of martyrs, and their fame extended rapidly throughout the earth. Churches were erected to them, and offices in the Breviary, both Gothic and Muzarabic, attested the efficacy of their intercession above. Nor were these honors paid to them in vain, for many a city did they save from destruction. They have thus far preserved their especial charge from peril of earthquake and cannon ball, and it is to be hoped that they will long secure to posterity the same gratification which has been enjoyed by past generations.

About nine o'clock in summer, the whole of Seville issues forth to enjoy the evening air on the Plaza Isabel, which is the favorite promenade at that hour. So following the current, I found myself in a large parallelogram, surrounded by stately buildings in the modern style, and half filled with an innumerable throng of all classes, some seated, some walking. Most of the men were smoking, and most of the women fanning themselves, with occasional intermixtures of conversation; but the great occupation of every one is to look and be looked at. On the first turn, I met some of my companions of the morning. They had done an immense amount of shopping— had visited every ladies' establishment in the Calle de las Sierpes and de los Francos, had caused half the goods to be taken down, and bought, I doubt not, five dollars' worth, that being the usual way in which ladies shop. The next day, however, was to be the grand finale, when all Seville was to be transferred to Lora. They were delighted with the city and its grandeurs, not thinking there could possibly be anything like it elsewhere. Though my young acquaintances had seen little of the world, it was surprising how entirely they possessed most of the advantages that travelling is supposed to confer, with the sole exception of their prejudices, which remained almost intact. They left next day in the afternoon train.

A public promenade is indispensable to every Spanish city, however small, and every Spaniard is sure to pass there some portion of the week. Particularly is this the case in Andalusia and Valencia. The unbroken clear weather continuing during a large part of the year, converts the occasional constitutional stroll into a daily habit, and an afternoon or evening walk is as much a matter of course, as attendance at Mass. Fortunately for strangers, they have thus, during the spring and summer, an opportunity of seeing a considerable portion of the population, without the necessity of resorting to letters of introduction, which involve the sacrifice of more time than a passing traveller can spare. Seville is the city where this, as all other national customs, is seen in its greatest perfection. In former times, the Alameda Vieja was the resort of the fashionable world, where valiant cavaliers, returning from the wars in Germany or Italy, or perchance America, hastened to pay homage to the fair dames, whose protecting images had cheered them through many a hard won field. In honor of its historic associations, two columns are erected at the farther end, surmounted respectively by statues of Hercules and Cæsar. It is now almost entirely deserted, except on certain holidays. The little square at the foot of the Calle de las Sierpes—made by the demolition of a part of the old palace of the Dukes of Medina Sidonia, the Guzmans—succeeded to the popular favor. But the great centre at present is the Plaza Isabel, on the site formerly occupied by the enormous Convent of the Franciscans, and a more beautiful scene than that it presented on the evening in question, cannot be imagined. The night was Spanish, and who can describe the glories of a Spanish summer night on the banks of the Guadalquivir? The mellow lustre of the moon seemed to have overflowed the earth, and the blue vault of heaven had given even to the stone buildings around an appearance of liquid silver. It was as though the air itself had a visible, tangible substance, and we were floating upon the bosom of an enchanted ocean. The lamps served but for ornament, and stood like little points of burnished gold. Not a cloud obscured the sky. Odoriferous breezes from the south wafted gently over, as if fearing to embrace too roughly the fair cheeks that sought their wooing. A quadruple row of chairs offered repose to the indolent or weary, and from time to time some young lady would take compassion upon a score of admirers, by remaining where all might approach within sound of her voice; but the more interesting part of the assemblage was generally to be found on the promenade.

The beauty of Spanish women has ever been a subject of
admiration to all who are endowed with a perception of the
lovely.   Yet, while acknowledging its irresistible power, there
is nothing so difficult as to explain the fascination which it
exercises; for, unlike the rest of their sex, the daughters of
Andalusia owe nothing to those artificial processes which may
be said to form a part of the female education elsewhere.
Their taste in dress is excellent, when combined with simplicity, as is generally the case; for they have by nature very
little disposition to the variety of colors, which appears to be
the ruling passion of Parisian circles.   The universal costume
in winter, and the usual one out of doors in all seasons, is a
dark colored skirt, called a *basquiña*, fitting close around the
waist and extending to the feet, which are thus concealed.   It
is sometimes kept in place by leaden pellets affixed to the
border.   The same innate sense of delicacy, or, perhaps, an
intuitive knowledge of the weakness of men in believing no
charms equal to hidden charms, preserves them from those
fearful exposures of neck and shoulders, which so shocked the
Japanese.   A delicate satin slipper encases a foot that would
not crush a daisy.   From the top of the comb, if one be worn,
gracefully fall the mantilla's folds across a gently budding
breast, where it is confined by the fingers of the wearer's left
hand, or at times the veil is thrown forward over the face,
when

> Tapándose la cara, ✦
> Descubren el corazon.

From the hair, massed above the temples, stealthily peeps a
rose, as if hesitating to venture its humble beauties beside such
loveliness.   Two little curls—*guedejas, caracoles de amor*—bear
it company.   A fan completes her costume.   Thus armed, the
maids of the Guadalquivir go forth to conquer the world.

The use of the black veil seems traditional in Spain, since it
is mentioned by the Roman geographers as a part of the
ancient costume existing in those provinces which had not
fully adopted the dress of the Conqueror, and they describe it
as frequently thrown forward over the face in the same style.
Just so has the dark cloak or *sagum* been perpetuated to our
day, both as a winter and a summer garment, notwithstanding
the unceasing war waged by foreign tailors and milliners and
native copyists.   In recreant Madrid, they have partly suc-

ceeded, and they have obtained a foothold even in Seville, so far as the men are concerned; but there are occasions when the old costume for the ladies is still *de rigueur*. The Church here, as in Rome, requires the female head to be covered. A person entering uncovered, would cause a general rush of the beadles, crying for life, " *Cúbrense vvm. Cúbrense vvm.*" On the other hand, I learnt by my own experience that it is not permissable to enter the Cathedral *embozado*—that is, with the cloak thrown over the mouth and left shoulder, in the Spanish style. Neither is it polite to retain the cloak in this position when addressing a person, for the same reason which required the old knight to withdraw his glove in shaking hands. It is a disarming. I agree with the new school, that after attaining a certain age and a certain degree of corpulency, the jacket without the cloak is not a very suitable garment for the men; but the national costume suits the ladies far better than any other style they can adopt, and it will be a sad day for them and for us poor men too, when they surrender themselves to the tyranny of the Parisian mantua maker. The mantilla is peculiarly becoming to the Spanish style of features, while the French hat presents the most odious and hidious contrast conceivable: the former lends additional attractions—the latter destroys those which already exist. One may be insensible to everything else, but the mantilla is irresistible. A *basquiña*, a Cinderella slipper, a mantilla or veil, a rose and a fan, are all that any Andaluza needs to bring the world to her feet.

But the fan! the magic fan! who shall describe its wonderful powers? Who can sound the depths of its mysteries? Every movement of this potent wand is fraught with happiness or misery. In their hands it positively speaks, and its gentle recognitions are far more winning than any assertions of the tongue. It is said to have a language, a sort of alphabet of its own, but that is doubtful. Its utterances are of the magnetic character, which need no interpretation, and are felt rather than learnt. The art of managing it was always to me an unfathomable science, and though I embraced every opportunity of becoming a proficient, and actually took two formal lessons, I failed utterly of success. It must be said, however, that my instructor had learnt by intuition, but unfortunately was not able to teach by the same method. I was always told that there was only one way of opening it, yet there are certainly five, for the theory is almost as difficult as the practice. But having, by dint of hard study, acquired, as you fondly imagine, the requisite theoretical knowledge, you desire to see it embodied in action. Your instructor shows how the fingers are placed. You are then told to do "so"; whirr! goes the fan, and it is all over before your eyes have caught the first movement. A gentleman present at my discomfiture, consoled me by saying that he would not respect a man who could acquire the art; that in men's hands it was a practical instrument for putting the air in motion. The ladies certainly do not so regard it.

I had been apprehensive lest this costume, rendered so poetical by the descriptions of travellers and the dreams of romancers, were not the true secret of the admiration which I had formerly carried away across the Pyrenees, and that it was a reflected, semi-poetic, semi-romantic, at all events unsubstantial conception. Such is not the case. On the present occasion the prevailing color, in accordance with the season, was white; and the mantilla was replaced by a simple lace veil, so that there is certainly some external attraction independent of dress. I attribute it to the combination of personal beauty, such as the world cannot surpass, with a grace of movement, an innate, inalienable elegance of manner, which no education can give and no words describe. An Andaluza is born, not made. Not too tall and never dumpy; (horrible word!) her person is so exquisitely proportioned, that without some measure of comparison, you would form no opinion as to her real size. An elegant fullness preserves her alike from the scrawny penury of the English or the corpulency of the Italians. Her lofty brow justifies her sparkling wit, and the delicate organization of her feelings and intellect is in harmony with the finely chiseled features. Luxuriant masses of dark, glossy hair, parted slightly on one side, and nobly arched eyebrows, are a fit setting to a rich Southern complexion, not of sickly yellow, but of a clear olive tinge, through which the timid blood, with every emotion, mantles to the surface. The pride of her beauty is the large, lustrous, almond-shaped, velvety eye, half covered with silken lashes, as if to screen her admirers from the danger of being consumed; but when aroused into activity, flashing forth pride, interest, inexhaustible love, with a fire more irresistible than that of a thousand suns. Then it is that, with an imperious wave of the fan, she bids you plunge into a maelstrom of vipers and you obey.

There is a widely diffused, but very erroneous belief among us that every Spaniard has perforce black eyes and a dark complexion. Such is far from being true even in Andalusia. Ladies of the better class, who are not exposed to the sun or wind, have beautifully clear complexions, though brunette. In Ronda, blue eyes form the majority, and they are by no means uncommon in other provinces. But the Spanish blonde is still a Spaniard, and her type of beauty very different from the insipid combination which often passes under that name in the north. There is the same smothered fire, the same deep expression in the eye, the same richness of complexion, which, in union with raven tresses, form an exquisite picture. Light-haired persons—*rubias*—are rarer, and of course much admired to look at, though every one falls in love with their dark-haired rivals. Of the luxuriance and elegance of their hair the ladies are justly proud, and no pains are spared to render it as beautiful as possible. The time devoted to this object is sacred in all classes, and if, in response to an inquiry or request, the ominous reply is heard, "*hombre! estamos ocupadas con el pelo*," it is useless to remain. Nothing short of another invasion of the Moors could arouse them. During the civil war Zumalacarregui, or Merino, for it is narrated of both, placed death for the men and loss of their hair for the women, upon the same footing, and found them equally efficacious punishments.

Spanish girls are taught to walk gracefully, too, as all girls should be, and since the narrowness of the streets prevents the general use of carriages, and the arms of gentlemen are seldom offered and never accepted, they avoid falling into the tottering shuffle, which is produced by the opposite customs. The walk of the Seville ladies is something peculiar to Andalusia. That they take steps is firmly believed because required by the anatomical construction of mankind, but in their case the belief is the result of induction, not of ocular perception. They glide over the earth as though supported by unseen hands, and disappear from your sight ere you can believe that they are actually moving. Who can gaze upon them without inwardly repeating the oft quoted, ever-applicable lines—

Avertens roseâ cervice refulsit
Ambrosiæque comæ divinum vertice odorem
Spiravêre; pedes vestis defluxit ad imos,
Et vera incessu patuit Dea.

The Andalusian foot is a marvel, both for size and beauty.
A lady will wear with ease the slipper of an ordinary girl of
fourteen. If any artificial means are used, the pressure must
be very slight, as the appearance is perfectly natural, notwithstanding the fact that they seldom adopt any other means of
locomotion. The development of the English understanding
is a subject of perpetual wonderment on the Guadalquivir,
where they are accustomed to compare its covering to a
twelve oared boat.

The graceful walk of the Sevillanas is not more peculiar to
them than the noble carriage of the head, due, doubtless, in
some degree to the absence of those fragile, yet cumbrous
ornaments which force others to assume a stiff and constrained
position. It gives them an air of haughtiness by no means
disagreeable, however, as you are quite ready to admit their
unapproachable superiority before they assert it. Every Andaluza has two points of beauty—fine eyes and hair. Then she
may have a good complexion, and she is almost certain to be
graceful. If to these she unite wit and cultivation, who so
daring as to deny her pre-eminence? Progress, perhaps mere
change, is desirable in many things in Spain, but that Heaven
may preserve her fair daughters from the hand of innovation
is the prayer of native and foreigner alike. It is scarcely possible that the best laid schemes of any power on earth could
effect an improvement. Better resign the Quixotic attempt,
and leave the lonely traveller despairingly to exclaim,

O! si yo naciera ciego,
O tú sin beldad naciera!

No wonder the hours glided by imperceptibly. About eleven
o'clock the company began to disperse. The music had taken
its departure at the appointed time, with praiseworthy punctuality, and in a half hour the square was deserted. Sta.
María was sending forth its booming peal of midnight, as I
slowly retraced my steps, through the silent streets, to my
domicile. In the meantime, everything had been arranged in a
style above criticism, though not in any excess of luxuriance.

The floor was covered with one of those beautiful mats, the art of making which has been handed down from the Moors, and is still practiced with much skill in various parts of the city, particularly by the gipsies. A table, a few plain chairs, a mirror, a cane settee and a wardrobe, completed the list of the furniture. All the linen was scrupulously clean. Upon this score I have never had cause to complain in the humblest posada. Wherever I have succeeded in getting a bed at all, it has been of the color of snow. Half the money a Spaniard spends on himself goes to his linen, which, if he can afford it, is embroidered in the most costly style. It is his luxury, and clean-shirt day is certain to find him in a good humor. There was a net over the bed, too, for there are mosquitoes at Seville, but such miserable apologies! No more to be compared with our sonorous and powerful beasts, the gallinipper grandisonens, than Mount Vesuvius is with Cotopaxi. Everywhere in Europe an American finds a justification for his national pride.

I was not in the humor for sleep. The spirit of the past was upon me with its recollections and meditations. The watchman under my window cried out, " La una de la noche y serê-ê-ê-êno," " Las dos de la noche," &c., &c.,) one o'clock at night, and clear, &c., &c.,) and he was crying the third hour when I retired only for a nap, for I was up with the sun. The guardians of the night in Seville remind one of a former generation, as they go about in their sheep skin cloaks, with long staves and lanterns. Indeed, they might be legitimately traced to the Addaraboun of the Moors, except that they were also provided with a dog to give warning of the approach of a robber, and perhaps to give the latter a friendly hint of the dangerous neighborhood. True they have the keys of the houses, and let in a belated occupant, whose porter has retired to rest, and they will also accompany you home, if you have lost the way, which it is very easy to do in these crooked streets, all resembling each other, but it is difficult to imagine how they pass the rest of the time. A fire is something unheard of, probably the oldest inhabitant has never known one to take place, and it seems no part of their business to interfere with a little peaceable fighting, unless it amount to an *émeute*. I remember once striking a Berlin watchman—who was springing his rattle with deliberate frenzy under the window—quite dumb with amazement, either at my ignorance or impertinence, by asking him the locality of the fire. He evidently thought I was attempting to "chawf" him. A Seville brother would, under similar circumstances, probably experience the same emotions as Schultz did. They are, however, standing, or rather sleeeping, evidences of the fine climate, for from the eternal fair weather and their continually crying out "Sereno," they enjoy that name throughout the Peninsula.

The next day, after a cup of chocolate, I strolled through the Gate of Jerez to the Promenade on the Guadalquivir, known by the appropriate appellation of "Las Delicias." It commences at the " *Torre de Oro*," which, after being attributed to various historical characters, is now believed to be Moorish. Could it speak, it might many a tale unfold. Treasures, both animate and inanimate, have been guarded within its walls. It has been a prison, too, and some have entered that little door, who were never to behold the day again. The Promenade lies between the river bank and the garden attached to the palace of the Dukes of Montpensier, whose orange trees suspend their golden fruit above the fair promenaders. Farther down it expands into a wood interspersed with alleys and flower beds. Most of the distance the river is straight, but at the end of the promenade gently curves south-westerly, so as to bring the whole city in view at the extremity of the vista. There are few as lovely scenes in Spain, and it is difficult to say whether it be more favorably viewed at sunrise or sunset. The stately Cathedral, with its delicate tracery of Gothic, towers above the trees, surmounted by the still loftier Giralda at its side. From this point can its vast dimensions be best appreciated. Various convents and churches bear it worthy companionship. On the western bank is the faubourg of La Triana, and in the foreground the triad of lonely palms, which every traveller should remember as sole living relics of the former conquerors. Between the two flow the pink and purple behued waters of the Guadalquivir, enlivened by numerous little craft and fishing smacks that ply to San Lucar and Cadiz; and if the hour be early, the steamer down the river will disturb the quiet of the scene, recalling you from your revery, and reminding you that you are not on the banks of the Tigris, in the reign of Haroun al Rashid. Over all reigns the indescribable charm of an Andalusian landscape, like the delicate odor of a bouquet. Though the middle of

the day is intensely warm, the character of the Spanish soil
causes a great radiation of heat during the night, and the configuration of the country keeps the air continually in motion.
In the morning, there is, consequently, a delicious breeze blowing along the river, which old and young are anxious to enjoy;
and as the population is very sociably inclined and abounds in
leisure, I frequently spent two or three hours in casual conversation with persons who seemed to have no more absorbing
occupation than myself. The winter, however, or spring, is
the heyday of Las Delicias. The air being then too chilly for
the nightly promenades on the Plaza Isabel, all people of
leisure (and how many does not that include in a Spanish
city?) meet here about an hour before sunset for every conceivable purpose. The fairer sex, I fear, to show a new mantilla, or to display the power of that most potent weapon, a
Spanish fan; the ruder to be remorsely slaughtered, willing
victims to the sweetest of sacrifices; the old to take in large
draughts of pure air, which here supply the place of the renowned medicaments of Brandreth and Jayne; the children
of the better sort to drive about in sheep and goat carts, or to
lead gaily caparisoned lambs with a string, while the humbler
class are intent in pursuit of *cuartos*, by offering lighted matches
for extinguished cigars. The carriage way is filled with equipages—some of most venerable appearance, others of the latest
elegance, and prancing steeds occupy the centre. Perfect
equality and good humor characterize the whole. If, amid all
these combustible elements, the old couplet,

> El hombre es fuego, la muger estopa,
> Viene el diablo y sopla,

or,

> Man is fire and woman tow,
> Comes the devil and gives a blow,

is sometimes verified by an example,·it is a not unnatural consequence.

The Guadalquivir—the poet-sung Baetis of the Ancients, the
Great River, the Wady 'l Kebir of the Moors—gives Seville a
pre-eminence over other Spanish cities, for none can boast so
noble a stream to do it homage. We, who luxuriate in the
majesty of the Father of Waters, may be disappointed at its
size, but in parched and thirsty Spain it has ever formed a fit
subject for poets and novelists. Even in our own distant

country its name is suggestive of visions, that, perhaps, have scarce existence beyond the boundaries of Dreamland. Springing from the Sierras of Alcaraz and Cazorla, and fretting beneath the enormous crags of the Sierra Morena, it pursues a south-westerly direction amid the fertile fields and olive plantations of the ancient kingdom of Jaen, by the cities of Baeza and Ubeda. Thence by Andujar, famous for its earthenware, and the steel-renowned Alcolea, with the noble bridge to Cordova, the city of the Caliphs, where it first becomes navigable. Thence to Seville, whose orange groves it threads, and turning the last spur of the Sierra Morena, winds its tortuous course through the uninteresting pasture lands below, to pour its waters into the broad Atlantic. It was distinguished among the timid mariners of the old world by the mysterious ebb and flow of the tide, and supposed moreover to communicate a golden tinge to the famous wool, famous even at that early day.

> Baetis olivifera crinem redimite corona,
> Aurea qui nitidis vellera tingis aquis.

In sculpture and painting, it still rejoices in its olive crown; but its waters no longer groan beneath the weight of treasure-laden fleets. It may be easy to find streams more beautiful than the Guadalquivir, as it is possible, perhaps, to surpass the Rhine, but there hangs about these two rivers an attraction which, though intangible, has a real existence, and which thousands of years and millions of castles could not give to the Seine or the Thames.

CHAPTER X.

THE CATHEDRAL · AND PAINTINGS.

Its Foundation — The Patio de los Naranjos — General Impression — Description—
The Retablo — Sacred Music — Sculptures — Paintings — Marshal Soult — The
Guardian Angels — Tombs — Church Feasts — The Virgin — Grand Effect of the
Cathedral — Paintings in La Caridad — The Museo — Murillo's Conceptions.

The principal monument at Seville is the Cathedral—la
Iglesia Mayor—the largest and grandest in all Spain, and for
impressive effect unequalled in the world, even by the Basilica
of St. Peter's. The characteristic excellencies of the principal
Spanish Cathedrals are enumerated in the following quatrain :

> Sevilla en grandeza,
> Toledo en riqueza ;
> Compostella en fortaleza,
> Leon en sutileza.

Tradition has pointed out the spot as the site of the temples
of the various religions which have successively ruled at Seville,
commencing with the goddess of the Phœnicians. The Moorish
Mosque, erected by Yusouf, the Almohade, and completed by
Yacoub al Mansour, his son, was, after the reconquest, purified
and consecrated to the worship of the true God, or, as the
Mohammedan authors complain, to the adoration of idols ; but
in the beginning of the fifteenth century, it had been so much
injured by earthquakes, that the Chapter determined to pull it
down, and to erect in its place a temple worthy of the city and
of their religion. In the year 1401, the Beneficiaries of the
Cathedral being assembled, it was resolved "that, inasmuch as
the Church is daily threatened with ruin, from the shocks it
has received, and is about to fall in various places, another be
built, such as shall find no equal, and shall correspond to the
greatness and authority of Seville ; and that if the funds of

13

the Church be not sufficient, everyone shall contribute from
his salary what may be necessary." (Digéron que por quanto
la Yglesia de Sevilla amenazaba cada dia runia por los terre-
motos que ha habido y está para caer por muchas partes, que
se labre otra iglesia tal y tan buena, que no haya otra su igual,
y que se considére y atienda á la grandeza y autoridad de Sevilla,
y su iglesia como manda su razon y que, si para ello no bastare
la renta de la obra, digéron todos que se tome do sus rentas de
cada uno lo que bastaba, que ellos lo darán en servicio de Dios.)
And one of the Chapter added: "let us build a church so great,
that those who see it finished will believe us mad." Most noble
resolve, most noble Chapter, and most nobly did they accomplish their proposed object! Without the aid of princes or
taxes, by their own savings and the assistance of alms from
the faithful, they erected the marvel of Andalusia. The exterior, like that of most Gothic cathedrals, is not impressive
when seen from near by; though occupying a large square, it
is not disfigured, as is usually the case, by mean houses. Indeed, it is rather fortunate than otherwise in its environs. To
the north, on the opposite side of the street, the houses are
preserved, as though the Moors had departed but yesterday;
and the little colonnade is said to be devoted to the same
trades that were carried on in the same place six hundred
years ago. On the east is the Archbishop's palace. The
Alcazar and the Lonja lie to the south, while the Cathedral
itself is surrounded by a terrace, slightly elevated above the
level of the street. The western front, as usual, is not finished.
A great many reasons are given for this peculiarity about
Spanish cathedrals. Some say it is to avoid a payment which
was due to Rome upon the completion of every religious edifice; others say to escape the effects of the "evil eye;" others
a prosaic want of funds. Be the reason what it may, Spanish
churches are seldom entirely complete. The entrance by the
north is through La Puerta del Perdon, which leads into the
Patio de los Naranjos, (the court of the orange trees,) surrounded on three sides by the lofty walls of the Parish Church
and the Library. The Patio. its fountains, the horse shoe gate
of the Perdon, are all Moorish and fine specimens. In the early
morning or afternoon this is a delightful spot to while away
the hour, listening to the bubbling of the fountains and the
conversation of the water carriers who come here to fill their

casks, while the breeze rustles amid the dark green leaves and yellow fruit of the orange trees, and the fairy Giralda towers majestically over head in silent beauty. Most of the Cathedrals, built upon the sites of Moorish mosques, retain the entrance court and the fountain for ablution, which was necessary to the Mohammedan worship. To the east of the Patio, near the library entrance, is the stone pulpit, which the inscription pronounces to have served St. Vincent and other persons of distinction in the Church. The Library itself, as most libraries, is uninteresting enough to the sight, but precious to the mind, as it consists principally of books presented by Fernan Columbus, with manuscripts of the great navigator himself, and hence styled *La Colombina*. It contains, moreover, a great many historical souvenirs of the re-conquest and subsequent periods. The Sagrario or Parish Church, on the opposite site of the Patio, would be considered handsome if it were not in such immediate proximity to the Cathedral. Some of its wood carvings are beautiful, particularly the altar-piece and the Sta. Veronica above; and a figure of St. John is also well worthy of remark.

The old Sagrario near the gate of the Patio, is converted into a sort of vestiary. The Cathedral, on my first visit, being closed, as the siesta was not quite over, I took a seat here to await the opening of the doors. The sun's rays poured fiercely down, but within all was delightfully fresh and cool. The altar-boys were engaged in the elevating occupation of standing on their heads for a wager, while in the next apartment, separated by a screen, some functionary snored away with the reverberating snort of a Mississippi high-pressure. The example was catching. I took one of the sweetest naps that ever fell to my lot. Soon the grating of the doors awakened me, and I entered the glorious edifice. Without all had been full of glare, almost blinding; here a faint, mellow twilight floated among the lofty columns, scarcely disturbing the solemn gloom which hushed one into an involuntary silence. The sound of footsteps was lost in its immensity, though its size could only be appreciated by comparison with some of the human species. Since leaving Seville, I have had an opportunity of revisiting most of the mediæval cathedrals, and I can truly say that none of them compare with this in inspiring the feeling of grandeur in the object and humility in the subject, which is the

peculiar merit of the Gothic architecture. I have twice been
to the Minster of Strasbourg for the express purpose of comparing them, but it has appeared cold and impressionless—
sterile, so to speak, whereas the soul must be hard indeed
that can enter here and not feel inspired with an overwhelming sense of awe and reverence. Its founders were truly
impressed with the divine conception of religion. Nowhere
else is the Christian thought so appropriately expressed in
stone; and if I were to select the two edifices of Christendom
that had most successfully attained the end for which they
were erected, it would be the Cathedrals of Milan and Seville,
the exterior of the former and the interior of the latter being
respectively all that could reasonably be demanded of architecture.

The ground plan is that of the Mosque, which preceded it,
being a parallelogram of some four hundred and fifty feet in
length and more than three hundred and fifty in width, with
large chapels on the northern and southern sides. Between
these are the five aisles, extending east and west, formed by
noble colonnades and surmounted by graceful arches, sustaining
the roof, some eighty or a hundred feet above. There are in
fact seven aisles, but two of them are occupied by the lateral
chapels. The centre aisle and the transept, forming the cross,
are more elevated, attaining the enormous height of a hundred
and forty-five feet, while the dome is still more lofty. Rich as
the Cathedral is in treasures of every description, in paintings,
sculpture, jewels, it contains nothing gaudy or striking, with a
single exception—no huge frescoes to divert the attention from
the great end of the architect. The eighty-seven windows,
painted in the most beautiful style of mediæval German art, to
represent Scripture scenes, some of them twenty or thirty feet
in length, are scarcely noticed. Everything has been made
subservient to the purpose of elevating the creature to the contemplation of the great Creator, in whose hands are all the
corners of the earth. Truly does it merit the distinction of
"La Grande." How much nobler an aspiration than that of
the Greeks, who sought merely to embody the highest conception of worldly beauty, and whose ideas of religion scarcely
rose above the ground on which they stood. And the conduct
of the worshippers here seems prompted by a sympathy in
accordance with the spirit of the place. Every purely worldly

enjoyment is banished. From this point of view the chairs of the French and the pews of the English churches are equally destructive to any elevation of feeling, inasmuch as they necessarily recall one from meditation on things above to the mere comforts of the body. Spanish ladies, if they desire to sit, have a mat carried by a servant and placed upon the pavement in the veritable Eastern style, while the men, noble and peasant alike, kneel upon the marble mosaic.

The internal arrangement of the Cathedral resembles that of most others in Spain. The centre aisle from the transept to within fifty or a hundred feet of the great western entrance, is occupied by the coro (the choir), closed toward the west by the trascoro, but open toward the high altar, which occupies a similar position on the opposite side of the *entre los dos coros*. Each is railed off by a handsome grating—*reja*—of ornamented steel, and a little gangway connects the two. The *rejas* in the Spanish cathedrals are always worthy of the attention of travellers, and give some idea of what the gold and silver and steel work in these churches was before the War of Independence. The whole high altar is a magnificent piece of skill and ornamentation, and the *retablo*, extending nearly up to the roof, is famous even in Spain. It is of *alerce* wood, and divided into forty-four compartments, which represent scenes from the Scripture history. Far up above, seemingly in the clouds, is a crucifix, projected apparently upon a back ground of dark velvet. At certain hours of the day, depending upon the season, the rays of the sun, through the stained windows of the cimborio or dome over the transept cross, fall upon this crucifix, which is thus brilliantly illuminated, while the rest of the edifice remains in profound gloom. The effect is beyond measure impressive. The coro is finely ornamented within, and above it are the grand organs, whose deep tones, swelling through the Cathedral on a feast day, and filling its recesses with the immensity of their volume, are indeed magnificent. One of them, built by Jorge Bosch, the largest in the world, contains a hundred and nineteen stops, and five thousand three hundred and twenty-six pipes; the other, by Verdalonga, is almost as large. Sacred music is still preserved in its purity and grandeur at Seville, resembling, in this respect, the cities of Germany. The artist, who performed on great occasions in 1852, was a master, and did full justice to the noble instrument, though this summer I heard no music that was remarkable. Around the coro and high altar, on the outside, are numerous small altars and chapels, containing many works of art, famous, some of them, for their excellence, others for their antiquity. Among them is a celebrated image, in wood, of the Virgin, by Montañes, probably the finest specimen of wood carving in Spain. It is perfectly exquisite, the embodification of the highest and purest style of Andalusian beauty, a Murillo solidified. A quantity of ornaments of a rich description, glittering jewels and costly silks, have been placed upon it, greatly impairing the effect; but a certain amount of silver about these images serves to heighten the relief, only it requires great judgment to know when to stop. For the artistic reputation of Spain, it is to be regretted that its sculpture consists almost entirely of either wood or earth in its various preparations. Its churches are crowded with images which, if in marble, would receive the unqualified approbation of the artistic world. As it is, they are generally hurried over with a passing notice, partly because when seen by strangers they have been removed from the situations for which they were originally intended by the artist, and partly because of the cheapness of the material out of which they are made, as though the excellence of the conception were not the same, whether executed in marble or terra-cotta.

The whole circuit of the Cathedral is a series of chapels and altars, with endless treasures of every description—a veritable museum. Its paintings would, of themselves, form a gallery as distinguished for excellence as for numbers. During a considerable part of the War of Independence, Marshal Soult reigned supreme in Andalusia, and, to speak in plain terms, robbed and stole whatever fell within his grasp. Nowhere in Europe did the Revolutionary Generals hesitate to melt down any ornament of the precious metals, however beautiful or sacred. Such conduct, though strange in those who came ostensibly as benefactors, might have been forgiven, but Soult, not content with this, by a refined species of robbery, plundered works of art. Some, in anticipation of this invasion of Vandals, had been removed to Cadiz, others hidden away in the vaults beneath, but such precautions did not always suffice, for the Chapter was occasionally compelled to produce its secreted treasures by the threat of a military execution. I was present, in 1852, at the sale of his collection in Paris—those very pictures seized here by fraud and violence—and I saw the agent of the Spanish Government bidding for the Murillo, its own property, now in the Louvre, which sold for the enormous sum of four hundred thousand francs. How the Allies could sanction the retention of them by Soult, and yet send back those which were in the possession of Napoleon, is inconceivable to an ordinary conscience. But the morality of the world is a strange science, and Europeans, who hold up their hands in holy horror at the thought of a Cuban filibuster, find nothing to blame in all this. A number of magnificent Murillos were, however, preserved. The first chapel on the left, entering from the Sagrario, contains a large altar piece representing San Antonio de Padua kneeling before the infant Saviour, which is considered by many the master work of the artist. Whether it be entitled to this pre-eminence may admit of a question, but it is a grand painting, one which improves with every visit. The picture is of large size, yet it would puzzle the critic to point out a fault. The somewhat unnatural subject, that is, unnatural when viewed from the experience of life, is clothed with dignity by the consummate hand of the master, and the devotion of the saint to a mere infant, produces none but the noblest impression. The " Guardian Angel," leading a little child by the hand, which is an altar piece near the western entrance, is entitled to all the admiration it has received. Nothing can surpass the benevolence of the Angel, who, with cherishing love and hope, points to Heaven, or the confiding trust expressed in the countenance of the child, as it clings to the hand of its protector. It is one of those pictures which remain in the memory, and seems a vision of some previous stage of existence, ere man had fallen from his purity. The Chapter House, too, possesses a treasure in the " Concepcion," which is, perhaps, unequalled among the conceptions; and another chapel, to the north, has a Madonna, by Alonzo Cano, that may worthily rank with the best. In the south transept is the celebrated " Generacion," by Luis de Vargas, commonly called "La Gamba," from the leg of Adam. I was never able to perceive the great merit of this painting, but every one else does. There can, however, be but one opinion about the miserable kitchen clock above, the only incongruous ornament in the Cathedral.

The Royal Chapel behind the altar, a church in size, contains a precious relic in the well-preserved body of St. Ferdinand, the reconqueror of Seville. The coffin in which his body was formerly enclosed still remains, with inscriptions in Latin, Spanish, Arabic and Hebrew. Here, too, are his sword and the sacred image of the Virgin, which hung at his saddle bow during the campaign. The original keys of the city, which were presented to him by the Jews and Moors on the surrender, are guarded in another part of the Cathedral. On certain anniversaries the body is exposed to view; guard is mounted by the picked troops of the garrison (this duty was formerly discharged by the master tailors of the Cofradia de San Mateo, among whom he was enrolled), and the flags are lowered before the saintly conqueror. In this chapel lies also the body of Maria de Padilla, formerly considered the mistress, now believed to have been the wife of Peter the Cruel. The tombs of Garci Perez de Vargas and other Conquistadores, are to be found in the various chapels, so that the Cathedral has been happily styled a Pantheon of Chivalry. The most interesting of all is that of Fernan Columbus, who is interred near the western entrance. A simple slab, let into the pavement, marks the spot, and on it are carved the caravels of the great discoverer, with the proud motto—proud in its simplicity—

> A Castilla y á Leon,
> Nuevo mundo dió Colon.

The remains of Columbus himself, after many translations, repose in the Cathedral of Havana, and should the project, avowed by western Europe of Africanizing the Island, be carried into execution, it is to be hoped that they will find an appropriate and final resting place in the bosom of the great American Republic. Filibustering, for this end, would deserve the approbation of the civilized world.

There are nine entrances to the Cathedral, one to the south, two to the east, three to the west, and three to the north upon the Patio de los Naranjos. Over one of these, *la del lagarto*, is suspended a wooden alligator, about which many marvellous tales are told, such as that it was a courting present from the Soldan of Egypt. In fact, it is, with the curb and other emblems beside it, merely symbolical of the cardinal virtues. The doors of the great western entrance are opened in summer for ventilation; but the iron grating is never removed, except to admit the monarch, or for the installation or burial of an archbishop.

Though the feasts of the Church at Seville are no longer celebrated with the pomp of former days, when a considerable portion of the wealth of the kingdom was in the hands of the clergy, they are still second in magnificence only to those of Rome. On such occasions, the Giralda is illuminated from its base to its summit, and as the flames flicker with the wind, the huge tower itself, like a burning arrow, seems to sway about in the heavens. The great Easter candle, formerly twenty-four feet in length, and weighing eighty arrobas (some two thousand pounds) is sadly reduced in its dimensions, but is still of enormous size, and the lofty *Monumento,* which is erected on the eve of Good Friday, and stands a pillar of fire in the general gloom of the Cathedral, yet displays its glories, far surpassing the descriptions given of the illuminated cross that used to be suspended in St. Peter's on the Saturday of Holy Week. Easter and the Feria, or fair, attract crowds from all parts of Spain, and not a few foreigners from the seaports of Cadiz, Gibraltar and Malaga. Then, Seville *ese Laberinto de forasteros,* combines every attraction, and the ceremonies of the Church, even to the eating of the Paschal lamb, are strictly observed. The market where these latter are sold used to be well worth a visit. Adult faithful throng to procure the holy symbol, while children embrace the opportunity of purchasing young pets, which are here great favorites. In the processions the image of the Virgin is conspicuous. Indeed, Seville has, during all ages, been famous for the honors it has paid to the Mother of God. Centuries ago, the dogma of the immaculate conception was fought and sustained here, and even passed into a shibboleth. As a question of revealed religion, every one must decide for himself. Regarding it from a merely human point of view, the worship of the Virgin appears to me very natural. What can be more worthy of respect, to go no further, than the ideal of female excellence? that ineffable purity and beauty of soul which doubles the enjoyments and divides the sorrows of life, which diffuses its rays over this weary pilgrimage below, and alone renders existence endurable? These may be mere phantasies of inexperience, the dreams of a bachelor. If so, it would be a sad mistake to exchange them for the commonplace realities of truth. If one may be pardoned for mingling things on earth with things above, I will confess that a visit to the Cathedral on a feast day could sufficiently explain to me the prevalence of this feature of religious worship, without the necessity of seeking its origin in the Roman Diana, or the Phœnician Astarte. Surely, no other spot on earth can offer such types of female loveliness as then crowd its spacious aisles.

As the excellence of the Cathedral does not consist so much in the contemplation of particular parts as in the general effect of the whole, it should be visited at all hours of the day in order to appreciate it fully. A stranger, with a guide and a guide book, will detect, perhaps acknowledge, its manifold beauties; but really to feel it, he should saunter in alone, with a mind free from preoccupation and ready to imbibe its mysterious influences. I was never more profoundly impressed than one evening, about sunset, in the month of September. The vesper chaunt had just ended, and the last notes of the organ, faintly echoing their mellow cadence, were dying away in the vaulted roof. Priests and choristers hurried out, with doubtless very prosaic feelings—it was their daily occupation—and I was left almost alone, with here and there a pious devotee lingering before some favorite altar. The expiring rays of the sun streamed in through the western portal, but were lost in the vast recesses of the edifice; the whole eastern portion lay shrouded in gloom. A faint gleam of light, struggling through the painted windows of the dome, fell upon the lofty crucifix, and seemed to point to the life of purity beyond. At such a time, one cannot but feel that there is an ethereal spirit within, a spark of the Divine essence, which would fain cast off its prison house of mortality and flee to the Eternal existence that gave it birth. This edifice is one of the few creations of man that realizes expectation. Morning, noon or night, none can enter without acknowledging that he stands on holy ground. The accessories, the trembling swell of the organs, the sweet odor of incense, the beautiful works of art, which elsewhere distract the attention, here combine in universality of grandeur to establish that harmony of the soul so conducive to devotion; and if the excellence of architecture consist in the accomplishment of the rational purpose assigned, to this must the palm be awarded. Political economists may reason that such an expenditure in unproductive stone withdraws from the general circulation a sensible capital; the severe reformer may preach against the adoration of saints and images; the abstract philosopher may denounce the appeal to the senses, but their remonstrance will fall pointless upon the heart. There are occasions when humanity rises above the earthly rules of logic, and acknowledges obedience only to those hidden laws which govern the divine portion of our nature, and whose sequence is beyond the reach of human intellect.

In olden times, the great city of Seville contained more than a hundred churches, besides hospitals and other semi-religious establishments. The various wars of the century, the suppression of monasteries and the confiscation of the church property, have reduced the number to a small fraction of what it originally was; and the works of art with which they were crowded have been transferred to galleries, oftentimes with ruinous effect, for they were always calculated for the precise position they were intended to occupy, with due regard to light and shade, and it rarely happens that they are, or can be suitably placed elsewhere. In no department has the genius of Andalusia been more pre-eminent than in painting. Murillo and Velasquez are but the brightest ornaments of a school, which numbered many others entitled to a high rank. The taste still survives, though the faculty of originating grand conceptions seems to be dormant, and almost every one here is capable of appreciating, if not of executing. Many of the Murillos have found their way to Madrid, and even further; but the best are, unquestionably, still in Seville. Between the city wall and the river is the hospital of La Caridad, which contains very fine ones. Hence was taken by Soult the Sta. Isabel, now in the Academy at Madrid. Two of those yet remaining are larger in size than Murillo was in the habit of painting; they represent, respectively, the miracle of the Loaves and Fishes, and Moses Striking the Rock. The composition of both has been criticised, and is, perhaps, faulty, as in neither is the principal figure sufficiently prominent. But in invention, drawing, coloring, they seem quite equal to the best. The San Juan de Dios had been to me formerly a disagreeable picture, on account of its dark back ground, and gloomy, forbidding manner, but I now acknowledge its excellence. The "Dead Bishop," by a less distinguished artist, is a revolting subject,

but a most admirable painting, if complete success in producing the desired effect be the true object of admiration. A
certain haughty prelate had treated the artist with a want of
respect, who, in revenge, determined to teach his reverence a
lesson of humility. There he lies in his coffin with mitre and
crook, the flesh seeming to fall from his bones, and the fright-
fully life-like worms crawling in and out. Pfaugh! Murillo
protested that he could not look at it without holding his nose,
and the proud Bishop, with unwilling regrets, confessed the
truth of the Preacher's words—"All, all is vanity."

The greater portion of the pictures which had belonged to
the suppressed convents, were subsequently collected into a
museum, where they yet remain, the old convent of La Merced
being appropriated for that purpose. As for those in the
church, I will not venture to give an opinion, for the workmen
were making some repairs, and my entry seemed always simultaneous with an increase of industry, producing such a dust
and noise that it was impossible to enjoy the fine arts. One
hall on the second floor is entirely filled with Murillos, which
seems to me a matter of regret. At least, I have always found
it difficult to bring away a distinct impression where there are
so many which necessarily resemble each other to a considerable extent. It offers, however, the best opportunity of studying the artist himself, and this collection reveals Murillo in all
his glory, though it is defective in representations of profane
subjects. The "Servilleta," which he painted upon a table
napkin, is deservedly admired, but the face is evidently taken
from some not very handsome reality, whom he has portrayed
more than once. The patronesses of the Giralda, the St. Francis, the San Antonio, and others, are much more to my taste.
Among them are two "Conceptions." An Andalusian courier
in the service of a friend of mine in Paris, vindicating the
superiority of Murillo over all rivals, acknowledged in them
an idea of the beauty of form and color, but claimed that his
countryman alone could bring out the "insides." The criticism was better than the English in which it was conveyed,
and is particularly applicable to the "Conceptions." Murillo's
success in this, the most difficult of all subjects, is marvellous.
Who but he has adequately imagined what Victor Hugo somewhere calls "le point mystic de la Virginité, de la Maternité,
et de la Divinité?" The task imposed on Spanish painters far

exceeded in difficulty the simple representation of the Madonna, who in unimpassioned repose idealizes freedom from earthly thoughts—a purely negative effect. Murillo has accomplished greatly more than this; he has embodied a conception of the most exquisite earthly loveliness, free from the taint of earthly passions; a picture of enraptured ecstatic beatitude, uncorrupted by the guilt of sensual gratification; a seraph who feels that she has unconsciously become the mother of the Saviour. Whether other artists could have equalled Murillo, is best answered by the fact that they have not done so. Even Rafaelle, except in the Transfiguration, has rested content with the comparatively expressionless purity and serenity of Greek sculpture, nor would his Madonnas ever convey the idea of a mortal who has immaculately conceived, and is to bring into the world the Son of the living God—the holy ambition of all the daughters of Israel. The one followed the classical taste of his age and country, the other the living, impassioned enthusiastic nature around him, and I have always thought that the greatest triumph of the Spaniard would be to place his master work between the frigid purity of the Madonna di San Sisto, and the sensual ecstacy of Correggio's Io. Then would deserved honor be accorded to him who first had united humanity and divinity.

THE ALCAZAR AND OTHER EDIFICES.

The finest, though not the purest, relic of Moorish art in Seville, is the Alcazar, which has served as a royal residence even from the days of the Romans. After the dissolution of the Cordovese Empire, Seville became the residence of one of the most enlightened families, that succeeded in establishing a dynasty upon its ruins—the Beni Abbad. Under them and their successors, particularly the Almohades, the Alcazar was greatly improved, if not rebuilt. But the finest portions date from the time of Peter the Cruel of Castile, whose alliance with the Moorish sovereigns of Granada and Africa enabled him to procure architects and workmen, and to rival the extinct glories of Cordova. Ferdinand and Isabella, and the Emperor Charles made alterations and additions, but some subsequent barbarian actually whitewashed the Moorish ceilings. It baffles ingenuity to conjecture the motive for such a performance. Since my last visit, the Duke of Montpensier, with the taste and liberality which characterize him, has caused much of it to be removed, and is attempting to restore the whole to its original state. A specimen of the old whitewashed portion has been retained for the purpose of offering a comparison. If his intentions are carried out, it will be almost as great an ornament to architectural Spain as the Alhambra. Indeed, I must say, that the Hall of the Ambassadors at Seville, barring the balconied windows cut into the *Media Naranja*, surpasses its rival, nor is there anything at Granada to equal the great court—the Patio principal—which, with its fountains and columns, is by moonlight really enchanting. It is some seventy feet in length, and some fifty in width, paved with the purest of white marble, and surrounded by an elegant colonnade. The decoration of the Moorish portion of the Alcazar is, if possible, richer than that of the Alhambra, and reasonably so, as the sovereigns of Se-ville, whether Christian or Mohammedan, were possessed of greater wealth, and had almost equal facilities with those of Granada; but beautiful as the Moorish Alcazar is, it lacks the charms of situation and the romance which lend such attractions to the Alhambra, and is moreover brought into too immediate contrast with other wonders to make its full impression.

The number of rooms, ancient and modern, is considerable—more than three score—but some of them are very plain in their decorations. The little chapel of Isabella, the Catholic, is a model of a royal chapel for devotion. Throughout the modern part are displayed the cypher of herself and her husband; that selected by Isabel was a bundle of arrows, the Spanish word for arrow (flecha) commencing with the initial letter of her husband's name; Ferdinand in turn adopted a yoke (yugo), the capital letter I, of Isabella, being written in Spanish as a Y. The motto, Tāto Mōta, has been erroneously interpreted to signify the equality between the kingdoms of Castile and Aragon, whereas none such existed or was contemplated. It has, with better reasons, been supposed to mean, simply, that it is as well to effect the union of the monarchy by marriage as by conquest. The gardens of the Alcazar are superb, and in spring the air is loaded with perfumes. One of the walks is lined with hidden fountains, whose jets arch over and drench the promenaders, and some unsuspecting attendant is generally made to suffer by way of illustrating the joke to travellers. It is not, however, half as good a plan as that of the facetious Archbishop of Saltzburg, whose dining table was surrounded with stone seats made hollow, for the purpose, with pipes running to his hand. *

The Alcazar is haunted by the uneasy shade of Peter the Cruel, about whose true character there is great difference of opinion among learned Spaniards of the present day. The impartial and inquiring spirit with which they have investigated this period of their history, is to my mind one of the evidences that the sound intelligence and critical judgment of the nation are rapidly awakening. Few princes have fared so badly in history as Peter. The vivacity and sternness of his disposition, his treatment of Blanche of Bourbon, his breach of faith toward the Moorish king, Abu Said, the cruelty of his vengeance were severely punished in this world by his premature death, and by the almost unanimous condemnation of historians. Of late, however, the foundations of this universally received opinion have been again investigated, and found to be liable to great suspicion. During the lifetime of his father, Alfonso XI, Peter and his mother were humiliated by the ambitious Leonora de Guzman, who aspired to substitute her own children in the place of the legitimate heirs. When he ascended the throne, a powerful feudal nobility, struggling to retain and enlarge privileges which were ceasing to be in accordance with the spirit of the age, and willing to embrace the opportunity afforded by the dissensions of the royal family of encroaching upon the prerogative, opposed continued obstacles to his government, and surrounded him with snares and treacheries, so that he knew not whom to trust. That his brothers acted toward him with dissimulation is certain, and his treatment of the Queen, his obstinate refusal even to see her, must have had some secret justification, otherwise his conduct would have been that of a mere insensate; nor is it to be supposed that the King of France would have quietly permitted the imprisonment and execution of an innocent daughter of the blood royal. The contemporary Spanish historians wrote under the influence of Henry of Trastamara, who had killed Don Pedro with his own hand, and thereby succeeded to the throne. What they say, therefore, must be taken with great allowance. We know that there was a very different narrative once in existence, though now lost or suppressed. The French writers are still less worthy of confidence, for their great leader, Du Guesclin or Claquin, was Henry's General, and is denounced by the Spaniards as a vile assassin for his part in the occurrence at Montiel, where he decided the fatal struggle between the brothers in a manner not easy to reconcile with the conduct of a *preux chevalier*. Pon Pedro had the additional misfortune of quarreling with the Prince of Wales, his only ally, about the pay for which that skilful soldier had bargained his services, and thus from none could he expect even justice. His friendship for Jews and Moors was considered a heinous sin at that day, but perhaps it was merely a liberality of opinion in advance of the age, and his unpopularity with the disorderly nobles of the realm, might well have been owing to the unrelenting severity with which he pursued offenders, whether high or low. Of this there are many authenticated instances. A striking one, in point, is narrated. Once upon a time a canon of the Cathedral having, in an ungovernable fit of rage at the bad shape of his shoes, killed the shoemaker, the family of the murdered man complained to the chapter, and the offender was punished by a suspension from his duties for a year. The son of the shoemaker avenged this double wrong by the death of the canon. Peter took personal jurisdiction of the crime, and having first ascertained what punishment had been inflicted in the previous case, imposed a similar one by suspending the young shoemaker for a year from the exercise of his occupation. Surely this was even handed justice.

Another anecdote is related of Don Pedro in this connection, which seems to me to have been strangely misunderstood. It is said that, being out alone one night, he had the misfortune, a very common one at that day, of crossing swords with a stranger, and killing him. Next morning he summoned the Chief of Police, and demanded the name of the offender. No one could tell. Peter commanded him to ascertain the author of the deed, and to place his bust on the spot. On the following day his own appeared, with all the regal paraphernalia, and it, or a pretended one, used to be shown in the Calle del Candilejo. His conduct in this particular has generally been construed into a poor and arbitrary jest in manifestation of his contempt for the law. But the idea of punishing a cavalier for the not unnatural consequences of an affair of gallantry, would have been considered in Spain at that day, and for many generations afterward, quite absurd. Besides, he could not be expected to hang himself. Yet it was his duty, as head of the State, to know the author of every evil deed, whether excusable or not, and the anecdote indicates a determination to punish, or at least expose, every offender, however great. Otherwise, the police would scarcely have dared to comply with his command. It would have been easy to feign ignorance, had they not known that such ignorance found no excuse in his eyes.

In view of such considerations, it has been proposed to substitute "El Justiciero" in the place of "El Cruel." Upon reading both sides of the question, it seems probable that Don Pedro was a person of bodily and mental accomplishments, of

14

a stern, unrelenting, passionate temper, soured by rivalry and
treachery; but that he was innocent of many of the crimes
imputed to him, and somewhat sinned against as well as
sinning; if occasionally violating the laws himself, yet demanding obedience to them from others, and frequently blameable,
not so much for what he did, as for the cruel manner in which
it was done. Doña Maria de Padilla, though living with him,
has escaped the breath of calumny except for her great fault,
and for that, many palliations are to be found in the prevailing
ideas of the age. It appears reasonably certain now that they
were privately married. She was pronounced to be his wife by
Don Pedro in his will, and through her daughter, Doña Con-
stanza, the Royal Dukes of Lancaster set up a claim to the
Spanish throne. The fascination which she exercised over this
blood stained man, like that of her unfortunate contemporary
Ines de Castro, over her husband Don Pedro of Portugal, cannot be appreciated by those whose fortune it has never been to
travel in romantic Spain. Various places in the city are connected with the traditions of their lives, and the baths in the
garden of the Alcazar are still called by her name.

There are in the city other palaces and houses of Moorish
architecture, better preserved than the Alcazar, and free from
the great confusion of styles which disfigure it. Seville is almost
the only place where such relics exist. The civil wars, after the
downfall of the Beni Omeyah and the inroads of the Christians, left little surviving of their former grandeur, and the
Moors of Malaga and Granada were too poor to erect costly
structures. It was otherwise with the great Christian captains
who victoriously marshalled the Conquistadores, and received
boundless grants of territory. Numerous palaces were erected
for them in the exact style of the country, without restriction
as to luxury or expense. Some of them contain half a dozen
or more Patios. One of the most perfect specimens, though by
no means the largest, is near the present Bank. I desired to
visit it again; but the good lady, without raising her eyes from
the floor, replied to the guide's request with the ominous ejacu-
lation, " estoy ocupada," which leaves nothing to be hoped.

One of the most celebrated houses in Seville is the Casa de
Pilatos, erected by a member of the Ribera family after a journey
to Jerusalem in the early part of the 16th century, and
supposed to be in imitation of the Roman Governor's mansion.

It was once a beautiful place, though suffered to go to ruin. A feeble attempt has been lately made to clear away the rubbish, and the marble courts, with their fountains, have been put in order. A peculiar and perfectly un-Moorish feature is the superb staircase, which may compare, *longo intervallo*, with that of the Palazzo della Scala. It can be seen at a glance that the owner's presence seldom enlivens this residence. Everything is in confusion. One of the best rooms is converted into a sort of painter's studio and old curiosity shop, in which, among other things, was hung a portrait of the fair mistress of the house, an Andalusian, and one of the most perfect types of Spanish beauty. The porteress, a sister of the artist, was very communicative, and set no bounds to her laudations of the painting and its subject. Like most other houses of state in Seville, there is a beautiful garden, with statues and fountains, all in a condition of neglect.

The finest structure in Seville, which has been erected since the days of Ferdinand and Isabella, is the Lonja or Exchange, lying at the south-west corner of the Cathedral. It is a noble edifice, built for eternity, and its massive architecture is worthy of the days when Spain ruled the greater part of the world. The shape is a quadrangle, some two hundred feet square, with a marble Patio in the centre. Unfortunately, its completion was almost simultaneous with the crumbling of the Empire and the decay of its commerce, and, like many of the Spanish bridges, it seems to be a display of prodigal munificence. The papers relating to America, were, in the latter part of the last century, neatly labelled and packed away here, and have never been disturbed since. As the building is fireproof, and apparently indestructible, they will be preserved to await the awakening into life of Spanish America, for whose history they are indispensable. The uninterrupted repose of these archives is conclusive evidence of the intellectual torpor that reigns over that quarter of the globe. The white steps of the Lonja, facing the gorgeous Cathedral, used to be a charming place to sit on winter nights, and meditate upon the past glories of Seville, when hundreds of ships yearly poured into her lap the treasures of the New World, and foreigners crowded from all parts of Europe to share in the golden flow. But, to descend from the sentimental, it must be admitted that my reveries were frequently disturbed by the snoring of the watchmen, who

made this and the opposite corner, at the entrance of the Calle
de las Sierpes, a favorite napping place.

The University is also modern, though anterior in date to the
Lonja. As a seminary of learning, it is in the natural condition which the long continued supremacy of the Inquisition
would lead us to expect, and is distinguished rather for works
of art than of intellect. The church contains some magnificent
sculptures by Montañes and Alonso Cano, but the most striking
objects are the tombs of the Ribera family, now merged in the
Medina Celi. They were removed hither upon the suppression
of the Cartuja convent. Over the tombs repose the grim
effigies of the old knights, and by their side lie the partners of
their honors and joys. The feet of the latter, in accordance
with the old custom, are, in every instance, carefully covered.
Whence this custom was derived I do not know, but so rigid
was it in old times, that the carriage steps used to be so constructed as to conceal these sacred objects from inspection, and
husbands went through life without having seen their wives'
feet. A fair Goth, who might easily have committed and been
pardoned grave peccadilloes, would have shrunk with horror
from such an exposure. As many of the Spanish prejudices
were prompted by the desire of distinguishing themselves from
the Jews and Mohammedans, it may be that a similar spirit of
opposition to the Oriental custom of covering the face induced
them to cover the feet. Whatever be the origin, this prejudice
was deeply rooted in the national feeling, and was one of the
regulations imperatively prescribed by the Inquisition for the
paintings of the Virgin.

The Riberas having left no male representative, are spared
the mortification of seeing their ponderous swords in the hands
of puny dancers around a modern court. The inscriptions tell
how they filled, in succession, the great office of Adelantado,
Mayor of Andalusia, at a time when such posts were entrusted
to none, save stern warriors, whose deeds were more sonorous
than their words, and whose leisure was more nobly occupied
than in the unmeaning gallantries of a subsequent age. It is a
pleasant thing to wander amid the resting places of a family
whose past is thus embalmed beyond the possibility of dishonor, and whose virtues are perpetuated in storied marble,
while none survive to awaken the envy or contempt of succeeding generations. There are many such in Spain; but the

evidences of their former grandeur have too frequently disappeared under the corroding influence of time and neglect. A noble monument of the munificence of the Riberas yet survives in the enormous Hospital la Sangre, without the walls, founded by a daughter of the house—a monument of art as well as of charity.

One of the lions of Seville is the tobacco manufactory, a vast establishment, with a number of courts. The operatives employed are enumerated at six thousand, of which four are women, their hands and tongues equally busy. A large proportion are gipsies, and such ugly creatures! I can honestly say that I never saw but one handsome *cigarera*, though they passed twice a day in front of my house. Whether it be the eternal odor of the tobacco, or the foul air generally, that produces this wonderful homeliness, no one can tell. Nor is modesty a prevailing characteristic, though there are exceptions to that. A great outcry is made in Europe against the government monopoly of tobacco, but it seems to me the most just of taxes. Tobacco is a pure luxury, which no one is compelled to use, though, in the language of the first discoverers, it does "tend to open ye pores of ye bodye and to disperse ye humoures of ye minde." Everyone is at liberty to pay the tax or not, as he sees fit, and surely nothing can be fairer. Another advantage is that it falls upon the men alone, for notwithstanding the prevalent belief, women seldom smoke in Spain. I have seen the commoner class indulge, but this summer I did not meet one such. The amount of revenue thus raised to the treasury is a serious item. At Seville they give you the only good segars that can be procured in Europe, and those at one cent are better than the French at six. The snuff manufactured here is mixed with a sort of ochreous-looking earth from Almayzaron, which gives it a reddish hue. I believe this has always been done, but in what consists the advantage I do not know. They seem to prefer it.

The streets of Seville are by no means fine, according to our ideas of space, in fact scarcely broader than alleys, though probably equal to the best of ancient Rome, and more airy than most in Italy. Not more than a dozen are wide enough to permit the passage of two carriages, and all run without the slightest regard to rectangularity. The Boulevards, the Rue de Rivoli, the Calle de Alcalá, Pennsylvania Avenue, are modern

notions, unsuited to the climate or the tastes of Andalusia.
Whatever they may thus lose in regularity of appearance
they certainly gain in comfort, where the sun pours down
with greater fury than in Africa itself, and where one of the
principal ends of street architecture is to exclude its rays. The
Calle de las Sierpes and that de los Francos, the principal shopping streets, are flagged entirely across, and in summer covered
with awnings, according to the usual custom in such climates.
They are, consequently, cool at all periods of the day, and as
the air is dry, there is no necessity for admitting the sun's rays
to dissipate the moisture. It is easily comprehensible how
travellers from the north, accustomed to the regularity of Paris
and London, and the grand thoroughfares of the former, are
disappointed at the first sight of Seville, of which they have
heard so much. But the climate, which enforces such rules of
architecture, brings, also, corresponding advantages, so that
the balance is restored. Its streets are not crowded by the
throngs that press the Boulevards or the Strand, yet the gay
balconies, the bright colors, which never fade in this dry climate, the absence of disfiguring rust, smoke and damp, the
very irregularity itself, more than compensate for the unhealthy restlessness of the north. In its multitude of flowers,
Andalusia resembles our own country. Every Patio and balcony smiles with them, and at certain hours of the day the
vendors fill the streets, crying, in local dialect—

> Flor' ! flor' ! flor' !
> Jasmin y alhelí !
> Rosa' de to' color' !
> Flor' ! flor' !

The taste for these simple ornaments is universal, and is
here abundantly gratified. All southern people have the
olfactory sense strongly developed, and nature seems to have
kindly considered this peculiarity in the formation of Andalusia, for every waste is overrun with aromatic herbs, which,
in some localities are used for fuel, there being no other. The
streets of Seville are redolent of the *Alhucema*. It serves in
all the houses to scent the fresh washed linen. A handful is
cast upon the *brasero*, and the article held over the rising
fumes; and the ladies sometimes stand over a perfumed bath,
such as is found in the Tocador de la Reina in the Alhambra.

The central market is a delightful place on a summer morning, on account of its exposition of flowers, and like every other establishment in Seville is amply provided with fountains, which serve to keep them fresh. By-the-bye, another curious article of sale in the same market were a number of crickets, enclosed in cages, keeping up a continual cri-cri, which seems to be a favorite music.

The private houses are mostly of modest height, rarely exceeding two stories. A few modern ones have been erected of three or more, but though they make a finer show on the outside, they are probably less comfortable and certainly less attractive than the others. All the older ones contain memorials of the preceding occupants; to pretend, however, to enter into an enumeration or description of the interesting relics of the Roman, Moorish or old Spanish eras, that remain, would be to invade the province of the guide books. Those from the Moorish days are more numerous and far better preserved than probably in any other city of Spain. Cordova has little besides the Mezquita, and the solitary boast of Granada is the Alhambra, while Seville contains numberless specimens, though no single one, perhaps, may rival the two mentioned. You have but to walk along the streets to be convinced of this fact. The old Moorish wall survives in part, looking just as in the illustrated chronicles of Don Pedro, and the bridge of boats used to be an equally characteristic feature, but that has given place to an elegant iron structure.

There is a good theatre at Seville. It was, however, closed during my sojourn on account of the summer heats. Though the modern drama took its rise in Spain, Spaniards are by no means so given to this amusement as the French or Italians who resort thither as almost the only place of public amusement. It here encounters the rivalry of the Paseo and the stirring Corrida de Toros, which are more consonant with the national tastes than regular theatricals. The Andalusians are probably the best judges in Spain of theatrical and operatic performances, but they are much better got up in Madrid, where they compare not unfavorably with those of Vienna and Paris. Indeed, the audience in both cities are no means critics. Classic dramatists, such as Calderon and Lope de Vega, appear seldom, as is the case elsewhere in Europe. Every place is overrun with translations of Scribe. I confess a pre-

ference for the Saynete, when I can understand it, which is far
from always, for the plot is characterized by the same intri-
cacy, and the words used have frequently no place in the dic-
tionary of the academy. Spanish tragic actors are apt to
overdo the thing; there is so much tragedy in real life in
Spain, that when they attempt to act it the result is generally
rant. I think it may be stated as a general rule, that cold
blooded people make the best tragedians, for with all their
efforts they can barely attain the appearance of nature, whereas the Spaniard starts from this point, and until half a dozen
victims or so are slaughtered, he considers nothing done—the
performance scarcely under weigh. Then, too, as has been
often remarked, people go to the theatre to see something different from every day life. Love and anger form the staple of
most dramas, and what author could concentrate these passions into greater intensity than is found in common Andalusian existence? But in comedy, founded upon national peculiarities, they are inimitable. In truth, Spaniards, though
without frivolity, appreciate highly a ludicrous idea, if another
be the subject, and their grave and serious exterior covers a
fund of humor. In the Saynete they are simply acting life.
The theatre is, particularly in Seville, a place of reception
also, which is very convenient for strangers. Otherwise, the
general arrangements are the same as elsewhere.

Dancing is, and always was, a part of the entertainment.
Spanish dancing from the most remote ages has been famous.
The Latin authors bear testimony to the ravishing effects
produced by the Gaditanas in the Eternal City, and describe,
though with qualified admiration, the warlike leapings of the
other provinces. Whether mankind originally sprang from
one stock or several, it is certain that the different nations of
the earth have become marked by very great peculiarities,
which no education can communicate, and which seem to be
radical, even in matters of comparative insignificance. It
remains to be seen whether the culinary taste of the great
powers can be reconciled even by a congress of *artistes*. No
Englishwoman could ever wear her dress with the taste of a
Parisienne; nor could either of them imagine, much less imitate the grace of an Andaluza. In these matters, the spiritless
uniformity that is creeping over the world is produced rather
by obliterating what is striking and national than by making

these peculiarities common to all. Spaniards may forget the fandango, but no one else will ever acquire it.

The origin and historic development of the Spanish dances is not easy, as the only sources of information are scattered phrases, culled here and there out the old authors; for the professors of the divine art themselves know their calling only as an art, not as a science. A great deal of confusion, too, has arisen from confounding pure Spanish with Moorish, and both with gipsy dances in general. The gipsies in Andalusia dance all;—but the gipsy dances proper, like the race, are derived from the far east, and have little in common with the Spanish. They are, for the most part, simply sensual, without ideality or poetry, except of the lowest order; and when gipsies undertake to render the Spanish dances, it is done with every license that the most prurient imagination can invent.

If the Andalusian differ on the one hand from the mere sensualism of the gipsy, they are equally removed, on the other, from the physical agility of the Slavonic polkas and mazurkas. They certainly belong to an age of the world and to a state of society in which persons sought enjoyment in witnessing the performance of others rather than in participating themselves, as was the case in the ancient world, and is still in the east. Every province in Spain has its peculiar dance, scarcely known beyond its limits, except upon the stage. The wide difference between them would manifest a great diversity of origin, which no competent person has taken the trouble accurately to investigate. Andalusians never indulge in the Jota, nor can the Aragonese supple themselves to the swimming Olé, yet each locality enters with such real gusto into its peculiar amusements, that a traveller who passes a dull evening in any village in Spain must be a veritable Heraclitus. Neither gout nor dyspepsia would be a sufficient excuse, for the climate is an uncompromising foe to both. The same general division, dependent upon temperature and temperament, obtains here as in the rest of Europe. Those of the north are characterized by agility and activity, those of the south by beauty and grace. Of the dances of the north-west I know nothing by personal experience, except what I have seen in the streets of Madrid to the music of the Zambomba, and that was not very prepossessing; but the Jota Aragonesa and the Manchegas of La Mancha are difficult to resist. Andalusia, however, is, as usual, the home of elegance in this department. The descriptions of Juvenal and Martial leave little room for doubt as to the identity of the ancient with those still in vogue on the banks of the Guadalquivir. Whatever changes may have been introduced by Moor or gipsy, they are certainly in their essence not to be derived from either of these sources, and if they existed in the east, it is strange that the Romans, ransacking the world to pamper their pleasures, could find them only in Bætica. From time to time, the names and peculiar developments have been altered and become obsolete. Thus the Zarabanda, once so famous, has, I believe, entirely disappeared; the fandango is of later origin, the bolero later still. The Church, while sparing the bull fight, has always set the seal of its reprobation upon them, but in vain; with more or less pruning they survive, and give unabated evidence of vitality. There is, however, one enemy approaching, whom they will scarce be able to resist—the spirit of money making. If the clammy hand of this spectre grasp them, their reign is over, and they must be content with an occasional appearance on the stage.

The foundation of every Andalusian dance is love in some shape or other, and the plot is so arranged as to exhibit, in its fullest power, the triumphs of this irresistible passion. For the most part the maiden is coyish, hesitates, resists, flees, relents, —displaying throughout all the attractions of which she is mistress. The lover pursues with palpitating heart; happiness is within his grasp, animation is suspended—but no! he is doomed to disappointment. The startled fawn bounds away. Again is the pursuit renewed, again is the cup of bliss dashed from his eager lips, until at length, unable longer to resist the intensity of fascination, she surrenders! the world has ceased to exist and time is no more! One can easily comprehend that such a performance upon the stage, cramped by the rules of art and the criticism of a strange audience, is very different from the natural effusion of joy and grace, which is its foundation, when danced in the familiar circle. Nothing can be farther from the regular ballet, with its artificial emotions and stereotyped smile, than the movement of the same actors surrounded by a group of sympathizing acquaintances. Its characteristics are not activity and skill, but pure, unaffected grace, and a complete identification with the spirit of the romance. For this reason strangers find Spanish dances of very difficult acquisition. I made an effort at the bolero myself, I fear with mediocre success, though my master was pleased to say that I was the best foreign pupil he ever had, the English being too awkward and the French too studied.

Once during my novitiate, an acquaintance—an *empleado*, as he was proud of recalling to me—took it into his head to celebrate some family festival with a *funcion*, and extended an invitation to me. On my arrival I found the company already assembled. As my friend did not serve her majesty in a very exalted capacity, there were no dukes or counts present, yet, judging only by their deportment, a stranger would not have ascertained the fact. The individual who took charge of me was, as I learnt, a distinguished barber, and consequently a personage of importance. Another very agreeable and stylish gentlemen was chief *artiste* at a confectionary. The performers were, for the most part, relatives and friends of the family, each accompanied by one mamá at the least. We took our seats around three sides of the apartment waiting for the signal. Soon, the tuning of the guitar and the preparatory click of the castagnette hushed us into silence, for the dance is a serious matter, and it is here strictly true as well as witty, "*qu'on n'écoute que le ballet.*" Spanish popular music has evidently little affinity with sustained melodies of Italy and Germany, but rather resembles that of Naples. It is almost always in the minor key, and for that reason, perhaps, more impressive, reminding one somewhat of the Highland ballads. There is something about it, an undercurrent of a mournful, unreposing character, by no means exhilarating when first heard. You soon perceive that it is in accordance with the serious, earnest vein which runs through the life of the nation. Their manner of striking the face of the guitar, from time to time, with the palm of the hand or the thumb—*golpeando*—heightens this impression. It is thus a suitable accompaniment to a Spanish dance.

The tuning over, business commenced. We first had *manchegas*, and *boleros*, and *jaleos* in abundance. Then came a charming dance—*El torero y la Malagueña*. The fair one enters, covered with a large mantilla, in the olden style, and wielding a fan. The torero follows, concealed up to his eyes in the ample folds of his cloak. He in vain attempts to spy out the lady, who avoids his glances by the aid of the mantilla, all the while skilfully enticing him on with her fan, as with a magnet. This coquetting is continued for a time, until the click of a castagnette is heard. She stops at the sound, her face is exposed, the torero approaches, cloak and mantilla are handed to the bystanders, and the couple bound forward in the undulations of the fandango. After this we had the world-renowned Olé, the perfection of its style. The performer has no companion, neither is she bound by any rules of art. No one can succeed who relies upon aught but inspiration. Science and education avail nothing. Compared with this, the others are the first rudiments of speech beside the wild oratory of an Arab chieftain. Every part of the dancer contributes to produce the general effect. The arms, the body, the feet, the flashing eye combine to work the audience up to a phrensy, and the influence she thus acquires over their feelings can be derived from no other source than the magnetism which philosophers have so often conjectured, but have failed to comprehend or explain.

But the most charming of all was the Vito, if I remember rightly. For this the guitars were laid aside, the music consisting in the clapping of hands in triple time by the whole company, intermingled with snatches of a wild, plaintive melody. One girl alone danced. She is supposed to be the belle of the village in the midst of her *beaux*. Commencing with a handkerchief wound about her waist, she dances around the circle once or twice, and, as she becomes inspirited, unties it and uses it as an additional means of forming those waving lines of beauty which artists have recognized. The person to whom she throws the handkerchief is the happy individual of her choice, and he is in duty bound to receive it on his knees. The point consists in dancing before each of her admirers, until, bewildered with the intoxicating influence, and in certain expectation that the guerdon has already left her hand, he falls before her, when she with a coquettish smile of triumph glides away to torture and disappoint another. The luckless wight is greeted with shouts of laughter, otherwise no sound is heard save the music. The use made of the handkerchief will be significant to students of Oriental manners. Several had been offered up to the pride of the dancer and the amusement of the company, when my turn at length came. I never before understood the fascination of the bird-charming rattlesnake. The effect was positively painful; I could see nothing, think of

nothing but the creature before me. Not particularly pretty,
she had become a divinity, girdled in mazy circles with pris-
matic hues of beauty, and appeared to undergo that species of
transfiguration which is recorded of some great orators. There
was no folly I would not have committed at the moment; and
when, in compliment to my being a stranger, she finally threw
the handkerchief into my lap, I felt disposed to burst into
tears or to scream, as though some great pressure had been
removed from the soul. Tradition tells that the Church, having once determined to suppress the fandango, concluded to
grant the criminal a trial before a court of reverend Judges,
arrayed in gown and cassock, previous to final condemnation.
At the appointed day, the advocates of the accused appeared
to plead his cause with castagnette and slipper. As the argument proceeded the Judges became restless, their stern physi-
ognomies relaxed, nervous twitchings manifested themselves,
until, unable longer to resist the contagion, they joined the
merry throng, and a unanimous verdict of acquittal was entered. If the incident be not true, it is well imagined, and
might have happened without violence to probability. Cato
himself would have relented before such an appeal. When the
handkerchief was thrown into my lap, I may, therefore, be
excused for having looked very foolish. It required some minutes to recover entirely. With this dance the *funcion* ended.
We smoked a paper of cigarettes, drank a glass of orangeade
and retired; Figaro and myself bearing each other company as
far as the Cathedral.

Across the Guadalquivir, in the faubourg La Triana, it is
usual to get up a *funcion de gitanas*—a gipsy dance—for the
entertainment of travellers, of course with a consideration.
Dirty, unwashed wretches, they do perform beautifully These
dances are, consequently, supposed by most strangers to be
peculiar to the gipsies, which is not the case, for every dance
danced by gipsies is not, therefore, a gipsy dance. There
are such, in the strictest sense of the word, but few would care
to see them repeated after one experience. Spanish dances
bear the mark of preceding ages in the certain amount of freedom allowable in a regular *funcion*, but banished from the stage
or private life. Our ideas of delicacy and propriety belong
essentially to the present century, and whether there were not
more real virtue under the old coarseness, than modern refine-

ment, remains still a question. As these dances are at present
pruned down, I certainly saw nothing to condemn here more
than in those countries in Europe, whence we draw our dances
of society. Surely it would be difficult to imagine anything
so ridiculously indelicate as the graceless haulings and hug-
gings of the half civilized Slavonic gyrations, which we have
naturalized among us. Terpsichore could never have presided
over such movements. The dances of Andalusia are the poetry
and ideality of motion, and the effect is precisely similar to
that of a gallery of ancient sculpture—the indelicacy is in the
mind of the beholder. Of course, the manner of their performance depends a great deal upon the performers themselves,
and so does the regular ballet. Like everything else in the
country, they are intensely national, characterized by the national virtues as well as the national defects, warm, poetical,
enthusiastic, superlative in both. All Spaniards have a great
indisposition to allow the sanctity of their persons to be invaded, even in a friendly way. A stab is more easily forgotten
than a blow. There is very little personal contact among
relatives in ordinary life, and the same feeling is carried into
this amusement. I do not remember ever to have seen a Spanish dance in which the performers touched each other; and the
disapprobation with which foreigners turn from the fandango,
cannot approach the disgust an old fashioned Spaniard would
feel for the *valse à deux temps*. Of the greater licentious tendency of the latter, I have little doubt. The parents of a
young gipsy, who will witness with applause and pride the
very questionable, or rather unquestionable evolutions of their
kinswoman, would, like herself, resist any unwarranted freedom suggested by such a presumption, with as much astonishment as fury. The number of dances is infinite, as every
person is at liberty to improvise a new one when under the
inspiration of the Muse. Some have penetrated, as summer
travellers, across the Pyrenees—such as the Cachucha, el Zapat-
eado, the Bolero, the Jota Aragonesa. The names of those
that remain at home is Legion. There is no difficulty in getting up a *funcion* in any village, however poor. A click of the
castagnettes and the whole world is alive. The first sound
behind the curtain of a theatre hushes everyone into attention. The contagion is very catching, too. Foreigners are
soon bitten with the mania, and the most refreshing chapter in

Allison, or even a number of the Congressional Globe, with an account of the last fight, would be powerless to withhold one from the circle. Who can measure the happiness which this innocent amusement pours into the tasteless cup of the poor? Among the nations which enjoy the credit of having made the greatest advances in civilization, all natural pleasures, springing spontaneously from everyday life, as green leaves from the bough, are banished. Have they been rendered the happier thereby? Are civilization and innocent, unpremeditated relaxation inconsistent? These are grave questions, scarcely in our power to answer, as there seems to be a current in events which we not only cannot control, but whose direction we cannot even ascertain.

Dancing in Spain was formerly not confined to social life. In imitation of, or rather in similarity to the customs of the Hebrews, it entered into religion, and on certain occasions, a party in full costume, with castagnettes, danced before the altar as did David before the ark. The time has certainly gone by for such a manifestation of devotion, though it survives in a sect in our own country. The national dances have also disappeared from polite society, at least they are danced only in private. I believe the young girls learn them; indeed I have known ladies of rank to devote much pains to their acquisition, but not for the ball room. No schooling could possibly be so effectual for the purpose of cultivating and developing the far-famed Andalusian grace. Certainly the Andaluzas alone can dance them as they should be danced, and were there nothing else in Seville, it would almost be worth a trip across the Atlantic to attend a regular *funcion*.

CHAPTER XII.

BULL FIGHTS.

Historical—Plaza de Toros—Majo and Maja—The Cuadrilla—Description of the
Corrida—The Novillos—Embollados—Breeds and Qualities of the Bulls—Progress of the Science—Its morality; its effect upon the audience; upon the economy—The Bull in Spain—Expense.

Seville being the home and headquarters of the fancy—the
aficion—this is the proper place to say a word upon the subject
of bull fighting, which no traveller in Spain could venture to
omit. Ponderous tomes have been written to discuss the origin
of this amusement. Some few facts are reasonably certain.
There is little ground for supposing that the Romans, or the
ancient Spaniards, or even the Mauritanians were acquainted
with the *Corrida de Toros*, although the practice of pitting wild
beasts against gladiators, or each other, was in great vogue
throughout the empire, as is attested by the magnificent ruins
yet surviving in the different provinces; and in cattle countries
people may have played with bulls for the amusement of the
populace, as in Thrace for example. But we first find the
veritable bull fight among the Andalusian Moors, and it was
the favorite diversion of the

> Caballeros Granadinos
> Aunque moros hijosdalgo,

who regarded it with ideas very different from those which
sustained the old gladiatorial sports. With the mob of the
Eternal City it was a mere scene of slaughter, a contest too
often between wretched captives who embraced this faint
chance of escaping an otherwise inevitable death. With the
Andalusian Moslems, it was a theatre for the display of manly
grace and prowess, and its actors the youthful gallants of the
court. But even with them it must have been of late origin.
I am not aware of any allusion to it under the dynasty of the

Beni Omeyah. War was still too serious and frequent a reality to admit of playing with its counterfeit. The only relaxations were literature and architecture. As in the progress of events, the Mohammedan thirst for conquest became slaked, and the pursuit of literature seemed to decline, these warlike amusements sprung up. From them the taste passed to the Christians, who could not quietly permit them to excel in a sport that elicited such applause from the fairer portion of creation. The Cid is said to have been one of the first Castillians who entered the lists. It is exceedingly probable that the Spaniards derived the thing from the Moors and the paraphernalia from the Romans, for the Plaza de Toros at present is a perfect representation of the amphitheatre. In old times the streets entering the public square were barricaded, and the knights, mounted on their best steeds, contended with the raging animals; their skill consisted then in not merely harassing the bull or saving the rider's own life, but also that of his horse, a much more noble object than the present. This was kept up at all events down to the war of the Succession, as is proved by the descriptions of travellers at that time, and even in this century the Corrida in small towns, which are without the luxury of a regular Plaza, takes place in the public square barricaded as formerly. In Seville, the present Plaza de la Constitution was the theatre. Corridas, in the ancient style, now take place at the "Fiestas reales," which are celebrated at a coronation in the Plaza Mayor, at Madrid, with great pomp and luxury, the horses being from the royal stables, and the combatants, gentlemen. But with these exceptions the old plan has gone almost entirely out of fashion, and the toreros (bull fighters) are as much trained artists as actors in a theatre. Sometimes *aficionados* (amateurs) from among the young gentry get up a *corrida*, which is then far more entertaining, as all their relatives turn out in a mass, and with redoubled interest in the performance. On such occasions the bulls are young, and are reduced to the level of their unprofessional opponents. The critic, moreover, can detect the want of that immensely developed strength in the wrist, necessary to keep the bull and the horse apart in the crush.

As bull fights, like horse races, resemble each other in their general traits, I shall describe one for all, without particular regard to the chronological order. I was in very good com-

15

pany that day, for as it was an unusual occasion—I forget precisely what—there was a general turn out, even of those who
were not in the habit of attending such exhibitions. The narrow streets were strung with vehicles, many coming from a
considerable distance, and filled with men and women in the
purest national costumes. Vendors of fans, fruit, orchata and
segars, surrounded the building, crying their wares at the utmost. We made our way with some difficulty through the
throng, and took our seats in a *paleo de sombra* (box on the
shady side) belonging to the family, for the boxes are placed
pretty much upon the same footing as those in the theatre. It
was a curious sight. The vast amphitheatre was crowded to
repletion. Circles of fluttering fans, variegated dresses and
flowers rose in tiers above each other, all resplendent in the
rays of a Seville sun, and offering to view a far more engaging
scene than any theatre. The boxes were occupied by the
beauty and chivalry of the land, and graced too by the presence of a member of the royal family. The arena itself presented the aspect of an exchange, such was the interested and
eager appearance of the men who moved about. Even the
neighboring house tops were covered by such as could not afford
the expense of entering the amphitheatre. The Andalusian
costume flourished in perfection, for this is a full dress occasion
—knee breeches, laced gaiters, opening to show a fine stocking,
silk *faja* or sash wound around the waist, neat fitting embroidered jacket, covered with tassels and glittering ornaments,
with a pocket handkerchief in each pocket, fancy neckerchief
passing through a ring, the whole surmounted by the *calañes*
hat. A long slender stick in the right hand finishes the complete *majo*. A Seville *majo* does not exactly correspond to
"dandy" in our tongue. There is nothing ridiculous about
him—quite the contrary. He must of course be the best dressed man on the ground, stunning in his attire; he must also
be the best horseman, the best handler of the knife, a dignified,
gentlemanly bully, insensible to fear, and to round off all, a
gallant man with the ladies. Then his position and authority
are undisputed. He reigns supreme, and moves about in the
throng, conscious that the eyes of envying youth are fixed upon
him. The *maja* is the female *majo*, minus his worse qualities,
and is altogether of a higher type than the manola of Madrid.
She is as fond of dress and resplendent in her apparel as the

majo. Therewith is united the unavoidable grace of her native land, and she is also *Salada! muy Salada!* No one can make a speech to her so witty, that she cannot return a still wittier answer. Yet appeal to those women, in whatever rank of life, and the genuine, unadulterated kindness of the Andalusian heart will pour forth.

The Plaza de Toros at Seville is one of the largest in the kingdom, some two hundred and fifty or three hundred feet in diameter. The arena is surrounded by a barrier some six feet high. This is, in turn, encircled by a gangway a yard or so in width, and then rise the seats in successive tiers. After these are the boxes. The arrangements, the entrances, and even the manner of designating the places, are precisely as in the Coliseum, except that the silken awning is replaced by the still deeper azure of an Andalusian sky. Measured by the standard of wages, the prices are high; the places in the shade (de sombra) costing most; then those which are in the shade part of the time and part in the sun (de sol y sombra); lastly, the sunny side, where the sovereigns roast in a temperature that would cause a sunstroke elsewhere, without seeming to suffer evil consequences from the exposure.

The goddess of Silence had been banished far away; a universal hum rose from all sides. The "human voice divine" vainly struggled for a place amid the clicking of fans, and the screams of the water sellers (whom I except from any suspicion of divinity), crying at their loudest, "*Aguá-á-áh! Aguá-á-áh! math frethca que la nié-é-ébe! quien quiere aguá-á-áh?*" (Water! Water! cooler than snow! who wants water?) Just as the appointed hour struck, a platoon of infantry, in full uniform, entered and took their seats. These serve the double purpose of repressing any riot that might occur, and of killing the bull, should he become dangerous to the audience. In the meantime, the dragoons had cleared the ring of stragglers, dogs, fruit sellers and dead heads. The corregidor then entered the box of state, the little flag was laid before him, and business commenced. Two alguazils now made their appearance, mounted on beautiful coal black Andalusian steeds, and dressed in the costume of Philip II's time, with slashed sleeves and waving plumes, to demand from the corregidor the key of the *Toril*, or place where the bull is confined. These functionaries are not popular, and are sometimes even jeered by the disrespectful mob, to which, however, they appear supremely indifferent. So soon as the object of their mission was accomplished, another door opened, and the cuadrilla, or company, made its appearance, glittering in their tight fitting garments. The two espadas, or swordsmen, marched in front; next come the chulos, two and two, and last the picadors, followed by the mule teams. The costume of the espada is the ancient dress of Spain, except that the materials are of the richest and costliest description. He wears a satin jacket and vest, embroidered with gold and adorned with numerous tassels; a silken sash encircles his waist; knee breeches, with silken stockings, enclose his legs. The hair is gathered sometimes into a knot, with a gaudy rosette, and sometimes enclosed in a net-worked bag. That of the chulos is similar. The picadors are more substantially clad, with the addition of an iron casing for the right leg, and a broad brimmed plantation hat. They are armed with a substantial pike, some nine feet in length, having a triangular pyramidical point of an inch inserted at the end, which is sufficient to prick the bull, and turn him off, without inflicting serious injury. The hero of the bull fight, next to the bull himself, is the espada; he is the star, the Corypheus of this dance of death. The cuadrilla is attached to him, travels about as a part of his train, and bears his name. On the present occasion we were to be rejoiced by the presence of the best espada in Spain, after the unapproachable Montes, assisted by some one, whose name I have forgotten, and whose performance was little inferior to that of the great master, so far as neatness of execution was concerned. The business of the *espada* does not commence until the third and last act of the play, when, as in the Greek tragedy, the hero succumbs to the decree of an inevitable fate. His is the crowning stroke. For weapons offensive and defensive, he has a Toledo sword, whence his designation, and a *muleta* (a little red flag upon a staff); but these, tiny as they seem beside the riotous strength and fury of his adversary, when guided by the cool courage of man, cannot fail of obtaining the victory. The chulos are entirely unarmed, except with the *capa;* their object being not to resist the bull, but to play with him and to aid the other performers, either by drawing him into a suitable position, or by enticing him off in case of danger. Their best defence is supposed to reside in their legs. The respective qualifications are, therefore, agility for the chulo, strength and consummate horsemanship for the picador, skill and dexterity for the espada. Imperturbable presence of mind and self-possession, and the absence of anything like a braggadocio courage, are indispensable to all. The relative rank of these parties, if measured by the standard of their pay, is the espada, the banderillero, the picador, and the chulo.

Having made their salutation to the powers that be, the performers dispersed to their several posts; the chulos, with their long cloaks (capas), or rather scarfs of bright colored silk, scattered themselves promiscuously over the half of the arena opposite to the door of the Toril; the three picadors took their positions in succession on the left of the Toril, a few feet in advance of the barrier, and facing to the centre of the ring. The espadas and the mule teams disappeared hastily, followed by the alguazil, so soon as he had thrown the key to the gate keeper. For a few seconds, a deathlike silence ensued; a pin might have been heard to fall, such is the intense anxiety felt to see how the bull will conduct himself on his first appearance; an anxiety participated in by the performers as well as the audience, for his deportment after the first surprise is the best index to his character, and it is, consequently, very minutely observed. The door opened, and out he burst with a terrific snort—an immense, powerful, red skinned monster, with a massive chest and an enormous pair of horns. He belonged to the class of *claro* or *sencillo*, who are frank, and free from sly tricks, and run directly at the object—the least dangerous of all. Astounded at the blast of trumpets, the shouts and waving of handkerchiefs, which greeted his entry, and blinded by the fierce sunlight, he paused for a moment near the centre of the arena, glared defiantly and angrily around and plunged at the first horse. The picador received him steadily on the end of his pike, and was fortunate enough to turn him off. The bull passed on to the second, who was not so lucky, but went down, without, however, serious injury; the third suffered the same fate. The bull took no further notice of them, but rushed on. He was in what is called the *levantado* stage, plunging at everything within reach, but not pursuing his advantage. A chulo next caught his eye. With a bellow that seemed to shake the earth, the furious creature bounded to-

ward him. The chulo ran for dear life; in vain did he seek
to distract the animal's attention by waving the scarf behind
him, and serpentining in his course; it was some distance still
to the barrier, and the enraged beast was gaining every step.
The *capa* and the chulo's handkerchief, successively dropped,
failed to arrest the pursuit, and as he leaped with the speed of
a bird over the barrier, the horns of his formidable adversary
entered the planks below him. Baffled in this attempt, the
bull trotted toward the centre. One of the picadors made a
challenge. Lashing his sides with his tail, and tearing up the
earth with his hoof, he roared back an indignant defiance.
Suddenly lowering his head he made a tremendous rush, and,
breaking in the guard, drove his horn deep into the poor
horse's side, who fell dead with scarcely a groan. The picador, caught beneath his body, lay perfectly still, which was his
only chance. By this time, the chulos had run up with their
cloaks, like a flock of martins, and tolled the bull off to another place. The dismounted picador was relieved from his
situation, mounted a fresh horse, the saddle and bridle were
taken off the dead one, and all went on merrily. The same
picador approached the bull a second time, but with no better
success; down he went again. This time, however, he was off
with a scratch. Two more horses were killed, and one badly
wounded, when the bull began to shrink from these bootless
encounters. He had received several severe wounds, and a
large red streak showed one of a foot in length across the
shoulder.

The trumpet sounded for the second act. The picadors retired from the scene, contenting themselves with riding around
the *tablas*, and the banderilleros entered, who are generally
taken from among the chulos, but the operation requires a
great deal more skill and self-possession than is necessary for
a mere chulo. It consists in sticking a pair of barbed darts, a
foot and a half or two feet long, ornamented with colored
wreaths of paper, or some similar substance, into the bull's
neck, one on each side, at equal distances. When well done it
is one of the most graceful operations of the ring, and appears
to be very dangerous, though they say it is not so to a skilful
person. The bull looked at the first banderillero rather with
an expression of curiosity than otherwise, as if wondering what
manner of man he might be. The banderillero stood his

ground, making a kind of expansive movement with his arms, like the wings of an artificial bird. He was an active, supple little fellow, quite a match for his weighty opponent. To solve the mystery, the bull made a rush; the banderillero stood lightly balanced on his toes a moment; the bull lowered his head for the final toss; the banderillero, leaning forward, planted the darts exactly, and leaped safely to the left, amid the thunders of the audience. " *Bravo, Pepe!*" "*buen par!*" (a good pair) continued for a minute or so; handkerchiefs were waved, and several hats thrown into the arena—a favorite method of manifesting gratification in Andalusia. How they ever managed to get the proper hat back to the proper person on such occasions was the mystery to me. It must be said, however, that they were shockingly antique specimens, worthy of Connaught. Once I saw a collection of hats, thrown into the arena, fare rather badly; for the bull, happening to pass along in no very good humor, took his spite out against these innocent coverings, and some of them were reduced to such a state, that, if found upon the head of the owner in the neighborhood of Donnybrook Fair, they would have been proof positive of a gay time and "illigant" amusement. But to return to the bull. Four successive pairs of banderillas were planted in fine style, all of which enraged him greatly. The trumpet now sounded the third and last act, and the espada, who had been observing the scene, and probably studying the bull's character from behind the *tablas*, leaped into the arena with a *muleta* in his left hand, and a long Toledo sword lying over it. He went to the box of the corregidor, and, taking off his hat, repeated the oath, which is to the effect that he will do his duty faithfully and honorably. It winds up with a flourish of the hand, and the hat is then thrown away. The matador is the general; the chulos are his aides-de-camp or adjutants, and play subordinate parts under his direction, and their aid is frequently necessary in counteracting the peculiar tendencies of the bull, as the matador is necessarily exposed in giving the stroke with uplifted arm. He approached the bull, and held the muleta with his right hand. The bull rushed at it. It was quickly lifted over his head as he passed under, seemingly much surprised at the sudden disappearance of his enemy. The *pases de muleta* were repeated several times until the matador became satisfied. He then shifted the *muleta* to his left hand, the long

sword dangled in his right. The bull made another rush.   The
sword entered his neck, separating the spinal cord, and he fell
instantly dead.   The matador then wiped his weapon upon the
muleta, bowed to the corregidor, and retired amid a fresh
shower of hats.   The band struck up a lively air.   Teams of
gaily caparisoned mules enter, one for every dead animal, which
were dragged out at a gallop; the horses to be sold to the glue
manufacturer, if there be one, and the bull to make beef for
the poor.   The fans now renewed their activity; the water
sellers recommenced their vociferations.   Fresh sand was scattered over the blood in the arena, and the previous combat was
already half forgotten, when the trumpet sounded for the entry
of a second bull.

   At first, he positively refused to fight, notwithstanding all
the insults and imprecations that were lavished upon him, his
owners and his ancestors.   The immense mass of heads became
furiously agitated, and the arena resounded with exclamations
of every kind.   The bull was called a coward and a mean rascal; the *Impresario* denounced as a rogue.   Above all resounded
the cry of *perros* (dogs); but no dogs came.   In their stead,
banderillas de fuego were ordered.   These are banderillas with
some explosive, detonating material within, which causes the
bull to bound about like a rocket.   A pair of them were placed
on him, and woke up his rage most effectually.   He proved to
be a *burri ciego* of the worst species, and was very dangerous.
All bulls whose sight is defective are dangerous; because, not
seeing clearly, they do not distinguish between the lure or
engaño and the individual, but generally make for the man as
the larger body.   This one gave a great deal of trouble; but
there is one fate for all bulls that enter the arena, and his was
no exception.   The third bull offered no new feature.

   I had attended the *apartado* in the morning, and, enlightened
by the remarks of the fancy around, had formed a sort of
opinion as to the virtues of the various animals that were to
appear.   The result of my cogitations was imparted to an
elderly acquaintance in the next box, who had attended ever
so many *funcions* in his life—somewhere up among the thousands.   We consequently waited with some interest to see the
gate of the Toril opened.   A middle sized, but powerfully built
black animal, with a most ferocious aspect, of the class called
revoltosos, bounded out.   A mass of shaggy hair hung between

his eyes, making him look still wilder. Without making the
usual pause, he made at once for the first picador; demolished
him in a twinkling; the second ditto. The third horse he
rammed up against the barrier, nearly crushing to death the
rider, who was saved by being drawn over it by his friends
on the outside. He then distributed his favors at large among
the chulos. The applause of the audience was frantic. My old
friend could scarcely refrain from embracing me, exclaiming:
" *Buen toro, amigo; verdad que es buen toro*," (a good bull, my
friend; really a good bull,) a gratifying criticism to the hero if
he only could have heard it. The bull continued to sustain his
reputation. One of the chulos, in making a *suerte á la Navarra*,
managed to trip, and was only saved by the capa falling upon
the bull's horns and blinding him. Twice did the bull jump
the barrier, the first time without harm done, for the gates
that open upon the arena are so constructed as to close the
passage behind the barrier, so that the bull must needs return
whence he came. The second time, however, a sentinel and a
water seller were caught behind. The former got past the gate
in time. The latter, being somewhat burthened, was a little too
late, and had no escape but by the arena. He got rid of his
water apparatus in the most approved style, and an exhibition
of speed was afforded us worthy of the Derby; no serpentining,
but a regular straight streak. The bull, following close behind,
spoilt his stock in trade for that evening. One of the horses
received a frightful wound. I watched the ladies of our party
to see what effect it would produce upon them. An expression
of intense and irrepressible disgust overshadowed their faces,
which they covered with their fans. The horse, however, was
removed, and all went on as before. One of the picadors
had aroused my dislike by seeming to push his horse on the
bull's horns, and I had been secretly wishing that he might be
punished for his cruelty. My wishes were gratified. The bull
rushed at him. The horse sustained himself, but the picador
fell as if struck with lightning. I did not see what had touched
him, but there he lay, motionless. The excitement and agitation of the audience were fearful. In their anxiety, they rose
from the seats as one man, and some of the ladies came near
fainting. I confess that my first emotion was that of satisfaction. He had received his reward in kind. But, as four of his
companions lifted the poor devil up, and carried him out of the

theatre of his humble triumphs, I could not but think how
nearly man is allied to the beasts of the field. This unknown
wretch, whose motives were probably as good, and his courage
as great as prompted Alexander or Cæsar, is converted by a sudden stroke, a material blow, into an inanimate mass of clay, a
mere dog's carcase. Can such a creature be endowed with immortality? Are not those internal whisperings which tell us of a
divine spark of life within, and a world beyond, where we are
to be immortal, the deceitful suggestions of pride? I looked at
my fair companions, radiant with beauty, which compassion for
the poor bull fighter had rendered almost celestial. My doubts
were removed, and I felt that the voice of nature can never lie.

It would be tedious to enumerate all the triumphs of this
bull. Five horses fell beneath his strokes; a proportionate number were wounded; one picador desperately bruised; another
carried out for dead; a chulo within an inch of the other world,
and a water seller frightened three-fourths out of his wits,
not to speak of the loss of his cooler. At length the trumpet
sounded; the glittering matador sprang into the arena with
alacrity, as if anxious to meet a foe so worthy of his steel. The
bull fought to the last. Twice did he receive estocadas; the
second time he sent the sword flying up among the seats. He
finally retired to his *querencia* (as any place in the ring that
the bulls prefer is called, and they frequently manifest such a
preference) near the barrier, and though almost exhausted,
with the bloody foam dripping from his mouth and his swollen
tongue lolling out, the fiery glare of his eyes showed the still
unsubdued spirit within. No enticement could seduce him from
his *querencia;* he was thoroughly *aplomado* (leadened). It was
necessary to kill him *á vuela pies,* a dangerous operation so
near the barrier, as by a sudden turn the matador might be
caught and crushed. A chulo took his position in front of the
bull, a little to the right; the matador lowered the *muleta*
nearly to the ground; the bull fixed his eyes upon it; his neck
became thus exposed; a rush forward, a spring to the left, and
the sword handle alone was visible behind the shoulder. The
blood gushed from the dying animal's mouth; he made a feeble
effort to turn upon his adversary, and sunk quivering on the
earth. The *puntillero* sprang over the barrier, and with a sharp
dagger, a *misericordia,* inserted behind the back of the head,
put a termination to his struggles. He presented a pitiable

sight when dragged out; a few minutes ago so proud and
strong, now, shrunk, as though consumed by some wasting disease.

As the afternoon was drawing to a close, it was proposed
that we should retire, and we turned our backs upon the arena.
In the distance, over the intervening houses, could be seen the
towering Giralda; the sunset light threw the color of molten
gold over it, and the massive Cathedral at its base, reposing in
silent grandeur with marble thoughts directed above. In what
contrast to the variegated throng of animated beings around,
intent upon the evening's bloody sport. Confused murmurs
had already begun to rise; it was evident that the time had
not been economized, and that the *angelus* would strike before
the appearance of the last bull. As the populace have been,
from time immemorial, rulers at these entertainments, their will
is law, and they are by no means backward in the expression
of it. The corregidor comes in for the greater part of the
cursing, which on such occasions is most freely bestowed. We
left them to settle their accounts together and retired. I will
mention, in passing, that the picador was not killed, but only
stunned, as we learnt next day.

During the winter and the intense heat of midsummer the
bulls are not in fighting condition; in the one they are be-
numbed by the cold and in the other debilitated by the heat
and the want of pasturage. Their place is supplied with
novillos, or young bulls, four years old, which are considered
playthings in Spain, and no real artist would consent to draw
his sword against such sucklings. As I have described the
best bull fight I ever attended, it will not be amiss to describe
the worst, what the Spaniards call a *Gallegada* of novillos,
because the performers are either awkward fellows picked up,
as it were, from the water carriers (gallegos), who do not make
a regular profession of it, or else mere beginners. There was
the usual parade and ceremony, with the addition of a monkey
perched upon a stake in the centre of the arena. Jocko's dislike of the bull and the bull's dislike of Jocko add some episodes
to the usual course of events. The picadors apparently did
well, because the novillo has not sufficient strength to drive his
blows home, and was still too much of a boy to be indifferent to
the prickings of the spear. But he made up upon the chulos,
knocking down at least a dozen, for they generally ran directly

before him. It was thus a mere question of speed, and many a
rent garment attested the superiority of the bull's legs. The
first espada was the worst I had ever seen, and I would have
thought him the worst in the world, if I had not seen the
second. This fellow had a square block head, with closely
cropped hair of a blackish tinge. It was wonderful why he
had entered the business at all, as he seemed to have a mortal
apprehension of his foe. Holding the sword much as a boy does
a gun on his first going out, he would advance hesitatingly, make
a lunge, miss of course, and then give up. The bull would
seize him, and rip his clothes from Dan to Beersheba. Once he
was thrown up into the air five or six feet; of course no harm
done, as it is almost impossible to hurt a Spaniard of the
lower class, they are blessed with such unconscionably tough
bodies. I expressed my wonder that some damage was not
done. They exclaimed, " Oh! it is only a four-year-old! only a
novillo!" As an isolated fact this was doubtless true, but I
did not understand the logical sequence in the argument. It
seemed to me that the horn of even a four-year-old would be
a very unpleasant acquaintance to scrape. The fight still went
on. Once it was necessary for the *savant*—who was below for
the purpose of superintending, like Bob Acre's second—to push
the espada on to the bull; he finally ran outright, amid screams
of laughter from the audience. This was worse than usual.
Generally speaking, some five or six horses are killed even at a
Corrida de Novillos, and these are the entertainments that most
travellers witness. The ceremonies and the externals are
nearly the same, but in the spirit of the performance there is
about the same resemblance between the " novillos" and the
" toros" as there is between a militia muster and a charge of
Zouaves.

In cold weather there is another favorite amusement of the
ring, viz: the *embollados,* or young bulls with balls of wood on
their horns. Everyone is at liberty to jump in on these occasions, as it is a free fight, and a great many are counted out
before the entertainment is over. They pull him by the tail,
and he repays the debt, with interest, in the same quarter;
nothing is left in arrear on either side. I once saw a fellow
get alarmed and run directly from the bull, who followed, passing a horn directly under each arm; the runner instinctively
grasped the horns and was carried several times around the

arena by the now equally frightened bull, who knew not what
to make of the strange proceeding. After a certain length of
time several oxen are turned into the ring, in whose midst the
tired animal takes refuge. The *embollados* withdrawn, a clown
enters, clothed in some fire proof jacket, which is hung over
with packs of crackers and small Roman candles. Thus armed,
he plunges about in the crowd like a fiery serpent. This is
considered great fun.

Much care is taken in selecting bulls for the arena, and the
characteristics of the various breeds are well known. I think
it is the Bañuelos breed that have a long black piece of flesh,
like a proboscis, growing over the snout, which gives them a
curious appearance. Some others, also, have distinctive marks.
The races are kept pure to preserve the reputation of the herd,
as the owner feels as much interest in the performance as the
bystanders, and these mere external peculiarities are perpetuated through successive generations. The breed of the Duke
of Veraguas is said, at Madrid, to be the best. Travellers are
sometimes merry over the fact that the representative of the
great Columbus should take pride in breeding bulls for the
amphitheatre. But the descendants of the great Columbus
cannot be eternally discovering worlds; they are men like the
rest of us. The folly consists in attempting to make greatness
hereditary. Besides, the bull is considered in Spain as noble
as the race horse is in England or America, and those who
have ever seen him in his untamed glory, his neck clothed with
thunder, his tail lashing his sides, and the dust flying behind
his indignant feet, will admit that there are few more grand
or terrific objects. Surely, the proudest of English gentlemen
would be glad to add to his title that of breeding the best race
horse in the kingdom, and there is nothing ludicrous about
the corresponding taste in the Spaniard. Next to the descent
is the requisite of suitable age, which should be between five
and seven, when they are in their prime. The hair and skin
are good external indices to the mettle and character of the
bull. The former should be fine, and a plenty of it, glistening
to the light, and equally distributed. The latter soft and
supple to the touch. The color is generally uniform. I have
never seen a piebald or light shaded animal in the arena. They
are generally black or dusky red. The Andalusian from the
valley of the Guadalquivir, the compact Manchegan and the

active Navarrese hâve each their respective merits. Those
from Jarama, kinsmen of the hero of the Moorish ballad, still
preserve their reputation. Foreign bulls are by no means so
suitable for the purpose as the natives. The flesh predominates
too much over the nerves; and though larger, they are inferior
both in activity and endurance, and even in courage, besides
being spoilt by contact with man, which renders them cunning
and dangerous.

The whole knowledge of bull fighting is now reduced to a
science, and there was even a College of Tauromachy established in Seville, by Ferdinand, under the government patronage, from which issued many distinguished artists. The bulls
are classed according to their dispositions, and the art of
combating is modified to suit each class. From time to time
contributions are made to the art. The *vuela pies* for bander-
rilleros and espadas was invented by Costillares, who gave the
rôle of the espadas a development it never had received before.
Candido did the same for the *chulos*, Romero for the banderilleros. Hillo, who was killed in the beginning of the century,
reduced his experience to writing and transformed the whole
science. Perhaps the most distinguished of them all was
Francisco Montes, whose marvellous exploits are still the subject of narrative. No one ever equalled him in the magnetic
power which the human eye exercises over beasts. He would
mark a circle upon the ground within which the bull was to be
killed, and rarely failed in carrying out his boast. The science
has a technical language, more elegant than our race course
dialect, because it has been the subject of learned treatises. Of
course there is also a slang which is as difficult of attainment
as the Basque.

Spaniards are very sensitive about criticisms upon their
favorite amusement. If you associate with one any length of
time he is very apt to ask your opinion on the subject. It is a
shibboleth. If you like them, it shows that you are a Spaniard
at heart, "one of us." And they are indignant against en-
lighted travellers who complacently thank heaven for not
having made them like these bull fighting barbarians. The
slaughter of the horses I detest as an unnecessary cruelty to
one of the noblest of animals, which might be easily obviated
by fining the picadors for every wound their horses receive,
and rewarding them for every stroke they turn off. Spaniards
defend this part of the entertainment by stating they are the

veriest hacks, who, in other countries, would be sent to the
glue butchery, which is true. As for the men and the bulls, I
confess I have no scruples. The men are paid enormously and
have every pleasure possible. They are very rarely killed,
and there is always a chapel and a priest in the building to
give the last unction to such as require it, besides a hospital
for the wounded. Far more lose their lives in the mountains
of Asturia, in the chase, or waste away in the manufacture of
articles of pure luxury, than die in all the bull rings of Spain.
We might as well think of crying over the exposure of a soldier's life, who is frequently dragged against his will to fight
battles in which he has not the slightest interest. When foreigners cease to wage wars of territorial aggrandizement, their
virtuous indignation against the Corrida de Toros will be
worthy of notice. The bull has still less reason to complain.
Surrounded with the pleasures of barbaric domesticity, he
spends his life in the midst of luxuriant pastures, where he is
rarely disturbed by the face of man. Every bull must die at
last, and it is a mere balancing of enjoyments to say that it is
better to work in yokes until he is old, and then be fattened
and killed in the butcher's stall, than to lead the jolly life of a
monarch, roaming his native fields, and die in the bull ring,
preserving his freedom to the very end. About the abstract
cruelty, there is something more to be said. It is undoubtedly
wrong in the abstract to take the life of any animal without
some sufficient reason; but as everyone judges of the sufficiency of the reason for himself, it becomes a practical question
of comparison. We consider the pampering of a luxurious ap-
petite amply sufficient excuse for the wholesale slaughter of
pate-de-fois geese; and the most reverend bishop in the land
would hesitate to interpose his crook between an innocent
lamb and the blood-thirsty butcher. We go with eagerness to
the chase, not for the prosaic purpose of procuring a haunch of
venison, but to enjoy the fun, to see the frightened deer course
before the hounds, and bring him down at a hand gallop. How
many of us take compassion at the sight of his tearful eyes?
And do ducks and fish, or even the writhing worm that squirms
upon the hook, escape their fate? There are some people who
fish for fish—practical geniuses—but the great majority fish
simply for the sport. Philosophically and morally speaking,
there is as much cruelty in the one as the other. But the bull
is a large creature, the bird or deer a small one, killing the one

is cruelty; killing the other, sport. Just as a large conqueror
is to be placed upon a pedestal—a small one (*vulgo*, robber) to be
suspended from a gallows. From the mouth of a pious Brah-
min the reproach would be justifiable; but when we consider
that dog fighting and boxing are favorite amusements in the
most enlightened portions of the world, attracting vast crowds
from all quarters, even across the Atlantic, we can well understand the indignation with which the Spaniards regard what
they consider a vaporing hypocrisy.

   Nor does the practice of travellers coincide with their professions, for however loud may be their outcries at the first
exhibition, they seldom abstain from the second. The fact of
their reiterated visits shows that there must be some attraction apart from the destruction of the animals, and so engrossing as to deaden the painful impression which the latter produces. The different characters of the bulls; the skill of the
Torero; the fertility of his resources; the exhibition of calm
valor; the triumph of human intelligence over brute force—these
are the great attractions which entice them to the spectacle.
They forget, or do not heed the fact, that the death of the animals is the price of this gratification. Neither do we in accepting an invitation to a convivial entertainment, reflect upon the
number of pheasants and snipe that are to be slaughtered for
our palates. I should be sorry to see the Corrida de Toros introduced into my own country, because it is not an institution,
just as I would look with little pleasure upon the establishment
of a democratic republic in Europe. But that is very different
from condemning the bull fight in Spain, or a republic in
America. Each of us digests, assimilates and thrives upon
poison. A vast allowance must be made for the idiosyncrasies
of nations as well as individuals. Innumerable institutions
productive of benefit to one race or civilization, if transplanted,
would give rise to unspeakable evils.

   Another objection against bull fighting is the effect it is supposed to have upon the audience. Unquestionably the intense
excitement of the spectacle, and the furious passions which it
calls into life, with the sight of blood, are calculated to produce a very great effect; but all this is, comparatively, lost in
admiration for the skill, the cool courage, the triumph of man
over mere brute force, of which the Plaza de Toros is the theatre. I defy any one to see the matador clad in tissue, standing
face to face with the monster, without feeling that there is a

grandeur in the scene far beyond the mere contest of two animate creatures. It inculcates, moreover, the great lesson of
freedom—self-reliance and individuality—and the continuance
of this spirit is the best safeguard against despotism. The
government may be as oppressive as it pleases upon the court
circles, and misrule the country in its foreign relations, but let
it continue to keep its hands off the Spanish people; for so long
as these qualities continue to be practically admired and vividly exemplified before the eyes of the populace, any attempt
to establish one of these intermeddling domestic tyrannies that
seem so fashionable in Europe just now, will be met by a
thousand knives from every mountain pass in the Peninsula.
It is, moreover, eminently a national amusement, and a firm
rock against the invasion, the inconsiderate adoption of foreign
modes of thinking and acting, which is fast reducing the world
to a tiresome uniformity. The mantilla reigns here supreme,
and the *majo* is considered eminently suitable. There is necessity for some such institution even in Spain, for a considerable class, from believing that there was nothing good out of
their country, have come to think that there is nothing good in
it, and denounce every national peculiarity as a relic of barbarism, fearful lest the Pyrenees should be regarded the western boundary of Europe.

Ladies seldom attend the Plaza de Toros, but they do upon
grand occasions, such as that I have mentioned, not so much,
however, to view the contest, as to see and be seen themselves,
just as with us people crowd to the opera, who could not distinguish Yankee Doodle from Mozart's Requiem. They are
greatly shocked with the disgusting portion of the spectacle,
and proportionably delighted with every display of manly
prowess. Spanish ladies are courageous themselves, and admire the quality in others. It may seem strange that they
ever entered such a place in the beginning; but, in truth, they
are taken there when small children. It is the only amusement in most provincial towns, and the effect produced by the
arrival of a Cuadrilla, is similar to the excitement of a travelling circus in the olden time. The whole town is in commotion; gaily-dressed cavaliers, in the costume of the middle ages,
prance about on fiery steeds; the sound of tambourines and
castagnettes re-echoes in all the streets; work is laid aside; it
is a Corrida de Toros! If the children are good, they are

16

allowed to go; so that the Corrida de Toros is associated in their minds, with holidays, fine dresses, cakes, and a multitude of other infantile joys. When they grow up, they hear themselves styled barbarians by ignorant and unreflecting book makers, who, perhaps, have a mind to every species of sin except this. As far as my knowledge goes, the only recollections that Spanish ladies bear away, are those of the gallant feats of horsemanship and the daring confronting of danger. They always cover their faces with the fan at the bloody portion of the tragedy. I have not found them less compassionate, gentle, lovely or lovable, afterwards than before, and I can only say that if they are injured by attending the spectacle, it is wisely so ordained by Providence to reduce them to the level of ordinary mortals—otherwise some of them would be unfitted for the earth.

Political economists have supposed that bull fights interfered with the increase of cattle by the great destruction of animals; but all of us who live in a racing country can testify to the contrary, and experience has proved in Spain that nothing would be more ruinous in this respect than their abolition. Only a portion are reserved for the Plaza, and those the very best of the best breeds. They are tried when young, and if they show any backwardness in facing the spear, are immediately destined to peaceful pursuits, so that the number of saleable cattle of good stock is really increased. From time to time bull fights have been suppressed, or, at least, an attempt has been made to suppress them. Godoy's was the last; and it may be that detestation of him caused the Toros to be a greater favorite than ever. The taste at present is certainly becoming stronger, and I found that bull rings had increased, since my last visit, far more rapidly than churches. No government in Spain could suppress them now, any more than it could abolish the right of going armed.

The progress of civilization and the greater diffusion of well being seem to have filled the Plazas, and attracted men's minds irresistibly toward this manly sport, so little in accordance with the effeminate industry which has taken possession of the human race elsewhere, as if to counteract the universal tendency of events. As a general rule, the bull fighters are from the lowest ranks of society, but, of late, I have been told that persons of much respectability have been unable to withstand the attraction, and have entered the profession. One

particularly, was mentioned, a person, by birth and fortune,'
entitled to take a place in society. I think he was a native of
Old Castile. His true name I have forgotten; he was familiarly known by a soubriquet derived from his lowness of stat-
ure, *el chico*, or some such appellation. In truth, the bull, and
everything connected with him, has a prominent place in the
thoughts of Spaniards of all ages and classes. He is a matter
of affectionate sport to them. Once, in a miserable little village, where I broke down, and was compelled to pass the day,
a young calf took a freak into his head of running at the children, and knocked down some half a dozen. Instead of interfering, the fathers and mothers laughed heartily, as though it
were a capital joke. They are entirely without fear of the
whole species under any circumstances. If they pass one on
the road, they shake their cloaks at him and taunt him. If
they meet him in the street 'they give his tail a pull. In the
villages, for want of the great tragedy, he is led through
the streets with a slack rope, so as to allow him to run at the
passers by; and it was formerly a famous joke in Tarifa to
turn one loose in the town, to the amusing consternation of
travellers. The Corrida de Toros occupies, more or less, the
minds of every age and occupation. It has a place in feasts of
the Church and feasts of the State. It is imitated in the nur-
sery, and danced on the stage. The adverse criticism of travellers, and of their own countrymen residing abroad, may
gradually inspire a conventional distaste for it in the higher
circles as something unfashionable, but at present they fall,
and will, for a long time, continue to fall without significance
upon the ears of the great body of the Spanish nation. So,
" pan y Toros."

The Corrida de Toros is an expensive amusement, and
always undertaken under the patronage of the government,
seldom by private enterprise. The places are high, compared
with the price of labor. I subjoin, by way of an example, the
following list, taken at random from the Madrid hand bills.
The value of a *real vellon* is five cents of our money.

		Sun.	Sun and Shade.	Shade.
TENDIDOS...	Barreras y tabloncillos....	6	6	10
	Asientos sin numeracion...	4	4	6
GRADAS	Delanteras y tabloncillos..	10	14	16
	Centros.................	8	10	12
ANDANADAS .	Delanteras y tabloncillos..	12	16	22
	Centros.................	8	12	14
PALCOS ....con diez entradas.........120........140..........200				

Meseta del toril—Primera fila, 10; Secunda, 8; Tabloncillos, 6; Centros, 4.

ENVIRONS.—HISTORICAL.

The ancients, with a due appreciation of the pleasures of
life, placed the Elysian fields on the banks of the great river of
Andalusia; and Tharsis, the grandson of Japhet, is claimed by
the Spaniards to have colonized the islands near its mouth. At
present they have become fertile wastes, the abodes of vast
herds of cattle, seldom invaded by any except sportsmen and
herdsmen, wild as the cattle they guard, who are said to rival
the Balearians in their skill with the sling. It is their only
defence against the enraged animal when separated from the
rest of the herd, for though insensible to wounds elsewhere, the
slightest stroke with a stone upon the horn, is said to render
them quite manageable. All the lower valley of the Guadalquivir is thus surrendered to nature, but the immediate neighborhood of Seville is charming, though entirely devoid of what
constitutes in temperate climates the delights of the environs
of a great city—neatly painted cottages, honeysuckles climbing over arches and gates, and velvety turf. Of all this there
is nothing, not only here but elsewhere in Andalusia. In its
place is the extended valley of the Guadalquivir, luxuriating in
oranges and olives, wild thyme, lavender, and a thousand name-
less herbs, whose sweet perfumes fill the air, as they lie crushed
beneath your horse's hoof. During the flowering season of the
orange, Seville appears one gorgeous bouquet, an enchanted
Paradise, with lamps of gold hung in a "night of green." The
country to the south-west is still called by its Moorish name of
Axarafe—the hilly region—renowned for its fertility, and celebrated in their poems as the diadem of Seville. Some few

miles from La Triana, the landscape is bounded by a spur of
the Sierra Morena, extending toward the Guadalquivir. Its
slopes, covered with olive plantations, and its summit crowned
with villages and half deserted convents, might well justify
the appellation of " The Mountain of Mercy," which it is supposed to have borne in the time of the Moors. The road that
branches to the left leads through an orange grove to the village of San Juan de Alfarache, formerly a miserable collection
of gipsy cabins, but which have now disappeared, giving place
to neat, clean houses. Whether it be the site of the famous
Osset, the Julia Constantia of the Romans, is more than I can
undertake to decide. *Faraj* in the Arabic signifying " to split
or divide," the name of the present village is supposed to be
derived from the cleft in the Cuesta. Ascending that and
winding around the parapet, the path conducts to the little
church whose terrace offers one of the most exquisite views
that can be imagined. It comprehends the whole of the Vega
of Seville to the Sierra Morena and the hills of Carmona,
through which flows the Guadalquivir, in graceful curves, directly toward the foot of the cliff. At this season the fields were
bare, and clouds of dust arose from time to time obscuring the
horizon. But in winter or spring, when the setting sun throws
its purple light over the city and the fretted cathedral, embowered in green and golden orange groves and surrounded by
verdant fields, I know nothing in Europe to surpass the beauty
of the prospect. It is the true garden of the Hesperides, whose
golden apples might worthily employ the labors of a demi-god.
The walk back may be diversified by keeping along the river
bank nearly as far as the Triana and crossing over in a skiff to
Las Delicias. A curling wreath of smoke from the porcelain
manufactory of Pickman & Co., was at present rather an incongruous element in the picture, but the great success of this experiment, in furnishing Spain with home manufactures, may
justify in some measure the outrage done to the landscape.

Farther to the north-west, upon the same range of hills, is the
town of Castilleja de la Cuesta, which also has a fine view, but
is more interesting to Americans as the residence and death
place of Fernan Cortez, whose house is pointed out. Beyond
this there is nothing to attract one to Castilleja, though the
ride is a pleasant one. Some distance to the right in the plain
are the ruins of the ancient city of Italica, itself built upon

the ruins of a still more ancient Iberian or Punic city by Scipio, as a retreat for his veterans. Celebrity is conferred upon it by the singular felicity of having given birth to three of the greatest and best of the Roman emperors—Trajan, Hadrian and Theodosius.

> Sola novum Latiis vectigal Hiberia rebus
> Contulit Augustos.

As if satisfied with having conferred so great a boon upon the world Italica ceased to exist, and little is left of its former grandeur except the ruins of the amphitheatre, which has served as a quarry to Goths, Moors and Spaniards. It resembles others in Italy and France. The crumbling seats and subterranean dens for the wild beasts are tolerably distinct, but by its size alone would you be able to form some idea of the importance of the city. That the decline of Italica was owing to the founding of Seville is scarcely credible, as the latter existed in the time of the Phœnicians, and the Roman aqueduct shows it to have been a place of note before Italica had lost its pre-eminence. Seville, however, was a favorite of Cæsar and of nature too, for a capricious change of course in the Guadalquivir is said to have accomplished the final ruin of its rival. The traveller is often struck with the utter disappearance of Spanish cities, which are known to have been flourishing centres of influence since the period of authentic modern history. The famous cities of Azzahra, of Azzahira, of Calatrava, the headquarters of the commandery of that name, of Alarcos, of Bilbilis, have vanished without leaving one stone upon another to mark the site of their existence, and were it not for the solid Roman relics, Italica would be known only by tradition. A few olives and the cool fountain are the only evidences of life. In its place has sprung up the Spanish village of Santi Ponce, distinguished for its fairs, the delight of majos and majas, one of which was memorably honored by the presence in full maja costume of the future Empress of the French, who in her youth used to do a great many things that might as well have been left undone.

The history of Don Alonso Perez de Guzman and the siege of Tarifa is familiar to readers of Spanish history. The Roman courage and fortitude with which he sacrificed his son rather than surrender that key of the kingdom to its enemies, received their reward in the heroic, romantic fame which has thrown a halo around him, and elevated his family to a distinction among the princes of the earth which few have attained. Scarcely a chapter in the history of his country can be written without mentioning some one of this illustrious house. Nor are its glories confined to Spain. The neighboring kingdom of Portugal owes a second birth to one of its fair scions. At present, the great Dukedom of Medina Sidonia, with all its immense possessions, are merged by marriage into another family; but soon three of the thrones of Europe will be occupied by the descendants of three of its beautiful daughters,— Leonora, Luisa and Eugenia,—who felicitously appeared upon the stage at a change of dynasty in every respective instance, and added no little to the stability of the Governments in which two of them were required to participate. The old hero, with a proper regard for the welfare of his soul in the next world, founded, near these ruins, the convent of San Isidro del Campo, in which the bodies of himself and his wife lie interred. A large portion of the building has been destroyed by the ravages of war, but enough remains to shelter the last resting place of the great founder, and to recall to the wayfarer one of the most striking and chivalrous incidents in history.

On the opposite side of Seville, a couple of hours' ride toward Carmona, is the city of Alcalá de Guadaira or de los Panaderos (the Bakers), a most picturesque spot, with a fine old castle overhanging the stream. Leaving Seville in the afternoon, the entry into this cool valley is delicious, and an artist would never become weary of its romantic scenes. The former road to Cordova passed through it; but now an especial visit is necessary, which well repays the trouble. Owing to some peculiarity in the water, probably, the bread made here is considered the best in Spain, and is carried into Seville early in the morning. Those who have eaten it any length of time will not dissent from the general opinion. With the exception of that from the Banat of Temeswar, there is no flour in Europe to compare with the Spanish; and I have seen it stated somewhere, that Haroun al Rashid would eat no other. The bread is differently made from that of Paris, being much more compact and whiter, and, at first, has not the taste which is so pleasant in the latter, but it grows upon acquaintance, and is exceedingly wholesome. A loaf, with a cup of Spanish chocolate, is a breakfast for a king. The ancient name of Alcalá was Hienippe, said to signify "the City of Springs," which abound, and whose limpid waters were carried to Seville by the aqueduct Los Caños de Carmona, a Roman work, repaired by the Moors. The present name signifies "the Castle of the river Aira," and both are appropriate.

In some respects, the early history of Spain is less satisfactory than that of any other country in Europe. Possessing no written language that has survived to our day, at least none that is intelligible, it must be sought, for the most part, in the records of the Greeks and Romans, aided by a few disjointed fragments of Punic, and the scanty relics of the previous age, still existing in the names of localities. These throw glimpses of light back to a period far anterior to the colonization of other European countries, but so faint as to stimulate rather than satisfy curiosity. Critics have struggled to trace a connection with various tribes on the plateau of Central Asia—by a comparison of customs and habits, as described by Strabo—with how little success every one must acknowledge who has investigated the subject. Among the different problems, none offer more than the origin of the names of Seville, Andalusia and Spain. At the same time, there are few more attractive subjects of speculation; for, under the guise of a mere philological dispute, they carry us back into the very recesses of antiquity. The only literature of the Western World, or, at all events, the only writings which have survived to us, with a few insignificant exceptions, are the Hebrew, the Greek, the Latin, and to them may be added the Arabic, every one of which has been spoken in Spain, giving different names for the same locality, sometimes differing in signification, at others merely offering a confusion of sound. Of the latter, the derivation of the Spanish word "sierra," a mountain chain, is a fair example. Both etymology and the appearance of the mountains themselves, would justify the derivation from the Latin "serra," a saw, to be found in the old Italian and romance, as the Monserrat (i. e., Mons Serratus) of Catalonia. Other philologists, among them, the learned Gyangos, derive it, with equal plausibility, from the Arabic "Sehra," an uncultivated region, allied to Sahara, as the Sierra Morena of Andalusia, which was called by the Romans, not "Serra," but "Mons" Marianus. I venture to prefer the former; but, among such doctors, who shall decide? Perhaps both languages have been correctly appealed to.

First, with regard to Spain itself. The Greek word was Hesperia, the land of the Evening Star; the Latin, Hispania, whence, evidently, the modern name. The word "Iberia" was probably—as savans are said to have discovered by the aid of investigation into the language of people of whom the Greeks were ignorant—a simple corruption from Aber or Eber, meaning "a river" in the dialect of one of the tides of population which swept over Europe in its earliest ages, leaving this root everywhere. By the Greeks, it was ignorantly extended to the country itself. What was the aboriginal designation of the peninsula, or whether it had one designation, is utterly unknown. Wilhelm von Humboldt and others have advanced theories, and sustained them, with an immensity of erudition; but the world is far from being convinced. Humboldt's theory is, that the Basques were the original inhabitants, which position he fortifies by the names of places scattered over the peninsula that can be traced to no other language but the Basque. He then maintains that the Basques were the Iberians, but they certainly do not so call themselves in their own tongue. Nor can the words Iberia and Iberians be traced anterior to Scylax. On the other hand, the Celtic scholars think that they find equally as conclusive evidence of Gallic predominance in such words as Asturia—as-thor; Artabor—ar-ot-aber; Celtiber—Celt-abor; Celtiaca—Celt-ac'h. And national pride, too, enters into the investigation, inasmuch as Cæsar says that the Gauls were called Celts in their own tongue, and the French consider themselves the embodification of the race, of which they form a part, so that each succeeding critic leads us further from a harmonious conclusion. But we do know that the Phœnicians had settlements, or, at least, commerce with Spain before the days of the Greeks and Romans, as is proved by the Old Testament and by the Greek navigators themselves; and the interesting column described by Procopius, if not a forgery, which there is no good reason for supposing, shows that one emigration took place in consequence of the invasion of "the robber," Joshua, the son of Nave (Nun). The traditions of the Spanish Jews, adopted, in part, by the native historians, point likewise to an early exodus from the same quarter, which could only have been accomplished by the southern route. To the East, then, must we turn, and imagination has run riot with fabulous kings—Hispanus, Hispalis, and a long list, whose reigns have been illustrated by the glowing eloquence of Mariana. According to these historians, Hispania comes from Hispanus. Aldrete labors to derive it from the god Pan, prefixing first an S, which was not unusual in Latin, and then prefixing an initial vowel, because, forsooth, the Latin, like the modern Spanish and Italian, abhors an S impure. Why, then, did they prefix it? The true explanation is both simpler and more natural. The Phœnician word *Span*, or *Saphan*, is said by the learned to signify a "rabbit," and also "secret," "hidden." Now, the Roman historians almost always speak of the country under the name of Hispania, not Iberia, and their medals and coins, of which two are given by Florez, struck under the Emperor Hadrian—a Spaniard himself—represent Spain under the figure of a woman, with a rabbit at her feet, and the country was, moreover, frequently designated "cuniculosa." The peninsula was famous in ancient times for its abounding in these creatures. They formed a large item of export to Rome, and modern travellers, including Gil Blas, can vouch that the animal, or his feline representative, is still a favorite dish in the Spanish cuisine. In this instance, therefore, the critical acumen of investigators seems to have attained quite a satisfactory conclusion.

But the Phœnicians found the country occupied, and who were these occupants? The literary world seems to have settled into the belief that Europe was peopled by successive emigrations from Asia, passing up the valley of the Danube and descending into the peninsulas, and that these emigrations sprang from one source, which we call Caucasian. It has, however, been suggested, with much show of reason, that the aboriginal population of the south-west, though Caucasian, entered Europe across the Straits of Gibraltar, after making the southern circuit of the Mediterranean. Those straits were once much narrower than now; even the rate of their widening has been ascertained by a collocation of historical statements; and the tradition of their having been opened, at some remote period, by a god, fanciful though it be in its particulars, is evidence of the general truth of their having once been closed. After this followed, perhaps, an invasion from the north—the Celts or Iberians, if there were any such. Then came the Phœnicians and Carthaginians from the south. Then again the Romans and Goths from the north. Then the Arabs from

the south, until the Spaniards and Portuguese themselves became conquering nations, and extended their rule over America and a considerable portion of Africa, Europe and Asia.
The Peninsula was thus the common meeting place or battle field of rival immigrations; all, perhaps, branches of one
great race, and finding a common origin in Asia.   From which
of these emigrations did the "doctissimi" Andalusians inherit
their "gramatica et antiquatatis monumenta conscripta ac pœ-
mata et metris inclusas leges a sex millibus annorum?"   From
the North?   No northern nation has ever possessed such.   Letters and learning were transmitted from the East to the Asiatic
Greeks.   By them, in turn, to Greece proper, and thence diffused over the northern tribes of Europe as they successively
came within the sphere of its influence.   From the Basques?
Who they are, what they are, and whence they came, no one
can say, but not a single ancient author mentions them otherwise than in the rudest state of semi-barbarism, nor have they
any written records.   Did the Andalusians invent and bring
forth a local civilization, which was doomed to perish from the
earth without influence upon, or connection with, the general
progress of humanity?   Such was, apparently, the case in
Peru; but the received tradition of the Incas derived their
laws and learning from an external source, and this seems to
be universally true.   The wildest fable never imagined an
autochthonous civilization; the divine fire has always been
procured from heaven either by gift or by stealth.   If, therefore, we pursue the analogies of history, guided by the few, the
very few landmarks still existing, it would seem that Spain
was inhabited by a race anterior to the Phœnicians, Celts and
Iberians, a race somewhat enlightened, entering by the south
and, subsequently, yielding to the attacks of northern barbarians—more than this, no one can venture with any confidence
to assert.

The derivation of "Andalusia," though by no means so remote,
offers likewise great philological and historical difficulties.   It
is indisputably derived by us immediately from the Arabic, in
which it was used to signify the whole of Spain, or at least the
Mohammedan portion of it, and passed over to the Christians,
with the latter signification, at a time when the Moorish possession did not extend beyond the Sierra Morena.   Casiri, and
his opinion is adopted by the Padre Florez, traces it to the

Arabic Handaloŝ, equivalent, as they say, to the Greek word
Hesperia; and the Geographus Nubiensis, whom Florez quotes,
pronounces it the same country that was styled by the Greeks
Hispania. But why should the Arabs have omitted the initial
Hha in a word of their own language, seeming to delight in
these guttural sounds? On the other hand, Al Makari quotes
the works of Arabic authors, now lost, who derive it from a
race of barbarians that settled there. Such is the opinion, too,
of Gyangos, and to this must be added the fact that the Spanish
chroniclers frequently translate it " Vandalusia," and derive it
from the Vandals. The Arabs having no V, might well substitute in its place the simple breathing. But, reply the former,
the Vandals remained too short a time in Andalusia to impress
their name upon the country, and in fact never did, which is
true. The Arabs, however, meeting the remnants of those who
had crossed from Spain to Africa, and being, moreover, very
incurious about such things in the outset of their career, might
reasonably suppose that the country whence the Vandals or
Vandalocii last came was Vandalia or Vandalusia, or, in their
tongue, Andalus. Similar mistakes are of frequent occurrence
in the history of other countries, particularly in our own, as
exemplified by the Indian names. As cumulative proof it may
be stated that they call Western Mauritania, not Handalus,
but Al Magreb, the real word, which sometimes is applied to
the whole west, including Andalus.

The name of Seville can be easily traced through the Ishbiliah
of the Moors to the Hispalis of the Romans, for which all sorts
of fanciful derivations were given, among them that of " a palis"
of San Isidro, whereas not only is Seville not built upon piles,
but it would require no inconsiderable force to drive one into its
firm soil, though it has been subject to inundation. The Phœnicians again afford the key to this riddle, offering, as they say,
the word *Spela* or *Sephela*—a plain—which suits the situation
of Seville exactly. Indeed, most of the riparian and maritime
cities lying to the south and east were founded by, and derived
their names from the Phœnicians. Gaddir, the Roman Gades,
and modern Cadiz, for instance, is said to signify, in Punic,
" enclosed," or as others say " separated," being upon an island.
Moreover, the Book of Joshua mentions a King of Geder in the
" old country." Carthagena, Malaga, Cartheia have the same
origin. It is a compliment to the discernment of these naviga-

tors, that the points selected by them should still be the commercial outlets of Spain.

All this will perhaps appear very incongruous in a book of travels, but it shows that Spanish intellect has been by no means so profoundly asleep as has been generally supposed by us, since it is not a mere dispute about words, but an effort to search out the early history of their country, which lies concealed in those words.

Over the gate of Jerez, leading to the Paseo, is the following inscription :

Hercules me edificó,
Julio Cesar me cercó,
    De muros y torres altas ;
El rèy Santo me ganó
Con Garci Perez de Vargas.

According to which, Hercules was the founder of Seville, and such is the unanimous assertion of the old Spanish historians. Foreigners are disposed to be mirthful over the matter, and pronounce Hercules a myth. If by Hercules is meant any one individual, who performed all the wonderful feats mentioned in the Mythology, the assertion is of course correct. But that Hercules was originally a Phœnician or Egyptian hero, and that there were many such, is equally true. In truth every great pioneer was a sort of Hercules, and their several deeds, magnified by the credulity of a primitive age, were consolidated and contributed to swell the reputation of the demigod. Had it been the fortune of Daniel Boone to flourish when the art of writing was unknown, and the colonization of wild regions a thing of slow progress, the Kentucky bear would have stood by the side of the Nemean lion in the wonder of posterity. That the (or a) Phœnician Hercules therefore founded Seville may or may not be a fact, but there is nothing about the assertion impossible or improbable. Most of the legends of marvellous antiquity, which are spread through the localities of modern Europe, arose in the middle ages, but these traditions of Andalusia were current at a period long anterior, when tradition was history, and it was supposed, even in the days of Rome, as appears from a previous quotation, to have laws dating back six thousand years.

Whoever founded Seville is entitled to the thanks of subsequent ages, for at all times and under all people it has been a favorite residence. Cæsar distinguished it greatly and bestowed upon it his name—Julia Romula—and made such improvements as to be considered its second founder. Being the only one of the great Roman cities upon the Atlantic slope, it was celebrated for a phenomenon in nature unusual to them,

Fulget precipuis Parnasia Castulo signis,
Et celebre Oceano atque alternis aestibus Hispal.

To the Vandals it was a capital, and likewise under the first Moorish conquerors. Its Bishop, Oppas, a relative of Wittiza, played a prominent part in the treachery which resulted in the battle of Guadalete; and the wife of the last Gothic king secured the clemency of the conqueror by sacrificing her widow's weeds to the son of the caliph's lieutenant. The Beni Omeyah established the seat of their Government at Cordova. Upon the downfall of this dynasty Seville fell to the Beni Abbad, who were compared to the Abassides of Bagdad, for their generosity, virtues and misfortunes. The fate of the last of the line—Al Mutaded—illustrates the dogma of the prophet, that no one can escape the destiny graven upon the eternal tablets. The Christian power having increased in proportion to the decline of the Mohammedan, he found himself under the necessity of seeking aid from abroad, and for that purpose turned his eyes toward Yusef ben Taxfin, the great leader of the Almoravides. His brother kings warned him against the danger of seeking an alliance with so powerful a friend, quoting the pithy proverb, "a kingdom without heirs and one long sword do not find room in the same scabbard;" to which he replied with equal point, "better be a driver of camels than a driver of pigs;" that is, better be a servant of the Mohammedan and guard his camels, than of the Christian with his unclean swine. Yusef came, and the battle of Zalaka, in which the Sevillian king behaved as became a gallant soldier, rebuked the pride and insolence of the infidel. Before the battle, Alfonso wrote a long letter to Yusef in a grandiloquent style, boasting of his resources and depreciating his adversary. Abu Bekr, the secretary, composed a similar reply. "It is too long," said the old warrior; "bring me Alfonso's letter," and he wrote thereon these simple words, "he who lives will see." Well might the Christian king tremble at its brevity. The war being over, Al Mutaded invited his guest to Seville. When the beautiful city, with its gardens and palaces, and its spacious river, covered with the commerce of Africa and the East, burst upon the sight of the Almoravide, his heart was filled with envy and treachery. A few months more, and Al Mutaded implored the aid of the Christian against his former friend, but in vain. The latter part of his days were spent in easy captivity in Africa, afar from the perfumed banks of the Guadalquivir. Of Al Mutaded's gallantry, a curious instance is narrated. One of his wives happening to see some countrywomen up to their ancles in mud selling milk, exclaimed, with the natural discontentedness of her sex, "I wish I could do as these women are doing." ·Whereupon Al Mutaded ordered the palace floor to be covered with a compound of musk and such like substances, mixed together with rose water, so that the Sultana and her maids might paddle about to their content. His courage and literary taste were equal to his gallantry; and, notwithstanding some serious defects, Al Mutaded may rank among the greater of the Mohammedan Emirs.

The Almoravides were succeeded by the Almohades. At length, the edge of the sword was turned to the destroyer; and St. Ferdinand, on the 27th day of November, 1248, after a fifteen months' siege, planted the banner of Castile upon the Giralda. Mohammed, surnamed Al Hamra or "the Red," the founder of the kingdom of Granada and of its famous castle, who in his quality of vassal to the Christian king, had borne a prominent part in its capture, returned to his mountain home, saddened by his success against the last remnant but one of the great Moorish empire of the West.

From that time until the conquest of Granada, Seville continued to be the principal residence of the Spanish monarchs while engaged in the final contest. The extinction of Mohammedanism was simultaneous with another event, which raised Seville to the summit of wealth and distinction — the discovery of America. Strange that Columbus, after being repulsed from every other maritime court in Europe, should have laid the fruits of his inspiration at the feet of Spain, as if in fulfilment of the prophecy of Seneca, himself an Andalusian, who, in the Medea, sang, centuries before —

> Venient annis sæcula seris
> Quibus Oceanus vincula verum
> Laxet, et ingens pateat tellus,
> Tethysque novos detegat orbes,
> Nec sit terris ultima Thule.

For many generations Seville enjoyed a monopoly of the American trade. Hence sailed the fleets which transported to the simple natives of the New World the wonders of Europe,

and hither they returned freighted with the silver and golden
sinews which sustained the mighty power of Charles and Philip,
and enabled them to keep so large a portion of Europe under
their influence.   That Seville should have been a great centre
of refinement and luxury is natural.   Its merchants became
princes, and its noble houses, its Guzmans and Ponces de Leon
ranked with the kings of the earths.   At the same time, the
facility of acquiring competence and position infused a new
spirit into the lower classes, and tempered the preponderance
of hereditary power.   Great as Seville was, the reports of its
magnificence, and especially of its manufacturing development,
were much exaggerated.   Capmany has reduced them within
proper dimensions.   He has labored to show that Spain never
was a great manufacturing or commercial nation, and that the
trade of Seville was, to a considerable extent, in the hands of
foreigners.   He certainly has not been led astray by national
vanity; and those who follow in his footsteps have improved
upon him to such a degree as to deny the country any industrial development whatever.   It is true and natural that the
peaceful arts should not have received extraordinary attention
where the sound of the bugle was seldom hushed upon the
border, and the tramp of the war horse was sweeter music
than the hum of the spinning wheel.   But there was also an
industrial class.   Formerly in Burgos one *Cofradia* alone could
not contain by law less than fourteen thousand members, a
number greater than the whole population of the city after its
decline.   We all have read, too, how, in the times of Edward VI
and Elizabeth, the present of a pair of silk stockings out of Spain
was sufficient to set the whole circle of court ladies into a flutter
of envious excitement, just as, during the reign of their ancestors,
the daily renewal of fresh straw upon the floor of a great nobleman's mansion was considered a mark of extraordinary luxury.
And we know that every article of manufacturing skill used in
England, from powder to looking-glasses, was imported from
France, Italy or Spain.   In fact, Spain was to Europe of
the sixteenth century what France is now, the centre of fashion
and elegance.   The names of many of the streets, such as Calle
de los Francos and de Genova, would demonstrate the presence
of a large foreign population.   But such is always the case.   A
very large proportion of the population both of New Orleans
and New York were born out of the limits of the United
States, yet they are, none the less, great American cities.

The effect of the discovery of America upon Seville was similar to that of the discovery of the California mines upon San Francisco. Crowds from every nation eagerly rushed to participate in the golden wealth, and in their train came the arts of more industrious races. Considerable part of this influx halted at Seville, for the regulations were very strict in pre-- venting unauthorized persons from proceeding to the Indies. After the furor of energy had subsided, came, in usual turn, the reign of the elegant arts, the famous schools of painting and sculpture, and a literary taste, which prove that the banks of the Guadalquivir were still the seat of Spanish refinement, though the Court resided elsewhere. Hither came all who were characterized by profundity of acquirement, elegance of sentiment, or a taste for the humanities. Nor these alone, but with them the miserable and unfortunate of every class, so that it was styled "refugio de pobres y amparo de desdichados." The absence of the frivolities, the phlegmatic dulness and tyranny of the Court was probably beneficial, for the effect of the influx of American wealth upon the Government, and the freedom of the nation at large, was by no means beneficial. It made the monarch independent of his subjects, and thus gave him a stand-point whence to wage war upon their liberties. The adventurers, too, scattered over an immense territory thousands of miles from home, and surrounded by enemies, demanded a strong central power inconsistent with, and de- structive of individual independence at home. Madrid was the seat of this political government, but, in other respects, scarcely more than the capital of New Castile, enjoying about as much. pre-eminence as is accorded by us to Washington city. Anda- lusia was by far the wealthiest province, and its Captain- General almost independent of the central power. The consti- tutional regime, which succeeded Ferdinand, struck a great blow at the importance of the provincial cities. The authority of the Captain-General was confined almost entirely to military matters; the central government extended the sphere of its influence, and the minds of men became gradually turned toward the capital. And the completion of the railroad system will have some effect in the same direction. So that Seville is no longer the capital of even the four kingdoms of Andalusia. It is a charming residence, but it is indebted therefor to advan- tages which no Government can confer, and none take away.

17

SOCIAL LIFE.

Before leaving Seville, I should say something about the people and the social life in Andalusia, of which it presents the fairest type, and to do so properly, it is necessary to consider somewhat the physical and the external conditions that influence more or less every people in the formation of their habits, and through them of their national character. The fine climate of the south of Spain causes a considerable part of the day, and also of the night, to be passed in the open air, whether within or without the dwelling, a circumstance that travellers do not sufficiently bear in mind, and are hence frequently deceived by appearances of publicity, which they hastily misconstrue into want of delicacy and proper reticence. They remark an absence of that sensitive shrinking from the public view, that secrecy of internal life existing in colder climates, but which is no evidence of modesty there, nor is the absence of it evidence of the contrary here. Both are habits of life, attributable to the peculiarities of the nature around them. In no part of Andalusia is there any real winter. There may be a cold wind, a slight frost, and at times a handful of snow in some localities, with enough variation in the seasons to brace the frame and stimulate the intellect, but no weather that would render one of our rousing fires endurable. As for colds, rheumatisms and aches, they are utterly unknown. The purity of the sky is seldom marred by a cloud. It is said, with probable truth, that there has never been a day since the creation of the world, in which the sun wholly refused to shine upon Seville, and its

climate possesses the further recommendation of healing all
wounds but those of the heart.   To this should be added the
elasticity of the atmosphere, which renders even the midsummer's heat exciting rather than debilitating, and the universal
good health that gives no excuse for dying.   The vigorous old
age of the Andalusians is astonishing.   Innumerable of the
great historic characters have exceeded the limit of four score
and ten in the full enjoyment of their faculties.   The habit of
living in the open air, and the freedom from those vast encas-
ings of garments, which restrain all natural movement and
convert human beings into walking bales of merchandize, have
doubtless much to do with the Andalusian grace, so proverbial.
Whatever be the cause, they are graceful, active, nervous and
capable of immense endurance.   They are temperate to an extreme.   Even in the Moorish days the Sevillians were renowned in this respect, and a historian mentions that contrary to the
law of the Koran, it was not considered improper to drink wine
in Seville, as indulgence never led to intoxication.   Any modern
Englishman or Dane, not to speak of "the old folks," would
drink enough at a sitting to send a company of Spaniards to
the asylum.   The ordinary beverage is water or other refreshing and harmless liquids, which are sold at the corners of the
streets. . In Seville temporary stands are erected in every place
where men congregate or pass, and furnish *orchata, naranjada,
agraz,* and similar compounds, far more suitable to the climate
and natural taste than the euphonious cocktail.   The naranjada
is made of orange, the agraz of unripe grape; but the most common drink of all is pure water, with an *azucarillo* or *panal,* a
porous, spongy stick of sugar, with a drop of lemon dissolved
in it, which can be procured at all times.   The shop is protected from the sun by branches of orange or fig, and the water is
kept cool in the *alcarrazas,* of which I spoke at Andujar.
Spaniards drink water upon all occasions and at all hours,
morning, noon and night, particularly after chocolate, which is
made thick, and is supposed to have bilious tendencies unless
thus counteracted.   Localities are praised by the mention of
their springs and fountains, not of their vineyards, nor does the
product of the latter form an endless subject of table talk.   In
this respect the whole country is alike.   Of intoxication they
have absolutely no experience, and nothing gives greater disgust than drunkenness or gluttony.   A Spanish soldier will

march all day on a cup of chocolate and a crust of bread.
Owing to the dry climate, food is said to contain more nourishment here than elsewhere.   At all events, so it is that they are
as temperate in eating as in drinking, and as for the ladies, I
think they live mostly on air.   Society in the rest of Europe
revolves around the table.   In Andalusia it must be sought on
the Paseo or in the Tertulia, and the idea would not naturally
enter a Spaniard's head of showing his respect or friendship by
inviting you to dinner, though you may perhaps be asked to
stay and try the "*fortune du pot.*"   Many foreigners cannot comprehend how it is that they deliver letters of introduction and
never once see the color of the host's mahogany.   To their
entire freedom from physical suffering, and this abstinence
from over indulgence in the pleasures of the table, may perhaps be traced the cheerfulness of disposition, or rather the
absence of peevishness and spleen which characterizes the Andalusians.   A Spaniard seldom complains.   Notwithstanding
the violence of their emotions, suicide is never resorted to.
Indeed, in this beautiful land, this *Tierra de Dios*, the usual
causes for self-destruction can scarcely be said to exist, and the
only occasion which could justify such an act would be the eve
of one's departure.

The Andalusians have not yet, as a general thing, adopted
the late hours of Madrid.   The almost universal habit in summer, among the men, is to rise early and to break the fast
with a cup of chocolate, taken in bed.   This is the *desayuno*,
literally, the " unfast."   After that is the promenade for
pleasure or business, as the case may be.   Formerly, the principal meal was taken about noon, but customs vary in different
classes of society, though the nature of the climate imposes a
certain similarity.   The names of the meals are derived from
the Latin: *Almu erzo*, the regular breakfast, is traced to "*mor-
sus*," though the article prefixed is suspicious.   It would thus
signify " a bite," which is in harmony with the habits of the
Romans, whose only formal meal was the supper.   So *la méri-
endá*, the lunch, comes from *meridianus; la comida*, dinner, from
comedere; la cena, supper, is the same in both languages.   The
siesta, in the hottest part of the day, is peculiarly Spanish, and
woe to the unlucky wight who disturbs that sacred period.
Doors and shutters are closed.   The master and mistress, the
man servant and maid servant, the cattle, and the stranger

.within their gates, are wrapped in profound slumber, and few inducements, short of salvation, could prevail upon them to forego this enjoyment. At three o'clock, the whole world wakes up; the afternoon cathedral service commences; buyers and sellers smoke a cigarette, and start afresh, and the dogs and cats, after a profound yawn, and a good stretch of the hind leg, renew the never varying round of canine and feline existence. As I have said, the promenade in winter on the banks of the Guadalquivir, and in summer on the Plaza Isabel, between nine and eleven o'clock in the evening, is also indispensable.

But the charm of social life consists in the Tertulia or evening reception, for which the domestic architecture seems exactly calculated, though it is a more difficult task to decide whether the architecture has exercised more influence over their habits of life, or these over their ideas of architecture. The plan of the houses is similar to that introduced or adopted by the Moors, and is eminently suited to the climate and the people. The outside rarely presents anything to admire—a white wall, with large grated balconied windows, in which the occupants can sit and look up and down the narrow street. In winter this is the favorite place for the ladies, and it is through these iron bars that lovers are permitted to whisper their vows. In an evening's walk one can see the faithful swains thus engaged in what is called *pelar el pavo*, nor are such interviews considered improper. The entry into the house is by a little hall or vestibule, some ten feet or more in width, and the depth of a room, with massive folding doors upon the street, which are seldom closed till past midnight. At the foot of the hall is an ornamented grating, giving admission to the Patio, the principal part of the house—an open court, square or oblong, varying from fifteen to fifty feet in size and paved with marble. In the centre stands a fountain, whose flowing waters help to lower the temperature. Around runs an open corridor with a colonnade, upon which the ground floor rooms open. The upper part of the house is similar in its arrangements, except that the corridor is generally closed, with windows giving on the Patio. There is still another court for the offices, and in grand establishments several. It will be seen at once that the upper portion is most exposed to the sun, and consequently the winter residence, and it is furnished accordingly. In January artificial

warmth is occasionally desirable, even at Seville. In the total,
absence of fireplaces, a few coals are placed upon a *brasero*,
and the company sit around holding out their hands to catch
the little heat it evolves. The first time I took my place in
the circle around this caricature of a fire, it was difficult to
refrain from smiling, as it gave us the complete air of a collection of beautiful, half-frozen witches. As soon as the rainy
season has passed and the warm weather commences, the
family move down below, flowers and odoriferous shrubs are
placed in the Patio, the piano in one corner, the guitar in
another, an awning is drawn over it during the daytime to
exclude the sun, and summer life commences. It is here that
the ladies of the family sit in the cool of the evening to pursue
their occupations or to amuse themselves with music and
company. Rigid formalities and their attendant cares and
anxieties are forbidden entrance. In common with most
warm-tempered people, their address is at first somewhat ceremonious, but the manners of the better class are eminently
frank, if there be no cause for suspicion. So soon as a faint
intimacy is established, the title and surname are dropped; it
is simply Francisco or Manuel, and Paca or Pepita, and how
pretty even the harshest appellative sounds when thus spoken.
Affectation, the vanity of display, indifference to or forgetfulness of the rights of the rest of the company, have no place.
Everyone respects himself, and while vindicating his own
equality, yields respect and equality to others, whatever may
be the difference of titular distinction; and any attempt at display or effort to engross the conversation by a speech or a
lecture, however brilliant, would be considered in exceedingly
bad taste. Without this sense of assured position there cannot
exist the perfection of manner, for there will either be an
assumption of superiority or an acknowledgment of inferiority,
and both are equally fatal. Hence it is that American gentlemen, like the Spanish (who are thoroughly Republican among
each other), have always been considered the best models of
good breeding, feeling within themselves that consciousness of
personal dignity and equality, needing no effort to procure
their recognition, which elsewhere must be found, if found at
all, only in the highest ranks of the aristocracy. A stranger,
judging them by their formal, external demeanor, is quite

unprepared for the charming freedom which reigns in the
domestic circle

Upon the delivery of your letter of introduction, a Spanish
gentleman immediately presents you with his house, *Mi casa
está á su disposicion* or *esta easa es suya*, without thereby intend-
ing to make you a conveyance, and give you the right to institute an action of ejectment, which would involve you in all the
troubles of housekeeping, but merely to inform you that you
are welcome in the evening, if you can find any one in. Do
not think, however, that he or the household are going to put
themselves out in the slightest degree. Some families are at
home on stated evenings, and it generally happens that you
find them in, but if you do not, why you can pass on to another
acquaintance, and there is no offence meant and none taken.
Nothing can surpass the fairy aspect of a family evening party,
viewed from the grating. The suspended lamps give just
enough light to see the sparkling drops of the fountain, and to
recognize the ladies, half hid among the flowers. With their
beauty, so suited to a scene of the kind, they scarcely seem to
be of this earth. You enter, are welcomed, pointed to a seat.
If the ladies of the house be agreeable you are seldom the
only guest. The time flies by, chocolate, sweetmeats, perhaps
ices, perhaps pure water, help it along. The watchman cries
the hour in your hearing. Heavens! can it be so late? You
place yourself at the feet of your fair entertainers (*me pongo á
los piés de vm. señorita*). They kiss your hand (*beso la mano á vm.
cabellero*). You skip along the street as though supported on
the airy pinions of the wind. You dream of black eyes and
glossy hair, of guitars and delicate fingers, of fairies seated in
opening rose buds, waving their fans to you and enveloping
your eyes with tiny lace veils.

But my lady readers will exclaim, what is all this rhapsody
about? You go into a house with a court; see some ladies
with fans and guitars; you drink a little water, eat a cake, and
come out raving about fairies and angels. We see nothing
wonderful in all that. There must have been some very intellectual conversation; pray, what were you talking about?
Alas! you cannot tell. You do not remember three words that
were uttered. It was very witty, very graceful, very charming; even the pauses were delicious, but exactly what it was
you cannot recollect. It did not impress you as displaying

profound erudition. Indeed, the education of Spanish ladies is
generally somewhat neglected. They learn from books little,
except the rudiments, and of the outside world beyond the
Pyrenees have exceedingly confused ideas. A young Aragonesa, who had just left school with a prize, and was full of
intelligence and patriotism, once asked me if Morocco and
America were not near each other. There are numerous exceptions, but reading, writing, a little arithmetic, geography,
poetry, Spanish history, and the lives of the saints, with a tolerable knowledge of French and music, is all one need usually
expect. Of the whole list of "ologies" they are entirely innocent. Your lady questioners turn away with indignation, and
ask how a woman can be agreeable who is ignorant of con-
chology, does not know sienite from hornblende, and could
not solve a quadratic equation to save herself from eternal per-
dition. For answer, I refer them to the Emperor of the
French, who laid the loftiest diadem in Christendom at the
feet of one of Andalusia's daughters, and has seen no reason to
repent the sacrifice. The truth is, that the whole charm of
either man or woman does not consist in the amount of the
outside world which they have managed to cram into the
inside of their brains—a system that should be styled inducation
rather than education. You would be very much shocked, in
walking through a flowery grove at sunset, if your companion
were to break away after some new species of the Hygomedon
Septentrionalis, or the jaw tooth of a decaying red-sandstone
monster. I am sure that no Andaluza would, but in these matters everyone must follow his own taste. Were some beneficent divinity to present the author with a pencil dipped in the
hues of the rainbow, he might undertake to explain the mystery of their powers of fascination; without such supernatural
aid he would probably meet, at least deserve, the fate of Prometheus. The women of every country have some peculiar
attraction. To these alone is it reserved to unite all. Their
inexpressible beauty has, doubtless, much to do with it, and it
certainly is beyond description. The most crazy dream of
poetry in its wildest conceptions never surpassed this reality.
The mere contour of the face is a small part, for her beauty,
like that of her country, is subjective, and consists rather in
the expression, in the mingled softness and fire, the enthusiasm
that sparkles forth. Those unfathomable eyes are but the

windows of the soul, and that inimitable grace of person which enchants the beholder, is only a part of the harmony of the universe that seeks in her a connecting link between our mortal cloaks and the mystic music pervading creation. While in repose, the expression of her face, in tender sympathy with the soul, is pensive, even melancholy, but, upon the approach of a friend, she returns to earth like the awakening of a morning in spring. Every feature beams with attraction, and precious pearls drop from her rosy lips. Who that has a heart to lose, could refuse to lay it at her feet? Ah! Love was surely born in Spain. Artless and unsuspecting in her thoughts, she receives every expression of admiration without vanity, and seems to value it rather because of the source whence it proceeds, than as a tribute to her own charms. The simplicity of her manner is only to be equalled by the kindness of her heart. All this, united with an ardent temperament, renders her capable of the noblest deeds of self-devotion, of which the maid of Zaragoza is no isolated example. The great peculiarity of Spanish women is their sincerity and open-heartedness. They will speak to you with praise of the ladies of other countries, admire their beauty and good qualities, but add *no tienen franqueza como nosotras* (they are not frank as we are). Spain is no land of hypocrites. It is the absence of this frankness which makes women *rusée* and fickle, defects thoroughly detested by both sexes. The character of a flirt, or whatever may be the proper appellation—I mean a beauty—who delights in general admiration, and makes use of her charms to bewilder the susceptible, without experiencing any emotion beyond that of gratified vanity, who, in a word, thinks only of herself and her triumphs—is as little understood as admired. Not that they are by any means indifferent to the good opinion of the other sex, for after all they are women:

> En palacio la Princesa,
> En la ciudad la Señora,
> En la aldea la pastora,
> Y en la Corte la Duquesa,
> Madre! á ninguna le pesa,
> Que le digan que es perfeta.

And custom has rendered it not impertinent to express admiration at the sight of a beauty, if done in the delicately courteous manner usual in this section. But this of itself is not sufficient.

Indeed, few Spanish ladies have any ambition to act the part of *belles;* to be the recipients of a thousand little familiar gallantries which mean nothing, and pass away, and are forgotten, like morning shadows. Others may be satisfied with formal and ceremonious courtesies. The homage they require is such as should be paid to divinity on bended knees, yet so irresistible is the infatuation inspired by these daughters of the sun, that the helpless worshipper is too happy to obey their imperious commands. When the system of gallants (*cortejo* was the Spanish word) prevailed in Europe, travellers wondered at the slavery it imposed in Spain. The cortejo was bound to be ever present. If a shawl, glove or fan was to be picked up, he was always on hand, and any disposition to be *volage* discredited him in the eyes of the whole community. Sincerity and constancy in the women correspond to obstinacy or tenacity in the men, for which they have been famous since the days of Hannibal. Spanish women are passionate, and if they do fall in love it is a serious matter. When they give their hearts, it is forever. Self is forgotten, and their whole existence wrapped up in devotion to the object of their choice. Three-fourths of the misery, and no inconsiderable portion of the crimes, of such frequent occurrence in the Peninsula, are attributable to this cause. The lower classes still use the dagger to revenge themselves upon a rival or a traitor, and if the higher ranks are less demonstrative, it is not because they feel less keenly. But can a woman inspire devotion who is incapable herself of jealousy?

You are seldom left in doubt as to the position you occupy in her estimation. One consequence is, that the system of marriage sales which reigns in England and France has only moderate sway in Spain. In France, young ladies have no liberty whatever. It would be an insult to venture beyond the merest formal courtesies. They are taken from the convent, and remain in a most irksome state of restraint until marriage—to which event they look forward as the door of freedom—and accept any suitable *parti* who has been selected by their parents. In England they have full liberty, but the same end is attained in a very different way. Mamá and the daughter go out to the chase together, and any poor fellow who has a title or a fortune is hunted down remorselessly. The practical results of this system seem to be better than that of the French, but in itself it is infinitely more humiliating and disgusting. In Spain, a medium

between the two prevails. They have far more liberty than in
France, far less than in England. Young people are allowed to
say agreeable things to each other, and insinuating compliments frequently pass. But whatever be the restraint imposed,
few Spanish ladies would sell themselves or allow themselves to
be sold by their parents. Of course, in an old country where
wealth is not easily accumulated, some regard must be had to
that commodity. Probably every woman would like to make
what is considered a good match, and sometimes there as well
as elsewhere

> The Knave of Diamonds tries his wily arts,
> And wins (Oh! shameful chance!) the Queen of Hearts.

But it is, nevertheless, a truth that six marriages out of ten are
made against the better judgment of the parents, though I
cannot say that in the long run the parties seem any the happier therefor. Love often overrides prudential considerations.
"At first sight they have changed eyes;" and, if the history of
Doña Clara de Viedma and Don Luis is no longer re-enacted
in all particulars, the spirit which dictated it still survives.

After a certain age, women necessarily change the object of
their lives. The disposition and the power to attract the homage of the other sex alike diminish, and more serious subjects
fill their thoughts. In those countries where the principal
object of every woman's existence is to get married, the match-
ing off of daughters is the absorbing occupation of old age;
and so powerful an instinct has nature planted in the mother's
breast for this purpose, that the ordinary feelings of delicacy
are quite forgotten. Every humiliation is cheerfully submitted
to which can conduce to the success of the cherished purpose.
There is nothing of all this in Spanish society. If ladies do
not wish to marry, they can remain single or enter a convent,
and both are honorable alternatives. Old maidism is not considered such a dreadful condition as to be avoided by the sacrifice of everything that could render married life endurable to a
Spaniard. Relieved from this great burthen of marrying off
their daughters at every hazard, the mothers are apt to devote
their time to religion and charity, and nothing can be more
charming than the family circle presided over by such an one.
The sons and daughters are not made to feel that their longer
presence in the mansion is irksome, and that it is time they go

forth to seek their own nests. They in turn repay this fostering
love with the purest filial affection. Every traveller must have
met, in his limited experience, instances of touching devotion
on the part of widows' sons. The mother of my Madrid hostess
was still living at Seville, and one of her sons had remained
single in order that he might the better discharge his duties to
her. Such occurrences are still more common in the higher
ranks. The cultivation of this reciprocity of generous feeling
throws a charm over the homeliest face; and the absence of
selfish purpose renders the company of elderly ladies far more
agreeable than what can be found in a state of society where
females, who survive their attractions, take to opium, women's
rights associations and Exeter Hall meetings, or, perhaps, still
indulge in the delusion of rouge and powder. Of course, all
this does not apply to Madrid, though there be more exceptions
there than is generally supposed. In too many lofty instances,
the eve of metropolitan life, like its morning, presents nought
but frivolity and dissipation.

I have said that Spanish women are imperfectly educated,
and I might add that they seldom travel beyond the limits of
their own province. There are exceptions to both statements;
such is, however, the general rule. Yet, the term "ignorant,"
in the signification it conveys with us, is entirely inapplicable,
unless ignorance be defined the mere negation of acquired
knowledge, and in that case the "ignorance" of Solomon would
astonish a modern boarding school miss. In those countries
where learning is forced upon everyone, the want of it, in certain classes of society, is evidence of stupidity, and the two are
considered synonymous. But the natural vivacity and bright-
ness of the Andalusian intellect and the cultivation which it
receives from conversation, make ample amends for any deficiency of mere knowledge, and the women still retain unim-
paired the charms with which heaven originally endowed them.
What particularly distinguishes the Andaluzas throughout
Spain is the indescribable thing called *gracia*. It is not simply
wit nor grace, but a combination of both, welded together
with some celestial cement, I know not what. You never con-
found the "*Sal Andaluza*" with that from any other province.
It has as distinct a character, and almost as great a fame, as
the attic salt of antiquity. The most indifferent and insignificant occurrence served up with this condiment becomes most

palatable, and all the ladies have it in the purest form. Andalusia has been the home of genius from the days of Trajan and Seneca to our own. Either the locality or the climate seems to develop that fervid imagination, without some of which there is little talent even of the order called practical. The men do not make such good soldiers, for that very reason; the restraint and *ennui* of a camp life is too irksome. But as rulers, generals, orators, poets and painters, they have always shone pre-eminent. These same endowments distinguished them in the time of the Moors, and still more among the Romans:

> Aliæ gentes quos fœdere Roma recepit
> Aut armis domuit, varios aptantur in usus
> Imperii,   *   *   *
>   *   * Fruges, æraria, miles
> Undique conveniunt, totoque ex orbe leguntur.
> Hæc generat qui cuncta regant; nec laude virorum
> Censeri contenta fuit, nisi matribus æque
> Vinceret et gemino certatim splendida sexu
> Flavillam, Mariamque daret, pulchramque Serenam.

Nor are the lines of the Roman poet less applicable to modern than to ancient times. Scarce one of the great men of the Spain of this century first saw the light north of the Tagus, and among the rival claims of the other sex few will hesitate in awarding the golden apple. In addition to gifts of intellect, they possess all the Oriental grace of narrative. A lady once undertook to tell me an incident from one of the old Spanish chronicles. The bare facts I knew already better than she, as I had read them in the book itself, which she evidently had not. But what a difference in the style of narrative! In my hands it would have been the text of the opera without the music; in hers, it was a poem set by Mendelssohn. They have a great deal of vivacity, yet they are by no means so given to gesticulation as the French, nor have they that sort of fictitious excitement unaccompanied by real passion. But they make great use of those natural gestures which are the appropriate aids of expression in persons who feel strongly. The fan is invariably appealed to; the elderly ones of the old school invoke the saints on slight provocation, crossing themselves all the while devoutly; and all ages have an inexhaustible fund of conversation, which, whether instructive or not, is amazingly agreeable. Their brilliant, florid imaginations, and the facility afforded by the *assonante* rhyme, render poetry an almost universal gift. One accomplishment they possess to perfection. I cannot say they learn it, for it seems to be born within them. I mean the guitar. Having no conception of the abstruse mathematical music that subordinates the voice to the instrument, they touch inimitably well this, which has very little power, except as an accompaniment, and they have by nature an exquisite taste, which impels them to make every thing subservient to the principal end, so that you are never tempted to forget the music in the skill of the performer, or in admiration for some artistic fingering. The music of an Andaluza seems, as it were, to have become a part of herself, and to be but another natural means of giving utterance to her thoughts and feelings. The men, in turn, all sing. I rather think the taste for serenading has died out in the large cities upon the highways of travel, but in smaller and remoter towns it is still the nightly occupation of the young gallants, who pass the evenings under the balcony of their mistress, and are rewarded by a conversation through the grating of the window. Every.guitar player in Spain, however, is by no means a skilful performer; a great deal of what one hears is mere strumming.

The influence of Murillo is still felt, though his excellence be not equalled, and it is said that if all the paintings in Seville were put in a row, they would reach to Madrid. There is an astonishing disposition to appreciate the beauties of the art, even if there be a deficiency of scientific knowledge. Persons from whom you would little expect it can give a passably good opinion on the subject, and there is nothing more agreeable than to listen to a young Andaluza, while she hesitatingly points out the excellencies of some favorite picture, and gives her reasons for the preference. Her own nature seems to reflect upon the object, and she discovers far more beauties than the artist ever conceived. In particular, do I remember one such conversation upon Murillo's "Guardian Angel," which first elevated me to an appreciation of its perfection. On the other hand, they seem to me deficient in the power of discovering defects, and both are necessary to correct criticism.

An idea has obtained circulation abroad to the effect that Spanish ladies, particularly the Andaluzas, spend their days in idleness. Nothing, in my opinion, could be farther from the truth. Women here certainly do not perform the onerous and unsuitable tasks which are imposed upon them in less gallant countries, nor do I think they should. Nature never intended the weaker sex to do the work of the world. But every young lady of the better class possesses a knowledge, more or less thorough, of the art of housekeeping; though it is true that the simplicity and temperate habits of the Spaniards render this a comparatively light duty. The dwellings in Seville are models of neatness, and not surpassed in Holland, and travellers, who have penetrated into their interior life, will sustain me in saying that the scene presented by the second Patio, so far from being one of idleness, appears rather to be an imitation of the mansion of Penelope as drawn by Homer. An Andaluza would be surprised to learn that there are countries in the world where it is considered little less than disgraceful for ladies of fashion to manage household affairs.

The family relations in Spain are very pleasant. Parental tyranny, and the consequent quarrels between father and son, are rare exceptions, nor is it thought necessary that the heir and the ancestor should be of opposite opinions—rather the contrary. There is a most respectful deference of manner, but it partakes of the nature of friendship, and there is little exercise of authority for authority's sake. I think that this is the reason why the children have so much ease of manner, without being forward. The plan of separating them from the family circle just at the age when their characters are forming, is not fashionable, nor have young ladies' boarding schools yet been introduced. The girls are either taught by instructors who come to the house, or by their relatives; the boys go to the local school. The son is thus the friend of the family, and feels that the paternal house is his home. In America, it is necessary to introduce boys early into life, because with us everyone must be essentially the architect of his own fortunes. There is no such thing as a fixed position. The wheel of fortune is continually revolving, and he who remains quiet is sure to be crushed. But in Spain, as in most European countries, society is comparatively stationary. The contest cannot begin until the recruits have been educated and introduced into the world by those who have already obtained a position. The noble spectacle is unknown of a young man, without the adventitious aids of wealth or birth, commencing at the lowest round, and by virtue, talent and industry, in a score of years attaining a place among the honored of the land.

The relation of husband and wife is probably more satisfactory than is the average of the rest of Europe. In the lower classes it certainly is, for elsewhere in Europe virtue can scarcely be said to exist among the inferior ranks, and I can truthfully assert that in an evening's walk down the principal thoroughfares of London, I have beheld more infamy than in all Spain put together. But regarded from our point of view, it is still bad enough. Yet here, also, a difference of customs has given rise to a great misconception on the part of travellers, for certain things are said, and certain things are done, innocent in themselves and in their effects, which elsewhere would be considered evidence of great impropriety. So, on the other hand, an unmarried lady's going out alone, or accepting the arm of a gentleman, occurrences certainly not unusual in America, would almost ruin a reputation in Spain. A few years ago it would have been considered a dreadful thing for a *novia* to shake hands even with her cousin. Then, too, nothing is concealed. Whatever evil exists is visible. The fair fame of the country has suffered much from one class of travellers who, ignorant of the language and the people, have thought it worth while to digest the fables of the *valets de place*, and still more from another class who have learned just enough of both to mislead them. Yet through the alembic of one or the other of these are our ideas of Spanish manners for the most part distilled. Whatever laxity of morals may exist I trace to the particular circumstances of the last hundred years. Formerly, Spain was distinguished above all other countries by the sanctity with which the marriage tie was regarded. Unfortunately, the present queen—placed by her position at the head of society—has given a shocking example of want of propriety. Her father and mother before her, and her father's father and mother, were among the worst of the race; and the effect of a sovereign's influence, for good or for evil, is exemplified, to our own knowledge, in the English court, which, from being under George IV, the most corrupt and licentious in Europe, has become one of the most correct. Could the Dutchess of Montpensier be substituted for her sister, a complete restoration of the old Spanish manners might be accomplished. All that I have said, however, applies rather to Madrid, where the queen's example is felt, and where the fashion of mercenary alliances, with their inevitable result, has been imported among other foreign barbarisms, rather than to the provinces. The most conclusive testimony in favor of the Spanish fair is the esteem in which they have been held when married into other countries. Blanche of Castile, St. Isabel, and the present Empress of the French, will sustain my assertion. I remember a touching instance of marital affection which occurred even at Madrid during my sojourn. A man in the humbler walks of life was murdered in an affray. His wife was sent for. Upon entering the shop where the dead body lay exposed, she uttered a piercing shriek, and exclaiming, "During twenty years we have never had an unkind word," fell dead by his side. I did not witness the scene, but it is a very natural one in Spain. When happily married they bring a full and overflowing measure of love, far beyond what any mortal has a right to expect, uniting the sterling qualities of the sex, sincerity, constancy, devotion, reverence, with those adornments which form the charm of life, and I have yet to learn that Juno is the less to be admired or respected because encircled with the magic cestus.

It would be unjust not to lay a considerable portion of the blame for such derelictions, when they do occur, upon the men, who in this connection have somewhat fallen from their former distinction, and in so falling have shaken one of the noblest pillars of the temple. It is no longer strictly true, as was said in the Romaunt of the Spanish Ladye's Love, that

> Spaniards fraught with jealousy we oft do find,
> But Englishmen throughout the world are counted kind.

Give them, however, their due. No Spanish peasant, not to say gentleman, would feel the pangs of wounded honor assuaged by the scandal of a public trial and a verdict for ten thousand pounds. Something is due to them for the past if not for the present, and when the history of European civilization is truly written, it will be found that women are indebted for their present elevated position more to the Peninsula than to any other portion of the globe. In the lower empire they were placed upon a footing of apparent equality, which, by depriving them of the support that the strong and generous are ever ready to extend to the feeble, produced, in fact, the greatest inequality. Women being by nature not so well fitted as men

18

to cope with adversity in the great struggle upon earth, have, fortunately for them, been furnished with powers of fascination and attraction which restore the balance. There is a natural disposition, on the part of everyone, to protect those who are incapable of protecting themselves, and hundreds will rush to the defence of a child where a man would probably be left to his own unaided exertions. The child will grow to be an adult not only in appearance, but in reality, but the woman must remain a woman, unless the powers beneath unsex her. The Romans, by giving her equality, thus, in truth, render her less equal than before; and the world had sunk to one level of materialism and selfishness when the Christian religion sounded forth the novel doctrine that the weak and humble were more honorable, in the sight of the Creator, than the mighty potentates of earth. To attribute a considerable amount of virtue to the barbarians, who overran the empire, has been a favorite error. Their disposition to blood and violence, and their intense sense of personal independence and dignity, prevented them from utterly yielding to the debaucheries of Rome, but they surely evinced little appreciation of that spirit of charity, of gentleness, of forgiving love, which it was the object of the Evangile to preach. This, the true spirit of modern civilization, is due solely to the religion of our Saviour. Fortunately for us, the tendency of the third and fourth centuries to fritter away its essence in fruitless discussions about the nature of the Divine person, and, on the other hand, to convert what was given us as a consolation here, and a hope hereafter, into a repulsive system of terror, was corrected by the honors paid to the Virgin, each representing respectively the influences that were to effect the salvation of the race; the one threatening despair and endless misery to the wicked; the other promising hope and measureless bliss to the virtuous. For this purpose it matters not whether the Virgin had a large family, or whether she were not simply a mortal, or whether she had ever existed. It was not a question of fact but of belief. Shrines were erected to an immaculate being, uncontaminated by the vices and frailties of humanity, yet sympathizing with its wants and necessities; a being of ineffable softness and love, the most powerful intercessor with the terrific Judge, who was justly incensed against His rebellious creatures—and this being was a woman. I have already stated that the worship of the Virgin was widely diffused throughout Spain, and almost peculiar to that country. It is very possible that the mere ceremonial, the gaudily-dressed images, the processions, the wax *votos* hung up at her shrine were imitated after Pagan sources. But those who go further and compare the worship itself with that of Venus Salambo, Diana of the Ephesians, or Cybele, are as ignorant of the history of civilization as of religion. The fairest of the daughters of Eve on earth, she was considered their protectress in heaven, ever attentive to the plaintive cry of the afflicted and deserted. The impersonation of female excellence and purity, she was the unapproachable model which all strove to imitate. The names of half the girls in Andalusia are still derived from her virtues or the several incidents of her life— Dolores, Mercedes, Rosario, Concepcion; and the memory of their guardian is constantly kept in mind by the custom of celebrating the feast of their baptismal saint, rather than the day of their birth.

The invasion of the Mohammedans exercised also a powerful effect upon the position of women in Spain from a very different point. The Mohammedan civilization was a strange mixture of Jewish and Christian precept, engrafted upon a stock which we are disposed to consider as originally and essentially Oriental, though it is very questionable whether the qualities and manners that we consider Oriental were not for the most part introduced into the East by the followers of the prophet. Borrowing the spirit of ceremonial observance from the Jews; from the Christians the doctrine of universal charity and liberality, and also its promise of a future Paradise for the good; from his own countrymen the manners and thoughts of every day life, he concocted a system which, as a worldly-wise scheme, was certainly a great improvement upon what then existed in a large part of the world. One striking feature of the Mohammedan civilization was the jealousy with which women were regarded as something too precious to be looked upon with ordinary eyes. The Moors of Andalusia, owing to their superiority in war and the brilliancy of their intellectual cultivation, exercised an immense influence over the neighboring Christian nations, and were themselves essentially impressed in turn. Eight centuries of civil and military rivalry developed all that was noble and generous on both sides. Much greater freedom was allowed to the Mohammedan women in Andalusia

than in the East, and something more was demanded than
beauty.   Poetry, music and other accomplishments are as
much dwelt upon in the description of their favorites as the
charms of person, and their literary women fill no small space
in the biographical dictionaries.   To judge of the relation of
the sexes in Moorish Spain by the habits of the Turks, a coarse
sensual race, or by those of their fallen brethren in the Barbary
States, would mislead.   The appearance of women in general
society was of course unknown, but they bore their part in
domestic entertainments.   The beauty and attractions of their
Christian captives heightened the refined education of the Cordovese Court, and produced in the men an elegance and respect-
fulness of intercourse, and a purity of love which surprised
their contemporaries out of the Peninsula.

The position of women in Christian Spain was subjected,
therefore, to four very different influences.   The Teutonic element from the North would reduce them to the level of our
Indian squaws, the servants of their lords; the tendency of the
Roman was toward equality; the Moorish made them the
centre of love and gallantry; the worship of the Virgin secured
for them the respect which virtue and purity are ever entitled
to command.   Imagine, now, the home of a Christian knight, a
Castro or an Osorio in some fastness of Leon.   Far from the
remains of ancient corruption, his castle lifts its battlements in
virtuous solitude.   Instead of frivolous intrigues, his whole
energy is devoted to maintaining the sanctity of his fireside
and the honor of his religion.   Bearing aloft upon his banner
the image of the spotless Virgin, he and his followers rush into
the thickest of the battle.   Protected by her guiding hand,
he returns crowned with laurels and enriched with the spoils
of the infidel, and at his castle gate is welcomed by the companion of his life, the humble kinswoman upon earth of her
whose powerful protection in heaven has brought him once
more safely to his home.   The combat of Garcilasso and the
Moor, for the honor of the Mother of God, is narrated of three
different persons, and, doubtless, such contests in her behalf
often occurred.   Is it unnatural, then, that some portion of the
adoration, considered so justly due to the one, should have
been bestowed on the other?   With the Moors, the feeling
toward the sex was rather a species of gallantry, which, uniting
in the Spaniard with the other and nobler sentiment, formed

the highest type of the cavalier. The Spaniard could not be said to love his mistress ; it was rather a worship, an adoration as of a goddess. No impure thoughts entered into the relation. A chivalric devotion, and an almost unearthly respect on the one side, were rewarded with a love and fidelity without bounds on the other. Whoso would fully appreciate the superiority of Castillian civilization and manners in this connection, let him compare life as portrayed in the old Spanish ballads with that represented in the licentious Decameron of Italy, the Fabliaux and the songs of the Troubadors in France, or the Saxon grossness of Chaucer, and form his own opinion.

At the close of the Moorish wars, with the capture of Granada, the Spanish dominion began to extend itself over the continent, and with their dominion their ideas. For a century and a half, not only was the Spaniard feared as a subject of the greatest monarch in Europe, but what is more, he was respected as the most loyal and lofty toned cavalier, and the most elegant gentleman in the civilized world. Then came the reaction. Piece by piece was lopped off from the decaying empire. The race of her warriors became extinct. The later Bourbons were surrounded by men whose hereditary wealth and honors placed them above the necessity of exertion, and whose leisure was consumed in the frivolous pastimes of an imbecile court, at which they were compelled to reside. The age of Louis XV of France, and of the Georges of England, found admirers and imitators in Spain. Manly occupations fell into disuse, and ceased to excite even respect. Fortune was to be courted, not on the battle field amid labor and danger, but in some miserable Palace Camarilla. What should have been an amusement of leisure hours became the great business of life, and the destinies of the nation were wielded by the fashionable actress. This was the gay circle of the metropolis. Ladies were, fortunately, removed from its vortex, and preserved their former character unspotted, because fashion had rendered another class the centre of such attractions. So that society in Madrid, at the end of the last century, astonished rather by its absurdity than its immorality. The conduct of Ferdinand VII, after his restoration, drove the liberal party to seek sympathy beyond the borders of Spain, and thus opened the door to the sensualism and materialism of the French revolution. The effect upon Madrid society in many respects, particularly in loosening the bands, has been deplorable. It is difficult for the serious, earnest Spaniard to become a mere Boulevard trotter; but the young men are doing their best, and the herd of Pollos bid fair, in time, to equal the kindred spirits of other lands. I repeat, however, that this, in the main, is confined to Madrid, and that gentlemen from the provinces preserve very much the characteristics of other days. Their intercourse with the fairer sex is marked by an enthusiastic devotion, a genuine admiration, accompanied by an absence of frivolity and a forgetfulness of self, which render their humility an acceptable offering on the altar of beauty. Woman is respected by them because she is woman. Like our own, no Spanish gentleman would hesitate to yield her the inside of the walk, or the best seat in the diligence; and no Spanish lady, unlike some of our own, would neglect to acknowledge even this trifling courtesy by a smile which could compensate for far greater sacrifices. Books of travel, founded upon data furnished by the scandal of the court, are utterly unreliable, and such a method of judging Spain would be as unfair as the course pursued by certain strangers in putting forward Washington and New York as models of American manners or morals. Yet life at the capital has not been entirely without effect upon the nation. The Spanish husband of the nineteenth century is not the equal of him of the sixteenth; and what was said at the beginning of this episode is true, that the decline in the virtuous tone of the marriage relation, culminating in a few striking instances in Madrid, which have been, ignorantly, considered criterions of Spanish society in general, is attributable principally to the men.

In the estimate I have given of Andalusian society, I may be mistaken. Of course, there are old women, and ugly, very ugly, women, and disagreeable women, and frequently disagreeable men; but, upon the whole, I have found the intercourse most pleasant. The opportunities enjoyed by a traveller, and his means of forming a dispassionate judgment, are naturally limited. It is difficult for him to avoid hasty generalizations from a few portraits in his own experience. It may be that at forty, and under different circumstances, my own conclusions would have been otherwise, and truth compels me to state that I have seen many French and English, who have long resided in Andalusia, and whose opinions are very different from those which I have expressed. They complain that the society is wearisome, though they admire the country. But it may admit of a question, whether these two nations are capable of appreciating the peculiar character of Spanish ladies. The earnestness, the enthusiasm with which they regard every object of interest are not suited to the gay and thoughtless gallantries of the one, or the heavy phlegm of the other. The dreamy German is a greater favorite, and I have never met one of that race who was not satisfied with Spain and its inhabitants. Surely, there may be some enjoyment in social intercourse, though it consist not in *badinage* at a *petit souper* or solid conversation around a smoking joint of roast beef.

The summer had now passed away, and the hour of departure was approaching. My second visit to Seville had sped like a dream. The almanac alone served to mark the days as they flew by. Upon the first entry it is natural to feel some disappointment at the external appearance of a city that fills the world with its fame; but after a residence of sufficient duration to investigate its hidden treasures, to appreciate its unostentatious life, and become acquainted with its delightful society, most strangers will agree with the natives in exclaiming:

> Quien no ha visto á Sevilla
> No ha visto maravilla.

It seems as if nature, exerting her utmost powers, had succeeded in making a paradise where beauty and happiness found an eternal abode. It was difficult to feel that the time had come to say farewell, as I took my last walk on the banks of the Guadalquivir. Its placid waters were resplendent with the glories of the sunrise, as they had been morning after morning, to be·succeeded by the milder beauties of a cloudless night. The graceful trees would continue modestly to gaze at their image in its mirror, the Cathedral to rear its noble form against the azure sky, but my place would be occupied by others, wanderers like myself. Why not eat of the lotos, and let life glide by in this fairy dream-land? Alas! it is not written in the book of fate that the measure of human felicity should be filled upon earth. Perhaps Andalusia, too, has its dark side, which a prolonged residence would bring into relief, for "Wo viel Licht ist, da giebt es starken Schatten." And visions of home, of sweet home, rise before me. Adieu! fair Seville.

CHAPTER XV.

CORDOVA.

The morning was spent in bidding adieu to those fairy scenes
which a presentment told me I was never to behold again, and,
at three o'clock, the train to Cordova was gliding with us up
the river bank. One by one the lofty edifices disappeared
behind the luxuriant vegetation. For a long time, the Giralda
continued alone to tower over the plain. It, too, at length
faded from sight, and Seville, the glory and marvel of Andalusia, was gone.

The sun was intensely bright, and the heat corresponding.
The air, near the parched earth of the hills, danced as if over a
cauldron. On its mountain cliff to the east glittered the city
of Carmona, its long white walls sparkling like the jewelled
crown of a magician. Illuminated by the rays of the western
sun, it continued to form a conspicuous point in the horizon
until we reached Lora. My only companion in the carriage
was a young gentleman of distinguished family in Cordoba,
who was returning from the watering place of San Lucar.
The season was now over, and every train bore the visitors back
to their winter homes. It can hardly be said that such places
are resorted to by Andalusians for the benefit of their health.
In this climate our long catalogue of slow diseases is scarcely
known. Consumptions, rheumatisms, dyspepsias, rebellious
livers, have no place, and even wounds (as I have said) heal
with proverbial facility in the valley of the Guadalquivir, which
is fortunate where the knife is so frequently called into action.
Its inhabitants enjoy robust, vigorous health until envious

Atropos grasps her scissors, when some violent inflammatory affection puts an end to their existence in the space of a week. Humboldt mentions some country in South America where the population is long lived,—no one ever really sick, yet no one ever really well. Such is not the case in Andalusia. Health, both physical and mental, is the normal state, and the longevity of its population, particularly in favored localities, has been proverbial. The climate, too, of every portion of it, except about the mouths of the rivers, is endurable throughout the year. The fashion, however, of spending July and August at some bathing place is coming into vogue, and it is possible that in a few years they will imitate the remainder of mankind in restlessness. The famous Merino sheep (*trashumantes*) set an example to Europe in this respect. As soon as the warm season commences they manifest an uneasiness, and will sometimes wander away of their own accord, and the excellence of their wool is the best evidence of the wisdom of these summer peregrinations. My companion was full of the pleasant incidents of the summer. We soon passed by a herd of bulls growing up for some future contest. This changed the subject. I have said before that you are invariably asked your opinion about bull fights. I gave mine to the effect already stated. He was willing to compromise with my horror of the horse killing, which I pronounced unnecessary cruelty toward a noble animal that, blindfolded in the arena, was alike unable to defend itself or to escape. To this he could make no satisfactory reply, and was driven to excuse it upon the usual ground that the horses were very old, and already worn out. But I have already given the pros and cons of the argument, and refrain from repetition of them. He himself had at times appeared in the ring on some special occasions, when only gentlemen amateurs participate, it being quite the fashion among the young gentry to patronize bull fighters and bull fights as the true national pastime. Finding that I had a taste for the amusement highly creditable to an outside barbarian, he gave me several wrinkles on the subject, which I carefully treasured up.

We passed leisurely up the valley, halting a considerable time at the different stations, Palma, with its lofty church, Lora, Peñaflor, looking gracefully down upon the old Moorish mills in the river, the castled crag of Almodovar to Cordoba, where I parted from him, placing our houses mutually at each other's disposal, a very cheap proceeding on my part. I was unfortunately out next day when he called, so that our acquaintance ended with this Spanish courtesy.

The Patio of the Fonda was crowded when I arrived. A sturdy old Asturian, who served me at table, expressed great contempt for the cause of the assemblage. Some person of the neighborhood of no great repute, as he said, had been appointed to a high post under the government, and was on his way to Madrid to enter upon the discharge of his duties. His friends had met to see the rising sun mount the heavens, and perhaps to bask a little in its invigorating rays. In Asturia he was sure they would not bow down before any man. Perhaps not; but then Asturia must be different from the rest of the world. I fear his patriotism overcame the impartiality of his judgment. The administrador had at least one redeeming thing about him—a very graceful daughter—and that made amends for a great many of his sins. The party soon took their leave in the Madrid diligence, and we were left to our slumbers. Mine were not very pleasant, as they were interrupted continually during the night by the entry of what seemed to be an army of cats, who chaunted every species of music, from the dulcet notes of the solitary serenader to discordant squalls that would have been no discredit to the most ancient married couple in Christendom. The contents of the wash basin had great effect in restoring harmony so long as the ammunition lasted; shoes were then called into requisition, but the enemy appeared to have a particular fancy for this skirmishing, and finally ended the contest by posting a couple of sentinels on the window sill, while the main body took up position on the little roof below. At daylight I was glad to leave the field to them and start off on a walk around the city.

Cordova has been a city of note from the earliest historic times. Strabo points out it and Cadiz as especially worthy of remark, the principal inhabitants of the surrounding country being attracted to it on account of the charms of its situation. A colony of patricians from Rome gave it reputation in the social world, and developed its literary genius to an extent that astonished even the Mistress of the Empire. Under the Gothic dominion it was, distinguished only in ecclesiastical annals, though Almakari enumerates it among the four resi-

dences of their kings. But Punic, Roman and Gothic Cordova
are known only through history. For the traveller it dates
from the time of the Beni Omeyah, who made it their sole
capital, and the great centre whence learning and civilization
were diffused over Western Europe. Abd-er-Rahman, the first
of the name, after a thousand hair-breadth escapes by flood and
field, having been invited by a portion of the Andalusian Arabs
to assume the caliphate in Spain—and thus relieve them from
the satraps of Damascus and the anarchy under which they
had suffered for half a century—landed in the year 756 at
Almuñecar on the coast of Granada, and, after many long years
of civil war, succeeded in crushing all opponents and firmly
establishing himself in Andalusia. The horrible manner in
which his family, with this solitary exception, were extinguished by Asseffah, has secured for them a larger portion of
historic sympathy than they could perhaps justly claim; and it
may be safely said that no one would have thought them
worthy of continuing to reign had not this, their last hope,
caused the power, which had set in the east, to rise so glo-
riously again in the west, and thus redeemed the honor of his
family. I know no other royal family which produced so
many estimable individuals, or which has displayed such indis-
putable talents for governing, as the Beni Omeyah of Spain.
Three of them of the same name—Abd-er-Rahman—were endowed with nearly every virtue one could desire in a sovereign.
Courage and skill in war, sincere religion, patriotism and a
refined taste for the elegant arts and for literature, have placed
them in the front rank of princes. To them should be added
Al Mansour, who may properly be considered of the dynasty,
though not descended from them by blood. Under the wise
rule of these sovereigns, Andalusia became the first country in
the civilized world. Mohammedan historians and travellers
found their copious language scarcely adequate to the description of its marvels. The banks of the Guadalquivir were
lined with stately palaces a distance of four and twenty miles,
and the wanderer from Bagdad could saunter along ten miles
of artificial lights, at a time when Paris and London were miserable collections of hovels and miry lanes. Learned doctors
and elegant poets crowded to it from every quarter of the east.
Its schools of philosophy and medicine attracted students from
all Christian Europe, who, returning, introduced a taste for the

long forgotten literature of the Greeks, and for the teaching of
the great master who so long held Europe in bondage. The
mild but firm government of the Beni Omeyah secured tranquility at home and respect abroad. Three hundred thousand
respectable residences and eighty thousand shops in Cordova
alone attested the excellence of a government which could
attract and maintain such a population. Nor were these material benefits the only jewels of their diadem. Justice and
religious tolerance supported their throne, and rendered their
rule more tolerable to the subject Christian population than the
persecutions of their own brethren of the faith in other lands.
It is a striking testimony to their wisdom, that the Mohammedan rulers were seldom, if ever, disturbed by insurrection
among the subject Christians at home. All, of whatever religion, enjoyed a certain limited amount of freedom, faithfully
secured, and persecution for opinion's sake was almost unknown. The followers of the Prophet, with a profound insight
into the philosophy of mankind, distinguished those who
thought this world the be-all and end-all of humanity, and
the earth sufficient unto itself, from those who, clinging to
a higher, nobler being to rescue them from the abasement of
materialism, rested their faith upon a divine revelation—the
Christian, Jews and Magians. For the former was death, for
the latter peace and protection, upon condition of tribute.
Hermits and others of holy life were sincerely respected, as
performing the precepts of the Mohammedan religion, although
devoid of the true faith. We are all familiar with the Palace
of Chosroes and the windmill of Potsdam, but though these
instances of self-restraint on the part of great sovereigns are
in the highest degree creditable, they do not equal a somewhat similar one related of Abd-er-Rahman I. After the conquest of Cordova by the Mohammedans, the principal church
had been divided in two portions, one for the Mohammedan
faith, the other for the Christians. This arrangement continued to be satisfactory until Cordoba became the capital, and
the increased number of the faithful required an enlargement
of the mosque. For a long time the Christians obstinately
refused to sell their portion, and the negotiation was about to
be broken off, when they finally agreed to accept the enormous
sum of one hundred thousand dinars and the privilege of erecting a new church entirely dedicated to their own worship.

This last condition was particularly difficult to grant, as the Mohammedan policy was to allow existing churches to remain, but on no account to permit the erection of others. The Christians, however, were inexorable, and carried their point. The whole church was pulled down, and upon its foundation erected the magnificent Mosque which is still the wonder of Moorish Spain. When we reflect that this occurred not a century after the conquest, and that the question was one of religion between opposing creeds, the justice and self control of the Cordovan Emir will appear in a brighter light than his better known rivals, Frederic and Chosroes. Such instances of respect for private rights were frequent at Cordoba. At a subsequent date the Hagib Al Mansour, wishing to enlarge the mosque, summoned the owners of the adjoining houses to place what value they pleased upon their property and yield it to the public, which they all did with the exception of one old woman who refused positively, unless another house were procured for her with a palm tree exactly like the one in her yard. After much difficulty, a house and palm tree, answering the description, were purchased at an exorbitant price, and the good woman's torn down.

The government established by the Mohammedans in Spain was purely military, for they seem to have had no disposition to propagate their faith or to punish dissenters. The tax upon infidels amounted generally to a fifth. They were not allowed to prevent persons changing their faith, and were confined in the celebration of their observances to the interior of their churches; otherwise they lived without apprehension of interference and in full enjoyment of their property. Mohammedans have a profound horror of the worship of images, yet the sanctity of the Christian churches was never violated therefor. They contented themselves with being the political and military aristocracy, leaving commerce and agriculture open to a fair competition, and allowing each nation to be judged by its own laws and officers. Whatever relics of slavery might have survived the fall of the empire, or been introduced by the Goths, disappeared. It was, thenceforth, confined to captives in war. Conversion to the faith worked of itself a manumission, and as slavery was confined to domestic servitude, the freedman frequently attained the highest position in the confidence of his former master. It is no wonder, therefore, that the subject Christians of the common class were contented with a lot far better than they would have enjoyed in any Christian country of Europe.

Abd-er-Rahman I, the Enterer, as he is called, was of a melancholy temperament, and in this respect his history has always recalled to me Charles V and Sertorius, whom he resembled in artistic and literary taste, as well as in deep poetic feeling and high talent as a ruler. Plutarch mentions that when Sertorius was on the point of recommencing the struggle in Spain, he encountered, at the mouth of the Guadalquivir, some mariners just returning from the Fortunate Isles, with glowing accounts of the peaceful delights of that favored spot, far removed from the clash of resounding arms, and the vain struggles and toils of earthly greatness; and that the hero long hesitated whether he should not forswear the world and its deceitful pleasures for happy obscurity in the Atlantic waste. So it is narrated of Abd-er-Rahman, that once in Seville, or, as others say, in his garden, Rissafah, near Cordova, the sight of a solitary palm, like himself a stranger, caused him to utter a pathetic lament, which passed from mouth to mouth throughout Andalusia, and has reached our day. The most exalted genius, such as that of Napoleon or Cæsar, however much it may arouse our admiration, can never attract us as does the sensibility of the heart, which, suddenly overpowering the great man, renders him once more to the purity and innocence and even the weakness of childhood. All can esteem and covet earthly distinctions, and the feeblest are willing to struggle for their possession, but the truly great alone can appreciate them at their real value, and voluntarily renounce their phantom delights. It is fortunate for mankind that many can admire, though few may imitate, the great Emperor Charles in exchanging the crown of the world and the adoring incense of millions, for the quiet of a secluded convent in the mountains of Estremadura.

Meditating upon the character of the Arabian Emir, I reached the great mosque whose foundation he had laid. Its outside gives the traveller no warning of the beauties within. It presents simply a blank castellated wall, some forty feet in height, with scarcely any ornamentation. But entering the *Patio de los Naranjos*, or Orange Court, you are immediately translated to the East. Fountains and orange trees, with scattering palms; a solitary water carrier filling his cask; a couple of priests promenading in front of the edifice; a few closely enveloped females, hurrying to early mass, might make you stop to reflect whether it be not really Damascus or Jerusalem, rather than Christian Andalusia. The nineteen entrances that formerly adorned the front of the mosque are closed, except one, by which you enter into a fairy scene of the days of Haroun al Rashid. On every side extends a forest of columns, faintly illuminated by the early light struggling in. The deep silence which reigns around; the long vistas with graceful arches; the apparent solitude of the place, recalled the pine forest at sunset. To describe such a structure is difficult, as I have always found to be the case in the architecture of the Moors. It is not intended to effect one grand distinct impression, as that of the ancient Greek or the Gothic, but the aim of the artist seems rather to produce the confusion, the bewilderment of perception which causes the soul to sink into a dreamy forgetfulness of all that lies without the enchanted walls, and is accomplished partly by a minuteness of detail which defies investigation. Having seen it once before and retained a very vivid impression of it in my memory, I concluded that a guide would be unnecessary, but I soon became convinced that the effect was of the indistinct character I have mentioned, and even now, after having again gone over it carefully with a guide, I am convinced that I should not be able to draw a reasonably correct plan. It is an involuntary tribute to the success of the artist. Even in its present condition the mosque is an object of unfeigned admiration to the world. What must it have been in its glory? The accounts differ as to the number of columns; some place it as high as fourteen hundred. Nineteen longitudinal and eight and thirty lateral aisles were resplendent with ten thousand lamps and more than two hundred chandeliers of exquisite workmanship. Wax and oil lights alternated with varying effect. Golden doors contrasted with a pavement of marble, mosaic, and even silver. Every successive sovereign sought his highest glory in adding to its magnificence; but it was reserved for the famous Hagib Al Mansour to perform the work most acceptable to the worshippers of the Prophet. Returning from the celebrated expedition in which he had ravaged the uttermost parts of the Peninsula, and reduced the rising kingdoms of Leon and Navarre to the verge of annihilation, he caused the bells of the church of St. Jago de Compostella to be transported upon the backs of his captives to Cordova, and there hung up to the glory of the One God, and to the confusion of all Trinitarians. Vast throngs of Christians had been brought to work in the contemplated enlargement of the mosque, a spectacle peculiarly edifying to the true believers, and meritorious on the part of their general. It is a remarkable feature in the edifice that most of the columns are taken from ancient ruins, and placed without the slightest regard to the order of architecture to which they originally belonged; but this anomaly has no influence upon the general effect of the mosque, and would escape the notice of a casual visitor.

The Christian choir, or rather church, built in the centre of the Mezquita, after the conquest, has been universally condemned, and does sadly mar the integrity and uniformity of the Moorish plan. In itself it is very beautiful, but emphatically the right thing in the wrong place. The Ayuntamiento, or city council, is said to have protested against the right of the chapter to make the alteration, and to have appealed to the Emperor Charles, who, misapprehending the circumstances, declined interfering, and the sacrilege was effected. The Mohammedan mosque architecture is essentially defective in the absence of some one central point of artistic interest, the Kiblah answering that purpose indifferently. But this though, in reality, a defect, is an essential part of the idea, and the entire scheme would be falsified, were the baffled spirit of the beholder to find a resting place. Nothing, therefore, could be more unfortunate and inharmonious than this addition. The early Spanish reconquerors were not animated by the rage for change and improvement which seems to have come over their descendants, under the influence of the renaissance. It must be said, too, that so long as the Moors retained a footing in the country they were respected and their works preserved and imitated, but so soon as the last stronghold surrendered, they fell into contempt, were styled Moriscos, and any show of appreciation for the evidences of their past power and genius subjected the unfortunate person to the suspicion of the merciless Inquisition. Though this prejudice has disappeared from the enlightened classes, it still lingers among the ignorant. But the government has become alive to the necessity of preserving what yet remains. The gem of the whole Mezquita is the little octagon Chapel del Zancarron, formerly the sanctuary where was deposited the Koran, which is perfection itself, and has undergone little or no alteration. The scenes around had completely carried me back to the days of the turban and the lance; nothing could be further from my thought than religion in any shape, and I had even forgotten that we were in a church, when, descending the steps of the chapel, I saw a young lady stop and kneel at one of the side altars. She was dressed in the Andalusian costume, and her face a perfect type of Andalusian beauty. Crossing her hands, she gazed upon the altar piece with uplifted eyes, that beamed forth a devotion, unconscious of all around. How I envied her that period of prayer. What earthly delight could compare with the ecstatic purity of this communion in spirit with her Creator; and happy the soul in purgatory for whom it was offered. I remained in my place until her devotions were concluded, and she, with the duenna, had disappeared from sight amid the thousand columns. She had not even seen me, but Andalusian beauty has the effect of some tropical diseases—one severe attack undermines the constitution, rendering it incapable of resisting the slightest exposure, and a long absence in the chilly atmosphere of the north becomes absolutely necessary to restore the system to its previous insensibility.

Leaving the body of the mosque, I crossed the Orange Court, and ascended the lofty tower built somewhat after the style of the Giralda at Seville, but by no means so elegant. The general features of the view I have given already. To the west, rose abruptly the advanced ridge of the Sierra Morena, its many farm houses, villas and deserted hermitages, sparkling in the morning sun; to the east, the undulating table land, which stretched away to the Genil; between them flows the shining Guadalquivir, with its broad and fertile valley. The white castle of Almodovar stood like a sentry to guard the passage to Seville. Well might Strabo speak of the charms of the situation. The accounts of the Moorish historians, corroborated by the reports of the ambassadors, who were sent thither from time to time by the Christian potentates, leave no room for doubting that this now comparatively deserted plain was once covered with every evidence of an unexampled material and intellectual civilization, of which scarcely

19

a trace is left. What, however, surprises most is the total disappearance of the former city of Azzahira. Under the sixth Sultan of the Beni Omeyah, Abd-er-Rahman II, the Cordovese empire attained its acme of splendor. The numerous victories of this sultan procured for him the title of Annasir Ledin Allah, or Defender of the Faith, and he first assumed the title of Emir Al Mumenin, or Prince of the Faithful, which none of his predecessors had ventured to do, contenting themselves with the earthly power, and leaving the caliphate, or lieutenancy of God, to their rivals on the bank of the Tigris. A successful reign of fifty years largely increased his dominion and filled his coffers with enormous treasures. A considerable portion of Africa acknowledged his sway. His yearly revenues amounted to five million four hundred and eighty thousand gold dinars, from the taxes authorized by the Koran and the Sunnah; seven hundred and sixty-five thousand from the tax on markets and other illegal exactions; then came one-fifth of the spoil taken from the enemy, and, in addition to the whole, was the capitation tax upon Christians and Jews, which equalled all the rest. With this immense amount at his disposal he was enabled to gratify his hereditary taste for building. Among the various structures erected by him, the most celebrated was the palace of Azzahra, whose very site can no longer be pointed out. That it lay between Cordova and the mountains, at the foot of a lofty eminence, is all we know. It is said to have owed its origin to his desire to gratify the favorite sultana of that name, which, in the Arabic tongue, signifies "flower," and is still preserved in Spanish for the bloom of the orange tree. Authors vied in their descriptions of its marvellous beauty; and perhaps the most conclusive evidence of its supereminence is the fact that they dwell little upon the charms of the Alhambra, which yet is the wonder and admiration of our day. Ten thousand workmen and fifteen hundred camels were daily employed in its erection. Four thousand three hundred and sixteen columns of green and rose colored marble supported its roof; some from Rome; some from the country of the Franks; some presented by the Emperor of Constantinople; some from Africa, and the rest from Andalusia. Two exquisite fountains, the one of gilt bronze, the other of green marble, astonished the beholder. In the centre of the larger of the two floated a golden swan, made in Constantinople, above which hung suspended the famous pearl presented by the Emperor Leo. But the wonder of all was the Hall of the Caliphs, whose roof was of solid gold and silver, and whose doors of ivory and ebony, ornamented with precious stones, rested upon pillars of transparent crystal. In the centre was a huge basin, filled with quicksilver, the light from whose surface when in motion was sufficient to blind the incautious. It was here that he received the ambassadors of the various Christian princes who sought his alliance or his mediation. Nor was the mosque unworthy of the rest of the palace; though inferior in size to that of Cordova, it was considered even more beautiful. The grounds, including the neighboring mountain, were covered with every species of fruit and flower that could gratify the eye or please the palate; and if nothing had remained but the terrace of black marble, travellers would have had no reason to depart unsatisfied. Men of all ranks, professions and religions, came from afar to behold this wonder of the earth. It was the Versailles of its day. In the latter portion of his life, Abd-er-Rahman resided here exclusively, and the court and the famous body-guard of twelve thousand slaves, Zenetes and Andalusians, found ample room for their accommodation. Yet, the possessor of all this, in melancholy acknowledgment of the truth that "all is vanity," wrote, in the secrecy of his cabinet, for those who might read after his death: "I have reigned fifty years, and my reign has always been peaceful or victorious. Loved by my subjects, feared by my enemies, respected by my allies and by the greatest princes of the earth, riches and honor, power and pleasure, all were at my command. No earthly blessing was denied me. I have carefully counted the days in which I have enjoyed unalloyed happiness. I have found but fourteen." Gibbon had the bad taste to institute a comparison between himself and the sovereign of Spain, and to proclaim to the gratified world that he had enjoyed more than fourteen such in the composition of his history alone. Alas! how few there are who comprehend grandeur of the soul! With more dignity does Almakari exclaim: "Oh, man of understanding! wonder and behold the small portion of real happiness the world affords even in the most enviable position. The Caliph Annasir, whose prosperity in mundane affairs, and whose widely spread empire became proverbial, had only fourteen days of undisturbed enjoyment during a reign of fifty years, seven months, and three days. Praise be given to Him, the Lord of eternal glory and everlasting empire! There is no God but one! the Almighty, the Giver of empire to whomsoever He pleases!"

His son and successor, Alhakem, sustained the glory of the empire undiminished. During his reign, the Northmen or Normans, now in the height of their power (A. D. 965), landed in the Peninsula. The caliph hastened to the Court, ordering his admiral to fit out the fleet; but it was unnecessary, as the invaders were defeated and repulsed at every point. This was the second attempt of the kind that had been made, and the result is the best evidence of the comparative power of the Cordovese empire. Alhakem excelled all his predecessors in his taste for learning. He had standing agencies throughout the world to procure for him rare and valuable books, regardless of cost. The palace library contained such an immense collection, that the catalogue itself occupied forty-four volumes. Besides that, he himself wrote a voluminous history of Andalusia, which was highly praised for a merit very rare among Arabic historians,—sound criticism,—so that whatever he related was considered true. Unlike most literary rulers, his passion for literature and science involved no neglect of the more serious duties of statesmanship, and Spain was never so happy as under the government of the just and enlightened Alhakem.

His successor, Hisham, was a true *roi fainéant*, but beside him stood one of the most remarkable men that Islam has produced, Mohammed ibn Abi Amir, surnamed Al Mansour, the real caliph, who was yet content with a position corresponding to that of the mayors of the palace in France. As the hero of fifty successful campaigns, he probably displayed as much military talent as was to be witnessed in Europe until the rise of modern warfare. Nor was it simply in the field that he was great, but in every department of military organization and foresight, for to him might apply what was said by an Andalusian poet of another: " The general, in the morning of battle, awakens thousands, after which he himself goes to sleep." Like all great leaders, he knew how to mingle justice with discipline, so that he was alike loved and feared by his troops. A striking anecdote is related of his severity of discipline. In reviewing the cavalry, a strict silence was imperatively commanded, and even the horses, as it is said, were taught to refrain from neighing. On a certain occasion of this sort, seeing something glitter in the ranks, he was informed, upon inquiry, that it was the sabre of one of the soldiers. In vain did the culprit protest that the scabbard had slipped off while he was pointing to a comrade. Al Mansour would admit no excuse for a disobedience of orders. The offender's head was struck off, and paraded in front of the line on a pole. Doubtless such severity was necessary to retain his collection of Christian slaves and Berbers, whom he first composed into a standing army in place of the militia upon which Mohammedan powers generally relied. When Al Mansour had become rich, he determined to build the city of Azzahira, partly as a palace, partly as a fortress in which to guard his treasures. It was situated to the east of Cordova, and pronounced by historians second only to the palace of Azzahra. It, too, has left no trace behind. He is said to have transcribed the Koran with his own hand; and, in order to be buried in the full odor of sanctity, was in the habit, during his campaigns against the infidel Christians, of causing his garments to be shaken at every halt, and the dust collected into a bag. His winding sheet, spun and woven by his daughters from flax that had been grown upon the little paternal inheritance, formed always a part of his baggage. He was buried at Medina Celi on his return from his last campaign, and with him may be said to have perished the dominion of the Beni Omeyah. The ten preceding sovereigns of this line had reigned an average of twenty-six years, nor had the throne been once acquired by violence. In the next twenty-four it was destined to change hands fifteen times. Cordova, alternately a prey to rival factions, was ruined. Sacked by the fanatical Berbers, scarce one stone was left upon another. The famous palaces of Azzahra and Azzahira disappeared from the face of the earth. "The necklace was broken, and its costly pearls scattered," to be picked up in succession by the Almoravides and the Almohades. At length the fated instrument of Providence appeared in the person of St. Ferdinand. It had been thought that the ancient capital of the Beni Omeyah could offer a sufficient resistance; "but who can escape the fate which is engraved upon the tables of adamant by the hand of eternal Providence?" A few short days of siege, and a special bull from Rome announced to the Christian world that Cordova, the ancient, the renowned, the wealthy Cordova, the home of Osius and Eulogio, had been rescued from Paynim hands. Nor were the misfortunes of Islam doomed to cease here. Seville, too, after an obstinate resistance, fell before the conquering swords of St. Jago and St. Ferdinand. Four hundred thousand preferred exile rather than submission to the conqueror, and the roads to Granada and Malaga were worn away by the hurrying tread of fugitives. And now were the hearts of the faithful throughout Andalusia filled with grief and terror. Yea, into the farthest corners of the east, were the dreadful tidings borne. "Oh man! suffer not thyself to be led astray by the charms of this life."

"A frightful, an irremediable blow has fallen upon Spain; its sound has penetrated even to Arabia, and Mount Ohod and Mount Thalon are shaken with the echo thereof. Her provinces and her cities are converted into deserts. Ask now at Valencia where thou shalt seek Murcia? where Xativa? where Iaen?

"Where wilt thou find Cordova, the home of the intellectual? Where are all the learned who once sparkled on her bosom? Where are Seville and her exquisite environs? Where her river with waters so pure, so abundant, so delightful? As the lover weeps the absence of his beloved, so does afflicted Islam weep.

"Thou art content and free from care; thy country still hath pleasures for thee; but can any one have a country after the loss of Seville?

"Oh ye, who mount the bounding courser, who on the fields where the sword delights its fury, fly with eagle's speed!

"Oh ye, whose hands are armed with the gloved steel of India, who, in the dark whirlwinds of dust, glitter as the fire!

"Oh ye, who beyond the sea pass tranquil and pleasant days, who enjoy power and glory at home!

"Have ye not heard of the inhabitants of Spain? And yet messengers have gone to inform you of their sufferings!

"Those are covered with shame who so lately were flourishing and glorious.

"Yesterday they were kings at home, now they are slaves in the country of the infidel!

"Ah! couldst thou have seen their tears flow on the day when they were sold!

"Merciful God! must a mountain be placed between the mother and her children? Must the soul be separated from the body?

"And these young maidens, beautiful as the sun when, at his rising, he sows the earth with coral and rubies.

"Oh horror! the barbarian drags them away to humiliation; their eyes are bathed in tears, and their senses desert them, drowned in misery."

And now, in place of the elegant Moor, comes the heavy tramp of the steel-clad Christian, strong in chivalrous devotion to his faith, and in the assurance of victory. The Guzmans, the Ponces de Leon, the Toledos, the Cordovas press through her tottering gates on their march to cast the infidel dog from the sacred soil of Spain. Another religion and another civilization succeed. The defilements of the past are swept rudely away. Christianity resumes her ancient seat upon the banks of the Guadalquivir. But, in the meantime, rival cities have risen to eminence, and the glory of Cordova is gone. Every thing, even the names of the streets, remind one of the day when the Great Captain filled the wide world with the echo of his name. Yet nought tangible, except the venerable mosque, remains to attest the greatness of her who once sat upon the throne of civilization. The inhabitants have one hereditary boast left, of which they are disposed to avail themselves—the purity of their descent, and the blue blood of Cordova has passed into an adage even in our own tongue. The city certainly has been favored in a remarkable degree as the birth-place of eminent genius and talent, whether Roman, Goth, Mohammedan or Spanish. When the literary athletes of the Augustan age, having finished their course, laid down the lamp of learning, it was taken up by the children of the west. Cordova contributed the Senecas, Gallio and Lucan to a circle which included also Quintilian, Silius Italicus, Florus and Martial. The flame no longer burnt so brightly as when fed by Virgil and Horace, but its light has penetrated far into the future. The new religion subsequently sought here its firmest supporters. The erudition of Averroes and his countrymen cast a halo around the crescent, and the historians of Spanish literature make honorable mention of their successors.

But of all the distinguished men to whom Cordova gave birth, no one was more remarkable, or exercised a greater influence upon his age, than the famous Osius, its bishop in the third and fourth centuries of Christianity; and Spain has the more reason to boast of this worthy because his character presented many of the strong traits which have distinguished Spaniards at all times. As was fitly remarked, he seems to have been born a man without going through the preliminary feebleness of childhood, for scarcely had he attained legal maturity when his fame began to extend itself, not only in the Peninsula, but throughout the Empire. In youth he had the good fortune to bear witness to the faith under one of the last persecutions of expiring Paganism. At thirty-eight he was elevated to the bishopric of his native city, and from that time forth no movement could be inaugurated, no council held, no creed adopted, without the aid of the Cordovese saint. In the great contest against the Arian heresy, he was an acknowledged leader, and was called to preside over the assembled wisdom and piety of the world at the great Council of Nice, whose declaration of faith in its essential parts is attributed to him. Subsequently an Emperor of the Arian belief having ascended the throne of Constantinople, his enemies clamored loudly for his destruction. "True," said they to the monarch, "We have cast the Roman Pontiff from his seat, and have banished many bishops; true, we have filled the world with terror, but all this is nothing, so long as Osius exists. If he remains in his bishopric, it seems as though nothing had been accomplished, for his word alone is capable of turning the whole world against us."

He was ordered to conform to what was now the established faith. So far from complying, the unconquerable prelate replied to the Emperor in a letter worthy of being preserved through all time. Among the unwelcome truths which he dared proclaim to the imperial ear, was one that would sound strange from a Bishop of Cordova at the present day : " God has given to you the empire, to us the church, and as he who interferes with your government of worldly things, contravenes the Divine ordinance; so beware thou likewise of pretending to judge of sacred matters. Render unto Cæsar the things that are Cæsar's, and unto God the things that are God's. It is not given to us to have power upon earth, neither canst thou, who art Emperor, enjoy authority in affairs of religion." It was, however, of no avail, and the intrepid Osius, bowed down beneath the infirmities of a century, was banished to a rude

city in the inhospitable centre of Europe. Death anticipated
the triumph of his enemies, and at the extreme age of one hundred and one years he received the reward of the faithful.

"It would be superfluous in me," says St. Athanasius, "to
eulogize this illustrious chief of the martyrs, for the whole
world knows what he has suffered for the faith. What council
has been held over which he did not preside? What assembly
of Bishops ever listened to the eloquence of his reasons without being convinced? What church cannot remember, having
at some time been assisted or defended by him? What suffering spirit ever addressed him without receiving consolation?"
In the immense physical and mental vigor, the unconquerable
tenacity of purpose and the enduring courage of Osius, we
seem to have before us the ideal of Spanish character.

But this old Moorish tower has seduced me into a long
digression, owing, perhaps, to the fact that there is little to
delight the eye; for at the present season the fields around are
bare, and the beauty of the prospect thereby greatly impaired.
To be seen in its glory, one should ascend the Sierra Morena,
to the Convent of San Geronimo, some winter or spring evening, and then even the most indifferent will appreciate the
"amenitas loci." Descending from the town, I wandered to
the market, through the street of Gondomar, whose name is so
familiar to the reader of English history. Among the edibles
exposed for sale, were pine burrs and acorns; not our pine
burrs nor our acorns, which would puzzle the digestion of a
Spanish muleteer, or even the quondam cook at the Table
Mountain, but the fruit of the stone pine and of the sweet oak,
called *bellota*. The former resembles the almond, and the latter,
when roasted, is very passable. The bellota is supposed to be
the secret of the superior excellence of Andalusian and Estre-
maduran pork cutlets, with which every traveller is or should
be familiar, as it is in Spain a sort of shibboleth, and proves
the consumer to be neither Jew nor Turk. It was formerly
supposed that the fish, in passing from the Atlantic to the
Mediterranean, fed upon them also, and hence derived their
delicate flavor. After leaving the market, an hour more was
consumed in strolling about the narrow, hilly streets. · Cordova
presents by no means the beautiful appearance of Seville. The
outsides of the houses are seldom attractive; but there are
great people at Cordova, and very attractive ones,—at least

when away from home, as I have never remained there long
enough to form an opinion of the society by actual experience.
I asked a person at the hotel if there were many respectable
inhabitants. " Si, Si, Señor! hay Condes y Duques, y algunos
que valen mas aunque no tengan titulos, porque son ricos."
(There are Counts and Dukes, and others, who are of more
importance still, although they have no titles, because they are
rich.) This is the cry throughout Europe. The almighty
dollar !

I very naturally, in Cordova, cast my eyes about to find a
horse of the famous breed for which it was so celebrated. Not
one did I see above mediocrity. Nothing has so completely
gone to ruin as the stud, that formerly supplied Europe with
such noble steeds. The valley of the Guadalquivir seemed to be
peculiarly favored in this respect. The best were said to come
from the *loma* of Ubeda, above Menjibar, but more care was
taken with the royal Hara at Cordova, and that belonging to
the Carthusians, near Xeres. The genealogy of everyone was
inscribed in a book, and copied over his stall, with a care that
must have been inherited from the Arabs. There are one or
two great fairs still held annually, particularly at Mairena, near
Seville, and the Government has turned its serious attention to
the subject, but as yet without marked success. The real
Andalusian, when you can find one, is a charming animal,
strongly built, broad chested and browd, with long black mane
and tail sweeping the ground, and moving with a springy,
haughty grace, as if conscious of his superiority. With all their
fire, they are exceedingly docile and capable of warm attachment. It may be a fancy, but they seemed to be of a higher
order of creature than the regular race horse, whose intelligence has more of the instinct and less of the human. While
first in Seville I had one—whom I christened with the Moorish
name of Zaide—quite as intelligent as a dog, without any
special effort on my part to train him. The ancients fabled
the Spanish horses to have been begotten by the west wind,
but I should not judge, from their appearance, that they were
capable of great speed. They seemed to me rather intended
for war steeds and chargers of noble caballeros, than mere
coursers or draught beasts. The Spanish method of bitting and
training is not at all to my taste, and fails entirely in developing the powers and beauty of the animal. The decline of the

breed may be attributed partly to the rapidly increasing demand
for mules, and more still to the War of Independence, which
broke up all the old establishments. It will require great skill
and some expense to restore it.

As it was now growing hot, and I had seen all that was
curious, even to the *soi disant* palm trees of the caliph's garden,
I returned to the hotel, and, in company with a Swede, sat
down to breakfast. During this meal we enjoyed the pleasure
of having the mirror held up to nature by a gathering of
school boys who had stopped at the window on their way for
the purpose of inspecting any outside barbarians that might be
visible, and who were kind enough to give us, without charge,
the full benefit of their criticism. A breathless silence prevailed
as we took our seats, broken by occasional exclamations of
"*Mira! Mira!*" (look!) as either of us would make a movement. Having been on my legs nearly five hours, I felt somewhat tired and, forgetful of the principles of teetotal abstinence,
my first movement had been to drink off a bumper of Montilla.
This produced a general exclamation among the audience of
"*Mira! que va á emborracharse!*" (Look! he is going to get
drunk!) Presently the omelette was brought. "*Ahora empieza
la tortilla*" (now it is the omelette's turn), they exclaim,
delighted at the prospect of close action. From this their
remarks extended themselves to our personal appearance,
winding up with "*qué bigotes!*" (what mustachios!) Now, surrounded as we were by the relics of Mohammedan civilization,
an insult to one's beard could not be borne. With one accord,
therefore, we clapped our hands, which is the semi-Oriental
signal used in Spain for the waiter. "*Llaman á Pedro*" (they
are calling Peter), whispered the boys. Peter came, and, like
an old soldier, seeing either from past experience or by the
higher quality of intuitive perception, what was the trouble,
dispersed the enemy by one gallant charge with the brush
handle, and closed the shutter. My companion, no great ad-
mirer of Spain, was indignant at such conduct, more particularly since his mustachios reached to his ears and nearly around
his head; I thought it rather amusing. Tranquility restored,
we ate our breakfast and drank our Montilla wine in peace,
and with infinite relish. Montilla is too strong for a regular
drink in Spain, but as a sort of agreeable semi-medicine, it
would be invaluable. The taste is delicious; not too sweet; of

much body; tonic without heating, and a stomachic of the first water. Having expressed a desire to drink some of the best once in my life, as we had none in America, the Asturian had brought me this bottle, which he thought would fulfil my utmost expectations, and he was right. I had often heard it praised as equal to the Amontillado, but what I had hitherto obtained must have been of a very inferior quality—not to be compared with this bottle.

The morning work over, we sat on the shady side of the Court, and listening to the murmuring of the fountain, and enjoying the soothing fumes of our cigars, bade defiance to the noonday heat.

CHAPTER XVI.

CORDOVA, BY MALAGA AND ALHAMA TO GRANADA.

Depart with Arrieros—Goats—Historic Towns—Lucena—Antequera—Peña de los Enamorados—View from the Sierra—Down the Valley to Malaga—Grapes—The City—Inhabitants—Alameda—English Party—Spanish Curiosity—Sea Bathing—View from the Water—Visitors from the Springs—Journey to Granada—Velez Malaga—Spanish Riding—Horsemanship—The Bull—I am Assassinated—Alhama—The Posada—The Fair—Fandango—Morning Scenery—Shepherd Dogs—The Sick Morisco—Hog Lottery—Approach to Granada.

Cordova being a thing of the past rather than the present, is not a town to arrest the mere traveller long, and having visited it once before thoroughly, a day was amply sufficient to revive my recollections. As luck would have it, an Arriero—un hombre de confianza—was returning to Malaga that day, and, by way of varying the style of conveyance, I concluded to take passage with him. A moderate unambitious looking horse was provided, and the son of the Arriero, a model of taciturnity for an Andalusian, was attached to my person as a special guide, in order to relieve me from the necessity of remaining always with the train. So, as the sun began to decline, we took our departure for Malaga, across the country, by a new route, at least to me. Crossing the famous Moorish bridge over the Guadalquivir, we followed for some distance the Seville road, ascending the hill that bounds the valley to the south-east. The view over the city is certainly very fine, finer even than that from the opposite elevation, because, from this side the Sierra Morena itself, with its groves and villas, forms a prominent object in the landscape. At its base extended the valley; its grayish fields relieved by occasional villages, conspicuous among them always the castle-rock of Almodovar. For some leagues the road was uninteresting, though we did pass from time to time most picturesque thatched tents, with a wild robber-looking family seeking shelter in them from the sun, while a donkey and a couple of pigs, those never failing evidences of the Spaniard's orthodoxy, sought to accomplish the same, and on the outside. The heat was indeed terrific, not to use a stronger expression. No debility, no perspiration, but you felt as if on the point of crisping up, and it required all the aid of handkerchiefs and umbrellas to keep from shrivelling to a mummy. Late in the afternoon we passed several herds of goats, which merit remark on account of their beauty. They were as tall as calves, of a reddish brown color, and resembled somewhat our deer in appearance. The ancient Iberians are said to have been fond of goats. The taste is justifiable if they had such as these. Even Esau might have found some excuse. The animal certainly ranks higher in Spain than in most other countries. The long summer and the want of suitable pasturage render cow's milk a rare luxury, and that of goat's is substituted in its place. The former is, moreover, considered bilious in this climate. Every morning, early, the herdsman may be seen driving his charge through the streets, stopping at the houses of his customers to deliver the article fresh from the teat. I found it quite agreeable to the taste, and then it is pure, for the operation of milking takes place before your eyes, and there is no opportunity of appealing to the town pump, even if that science had been imported into these unsophisticated regions. Sometimes the goats escape into the mountains, where, after a generation, they become perfectly wild, and are hunted as game.

This part of the country was for a long time the march of the Moorish frontier, and its towns have each a place in history. All that lay upon the route were well built for the purpose of sustaining an attack. Some of the noblest titles and proudest families rose into consequence by virtue of their valor displayed upon these fields. Aguila, Ferman Nuñez, Cabra, Montilla, are familiar to readers of Spanish history. The latter lies a mile or so to the left of the road, built upon the long tongue of land which extends from the table land into the valley. It seemed at a distance admirably calculated for a frontier station. This is the region of the famous wine of which I have spoken. The country between the Guadalquivir and the Genil, over which we were travelling is very broken. Every village was set upon a hill. And what is unusual in Europe, they were all full of children. Not a beggar appeared

on the route, owing, perhaps, to its being so seldom travelled.
As we had started late, the night was ever so far advanced
when we reached Lucena, and the latter part of the journey
was performed in the dark, so if the country presents any
beauties they were lost to me. The Posada being seldom visited by foreigners, was, in the primitive style, none the worse,
however, for that, as we at least were not imposed upon in the
cuisine; no boiled beef broiled up into steaks, but a real *olla*
and *huevos con jamon.* Opposite to the Posada was one of the
handsomest private residences I had seen in Andalusia, three
stories high, with a magnificent marble court and beautiful
fountains. It was just finished, and had been dedicated to
some saint in gratitude for a narrow escape on the part of the
owner from an impending accident. The landlady asked me if
we were so devout in America. I replied, that if we returned
such costly thanks in my country for every escape from peril,
we would be soon reduced to poverty. My statement was
received without incredulity, as on this side of the water our
daily food is supposed to consist of bowie knives and revolvers.
The next day's ride was as uninteresting as its predecessor, as
far as the Genil, whose crystal waters we crossed at Benamejí.
Thence the road led over a Sierra, unrolling pretty landscapes,
down to the city of Antequera, where dusty, hot and travel-
stained, we found a hearty welcome in a tidy inn, which proved
eminently satisfactory after a long, and I must confess, tiresome ride. Nature doubtless puts on a handsome garb, in
spring or autumn, though I cannot speak from experience, as
this was my only journey here. She certainly wore a very
sombre russet at the present time. A traveller in search of
the picturesque would do far better to pass by Ronda or Alcalá
la Real, either of which routes would satisfy his expectations.
Nor can I boast of having found anything of noteworthy.inter-
est in the city itself, unless it be that, peering about in the
stable to look after the cattle, I saw several little Roman columns with Ionic capitals, which had been pressed into service
from some ruins, probably by the Moors, for the building was
old enough to have dated from that period. The ancient
castle on the hill was visited, and offered a fine prospect at
sunset. This completes the list of sights, so far as my observation extended.

A companionable, middle aged Spaniard, with a long gun,

had been my companion hitherto, but he left at Antequera for his home, and I was to continue the journey the next day with the Arrieros only. We started from Antequera without waiting for the rest of the train, as early as might be, to avoid the heat, if that were possible. The road commenced immediately its steep ascent of the Sierra, which extends to Ronda, forming the mountain chain, to which even Gibraltar and perhaps Centa belong, and which separates the Mediterranean littoral from the high lands of the interior. The view over the journey we had performed began to develop itself rapidly. The fertile Vega surrounding the city, which had scarcely the appearance of a town of our century, was still in the shade of the eastern mountains. Beyond it, toward the valley of the Genil, extended the broken country of Andalusia, its brown, dusty hue of the season, somewhat relieved by the salt lake, a unique feature in the landscape. The road to Granada wound around the lofty Peña de los Enamorados, or Lovers' Leap, which, in solitary grandeur, commands the approach to Loja. The tradition tells that once there was a Christian slave in Granada of such excellent disposition and exemplary conduct as to win the heart of his master's family, including an only daughter But alas! what hope was there for the Moorish maiden save in flight? They embraced a fortunate opportunity, and another soul was about to be gathered into the fold of the holy church, when the raging father appeared in sight, followed by his armed retainers. Knowing the fate reserved for them—death, or what were worse than death itself, a separation in life—the despairing lovers refused to surrender themselves, and by dint of stones, drove back the assailing party. At length archers were brought, when, seeing no longer hope of escape, the faithful pair, locked in a dying embrace, fell crushed at the feet of the relentless parent. One grave received them, and the still unforgiving Moslem returned forlorn and heavy hearted to his cheerless home in Granada.

Antequera is a place of considerable importance, as it is situated at the embranchment of the roads from Malaga, Granada, Ronda and Osuna, and numerous are the trains of mules that tread its rocky streets. But it occupied a much more prominent place in the world when it was a great outpost of the Mohammedan kingdom in the east of Andalusia. How often has the watchman from its castle tower seen the fierce battle

between cross and crescent rage beneath these walls! But its
fate was sealed in 1410, when it fell before the conquering
sword of Fernando. No sooner had the Christian taken full
possession, than a fierce contest arose as to who had been the
first to scale its walls. Many were the claimants for this distinguished honor, and great the rivalry. After much delibera-
tion and examination of witnesses, the judge decided in favor
of Juan Biscaino, who had died the soldier's death in the tower
itself, and was now in the far off land beyond the tomb enjoying the crown of martyrdom that fadeth not.

After a couple of hours' steep ascent we reached the Pass of
Escaberuzala, and I reclined upon a little pinnacle, surrounded
by immense misshapen rocks, to enjoy the view. A cooling
breeze swept up from the sea. As it is only a few leagues to
the coast, the descent is rapid and frequently precipitous. The
pass was at the head, as it were, of a vast funnel; on each side
extended the spurs of the Sierra, bounding the valley, and
separating gradually until they sunk abruptly down at the
margin of the shore. The valley deserved the name, in so far
as it lay between two mountain ridges—but of smooth green
meadow slope there was nothing. All was arid, distorted,
wild in the extreme, but grand, and beautiful in its grandeur.
Beyond extended the Mediterranean, presenting the curious
perspective appearance which the sea always has when looked
down upon from a great height. Far, far away to the south
could be dimly seen the mountain coast of Africa and the
many peaks of Atlas struggling, as of yore, with the weight of
the heavens. Imitating Isabella, I with truth exclaimed, "Marbella! Marbella!" A few Cortijos sparkling below were the
only evidences of life. Several trains of burden mules passed
by, the Arrieros singing occasional snatches of old border
ballads; and once a large vulture flew circling around, otherwise a dead silence reigned, undisturbed even by the humming
of a beetle, and the iron landscape seemed frozen into eternal
immobility. I remained a half hour imbibing the poetry of the
situation, when the increasing heat recalled the long journey
ahead, and slaking our thrist at a cold and deliciously pure
fountain that burst from the rock, we commenced the descent.
For many a weary mile we wound among the parched hill
sides. Finally we entered the region of the grape, and thence,
even to the gates of Malaga, our path was bordered by vine-

20

yards, pendant with the most luxuriant fruit I ever beheld. Some were at least (I fear to say it) an inch and a half in length, and so luscious as to be absolutely cloying to the taste. The great wonder to me was whence the vines procured suffi- cient moisture even for their sustenance. Water there was none, nor had any rain fallen for five months, and the air was as dry as the earth. The streams were exhausted, and families had even established themselves under the little bridges, such is the unchanging nature of the climate during the summer months. Deserting the road, a considerable part of the journey was performed in the bed of the river, which, with the thatched huts for the vineyard keepers and for the sale of commodities, resembled a street. In the rainy season the beds are quickly filled, and every rivulet assumes gigantic proportions as it sweeps down the mountain side freighted with its load of stones and sand. The temperature of the coast of Malaga is higher than that of the valley of the Guadalquivir or even of Africa itself, for the Sierra wards off effectually the winds from the north, and it may be truly as well as poetically said, that summer reigns throughout the year. Enormous cactuses, laden with ripe fruit, were evidences of a tropical luxuriance. A brisk breeze blowing up the valley all day had rendered the temperature endurable, yet we were not sorry on ascending a hill crest to see the city of Malaga smiling in the midst of its gardens. Its environs gave proof of commercial prosperity in numerous villas; and some tall, smoking chimneys had made their appearance since my last visit. The approach to a com- mercial city is generally more enlivening than that to an inland capital. It seems as though the inhabitants of the former sought their pleasure in fleeing without the walls where their labor is done and their wealth amassed. In the latter, exactly the reverse happens, as wealth is brought and pleasure sought within. So that while the environs of the one are brilliant with the overflowing of superfluous wealth, the traveller fre- quently enters the other without preliminary warning of his approach to a great centre of refinement and luxury. The contrast in this respect between Malaga and Madrid is strik- ing. Crossing the dry bed of the Guadalmedina, or the river of the city, I was soon lodged in a hotel upon the Alameda, and bade adieu to my silent conductor.

Malaga is one of the most flourishing cities in Spain, notwithstanding the shoaling of the harbor by the detritus of the mountain torrents, which impose the necessity of constant dredging. It naturally has a monopoly of the export of raisins and the various Malaga wines, the demand for which is increasing every year. In the last ten years manufactures too have taken a considerable start, notwithstanding the efforts of their English friends to persuade them that their only calling is agriculture, and that they should leave every other source of national wealth to foreign countries. Malaga has also another merit with a traveller suffering from the Solano, which was in full blast; it has few paintings or other works of art, whether good or bad. The Cathedral is an immense structure, but detains you a very little while. The Alcazaba—the ancient Moorish castle—is a magnificent feature in the landscape, from the water, but it is scarcely worth the while to enter unless it be for the view. This completes the list, so that Malaga is to the sight-weary traveller a sort of holiday—a day of rest. At this season of the year, the great attraction was the grape market, which offered such treasures as are rarely seen elsewhere. The size of the fruit was in some instances surprising, almost as large as a small pear, and its juice sweet as distilled honey. In fact, rather too much so for my taste. It is said, perhaps with truth, that a preference for acids over sweets is characteristic of habits which have departed from nature, just as old drunkards dislike champagne. Certainly, Spaniards of both sexes preserve their natural taste in this respect, if a love of sweets be the criterion, and Andalusia must be the country of nature, for among all its productions there is scarcely one of an acid character. The grape vintage is the busy time here, rendering the city for the time quite an emporium. The peasants flock in from the country and foreign vessels crowd the harbor, giving it quite a brisk appearance.

The society being commercial, is naturally more free and easy than that of Seville or Cordova; but, perhaps for the very reasons that render it so, is regarded as second rate by the blue blood that disports on the banks of the Guadalquivir and the Genil. Even the majos of Seville regard with contempt the feeble imitations of the coast. So far as outward appearance goes, the ladies certainly are far inferior to the high born dames of Seville, Cordova or Ecija. There is a want of that indefinable high bred elegance which seems to preside over the smallest movement of their proud neighbors. Nor do I find the climate as agreeable, though a perpetual spring does truly reign, and it is also said that there is not sufficient variety in the seasons to produce that bracing of the system which is requisite to the perfection of a climate. Hence, persons who reside a long time at Malaga are apt to suffer from a feebleness and distension of the veins. The Malagueñas have, however, a very fine Alameda, in the centre of the city, upon which to display their charms, and there are few more agreeable loung-ing places, after dinner, on a summer's eve.

Sitting there one afternoon, in the enjoyment of a segar and the dolce far niente, my attention was arrested by the appear-ance of an old woman, apparently sixty years of age, much bent and shrivelled, but still vigorous, and not easily alarmed, if one might judge by her gray eye. Her costume was humble and faded, and in the excess of the English fashion, her dress coquettishly held up in front of her right leg, while a parasol protected her features from the sun, which, however, was quite innocent of any amorous intent, as it had already descended below the house tops. A young girl and a boy accompanied her. Every eye was turned upon the party. A straggling collection of boys followed with evident amusement, and stood around their seat in wonder. I thought it a misplaced carnival joke, and that some wags had dressed themselves up to ridicule the English fashions. It was certainly the best imitation in the world. It turned out, however, that they were really from Albion's cliffs, and were much annoyed by the impertinent curiosity of their tormentors—so much so that they soon left the Alameda. It was only to bring up reinforcements, for they presently reappeared, leaning on the arm of an old man, who was provided with a good stout stick, and had evidently come to vindicate the right of his fair help-meet to an unmolested place on the promenade. I did admire the old fellow's pluck, for it required more than a soldier's courage to face the fash-ionable world at the head of such a harlequin-looking party. It was amusing to see the effect produced by General's stick and determined aspect, for the crowd kept at a most respectful distance, making every possible allowance for the length of his arm. They took a seat by me. The curiosity of the bystanders soon became satisfied, and it was now their turn for revenge. They had just arrived, and the effect which they produced upon

the Malagueñas was not greater than the effect produced by
the Malagueñas upon them. Everything excited their wonder,
and sometimes their merriment. The climax was capped by
the appearance of two uncommonly fat priests in low shoes and
white stockings, with the immense Basilio hats, a yard long
and turned up at the side, which still hold their place in the
Spanish clerical costume. Thinking after this that they had
had enjoyment enough for one day, the whole party retired.

Strangers are frequently much annoyed by the observation
which their foreign dress excites in Spain. But really it is very
natural. They go hundreds and thousands of miles to see the
Spaniards and their costume, and the Spaniards with equal
curiosity stare at them. We think that an Andalusian majo,
in his Figaro dress, is a fit object of wonder, and that a man
who dons such a costume has no right to object to a considerable amount of staring. But a Paris or London dandy is a far
more incomprehensible and amazingly dressed object in the
eyes of a Spaniard. Imagine one of them turned loose in some
primitive town in America! The number of travellers in Spain
is still comparatively few, and a simple stranger is of himself
an object of curiosity off the highways, but the appearance of
one of the ornaments of creation above mentioned is the signal
for a general turnout of the population—men, women and
children. I knew an Englishman at Madrid who was excessively teased on the Prado by this habit, but he was not born a
martyr, and half his time was spent in walking defiantly around
persons who had manifested more curiosity than was seemly.
His plan was a most successful one; it was as magical in effect
upon the unmannerly gapers as the "Perdóneme vm. por Dios"
is upon a beggar, for few people are willing to risk a fight for
the pleasure of being impertinent. The most dangerous thing
of all, however, for a foreigner is to adopt the full Spanish costume, for that requires a grace of movement, a springiness of
step which twenty years of straps and suspenders is apt to
impair if not destroy.

As Malaga affords facilities for salt water bathing, I pressed
into service a boy, one of the Gibraltar rock scorpions attached
to the hotel, as a guide. According to his account the floating
baths were magnificent. Mohammed himself could ask nothing
better. The first was moored in the dock, and every now and
then some refuse stuff floated by. I made decided objections to

the locality; the other was no better. The valet expressed surprise that I did not find the water clean enough, as he and all the other gentlemen at the hotel bathed there. I told him that there was nothing about which gentlemen differed so much as bathing, both as to the quantity of the water and its quality, and I forthwith stepped into a boat. In a few minutes I was in the blue water of the Mediterranean, beyond the entrance of the port, enjoying a gull's eye view of the scenery. From this point one has the finest view of the city and its surroundings. On every side is the noble amphitheatre of mountains; their base covered with vineyards and farm houses; their summits arid and barren, glistening in the noonday sun. Midway up was Colmenar, and, like a faint thread, the road to Loja, whence the views of the Vega of Malaga are so beautiful. The foreground was filled up with the city, flanked by the molehead and the Alcazaba. The huge Cathedral asserts its pre-eminence in the centre. Every traveller should take this prospect, as it is certainly the finest thing in Malaga, and then it is such a pleasure to be in the salt water of the tropics, knowing at the same time that there is not a shark within five hundred miles.

I had already once made the journey to Granada by Alhama and returned by Loja, both of which are well worth travelling, the former for its general interest, the latter on account of the lovely views of the Vega, as you descend in the evening the Sierra of Colmenar—not to be surpassed in Europe. I had therefore thought to go quietly snoozing in the diligence, but in the fall of the year one is apt to count without his host in this matter on all the frontiers of Spain, for the places are taken months ahead by persons returning from springs and bathing places. Such was the case now. The hotel was crowded with guests from Carratraca—a famous mineral spring in the mountains to the north-west—awaiting their turn. Failing in all my efforts to obtain a seat in the public conveyance, I made the best of a bad cause, arranged for two horses; bespoke a *bota;* saw the alforjas or saddle bags filled with what turned out to be one of the most abominable meals I ever ate, and retired to rest.

Before daylight Diego and myself were off on the road which skirts the hills along the Mediterranean toward Velez Malaga. The way was strewed with an uninterrupted succession of donkeys heavily ladened. As it was still quite dark, that is, as dark as it ever gets in the starry clime of Andalusia, we were always on the point of running some of the patient animals down; and the burden of one of them coming in contact with my knee, taught me, to my sorrow, of what it consisted—boxes of those dried grapes which form the delight of all American children, here called by the classical name of *pasa*. The recollections of infancy had very little effect, however, in assuaging the pain of the concussion. As day broke, the donkeys and dust seemed to increase, perhaps because rendered visible. Every mountain path added its contingent to swell the throng. Sometimes the road descended to the level of the beach, then mounted again to cross the winter torrents, *rios secos* at this season. Old watch towers (atalayas), built by Moors and Christians alike, many dating even from Hannibal and Cæsar, *segun dicen*, were strung along, some of them improved in the modern style of fortification, as outposts for the carabineers of the custom house, of whom we met from time to time a patrol—good-looking men, well armed and well mounted. For a long distance we kept the city in sight on our right; on our left rose the Sierra, crowned with vineyards and frequent farm houses, where the peasants were occupied in preparing the *pasa*. It seemed as if this occupation embraced all who were not engaged in driving the donkeys to the city. It was very pleasant to ride along the Mediterranean, in the cool of the morning, in the midst of the plenty and contentment which the vintage season produces. They might well be contented, for of all the gifts of heaven to man, the vine is the most beneficent. Its culture is light, and in its train follow temperance, health and wealth, a wealth too of which they cannot be deprived, as it depends not so much upon the wit of man as upon the natural gifts of soil and climate. After proceeding three or four hours, we turned into the Vega of Velez Malaga, which is without doubt the most fertile spot in Europe. It seemed as though there was not room for the products of its soil. Our own staples held a conspicuous place; maize, sweet potatoes, generally eaten here as a preserve, sugar cane, besides the cereals appropriate to a more temperate climate. The soil is composed entirely of the washings of the mountain streams for centuries, and is naturally fertile in the extreme; add to this an abundant irrigation, with the heat of a September sun, and its exuberant production is easily understood. The town of

Velez, with its white castle, backed by the naked Sierra Tejeda, formed a beautiful contrast to the rich green of the valley. Traversing a cool grove on the banks of the river, where numerous families had taken up their summer residence, we entered the city and proceeded to the Posada, where I took my siesta, as the rest of the journey bid fair to be as hot as it was fatiguing. A cup of chocolate and an *azucarillo* refreshed us, and a little before noon we started again   •

The carriage road ceases at Velez, and we ascended the spacious dry bed of the little stream, penetrating gradually into the mountain. For some time the aspect of the country continues the same—vineyards and long files of donkeys seeking the shade of the gigantic aloes and cactus hedges. By and by the productions of a tropical climate became rarer; the road a mere mountain path, crossing precipitous ravines on Moorish bridges, and winding among hamlets that seemed to hang upon the side of the rock. Diego had been very talkative all the morning, so long as we could ride abreast; but as in single file he was reduced to his own meditations, which were few, sleep asserted her empire. I first discovered the fact by seeing his horse leave the path and make straight for a house a little way off, which he would have entered, had not the shouts of the astonished females within awakened the slumbering Diego. Arrieros sleep and sleep profoundly a considerable part of their journeys. They tell of a merchant, with his train, who arrived, dozing upon a mule, at the village, upon the banks of the Tagus, by the usual road leading over the famous bridge of Alcantara, shortly after one arch of that structure had been blown up by the British, he himself being ignorant of the fact. The villagers could not believe but that the bridge had been magically repaired, and went back to see, when it was found that a narrow timber had been laid across the break for the goats. When the poor merchant saw the thread, the real bridge of the sword (Al Kantar al Seif) upon which he had been carried two hundred and fifty feet above the foaming torrent, his hair turned white. Spanish horses can safely be trusted in this manner for, being exceedingly sure footed, they go as safely without a bridle as with one, and the high peaked saddles assist the rider in holding on. Nature has kindly disposed that a horseman's members succumb successively in proportion to the necessity for their continued exertion. First the muscles of the neck; then the arms; then the back, and last of all the legs; such I believe is the universal experience of horsemen. Diego maintained that his seat was better adapted for the purpose than the European. Most Andalusians while on a journey ride *á la ginete,* a custom derived from the Moorish cavalry, who rode with very short stirrups, and were armed with an *adarga* or light shield and a lance. In the middle ages Spanish cavalry were divided into *castellanos* and *ginetes,* the former armed in full with heavy lances and long stirrups, the latter, as I have described, which was universal among the Moors, "ginete," meaning simply a horseman. Some of the late authors on cavalry tactics recommend a partial return to this manner of riding. There is no doubt that the present method in the British army, copied by them from the continent, is traceable to the mail clad knights—the Castellanos of the Spanish tactics—who could scarcely bend their knees on horseback, and is unsuited to the present age. The other, however, is as great an extreme. Reasonably short stirrups are of course desirable for a swordsman, but it seems to me that they involve a sacrifice of the solidity of the seat, and that an adarga and light lance would be poor matches for the mailed armor of an old knight or even the modern cuirassier; yet the experience of a thousand battle fields has proved that in an open hand to hand fight, activity and freedom of movement more than counterbalance the mere resistance of armor, and the Moors, once the best cavalry in the world, and now excellent horsemen, retain their short stirrup. Diego, however, carried his point about the sleeping.

The path now became steeper. Flocks of sheep began to make their appearance as we neared the summit of the Sierra, and the view behind us assumed the grand proportions I have described in passing from Antequera to Malaga, with the advantage this time of the evening sun and a clearer atmosphere, which brought the opposite coast of Africa into full view. Descending from the crest, we entered and crossed diagonally a broad level valley that extended a considerable distance and was covered with green, which appeared doubly beautiful by contrast with the bare mountain side we had left. Numerous flocks and herds were grazing, and one of the bulls made a show of attacking us, which would have been exceedingly inconvenient, as the skill of a bull fighter does not come by intuition, and the intense heat and hard day's ride had made a visible impression upon our animals. By pushing them into a trot we managed to put a precipitous gulley between our valuable persons and his taurine majesty, who contented himself with roaring and pawing the earth at us. He was a very good looking beast when seen across that obstacle, but I confess I was not sorry to lose sight of him. Down in the plains these embryo heroes of the bull ring sometimes give a great deal of trouble to passers by, particularly when they stray away from the herd, as this one had done.

We soon after entered a tortuous ravine leading over the northern barrier of the valley. I had loitered behind, lost in those meditations which the evening brings upon the traveller in strange parts, when I was aroused from my reverie by the sudden springing from the road side of a most unamiable-looking man, with a sledge hammer, who commenced addressing me in a strong dialect which I did not very well comprehend. I stopped, and, loosening my dagger, entered into conversation. His appearance was not prepossessing, but I thought that if a good five inch Toledo, on horseback, was not equal to a sledge hammer on foot, it was time to stop travelling. He wished to know if I had passed a certain friend of his proceeding to the fair at Alhama. I had seen no such person, nor anything like him. At this time a turn in the ravine brought Diego in view, who immediately came back at a gallop and prevented the denouement, whatever that was to be. He scolded me for stopping; said that the fellow looked like a "mala gente" (bad people), which indeed he did; that the Sierra was full of them, particularly as to-morrow was to be a fair, and called my attention to a cross which stood near by, very apropos to point his moral. These crosses or *milagro Andaluz* (Andalusian miracle) as they are called, are erected to mark the spot where a person has been found murdered. It used to be a custom for every passer by to throw a stone upon the heap, and to offer up a short prayer for the peace of his soul, but this custom is going out of fashion. People are too busy now-a-days. They are not always evidence of robbery, for love and jealousy come in for at least a half. I am sorry to say that this was my nearest approach to the pleasure of being robbed and buried under a wayside cross; and half of the terrific, petrifying, hair-elongating recitals that grace the books of travellers, have very

little more foundation. From the top of the crest the city of
Alhama appeared overspread with the roseate hue of sunset.
To the north and east were the lofty mountains of Granada
and the many peaks of the Sierra Nevada. On every side
extended the spurs that spring from these chains. Grandly
did they repose in their solitude. Dismounting, we led our
horses down the steep descent, and after a half hour's walk,
were in the precipitous streets of this romantic gate to the old
kingdom of Granada.

  I proceeded directly to a house where I had been entertained
on the previous visit with good humor and clean sheets, if not
with elegant fare in other respects. But the family had moved
away and the present occupants were not disposed to be hospi-
table. After one or two other fruitless attempts, we nerved up
our minds to try the Posada—a place to be avoided in a crowd
such as at present thronged the little city. Pushing my way
through the kitchen and among the mules, I mounted to the
first story to view the accommodations. Slender they were,
but the best—an uneven brick-paved room, with one chair and
a porthole for a window, by which I took a seat until Diego
had put away the cattle. This accomplished, he made his
appearance with Juana, the daughter of the family, who united
in her small person the weighty functions of chambermaid,
cashier and housekeeper. Juana was fifteen or thereabouts;
not pretty, but brisk and talkative, and disposed to render
herself agreeable as well as useful. I complained that the
house contained nothing, not even chinches. "Si, si, las hay!
hay todo! hay todo!" and she was not altogether wrong. A
ricketty table was brought first; then a grand consultation was
held as to the sleeping apparatus. It was finally concluded to
make a pallet upon the floor, as the best means of cheating
those travellers' enemies that lurk in the hiding places of bedsteads, and of which I have a wholesome horror. Next, supper
was brought up, in the best style of Alhama cookery. I will
not venture to say how much garlic and oil it contained, nor
how palatable it was after the journey. I ate in state, surrounded by the landlady, Juana and Diego. The latter was in
his element, delighted to have something to do. He informed
me privately that he was glad we had failed in obtaining lodgings at the other houses, as he would not have felt himself at
liberty to order about as he did here. The conversation turned

upon the annual fair, which was to commence to-morrow and
to last three days. The town was already thronged, and a
busy time was expected. Having received with due humility
the compliments of the hostess upon my practical appreciation
of her culinary skill (your mistress of the Posada likes to see
you eat heartily of her viands; it is always a strong point in
your favor, and shows that you know what is good—a Spaniard
of taste), I sallied forth to see the world.

The situation of Alhama is superb; evidently intended by
nature to be what it was, a fortress town in the days before the
invention of gunpowder. On three sides it is almost impregnable; one of them is upon the deep cleft in the mountain ridge,
through which the Marchan foams and boils—a scene of savage
grandeur. As the moonlight illuminated its recesses and
brought its old Moorish mills and ruined walls into relief, it
required little imagination to see the spirits of the warrior
Marquis of Cadiz and his turbaned opponents wandering over
the theatre of their romantic exploits. The Plaza above was
lined with booths, in front of which were collected numerous
groups, buying, singing, or dancing, as the fancy took them.
Guitars were numerous, some of them in the hands of no mean
performers. I do not remember ever to have seen a finer looking set of men; of the medium height, well and actively made,
and, what is better still, well behaved; no drunkenness, no
quarrelling, though it is very probable that many knives were
drawn before the three days had passed. After rambling about
sufficiently to satisfy my curiosity, passing a word here and
taking a *panal* there, for sociability reigns on such occasions, I
returned to the Posada. The sound of merriment saluted my
ears on entering. The room below, which served the threefold
purpose of kitchen, blacksmith shop and parlor, had been
cleaned, and a fandango was in full blast, with all the fire of
the uncorrupted Andalusian, Juana, the ubiquitous Juana, and
a young gallant, by name Jorge, being the artists. Juana was
fleeing from his enticements, Jorge pursued, Juana relented,
Jorge was but too happy, Juana was startled again into flight,
and so the miniature ballet continued, when at length Juana
could resist no longer, and surrendered to her pertinacious
besieger. The audience vociferously expressed their gratification, and a hail storm of hats fell at the feet of the dancers.
Juana then passed around the circle, giving us the customary

embrace, a dreadfully faint one, the only artificial part of the performance. If the exhibition was without the finished elegance of the stage, it had been much more naturally danced, and in the true spirit. After leaving the room below, I sat for a long time by my window, looking out upon the various companies of cloaked serenaders that passed up and down the street upon their mission of love. The twanging of guitars and the clicking of castagnettes continued past midnight, and it is probable that the dawn surprised many a reveller still abroad.

All of our countrymen have read Irving's Chronicle of the Conquest of Granada, and consequently know how Alhama was surprised and taken, and how profound an impression its loss made upon the Moors. They will remember also the dolorous ballad composed upon the occasion, commencing

Paseábase el rey Moro,

which Lord Byron translated. Its effect upon the Moriscoes was such that like the Ranz des Vaches among the Swiss in foreign service, it was forbidden to be sung after the conquest, and has never been printed. In 1852 I wrote back to a descendant of the Moors, who had acted as my guide, to send me a copy, which he did, appropriately surrounded with a mourning border and in a mourning envelope.

Daylight the next morning found us descending the zigzag path that leads into the valley of the Marchan. On the opposite hill, beyond the ravine to the left, was the Calvario or Calvary, a universal ornament of Spanish towns. Some place in the city of peculiar sanctity is selected as the commencement of the via crucis—generally a church; in Seville it is the House of Pilate; the several stations of the Passion are marked by a cross, and the spot of the Crucifixion by three. Some person was performing his devotions at one of them as we passed. Was he asking an exemption from the temptations which the business of buying and selling offers to the unwary sinner? or was it that he might not fall into the hands of honest thieves, who lurk about in the peaceful garb of horse traders? It would almost require a special interposition of Providence to protect him from either danger, whether of cheating or being cheated on such an occasion. We did not go out of our way to visit the baths of Alhama, as I had seen them once before. The word alhama means "bath" in Arabic, and very little improve-

ment has been made in the accommodations since the days of
the Moors. Their successors have retained the substance as
well as the name unchanged. The water is said to be highly
beneficial, but few resort thither except invalids, as the means
of approach require that the journey should be made on horseback. So crossing the river on a romantic Moorish bridge,
just before it enters the rocky cliffs that close in here upon its
banks, we ascended the Sierra which separates its valley from
that of the Cacin. The view of Alhama and the Sierra that
towers behind it was very, very fine. To borrow the imagery of
an old Andalusian poet, "morning had gone round like a cup-
bearer, and from the vase of light in her hand had copiously
poured forth the day." The summits of the Nevada and the
Tejada were already brilliantly illuminated by the sun, but its
light had not yet reached the city, which slumbered upon the
mountain side. Its narrow, precipitous streets could no longer
be distinguished; the white walls alone were visible, and it
seemed an eagle's eyry suspended beyond the reach of man. A
few hundred steps more lost it to our sight, and substituted in
its place the green valley of Cacin and the snowy peak of
Almuhacen, which was to be our beacon until we reached the
city of Jaen, I may almost say the Despeña Perros. On the
way down I stopped to talk with a shepherd, at whose feet
reclined two fine dogs. Three others were crouched among
the flock. They were beautiful animals, of the medium size,
with smooth, soft hair, and exceedingly intelligent countenances. He was willing to part with them at two dollars a
piece, and, had it been convenient to transport them to America,
I should have yielded to the temptation of purchasing a pair.
At night the sheep are gathered together, and all the fold surrounded with a rope stretched on stakes. The dogs seem tacitly
to divide among themselves the duty of walking around it from
time to time. They are fully as powerful as a wolf and almost
as fierce when aroused. On my previous visit, while mounting
the Sierra de Alhama toward the close of the first day's journey,
I had been struck with the graceful attitude of one near the
roadside. Seeing that we had stopped to look at him, he arose
slowly and walked away with an air of offended dignity, as
though he wished to express his dissatisfaction with our impertinent curiosity. The incident was insignificant, but there was
a majesty about his manner which seemed almost human, and

impressed itself on my memory. I made frequent inquiries
about the origin of the breed, but no one could enlighten me,
nor did it appear that any particular care had been taken to
improve it.

Thus far we had enjoyed the companionship of a person who
in outward appearance would have worthily passed for a
descendant of Boabdil himself. The Moorish cast of his features was heightened by the pallor of disease. He was returning from the baths of Alhama. A long white garment, a sort
of bournous, covered the greater part not only of himself, but
of his donkey, leaving only the face exposed. An athletic
peasant conducted the animal. Such a companion was not
inappropriate to the scene and its traditions. He left us at
Cacin, and our road crossing the valley and ascending the
opposite hill entered a country uninteresting in the extreme—
a bare, undulating plain, surrounded by mountain ranges. It
produced, however, capital grain crops. The sun came down
with an intensity that defies description, and one of our horses
having received a sort of sun stroke the day previous, it was
necessary to travel slowly. Diego went to sleep; I concluded
to follow his example. What became of his thoughts, I know
not; mine wandered home to the old plantation. I dreamed
myself once more a boy, playing under the noble forest trees
that border its lake. Birds sung in their branches, and squir-
rels skipped playfully about their venerable roots, while a
Southern breeze rippled gently over the water. The sound of
many oaths, classical and unclassical, arousing me from my
slumbers, dispelled the illusion. It was the dream of the fever-
tossed patient, who babbles of mountains and gushing streams,
for nothing could be in stronger contrast than the scene of my
vision and the reality around. Water there was none, nor did
a single tree enliven the prospect; on every side extended an
arid plain, bounded by stern, gloomy Sierras. Except for a
few dust brown villages and a narrow pathway, it might have
been the morning after the creation. Our horses had taken
the wrong fork, and were nearly at the foot of El Ultimo
Sospiro del Moro (the last sigh of the Moor), a hillock so called
because the unfortunate King of Granada, or perhaps the
banished Moriscoes at a later date, are said to have here taken
a last view of the fairy home over which the proud flag of
Castile was now floating. Crossing the fields, we re-entered

our path near the village of Garvia, whose environs seemed
blessed with an unusual number of murder crosses, most of
them, however, dating from the earlier part of the century—
the latest one (about two years old) bearing an indignant
inscription. Within the village all was festivity, as it was the
feast of the patron saint. Half the population, in clean shirts,
were assembled before the church. Various uniforms appeared.
A party of boys, with musical instruments, were parading a fat
black porker through the street on his way to the hog lottery.
He was evidently the centre upon which the feast was to turn,
and the eyes of the ticket holders already feasted upon him,
as, fluttering his party-colored ribbons, he grunted along to his
fate. The Garvians were evidently bent upon having a gay
time, and I have regretted ever since that I did not stop and
take a chance for the animal. Hog lotteries are a thing peculiar to Spain, and a village feast without a pig would be the
play of Hamlet with the part of Hamlet left out. Days before
the eventful period he is subjected to the ocular investigation
of all who can see, and the blind, a numerous class in Spain,
who cannot see, punch him with their sticks to ascertain if his
ribs are well covered and his lungs in a healthy condition. The
Spaniards are great lovers of bacon in every shape, partly, it
has been thought, to distinguish them from Jews and Mohammedans, who abhor the unclean beast. That which is fed upon
the *bellota* of Andalusia and Estremadura is unrivalled, and the
sweet hams from the neighboring mountain of the Alpujarras
enjoy a European reputation.

Leaving the Garvians and their pig, we entered the range of
lofty hills that bound the valley of the Genil to the south-east.
At length we emerged on the western side of the elevation,
and turning a shoulder of the *loma*, Granada and its glorious
environs lay in the distance before us. Earth, air and water,
and we may complete the list of the elements by adding the
solar fire, had done their part. All had worthily contributed
to unite, within the space of a few leagues, most of the external
charms of existence, and to create one of the most beautiful
spots in the world. To the right and left extended the famous
Vega, from the base of Almuhacen to Loja, its surface ever
green in the midst of drought, for its fertility is derived from
a perennial source. In the winter, while the snows of the
mountains are congealed, the benignant heavens send down

their gentle showers. In the summer, when for six months no drop of rain falls upon the parched earth, the melting ice of the Sierras kindly supplies the deficiency of the seasons, and the Vega blooms with increased luxuriance. Diagonally across the broad valley, through the blue haze, reclined the ballad-sung city, embosomed in gardens and vineyards, its dun, reddish castle above the trees hardly distinguished from the hills that formed the back ground.

> Que castillos son aquellos ?
> Altos son y relucian.
> El Alhambra era, Señor,
> Y la otra la Mezquita,
> Los otros los Alijares,
> Labrados á maravilla.
> El otro is Generalife,
> Huerta que par no tenia.
> El otro Torres Bermejas
> Castillo de gran valía.
> Si tu quisieses Granada,
> Contigo me casaría
> Daréte in arras y dote,
> A Cordoba y á Sevilla.
> Casada soy, rey Don Juan,
> Casada soy, que no viuda,
> El moro que á mí me tiene
> Muy grande bien me tenia.

The thousand canals sparkled in the midday light, but wherever irrigation ceased the bare hill side rose precipitously in barrenness; a dozen paces frequently sufficed to mark the transition from a land overflowing with every production of the tropic and temperate zones, to naked sterility itself. Above all was spread the pure panoply of a Spanish sky, so unfathomably deep and blue, the few healthy clouds that floated over seeming thousands of miles removed into eternal space. We soon descended into the Vega, and pursued our way across amid the humming of insects and the sound of rushing waters. Those who live in a country of large streams and continual showers know not the pleasure which water confers. With us it is a fluid for practical purposes, to drink, to wash with, or to sail upon; but in Spain it is more, it is the source of fertility, of wealth and comfort. It is inseparably connected with the Andalusian idea of pleasure; is a centre of association. It thus quickly assumes the hue of poetry, and ballads are sung

21

to its honor. The well by the wayside and the fountain in
the city, are yet in Spain what they were in the days of the
Old Testament, and to appreciate to its full extent the exquisite poetry of the Hebrews, or the charming simplicity of their
illustrations, one should have sojourned south of the Sierra
Morena. It required the desert of the morning to make me
feel the full charms of noonday on the banks of the Genil.
Exchanging salutations with crowds of peasants, the men in
half Moorish, half Spanish dress, the women in the glories of a
red petticoat, we approached the city, and crossing the river at
the foot of the shady Salon, entered about two o'clock the
court of the hotel, where I found my baggage awaiting me in
a charming apartment, which commanded a full view of the
Sierra Nevada.

Chapter XVII.

GRANADA.

Bull Fight—Cruelty—Promenades—The Inhabitants—Moorish Blood—Alhambra —The Hand and the Key—Patio de la Alberca—De Los Leones—Tocador—Restorations—View from the Torre de la Vela—The Vega—Generalife—The Cathedral—Chapel of the Kings—The Cartuja—San Juan De Dios—Old Streets— Albaycin—The Gipsies—The Dance—Expulsion of the Moriscoes—Romantic Character of their Wars—Origin of Chivalry—Pundonor.

As a bull fight was to take place that afternoon, I dressed in a hurry and made my way to the Plaza de Toros, where I was certain to find the world of Granada. The direction was unerringly indicated by the immense throngs that pursued the streets leading toward it. A great crowd surrounded the outside of the building; some talking, some selling tickets, others the fans which are used only upon such occasions, made of yellow paper and costing one cent. Nor was the aguador or water seller absent. There was much moving to and fro, mingled with a vast amount of standing still. It was a combination of militia muster, county court week and Fourth of July. Being late, I had to content myself with a seat among the sovereigns; on my left a Sergeant of Cazadores, on my right a dame not over fair nor young nor graceful. Behind me were several well dressed people, one of whom turned out to be a critic, fully saturated with Granadian "sal" (salt), by no means a refined article, though very salty, or as we would say, "spicy." The Cuadrilla was the same that I had met about in Andalusia, and was to meet again in Madrid—that of Sanchez (called El Tato), who ranks among the best Espadas of Spain. He is rather under the medium height, exceedingly graceful and with a face of girlish innocence. The performance was not very good. Tato made a particularly bungling business in killing one of the animals. The critic behind, who pronounced his running commentary at the top of his voice, kept calling out " *Verguenza, Tato! Dominguez le hubiera ya matado y olvidado*" (for shame Tato, Dominguez would have already killed and forgotten him). Dominguez is a rival Torero, and from the continued severity of my neighbor's critique, I began to suspect that he was in the interest of the other party. However, he did full justice to Tato, when, on another occasion, throwing a bespangled cloak over his shoulders, he entered the ring with the *chulos*. The bull was perfectly fresh and made frantic efforts to gore him, but in vain. Tato quietly stepped aside, lifting the cloak over the bull's eyes, who would turn raging around to repeat the operation with like success. It was a very pretty sight and the amphitheatre resounded with shouts of "Viva el Tato! viva la gracia!" One of the Picadors came in for his full share of abuse because he held his spear too short. The first five bulls afforded no new incident, and I would not have mentioned the fight at all, were it not for an exhibition of the most infernal barbarity and cruelty I ever beheld. The sixth bull had died on the way from Seville, and his place was supplied with one from the locality. He turned out a regular coward, or rather he seemed indisposed to hurt any one. As soon as it was ascertained that he would not fight, under any circumstances, it was determined to kill him *á palos*. At last a hundred persons jumped into the ring, and, by the aid of sticks, pieces of plank and what not, the poor devil was actually beaten to death. My disgust nearly boiled over as I left the place. But this was a rare exception, and I do not think it would have been permitted elsewhere. The lower classes of Granada are famed throughout Spain for their coarseness and brutality, qualities that they probably owe to their semi-Moorish ancestry. The Cuadrilla were staying at our hotel, and though not very refined in their manners, they certainly gave no indication of cruelty or brutality of disposition. Of course they had taken no part in killing the bull *á palos*. The old method used to be to introduce dogs, or to hamstring the bull with an instrument called a *media luna*, or half moon, a sharp edged crescent, placed upon a spear staff. Authors exclaim warmly against both. One of them even says that the *media luna* must have been the invention of a heretic! I have seldom seen either used. *Banderillos de fuego* are generally substituted, and an announcement is frequently made on the bill to that effect. If it be necessary to remove a bull from the ring, it can be very easily accomplished by introducing oxen; for half a dozen oxen will lead a whole regiment of bulls in any direction.

As the evening advanced I found myself on the banks of the Darro, in the midst of a throng of promenaders. The public walks of Granada are worthy of its situation. The river Genil, taking its rise in the eternal snows of the Sierra Nevada, courses southwesterly down the Vega, almost touching the hills, upon whose slopes the city is built. Nearly at right angles on the north comes the Darro, resembling rather a torrent, which, threading the ravine that separates the Alhambra and the Albaycin, traverses the city, going under the Plaza Nueva, and unites with the Genil before the latter leaves the city limits. On the banks of the one is the Carrera del Darro running past the hotels, theatre and café to the Genil. The latter rejoices in the Salon, one of the finest walks imaginable. True it has no Guadalquivir, nor does it possess that indescribable charm which hangs over marvellous Seville, but it need fear no other rival. The trees are noble, resembling more the productions of our own forest than the stunted dwarfs of Europe. Stone seats and marble statues ornamented its avenues, and alongside fretted the icy river, while the silvery beams of the moon, struggling through the arched foliage, threw a subdued light over the variegated groups, who, in easy conversation, glided past. The Granadinas are pronounced " muy finas"—partly because of the rhyme and partly because it is the truth. They are certainly entitled to a place in the front rank of Andalusians, and there is among them a much larger proportion of blondes than is generally to be found in Spain. The higher ranks, at least the few I have met, resemble those of Seville and Cordova, but the lower are a great mixture. Elsewhere in Andalusia there is by no means so great an infusion of Moorish blood as is generally supposed. The Saracens, like the Goths, swept over it, seizing the government, but leaving the original population almost undisturbed. After the battle of Guadalete, the latter, having occupied it some three centuries, retired to the north-west, and the former took their place during the next five, the bulk of the lower classes, in both instances, being still of the mixed character which formed the substratum throughout the Roman Empire. Upon the reconquest of the valley of the Guadalquivir, the greater part of the Mohammedans withdrew to Africa or to such parts of Spain as still remained in the power of their brethren. But Granada was very differently situated. Even under the Moorish domination there was much comminglement of races, which was greatly increased during the century subsequent to the conquest by the Catholic kings. The pure Moorish style of beauty is not to my taste. It is striking, but the contrasts are too sharply defined. The features do not melt into each other, as is the case in the Spanish countenance. The best specimens I have seen were at Tarifa. Those in Africa itself may be handsome, but they are not visible, while the Tarifeñas leave one half of the face exposed. They have fine eyes, yet the expression is without that *no sé que* which renders the Spanish maiden irresistible. It pierces rather than captivates, and evinces curiosity rather than love. But the men of pure Moorish blood are as fine a looking race as can be found, exceedingly well made and with an appearance of great muscular power. The violent prejudice still entertained by the Spaniards against any admixture of Arab or Jewish blood, has certainly very little foundation in reason, and meets no sympathy in other parts of Europe. They are both of the true Caucasian stock, of which they have given abundant proofs intellectually, and certainly if purity of descent is any recommendation, they are entitled to it, for no other nations have preserved their integrity so carefully. Many persons in our country have an idea that a Moor is a sort of negro. I have seen somewhere in Europe (Magdeburg if I remember correctly) an image of St. Augustine painted as black as the ace of spades, upon the strength of his African bishopric, and Othello is always presented with a most suspicious coloring, which is a stage absurdity. They are no darker than the Italians or Spaniards, and those from the mountains are as fair as the Jewesses from the mountain of Libanus. But the Moorish cast of features is as unmistakable as the Jewish, and there are abundant specimens in all the country of Granada.

The great attraction of Granada is, of course, the Moorish palace of the Alhambra, the finest specimen of an extinct civilization that exists in Europe. After the thousand descriptions that have been given of this fairy ruin, it would scarcely be possible to add anything new. Yet few travellers could leave Spain without seeing and speaking of a building which has aroused the unmingled admiration of Christians from the date of the Conquest to the present time. As children we have read and dreamed of what we were there to see, and as old men we reflect and dream of what we have there seen. Boabdil and the Sultana Zoraya, the rivalries of the Zegris and Abencerrages have formed the delight alike of the sunny valley of the Mississippi and of the snowy plains of Russia. Remote from the whistle of the invading locomotive, it has as yet lost none of its interest in the hackneyed description of professed travellers and salaried letter writers; but this is rapidly changing, and ere long the genius of the place will have fled with alarm from the tramp of sight-seers and the droning of guide books. Even seven years have made a difference, and it is already scarcely possible, during the greater portion of the year, to wander about its enchanted halls unaccompanied save by the shades of its former proprietors. I count it among my greatest privileges to have travelled here before the throng of visitors had rendered necessary those restrictions which effectually banish all illusions of the past.

From its situation, upon a lofty spur, over-looking the city and the valley, the site of the Alhambra was always occupied by a fortress, which was called the watch tower of the plain. It was left to Al Ahmar, the founder of the kingdom of Granada, to unite the security of a fortress with the charms of a Moorish palace. The whole hill is surrounded by a wall with lofty flanking towers, which were formidable enough at the time of their erection, and quite sufficient to protect the royal residence against the escalades and men at arms of the middle ages. Within is a large, motley village, under the jurisdiction of a separate governor, once a functionary of importance. The outside indicates the fortress, and is forbidding to the aspect. Its charms, in accordance with the Eastern ideas, were reserved for the eye of the master and those whom he chose to admit to the intimacy of his private life. Passing through the Puerta de las Granadas, we entered the grove which covered the hill side. Deliciously cool it was in this September sun. The instantaneous transition from the glare of the city to this shady spot, amid fountains and gardens and the warbling of birds, was magical. The reign of the enchanter had begun. On the

left ascends the path to the massive Gate of Justice, wherein
the King sat to exercise what has always been considered in
the East the most ennobling function of royalty. Over the
horse-shoe arch are a hand and key, whose interpretation has
puzzled the most learned of travellers. Some have supposed
them to be symbols of faith. The key is frequently mentioned
in the Koran in reference to the Gate of Paradise, in precisely
the same manner as in the Christian religion; and the figura-
tive manner of speaking of the keys of St. Peter is doubtless
derived from the same Oriental source. It is moreover said,
with what authority I know not, to have been the armorial
bearing of the Andalusian Moors. The hand has many mysterious significations. It has the universal one of power, firmness and protection, which has passed into all languages, until it
has lost its symbolical meaning in the frequency of its use.
Fortune-tellers have sought to read the human destiny in its
lines. Anatomists find it one of the distinguishing characteristics and excellencies of man; and to such extent have mate-
rialists carried their admiration, that I once heard a popular
lecturer dilate upon its glories as though it were the immortal
portion of our being, which caused one of the company wittily
to remark that the poor success of Lord Raglan, at that time
the subject of conversation, was probably owing to his having
lost one of these valuable appendages. The other signification
of the hand is mystically connected with the Mohammedan
religion, whose teachings involve one point of faith—belief in
the one God and his Prophet—and four of practice, viz:
prayer, alms, fasting and pilgrimage. Four of these precepts
have three sub-divisions each, and thus correspond to the three
joints of the fingers; the first has only two, and corresponds to
the thumb; so that the entire hand represents the whole duty
of religion. This is evidently one of those pious ingenuities of
which Europe also has been fruitful, but from it came the habit
of using the closed fist with the thumb, the representative of
faith, inserted between the first and middle finger, as a preservative against the "evil eye," the thumb being pointed toward
the obnoxious person. The Barbary merchants at Seville and
Gibraltar still sell charms in this shape, to be hung around the
necks of children. Under the Spanish rule the gesture thus
described came to be significant rather of contempt. As to the
meaning of the hand over the Gate of Justice here, the traveller

can select what signification he please, with as much probability
of being right as if aided by the most learned disquisition. Had
it been over the gate of the Palace itself, and the inscription in
the tower of Comares alongside, there might have been reason
for thinking it a protection against the "evil eye," but there
was no manner of necessity for thus protecting the whole
village, and that the founder should have selected the armorial
bearing of his enemies, the Almohades, whose empire he had
aided to extinguish by the capture of Seville, is improbable.
Taken in connection with the key, and in its position over the
entrance of the fortress, it was more likely a symbol of the
power and protection of God against all enemies, as the other
was a symbol of faith. But Allah is great! he only is all
knowing!

Passing through the Gate of Justice, we enter the precincts
of the fortress—whose first appearance is apt to cause disappointment—an irregular, open square, called the Plaza de los
Algibes, or the Place of the Cisterns, which lie underneath. On
all sides are uninviting buildings, among them the unfinished
Palace of Charles V, which would be a fine structure if
it were completed. Externally it is square, of mingled Ionic
and Doric. The interior is circular, with a double colonnade.
The architectural plan is certainly good, and had the original
idea been carried out it would have been a great addition to
the otherwise unattractive appearance of the exterior of the
Alhambra. To make way for it the winter residence of the
Moorish kings was destroyed, a matter of ceaseless regret to
the whole world, though, in the absence of contemporaneous
description, it may reasonably admit of a doubt whether the
winter home were constructed upon the same scale of elegance
as the portion that remains. The cold season with the Moors
was not a period of enjoyment, and the great Emperor was too
deeply imbued with the true artistic feeling to destroy what
was worth preserving. It is much more probable that he
intended to substitute in its place a palace in the northern style
of architecture, which recognizes the beauty of winter, and is
better suited to the temperature of that season in Granada, as
combining warmth with elegance, while the Alhambra should
be preserved for the summer's delight. The original entrance
in the time of the Moors was on the south, now blocked up by
the Spanish Palace. A small door, of most unpretending

appearance, was subsequently made to the west to supply its place, and by that we were, without preliminary admonition, ushered into the midst of its fairy scenes. And now the disappointment of the outside aspect gives way to an astonishment which few pens can describe. Within that coarse exterior glitters the sparkling diamond. Courts and airy columns, and orange ceilings, gardens, fountains, everything that could aid in banishing remembrance of the outer world, are here in profusion.

The first or entrance court, is the Patio de la Alberca, the Court of the Pond, which occupies the centre, its limpid waters sparkling with gold fish and reflecting the flowers around its edge. An ornamental rail encircles the whole. The former entrance from the winter palace was to the right of this court, and· the rooms for the attendants opened upon it. On the northern side rises the tower of Comares, and within it is the wonder of the Alhambra, the Hall of the Ambassadors. Whatever expectations may have been formed of the beauties of the Moorish ornamentation are here exceeded by the reality. But I am warned from an attempt at description by the failure of all I have ever read to convey an idea of its effect. Nor·is it wonderful that the artist should have thought it necessary to deprecate in an inscription the influence of the "evil eye." The size of the hall is not great, scarcely more than forty feet square, but the centre of its dome attains a height of seventy or more, whose sombre gloom adds indescribably to the general effect. The ante-chamber contains some of the best preserved portion of the old coloring, whose contrast with that of the restoration is humiliating to modern art. The views from the embrasured windows of the Hall of the Ambassadors are superb, and it is looking from them that Charles V is said to have exclaimed, "Ill fated the man who lost all this!"

Returning by the Patio de la Alberca, and passing through an ante-room, you enter the famous Court of Lions, whose long vistas and pure marble columns recall faintly the Mosque of Cordova. The fountain in the centre rests upon the backs of twelve heavy animals, which have euphemistically been called lions; while the delicate columns of the pavilions and corridors seem as though they would be crushed beneath the superincumbent weight above. Upon this court open two of the most celebrated halls in the Alhambra—that of the Abencerrages

and that of the Two Sisters.   In the former are still shown the
blood stains of the luckless cavaliers who paid the penalty of
love with the extinction of their power and almost of their
race.   Sad, that not only these marks, but even the narrative
itself were too probably an invention of the romantic Perez de
Hyta.   The name of the hall of the Two Sisters is said to be
derived from two slabs of marble which have been let into the
floor—a most prosaic derivation, but one that seems to be true.
On the east are three other halls, containing paintings of men
and animals.   In one are represented ten most venerable
bearded Moors; in others hunting scenes and even ladies are
portrayed.   That the second commandment should be thus
violated in the Court of Lions both by paintings and sculptures, is an astonishing and unique exception to the practice of
Mohammedans, who have been fanatical iconoclasts, and whose
reformation of the Christianity practiced in the seventh century
consisted principally in the substitution of an ethereal, inconceivable Deity for the gross materialism into which the world
was fast relapsing.   Such was the horror with which the
wooden and stone representations of the Great Jehovah filled
Mohammed, that he re-enacted the provisions of the Jewish
law in all their stringency, and few of his precepts have been
so faithfully obeyed.   These in the Alhambra were probably
the work of Christians, but the sin consisted as much in using
as in making them.

I have passed over the Patio de Lindaraja, the Royal Baths,
the Mosque, the Discreet Statues, charming as they all are,
without remark; but I could not venture to leave thus unno-
ticed the *Tocador de la Reina.*   A little corridor leads to the
pavilion so called.   It is open on all sides, its frescoed roof
being supported by slender marble columns.   The object for
which it was constructed is not with certainty known.   For a
long time it was supposed to be the Queen's toilet room,
whence it derived its name, and the perforated marble slab in
the corner to be the place where the Sultan stood to receive
the odor of the perfumes, a practice which I have known
myself to be indulged in.   But a dressing room in the open air
would scarcely accord with Moorish customs.   Others have
supposed it to be a mere mirador, a looking-out place.   But
the inscription around the Frieze is thought to indicate a much
nobler destination.   As my Arabic was not equal to the task of

deciphering the flourishes of the Alhambra, I must borrow
the following translation : "In the name of God the merciful !
May God be with our Lord and Prophet Mohammed ! To him
and his be endless happiness and salvation ! God is the light
of heaven and earth, and His light is like unto Himself. He is
like unto a lamp whose rays are many, while it is one. He is
the light of light, like a blazing constellation, which kindles
and illuminates, but is not itself consumed." Judging by this
inscription and its situation, the pavilion was probably the
Sultan's oratory, and what nobler spot could have been selected for the worship of the Almighty God ? The prospect is
enchanting. Perpendicularly below bounds the Darro, amid
pomegranates and figs, separating the hill of the Alhambra
from the opposite one of the Albaycin. Beyond this the view
embraces the city, the green luxuriance of the Vega, and far
beyond all, the Sierras Elvira and Nevada, towering with
barren sides and snow capped peaks into the very heavens.
On the left rise the blank walls of the Alhambra. The worshipper would seem thus to be separated from humanity and
its works, in order that his whole soul might be poured out in
abstracted devotion to its Creator. The example of the patriarchs who went up into a high mountain to pray, has been
abandoned in modern times for the charms of a fashionable
assemblage, the rustling of silks and odor of perfumes, with
the drowsy platitudes or, still worse, the thundering invectives
of a favorite preacher. For the inculcation of moral sentiments and the enforcement of moral duties this may be the
best plan. But for religion, for the appreciation of the bond
which unites the creature and the Creator, there must be the
solitude of the desert or the solemn grandeur of the Cathedral
at Seville. Yet neither the glories of the prospect nor the
beauty of the Tocador itself have preserved it from the desecration of scribblers, and the Joneses of England, the Schultzes
of Germany, and the Petits of France, vie with each other in
the race of immortality upon its walls.

I have not attempted to describe the Alhambra. That were
presumption. Even the genial writings of our own celebrated
countryman, whose name is a household word in the Palace of
Al Ahmar, seen tame and artificial beside the moonlit glories
of the reality. Of most of the great triumphs of architecture
it is easy to convey a reasonably distinct idea by the united

labors of pen and pencil. But the genius of Moorish art, like
the perfume of a rose, cannot be imprisoned in fetters. Its
thousand columns, its endless figures, its inscriptions torturing
the ingenuity, all combine to produce the indistinctness which
is its characteristic. As a summer palace it seems to be perfect. Its spacious marble courts, its delicate columns, its
bubbling fountains' and curtained doors suggest, irresistibly,
the idea of a refreshing coolness and blissful repose. The
Alhambra, however, to be appreciated must be seen by moonlight. Then, seated alone in the hall of the Abencerrages,
and looking forth upon the Fountain of the Lions, does it
become re-peopled with the spirits of by-gone days. Boabdil
and his queens, Zegris, Abencerrages, Gomeles, Gazules, Aben-
amars, crowd its audience halls, or saunter along its silvery
corridors, while the warning spirit points ominously to the few
sands yet remaining ere the Christian bugles shall sound at its
gates. The Alhambra is seldom mentioned by Arabic historians in any unusual strains of commendation. Ibn Batutah
does not even allude to it. We can thus form some conception
of the grandeur and beauty of the palaces of Azzahra and
Azzahira upon the banks of the Guadalquivir, which fire the
imagination of their writers. Indeed the city of Granada was
built in the decadence of the Moorish Empire, when its territory was restricted to the upper valley of the Genil and the
sea coast of Malaga and Almeria, and its treasury exhausted
by war and tribute, so that it boasts few edifices of note
except the Alhambra itself. The founder of the kingdom,
Al Ahmar, was the same I have mentioned as aiding St. Ferdinand in the conquest of Seville, and this was the last of the
great Mohammedan cities of Spain. And yet the ruins of the
Alhambra, the least celebrated of the Moorish palaces, is the
gem and wonder of our age.

The Duke of Montpensier and other enlightened spirits have
caused the work of renovation to be prosecuted in earnest. It
consists as much in undoing as in doing. The horrible, vile
tiled roof is to come down; the whitewash is to be removed,
and where the ancient work is irretrievably destroyed, an imitation, the best that can be, is to be substituted. As the place
is filled with workmen, the opportunity is eagerly seized by
amateurs of obtaining a piece of the genuine Azulejos. They
are open to approaches, and dispose of small bits at exorbitant

rates; but it is diamond cut diamond, for in ninety-nine cases
out of a hundred, the dear-bought specimens are the new manufacture, which cannot readily be distinguished by an unpracticed eye. The difference in weight is an infallible criterion,
the original being nearly twice as heavy. This mania for col-
lecting pieces of celebrated things, at any expense, whether of
purse or of honor, seems confined to the British dominion, with,
of course, a few imitators among us, as a portion of our population seems to have a happy facility in copying foreign, particularly British vices. Morality on the subject is suspended. It
is hardly possible to conceive what pleasure the possession of
such an article could give. The French excused their hauling
the Cid's bones about, by having thus saved them from the
English virtuosos. I once saw, with my own eyes, an American—a member of a church at that—knock off a statuette from
a tomb on the Appian Way, and think he had made a fine
"operation." The nose of the Venus de Medici, or the shank
of Apollo, would probably suffer the same fate, if a fair opportunity offered. On one occasion, at the Alhambra, I had
noticed a broken piece in the pavement, near the Hall of the
Baths, but had passed on without thinking more of the matter.
Presently an Englishman of the party remarked to me that he
had secured a fine specimen. I said nothing. His triumph
was of short duration, for the custodian was soon seen in confi-
dential intercourse with the guide, and Albion's son was summoned to restore the missing article, which he did with infinite
confusion. Yet I know that he was a person of honorable sentiments and would have scorned to do what he considered a
mean action. The most provoking thing about the affair was,
that the same piece had attracted the covetousness of three
others, at different times, and had been left loose as a kind of
bait.

The extremity of the hill or spur of the Alhambra is occupied
by the Torre de la Vela (the watch tower), whose bell is tolled
upon the anniversary of the surrender. It has little rest that
day, for when rung by the hand of maidens, it has the same
effect as the pistol of our ancestors in arousing gallants to the
duty of declaring their intentions, and the excellence of the
husband is proportionate to the vigor of the peal. There is
said, however, to be a certain age beyond which even this
expedient fails. On ordinary occasions it serves the more pro-

saic purpose of indicating to the farmers of the Vega the period
of irrigation. Formerly it was permitted to breakfast under
an arbor in the garden, which pleasure I enjoyed, but they say
that is now prohibited. The view is enchanting. At our feet
reposed the shining city of Granada, girted about by gardens
and noble walks. The whole extent of the Vega lay as a lake
of flowers and verdure, its velvety green interspersed with
sparkling villages, all embalmed, as the scene of some knightly
encounter between the Christian and the Moor. A network of
canals glittered amid the luxuriant products of three continents. Enclosing the plain, rose on all sides the wall of bare
mountain, while, overlooking the whole, towered, in snowy
sublimity, the Sierra Nevada, like some beneficent genius surveying in conscious omnipotence the glories of his handywork.
From its recesses trickled the gentle Genil, receiving at every
step the offering of its tributaries, and placidly gliding amid
flowery fields until the narrow gorge of Loja stole it from our
vision. " Why should Cairo boast her Nile, when Granada has
a thousand Niles in her Shenil ?"

The word Vega is supposed to be of Basque origin, and is
applied to any fertile plain between elevations; but that of
Granada, extending from the base of the Sierra to the city of
Loja, a distance of nine Spanish leagues, is called the Vega by
distinction. Take it all in all, there are few spots in the world
worthy of a comparison. A broad valley enclosed between
lofty Sierras, whose nakedness renders its luxuriance the more
beautiful, is fertilized by ample streams flowing from the eternal snows of the highest mountain in Spain. Thus are united
and brought within a small compass the whole range of the
vegetable kingdom. The fervid sun of these latitudes lends his
aid to the work of production, and the agricultural skill of the
Moor has been perpetuated to our day. It would be easier to
say what is not than what is cultivated here. The climate,
too, is beyond complaint, though the neighboring mountains
cause at times fierce winds to blow. One such in the month of
March compelled us to remain in doors a whole day, with closed
shutters, for the panes were all broken by its violence, and
the falling tiles rendered it dangerous to walk the streets. The
neighboring mountain of Parapanda supplies the place of a
barometer, according to the distich—

Quando Parapanda se pone la Montera
Llueve aunque Dios no lo quisiera.

Fulfilling the part of Mount Pilatus in Switzerland, of which there is a similar saying, its equal in elegance of diction—

> Wenn Pilatus trägt den Hut
> Dann ist das Wetter gut.

To all the attractions of nature it must be added that every foot of ground is hallowed by some romantic recollection. Here is the village of Santa Fé, built by the Catholic sovereigns during the siege, to prove their fixed determination never to abandon this cherished object. It was at this village that the deed of surrender was signed, and hence, too, did Columbus, with joyful countenance, set forth to the discovery of our own continent. Farther on is the magnificent estate of Soto de Roma, which, presented in succession to various warriors in token of national gratitude, now belongs to the Duke of Wellington. Here is the Sierra Elvira, famous in Spanish history for the defeat and death of the Infantas. Lost in that gorge lies Loja, and hidden behind yon Sierras is Alhama. Indeed what spot is there which has not been watered by the best blood of Moslem and Christian ?

Tearing ourselves reluctantly away, we descended into the valley of the Darro, and, passing along the base of the Alhambra, mounted the hill to the Generalife, a fairy spot of fountains and flowering avenues. The venerable cypresses which bore such false witness against the Abencerrages are still pointed out. The Generalife belongs to a noble descendant of the Moorish race. On a still loftier eminence to the rear is the Silla del Moro (the seat of the Moor), a ruin said to be of a former palace. The view from this point is more extensive than from the Torre de la Vela. It embraces the Generalife and the Alhambra itself, which lie as it were upon successive steps of the same hill. On the right is the precipitous ravine of the Darro, separating it from the Albaycin, in which the Moriscoes after the conquest were required to dwell. Their poverty and fallen fortunes are fitly represented by its present inhabitants. To the left are the groves of the Alhambra, and beyond the wooded ravine rise the Torres Bermejas. The teeming Vega blooms as ever, while around, far as the sight can reach, struggling Sierras lift their bare precipices toward heaven.

Returning by the grove of the Alhambra, we stopped at the

tower of the Seven Stories (los siete suelos). A little restaurant with a garden had been fitted up to refresh the thirsty. One of our English acquaintances in Malaga had recommended in the strongest terms a visit to the Torre de los Siete Suelos, not to see the old gate, nor to think about El Zagal or Boabdil —quite a different purpose—to drink a marvellous nectar called *Sangria*. What it was he could not exactly decide, but pronounced it worthy of the gods on a hot day. The *Sangria* turned out to be neither more nor less than sangaree, so that though I failed to obtain a new sensation, I learnt the origin of the drink and its English appellation. For the benefit of tyros in Castillian it may be well enough to say that *sangre* means blood, and the name is hence appropriate.

Among the modern buildings of Granada, the most conspicuous is the Cathedral, founded upon the ruins of the ancient Mosque, and preserving very nearly its shape. The interior is too full of light for my taste, but it is nevertheless a fine edifice, and some portions of it are magnificent. The high altar and the beautiful dome are especially worthy of admiration. One is surprised to see how much wealth it has retained, notwithstanding the strenuous efforts of invading armies to relieve it of that root of evil. As Granada was the birth place of Alonzo Cano, it is fitting that the Cathedral should be ornamented by the works of so distinguished a son, and such is the case. The specimens of his art are numerous and of the first degree of merit. There is a series of seven pictures by him, representing scenes in the Life of the Virgin. As is usual with a continued effort of this kind, some are good and others much below what might be expected. But unalloyed praise must be bestowed upon his various carvings of the Virgin. The heavenly expression which he has infused into the speechless wood surpasses belief. Every one of these is a treasure. But his Virgins, however beautiful, do not approach in sanctity the ugly image in the Chapel de la Antigua, which was brought by Ferdinand and Isabella to aid the siege. Like its sister of Guadaloupe, it has received the honor of bestowing a name on one of our islands.

By far the most interesting portion of the Cathedral is the Chapel of the Kings, which, though attached to the building, is on a separate ecclesiastical establishment, and devoted to the sepulture of the Catholic kings and their daughter and son-in-

22

law. The shades of evening were gathering as we entered the
sacred spot where repose the mortal remains of the great, the
wise, the good Isabella, the queen of queens, whose firmness
and intelligence equalled her gentleness. Among the female
sovereigns who have dazzled the world by their charms or
scandalized it by their crimes, Isabella of Spain stands alone
uncontaminated by the vices of her position, or the frailties of
her sex—surpassing Elizabeth and Catharine in wisdom, and
Semiramis in fortune, uniting therewith the peculiar charms of
her sex—virtue, submission, piety; alike beloved and esteemed
as a woman and a sovereign. The only blot upon her reign is
the establishment of the Inquisition. A great deal may be said
in her excuse or justification in this behalf. The whole of the
newly conquered country was filled with pretended converts to
the faith, who remained at heart its bitter foes. And as this
difference of faith involved in those days a difference of nationality, it became a political duty to see that the safety of the
State were not endangered by its enemies concealed within its
own bosom. Such was the Inquisition as first established—an
instrument against hypocrisy; and her meek and gentle spirit
would writhe in its prison house could it but behold this child
of hell, as it soon afterwards became, blasting and withering
the grass as it strode the earth, and scattering broadcast
anguish and misery unutterable. Strange fate! that the most
horrible of all human institutions should owe its establishment
to the best of sovereigns.

The faint twilight fell upon the marble effigies of the great
queen and her husband. Nothing can be more exquisite than
the expression of her face. It is that of the Christian who has
fought the good fight, and this fitful dream o'er, in the calm
repose of faith awaits the trumpet summons of resurrection.
Seldom has a work of art been in happier harmony with its
surroundings. On the adjoining tomb are similar effigies of
their daughter, Juana la Loca, and their son-in-law, Philip of
Burgundy. The whole in costumes remarkable for their simplicity. There was some difficulty about procuring the key to
the vault below out of the usual hours, and as I had visited it
upon a previous occasion, it did not seem worth while to insist.
The coffins are plain, entirely without ornament. The ceno-
taphs above had spoken of the glories of the past, the hopes of
the future; the shapeless, leaden boxes below told us of the

present, of the corruption of mortality and of the vanity of human greatness.

The rest of the Chapel is occupied by the high altar, which is ornamented with curious and very interesting carvings, representing the surrender and conversion of the captives. The banners used at the siege, with the sword of Ferdinand, are worthily deposited here. It is really pleasant to see the unity of the idea so exquisitely preserved. Nothing is calculated to divert the mind from the conquest, unless it be the tomb of Juana la Loca and her husband, which, perhaps, has been permitted to remain as a commentary upon worldly pride—that the proudest sceptre of two continents should descend to hands bereft of reason to grasp or appreciate it.

Of the various convents there are few at present worthy of a visit. The Cartuja, a little outside of the city beyond the gate of Elvira, is an exception. Though the Carthusians were averse to the charms of conversation, they generally manifested an appreciation of the pleasures of sight. The view over the Vega, from the convent terrace, is lovely, indeed, as every prospect over that magic vale must be. The cloisters within present a less agreeable aspect, being ornamented with frescoes of the cruelties inflicted upon the members of their order in England, under Henry VIII, as a set off to similar acts charged against their own faith. Both are, doubtless, correct in the substance of their accusations; power and fanaticism cannot be united without the effusion of blood, and history shows that Elizabeth and her father, considering the small sincerity of belief in either, were as little disposed to be tolerant as Queen Mary. But what did arouse my admiration were the marble and the tortoise shell, the ivory and ebony work of the chapel and sanctuary. Such things rarely strike me, but these are quite out of the ordinary range, and are not only curious, but exquisitely beautiful. The lines of color in the marble have been interpreted into various fantastic figures, and some strangely correct representations of our Saviour, crowned with thorns, are considered to border upon the miraculous. In surveying their unequalled richness of decoration, I could not but think if such be a Spanish convent, after its desecration, what must they have been at the beginning of the century. By thus ornamenting their abode, the Carthusians must have rendered doubly hard the duty of self-mortification;

for what could be more tantalizing than to be thus surrounded with so many of the charms of life, and yet unable to speak beyond the two gloomy phrases: "We must die;" "die we must." (Hémos de morir; ya lo sé.)

The marble here used came, for the most part, from Lanjaron. All the neighboring mountain ranges are full, and the whole of Andalusia abounds in vast deposits of every class, some quite equal to the best in the world. It is questionable whether any other portion of Europe be so well provided. They are found, too, in a greater variety of color. The abundance of so ornamental and useful a material, and the excellence of the climate, which prevents it from tarnishing, are two reasons of the extraordinary neatness of the houses in all this province. The Patios of the commonest dwellings in Seville are paved with it, whither it is brought from the Sierra Morena, the mountains near Ecija, and those of Ronda. On the sea coast the Italian marble was formerly employed as a part return trade for the exports from the Indies.

The once magnificent convent of Saint Jerome is utterly ruined, and even the tomb of the great Captain Gonsalvo de Cordova desecrated. It is an old tale, soon told: the French carried off everything that could be removed, and converted it into a stable. The so-called liberal mob completed what the French had left undone, murdered the monks and rifled the sepulchre of the Great Captain, whose bones are probably scattered in private cabinets, from Land's End to John o'Groat's. But one of the noblest monuments of a past age survives in the Hospital of San Juan de Dios, founded by the Saint himself, who died in the reign of Charles V. I happened to be there on the day of the patron Saint, in 1852, when the Hospital, with the exception of the dangerous and infectious wards, was opened for inspection to all who chose to enter. We followed along with the crowd. The appearance of everything was admirable; neatness and order reigned around; nor was this merely for the occasion, as the hospitals in Spain are better managed than anything else. Among the patients was a handsome young girl, with raven hair; her face slightly flushed, but without the appearance of suffering. Her suffused eyes rested dreamily and confidingly upon us as we passed by. I shall never forget the expression of that innocent face. One such look of relieved suffering would reward a lifetime of charity. As we went out of the great entrance, I placed two *pesetas* (forty cents) on the contribution table. "You are extravagant," said a friend. "After paying five for a gipsy dance, I think I can afford two to a hospital," and two other pesetas kept mine company.

As I had had some desire to see a gipsy dance, we concluded one day to mount the Albaycin, the gipsy quarter, and the home of the poor and squalid of every race, in order to engage the dancers ourselves. The old city was confined, for the most part, to the Albaycin, lying west of the Darro, which was formerly peopled by the Moors of Baeza, who removed thither after the capture of that city, whence its name. The Alhambra lies east of it, and the Antequerula between the foot of the latter and the Genil. Passing from the head of the Carrera del Darro, we entered the Plaza of Vivarambla, the great square of the Moorish city, famous for its bull fights and Djerids, where the lance was exchanged for the reed. Granada, formerly, had twenty gates, among them Vivarambla, the Gate of the River, or rather the sand, that has assumed its present name, by the same process which converted Al Hamra into Alhambra. The Spanish language has adopted the word *rambla* to mean the sandy bed of a river, when the water has been dried up by the summer heat. This famous square of the Romanceros, notwithstanding modern alterations, retains something of its ancient appearance, though, like the Gate of the Sun in Madrid, it is now in the centre of the city. Its poetic appellation has, with singular ill taste, been supplanted by the prosaic and chronic one of Plaza de la Constitucion—one of the inevitabilities of every Spanish town. From that we plunged into a labyrinth of narrow streets, which finally became zigzags, until we at length reached the habitations of the veritable children of Moultan, some dwelling in houses of the smallest dimensions, others in the more primitive style of caves. These latter were by no means so despicable as might be supposed, judging them by our own wet country. The earth is firm, and there is little or no moisture in this dry climate, so that the occupants were probably as well off as the more aristocratic dwellers in houses. The gipsies congregate in Andalusia and Barcelona. The former is their favorite of the earth, and they have all sorts of tender expressions for this land of choice. Here alone do they seem to have a fixed residence. The date of their entry into Spain is uncertain, but probably after the Moorish power had begun to decline. No allusion is made to them as having played any part in the rivalry of the religions, which they certainly would have done. They were required by the royal edict to adopt a residence, and to conform, at least outwardly, to the Catholic faith; but it seems doubtful whether they have any real belief beyond this existence.

Most travellers are wonderfully struck with the beauty of the young women. Elsewhere I might have agreed with the general opinion, but when compared with the pure blooded Spaniard, they fell in my estimation far below. Their complexion is that of a dark mulatto. The contour of the face resembles somewhat the North American Indian. Their eyes are their own—orbs of fire with no shades of softness, partaking as much of what is below as of what is above the earth. Toward other nations their chastity is absolute, admitting of no exception. But among each other the marriage tie once contracted they live the life of pigs; a strange medley of contradictions. The occupation of the men consists in a variety of petty employments—requiring no investment of capital, of which they are singularly deficient—smithing, shearing mules and dogs, farriery, swapping and selling horses, lying, thieving and roguing in general. The women help in these occupations so far as they can; make mats and produce vast quantities of young gipsies. The children pick up stray jobs, hold dogs' feet while the hair is being taken off by their elders, filch from the pockets of short men, or tall ones, if there be a bench near by, and make themselves useful to the tribe in a small way. In all Spain I knew of only one gipsy who followed a steady and respectable occupation. From time immemorial they have been tacitly allowed to govern themselves, under a captain of their own choice. But I was told that lately in Barcelona they had been brought under the jurisdiction of the common tribunals, and now stand upon the same footing with other subjects.

We stopped in front of a house and looked in upon a collection engaged in plaiting mats. A few of them, with coal black, dishevelled hair and intelligent, flashing eyes, did look very interesting, though there was wanting some element which is indispensable to beauty. We were welcomed with smiles, per-

haps it would be more strictly correct to say that our guide
was. Preferring to sit outside, rickety chairs were placed on a
little knoll in front, and we were speedily surrounded, the news
having spread that we were getting up a "funcion." The
young hopefuls were clad in extreme summer costume, consisting frequently of nothing but their own skins, which, it is a
thousand pities, they could not take off occasionally for the
purpose of having them washed. They were intent in pursuit
of coppers, and avowed their willingness to turn any amount
of somersets for a *cuartito*. Those of a more advanced age
were decently clad and behaved with perfect propriety. We
whiled away an hour in this outlandish company, making our
arrangements. Four of the young ladies were selected. One
of them was really good looking, with a frank, smiling countenance and glorious eyes; modest in deportment and evidently
a belle. I commenced a most innocent flirtation instanter.
With a parting recommendation to get themselves up in fine
style, we passed on to the church which overhangs the valley
of the Darro, to enjoy the *vista general*. The terrace commands the city and Vega, and gives in addition a fine view of
the Alhambra itself, which is directly opposite. Descending
thence by a precipitous Moorish street, the houses being within
touch on either hand, we called at the residence of an artist,
who was engaged by the Emperor of Russia to copy portions
of the Alhambra on a reduced scale. The work is beautifully
executed and faithful to the minutest line, for the present Emperor seems determined to follow the example of his father in
developing the taste as well as the material resources of his
vast empire. Proceeding on our way, the guide pointed out
one of the two houses that enjoyed the right of sanctuary,
which he assured us was still respected, though I think he
must be in error. We then turned into the Zacatin, the famous
shopping street both now and under the Moors. It preserves
its name and appearance with scarcely an alteration. An
awning drawn over excluded the rays of noon and rendered it
a pleasant resort for the idle fair of Granada.

After nightfall we assembled at the residence of the captain
of the gipsies to witness the *funcion*. The former dignitary
had died. His successor was a rather young man, of handsome appearance, and manners quite genteel. We foreigners,
three in number, took our seats in a row; the performers, con-

sisting of the four damsels and one of the other sex, who was
a famous dancer, sat opposite. The captain's wife held a central position with the collection hat in her hand, while the
native spectators scattered promiscuously around. The performance was opened by the captain, who gave us several
pieces upon the guitar. Those who have never seen this
instrument in the hands of a Spaniard, can form little conception of its powers. He had learned entirely by ear, yet his
performance was wonderful. Having satisfied us with his
music, he gave us a specimen of his skill, playing it behind
his back, and over his head, and under his feet, and finally
with his elbows. He then took a tambourine and knocked
himself with it all over, from his crown to his sole, in the style
of Ethiopian dancers, only more so. Our unqualified approbation was justly bestowed and gracefully acknowledged. The
space was now cleared for the dancers, who first appeared in
twos. Before taking her position, each gave her handkerchief
to one of the company to hold. My beauty completed her
conquest by the selection of her knight. There is nothing of
the Othello about these handkerchiefs, except that they must
be returned when called for, and it would be the height of
impoliteness to hand them back empty. I happened to have
some American cents, of the new coinage, which were distributed among the silver, and seemed to give great satisfaction. It is to be hoped that their dusky red hue did not cause
them to be mistaken for the more precious metal. It would be
as well not to enter too minutely into a description of the
dances. They are derived from Hindostan, and are supposed
to be identical with those which delighted the wits and joyous
revellers of the lower empire. One of the company had seen
them on the banks of the Nile, where they would be more
appropriate than in a modern ball room. In a historical point
of view they were interesting enough. Some of them were of
later origin and proper. One called *El Torillo*, or the Little
Bull, was an imitation of a bull fight, rather a difficult subject
to portray in a ballet. But I have seen Faust danced, and if
German metaphysics can be expressed in the poetry of motion,
why should not the bull fight have a trial? The sound of the
castagnettes had, meanwhile, collected an audience outside,
who mingled their applause with our own, the *gamins* diversi-
fying the entertainment by climbing the grating and slily

pulling our coat tails. An indignant exhortation from the captain, or rather a speech, consisting of some half a dozen score of Spanish and gipsy oaths, restored order. After a couple of hours I took my departure with the conclusion that I had seen gipsy dances enough to last me my lifetime. It is one of the orthodox sights, and has to be seen once, but the guide informed us that Louis Napoleon was the only person, in his recollection, who had ever called for a repetition.

Granada is no longer that centre of wealth which it was said to have been formerly. Manufactures and commerce there are none. The population is purely agricultural, and quite as great as the country can support, unless the science of production be improved. Its decline has been very generally attributed to the expulsion of the Moriscoes by Philip III, and this measure has been condemned under every point of view—economical, political and moral. About the political I think there is room for doubt. The conversion of the Moors after the conquest was purely nominal. Crowds were collected, a little water sprinkled over them with a brush, and the change of faith accomplished. To suppose that the opinions or sympathies of the baptized population underwent any alteration would be preposterous. They continued at heart as they had always been, not only Mohammedans, but Moors longing for the return of their countrymen, and ready to join an invading army, or to prepare their entrance. It is well enough at our day to speak of toleration and to condemn ebullitions of bigotry in the past, but such is not history. Questions of faith in those days were questions of nationality, and oil and water were easier to mix than Moslem and Christian, according to the practice of the latter. Compared with the Moors, the Spanish were in excess of intolerance; compared with other nations of Europe, they were disciples of a common faith, whose usual argument was the sword. We have had in our own country an experience of the inconvenience which results from the existence of an un-harmonizing, worldly and semi-political religion within our borders. Yet the handful of Mormons is nothing compared with the population of Granada, occupying the seacoast directly opposite to Africa, where their fellows were still in the enjoy-ment of pristine vigor. Few will doubt that in a political point of view the exodus of Brigham Young was an immense benefit to the State of Illinois. The humanity of the expulsion in

either case is another matter.   But in the affairs of the world
political necessity is apt to override all obstacles. The extreme
measures taken against the Moriscoes were harsh and harshly
executed; yet it is doubtful whether any of their neighbors
would have acted more gently.   Events of even a half century
later in America deprive us the privilege of casting a stone,
and the punishment of death upon a Jesuit for simply landing
upon the shores of England estops criticism from that quarter.

It must, however, have been a mournful sight to witness the
extinction of this gallant race, to which mediæval Europe was
indebted for so many ameliorating institutions—ameliorations
she has not been eager to acknowledge.   Most of what formed
the romance of earlier days throughout the Continent is traceable to the Peninsula, where the rude, sturdy Teutonic and
elegant, poetic Oriental were subjected to mutual influences.
One of the most conclusive evidences of the utter rudeness and
barbarism of Europe in the eighth, ninth and tenth centuries,
the darkest of the dark ages, is the unanimity with which the
feudal system was received.   This was a great progress, a
long step in advance, but how miserable must have been the
condition of society which required such a remedy.   It had no
existence in Spain, because the Spanish civilization had never
reached such a pitch of violence and anarchy as to require it.
About that time the Beni Omeyah were at the acme of their
glory, and the softening light of Cordova penetrated even to
the farthest corners of the north-west.   The Spaniard inherited
from his Gothic ancestors fierce courage, valor, the sentiment
of personal honor, the duel, the judgment of God, fidelity to
his chieftain, and the other points which characterized the
Teutonic civilization.   The Oriental to a valor quite the equal
of his rival, united other qualities which were considered no
less necessary to the character of a warrior, viz: poetry, grace,
elegant horsemanship, skill in weapons, gallantry, fidelity to
plighted word, and mercy to the conquered.   The result was a
military fraternity between the warriors of the two nations,
and a common military character to which the Teutonic
element contributed the strength and the defects, the Oriental
the virtues and elegancies.   Hence sprang chivalry, which
spread gradually over Europe, and contained the first germ of
civilization.   The contest of Reeds (juegos de Cañas, the Djerid
of the polished Moors) was imitated by the northern nations in

the joust and tournament. Indeed, it is questionable whether the institution of chivalry as described in the romances had a veritable existence out of Spain. No where else were celebrated *Pasos Honrosos* such as that of the bridge of Orbigo, in which Suero de Quiñones, aided by nine other knights, defied all passers by, in order that he might remove from his neck an iron collar which he wore in honor of his mistress. In this encounter more lances were broken than is mentioned in any similar trial. Wherever the Spanish authority extended, a taste for these encounters revived, though it had almost disappeared under the progress of political science. Giucciardini gives a detailed account of a battle of champions in the Spanish wars in Italy, merely from the point of honor. Numerous others are recorded, but all of date long subsequent to their origin in the Peninsula, whence they were indisputably derived. In one of the campaigns of the Hagib al Mansour, as far back as the tenth century, an account is incidentally given of a similar challenge on the part of a Christian knight, which resulted in the defeat of all the Mohammedan champions except one, who, mounted on a sorry nag, yet carried off the victory. Such contests, merely from a chivalrous desire to test the prowess of an adversary, were favorites with the Spaniards and Moors, and these gallant encounters lend a charm to their history which none other can hope to possess. They are justly entitled to the credit of having revolutionized war. Before their day, it was a brutal, bloody, ferocious means of destruction. Gentle mercy to the vanquished was as unknown to the Hebrews, Greeks, or Romans, as to the Franks or Anglo-Saxons. Hence arises the charm of romantic chivalry hanging around these Andalusian battle fields, which will be vainly sought elsewhere, for here alone was a distinction recognized between the armed foe, careering in the pride of equal strength, and the same foe dismounted and prostrate under the victor's feet. It is no wonder then that the gallant spirits of the rest of Europe should flock to Spain as the land of romantic adventure, and the proper theatre for the display of knightly prowess; that the Douglas should perish at the siege of Teba; that the Counts de Arbi and Solusber (as they are styled in the Chronicle) should fight by the side of the gallant hero of the Salado; that Lord Scales should come from the misty north-west to the siege of

Granada, and that Chaucer should consider the proudest recommendation of a knight—

> In Gernade at the seige eke hadde he be
> Of Algesir.

Yet what historian has had the justice to trace chivalry to its true source.   Spaniards have never been given to book making, and, verily, Esop's fable of the man and the lion is the experience of all ages.

The pundonor or point of honor, distinguished from the vengeance of the northern nations, sprang from the same origin. As the other quality mentioned above was derived from the Oriental, so did this come remotely from the Teutonic element, but modified in a similar manner by contact with the enlightened Andalusians.   To this day it is as unknown among the Italians or the Scandinavians as it was to their ancestors.   But to pursue, in all its developments, the influence of the Hispano-Moresco civilization upon the world would make a book, a history of the Peninsula, such as no one as yet has seen fit to write.   Without such investigation, it is scarcely possible to appreciate the Moors.   The work of Perez de Hyta bears upon its face unmistakable marks of relationship with Amadis de Gaula and Palmerin de Inglaterra, yet the spirit is doubtless correctly portrayed, though the narrative be mostly fictitious. But the Beni Serraj and the Zegris have alike disappeared, and they and their contemporaries are remembered rather for what they certainly did not than for what they did.

CHAPTER XVIII.

GRANADA BY JAEN TO MADRID.

Puerto de Arenas—Approach to Jaen—View from the Castle—The Paseo—To
Bailen—Menjabar—Despeñaperros—Leave Andalusia—La Mancha—Oil Jars—
Beggars—Arrive at Madrid.

It had been my intention to proceed by Murcia and Orihuela,
two of the most beautiful Vegas in Spain, to Carthagena and
palm-embowered Elche, but the cholera unfortunately was rav-
aging that country, and the seaports were all under quarantine,
so I must needs content myself with the inland route to Madrid, whither I was obliged to return.

At an early hour of the next morning, therefore, I was upon
the balcony waiting for the diligence to Jaen. The moon was
still silvering over the city, though the daylight was visible on
the peaks of the Sierra Nevada, coloring the snow upon their
bosoms with a faint rosy blush. Our road ascended quickly
out of the Vega, and afforded kaleidoscopic views of its beauties
under the varying aspect of the morning light, until turning a
shoulder in the ridge, we suddenly lost sight of Granada and
its glories: but our way was still enlivened by the appearance
of wild flowers and fields until we entered the Sierra Susana.
The pass is not a lofty one, and consequently presents nothing
that is entitled to be considered grand, but the passage through
the Puerto de Arenas is very curious, and is really a "gate."
It appears as though a perpendicular slab had been taken out
of the wall for the river bed, and so narrow is the passage, that
it is necessary to tunnel for the road, as there is absolutely not
room for both. Commanding the entrance to the kingdom of
Granada, it was often contested in the olden time, and its waters were as frequently tinged with human blood as any others
consecrated in the ballads. No place in the country could be
better suited for such a purpose. A few leagues farther on

opened to us the mountain panorama of Jaen, a truly magnificent prospect, with all the stern grandeur which so eminently
characterizes the mountain scenery of the Peninsula. The city
was still a considerable distance from us. It lies upon the lofty
ground in front of the Sierra, or rather upon the projecting
breast of the chain, and appeared to be half way to the heavens. Behind it rises the bare and cheerless mountain range,
which is so elevated, as, in winter, seriously to interfere with the
comfort of the plain by intercepting the sun's rays. The aspect of the city itself was consonant with the scenery around,
and it well deserved the appellation of the Citadel of Andalusia.
The old Moorish walls can be traced winding over the hills up
to the Castle, and the towers of its churches still give it the
appearance of an ancient fortress. Between us lay the broad
valley of the river Jaen. From reading the history of the reconquest of Spain by the Moors, and of the many notable feats
of arms that had been enacted in the neighborhood, I had
formed an expectation which was not disappointed by the
reality. It is the beau ideal of a Moorish outpost, and unites
all the elements of picturesque beauty which seem to have
guided those elegant Orientals in their choice of sites for their
cities. Descending from the branch of the Sierra which separates it from Granada, we crossed the fertile Vega and commenced the ascent, and after much shouting and trouble,
arrived at our destination in a clean street paved with rough
stones. As few travellers halt in this time-honored but somewhat shrunken place, the Posada was none of the best, and did
not exceed what a reasonable traveller might have justly demanded.

The boast of Jaen, in the way of sights, is its Cathedral—
a beautiful structure in the modern classic style—and viewing
the present condition of the city the wonder is, why such an
amount should have been expended in an unimportant town on
the side of a mountain. It is grand in dimensions, of a very
pure style of architecture, and abounds in beautiful marbles, all
from the neighborhood. It enjoys, furthermore, the reputation
of possessing precious relics, such as the handkerchief of St.
Veronica with the miraculous image of the Saviour's face,
which I did not see. But the true beauty of Jaen depends
upon its situation. Being thus at the base of a lofty Sierra, it
is abundantly supplied with fountains and deliciously cool

water, which will render any spot in Andalusia charming, and
the views from its Alameda are unsurpassed. The old Moorish
walls still exist, in a dilapidated state, and wind picturesquely
up the hillside to the castle, whence the prospect by sunset is
superb. The mountain chain behind, running north-west and
south-east, casts its shade over the valley even to the foot of the
ridge we had descended in the morning, alternating with the
green herbage of the river bank and the bare rocks beyond,
across and through which wound the white road until it was
lost in the distant Puerto de Arenas, at the entrance of the
valley of the Genil. To the left, at right angles, far below, was
the ever graceful Gaudalquivir, and crowning the valley to the
north rose, in the distance, the tremendous mass of the Sierra
Morena, while the peaks in front and on both sides were bathed
in the rose and purple light of the hour. Owing to the great
elevation of the city the prospect was extensive, comprehending a considerable portion of the kingdom of the name. No
wonder that it proved so long a barrier to the Christian power,
and that their armies had so often retreated from its walls
" farther than the Pleiades."

As the shades of night fell I returned to the uninviting
Posada, and was meditating upon the difficult problem of passing an evening agreeably in a strange place, with but little
prospect of a successful solution, when I found that my two
companions of the morning ride, who were returning from the
Baths of Carratraca, had taken a Samaritan's compassion and
had called to invite me to an evening promenade upon the
Paseo. The courtesy was as unexpected as it was acceptable,
and we took our place among the crowd to enjoy the glories
of a September night on an Andalusian mountain slope. They
soon met some ladies of their acquaintance seated in chairs
upon the side of the walk, and I was presented, in the informal
way usual upon such occasions, as a *Caballero estrangero*, who
had made the journey with them—and this seemed quite sufficient recommendation. In the course of the conversation I
found that the elderly lady was the mother of the two younger,
and the names of the latter were Clara and Eugenia. Doña
Eugenia was a blonde, with bright blue eyes (ojos zarcos),
glossy dark hair, and an elegant figure, such as nature kindly
bestows upon most Andaluzas of eighteen. She seemed a very
mountain rose—somewhat doubtful at first of the deportment

she should assume toward a person who lived the other side
of three thousand miles of water, but this soon wore away, and
we commenced our conversation about the Moorish war, which
at that time occupied all thoughts. The ladies were very
enthusiastic for the honor of Spain, and stamped their little
feet upon the ground when speaking of the insults which had
been offered to the garrison at Ceuta. Thoroughly Andaluzas,
every gesture, movement, thought, was grace personified. At
anything startling, Doña Eugenia, exclaiming " *Santissima
Virgin !*" would cross herself so prettily that even the Emperor
of Almagreb himself would have been converted. How the
hours flew by! Star after star waned before the increasing
brilliancy of the moonbeams, and eleven o'clock had passed ere
we took leave of our fair companions and one of the gentlemen
at the grating of their door. I lingered a moment until Eugenia's lace veil disappeared behind the sparkling fountain of the
Patio, and checking a rising curiosity, supposed to be peculiar
to our country, expressed sincere thanks to my entertainer for
the pleasure of the evening, as we parted at the door of the
Posada.

The next morning was wearisome enough while waiting for
the diligence from Granada. Beyond what I mentioned, Jaen
offers few attractions. According to the Moorish accounts, it
was once celebrated for its silk manufactures, and Al Makkari
says it was called Jaen al Harrir, or Jaen of the Silk ; but manufactures have disappeared, and it is now the residence of a
purely agricultural population. The neighboring country, like
all that which borders upon the Guadalquivir and its tributary
streams, was, and is yet, famous for its horses, which, in better
days, were little inferior to Arabs. Of products of the soil it
furnishes a superabundance, for though the mountain sides and
elevated plains are comparatively sterile, its valleys riot in
fertility.

About noon the diligence made its appearance and we thun-
dered down the slope. A journey of three or four leagues
brought us to the valley of the Guadalquivir. The Pride of
Betica was so reduced in dimensions that I did not recognize
it at a distance, and was surprised to see a strange and unusual
airy structure extending across a part of the valley, and a clus-
ter of tall chimneys upon the summit of the distant ridge to the
north vomiting forth their smoke against the cloudless blue of

the sky.   The latter were at the famous mine of Linares, celebrated even in ancient days for its stores of lead and copper, and the former was the suspension bridge of Menjibar.   How misplaced and unnatural it appeared in this land of massive masonry! for Spain is distinguished by the almost unnecessary solidity of its public edifices.   Both were unusual sights in a country where the traveller seems to have left modern inventions behind him.   Passing over the bridge we continued our way to Bailen, where it unites with the grand route from Seville, and we retraced slowly the road which I had descended a couple of months before.   The good meal at Bailen prepared us for crossing the Sierra Morena, and a detachment of beggars welcomed us into and out of the town wishing us a good digestion—and the poorest beggars I had seen for many a day.   A gentleman from Madrid here entered the berliña and gave me the pleasure of his company to Tembleque.   He was on his way to bring his wife to Andalusia to spend the winter for her health.   Fortunately, I had met and exchanged cards with a friend and schoolmate of his, which at once placed us upon a footing of friendship, and caused him to supply me with notes to his family and friends in Madrid, which, to my regret, I had not time to deliver.   His manners were courteous and his information by no means restricted, so that his society converted a tedious into a very pleasant journey.

Passing through Carolina, Las Navas, and other villages of what are called the "Nuevas Poblaciones," we commenced at Sta. Helena the long ascent of the Sierra Morena.   This famous pass, which connects Andalusia with the interior, is known by the name of Despeña-perros, interpreted by some "throw the dogs (*i. e.* the enemy) over;" by others as signifying a place where a dog might easily fall over.   In former times it well deserved its name, as the most break-neck place in the four kingdoms of Andalusia.   By the enlightened efforts of the Count of Florida Blanca, in the reign of Charles III, a magnificent road was constructed, quite equal to any of those which have been subsequently made in Switzerland, except that there are no avalanches to be guarded against.   At this season of the year much of the splendid masonry work seems to be an unnecessary waste of labor; scores of bridges, built in the most massive style, span tiny rivulets and ravines, which are now perfectly dry, but in the winter and spring become

23

furious torrents, sweeping everything before them. The scenery
is of the grandest description. On each side of the road stand
lofty crags of brownish rocks, rearing their perpendicular sides
until they are lost to view—monarchs in the solitude. Tropical
vegetation is soon left; all the grades of the temperate zone in
turn disappear; a few firs struggle out from sheltered crevices,
but even these cease, and the wildest solitude reigns over the
face of nature. Descending into and crossing a deep and broad
ravine that makes its way up to the north-west, we commenced
the final ascent of the pass itself. In spite of the warnings of
robbers, which the neighborhood of the far-famed Venta de
Cardenas rendered not altogether pointless, I dismounted and
walked on ahead of the toiling mules. A perpendicular mountain side bounded the way on the left, a precipice on the right.
From the depth below rose, on the opposite side, the naked rock
to an equal height. Reaching the summit, I sat upon the
parapet awaiting the arrival of the vehicle. The situation was
indescribably lonely. It was just midnight. A cold wind
swept up the valley, and the moon threw a pale light down
into the gorge, causing each rock to assume fantastic shapes,
and peopling the solitude with giant forms. An open space to
the north, faintly illuminated by its glimmering rays, represented the vast plain of La Mancha. In front frowned the
beetling precipice, and above and around reigned the quiet of
desolation, unbroken save by the rumbling of the diligence in
the valley below. The cheerless aspect without reacted upon
the spirit within; it was natural to feel gloomy in such a place
at such an hour and on such an occasion. At the foot of these
mountains lay romantic Andalusia. How different were the
feelings with which, on first crossing, I had here welcomed the
Land of the South! I was now to say farewell; farewell to its
olives and citrons; farewell to the sweet song of its nightingales; farewell to its gentle zephyrs, laden with the perfume of
the rose and the violet; farewell to the golden waters of its
Guadalquivir and to the purple light of its sunsets; farewell to
those whose memory lends an undying charm to all that is and
exists in this glowing land; farewell! a long farewell!

The descent into La Mancha is by no means so great as into
Andalusia; the table-land of the interior being scarcely less
than 2,000 feet above the level of the sea. Manzanares and
Val de Peñas seemed dustier and poorer than ever. On every

side extended an arid, treeless expanse. The road was thronged with vehicles returning from the transportation of oil and wine. Each contained one huge earthen Ali Baba jar, some six or eight feet in depth and of a diameter in proportion. Rows of vehicles would follow each other, the drivers for the most part quietly asleep in the jars, trusting the mules to "take to the right," as the law directs. This confidence was not often misplaced, for the Spanish mule is exceedingly sagacious. I have seen them in scavenger carts arrange the supporting stick themselves when told to halt; and a team of eight is frequently guided at half speed by the voice alone, every one seeming to recognize his name and to distinguish " *Capitana-á-á-ah* " from " *Machô-ó-ó.*" Several times we passed companies of soldiers on their way to the camp at Algeciras. Their spirits were good, and the rate at which they moved surprising, though it would have been a great saving of human legs to have taken the railroad to Alicante and gone thence by sea. It may be that the rumors of the cholera caused this route to be preferred.

At Tembleque we halted to await the train from the east. The same boys were there to ask for coppers; one was deaf and dumb. To him I gave two—one for each affliction. The rest of the passengers asked me if we had beggars in America. I replied no; at least not in that part of the country which was known to me; that every honest, industrious man could at least gain a livelihood, and though there were many disagreeable things home, this alone would compensate for them all if one were reduced to a comparison with Europe. They agreed with me in the conclusion, but evidently did not comprehend how such a state of things could exist, as the idea of one class having nothing to do and living upon another class, who frequently cannot find sufficient honest employment to eke out a support, is deeply rooted in all European systems. A long train of freight cars was drawn up in the station, to avoid the trouble of going around which, I was about to pass between, but was stopped by the guard. This caused me to mention for their doubting admiration another precious privilege of the freeman in America, equally incomprehensible, viz: that of getting yourself killed, whenever you feel in the humor, without the hindrance of officious philanthropists in police uniform.

As the train approached, we were driven up on a car and took our place in line. Ocaña, the avenues of Aranjuez, Madrilejos whirled by in the dark, and about eleven P. M. the lights of "La Corte" appeared in the distance.   In a half hour more I was seated in my former apartment, welcome, although without the loaf of Seville bread, which my hostess had requested me to bring, in order that she might win her bet with a Madrileña as to its superior quality.

MADRID AGAIN.

Madrid appeared under a different hue by comparison with Andalusia. The temperature had lowered considerably, and the nights were cold, yet the streets had a glassy look about them, in sad contrast with the awning shades of the Calle de las Sierpes at Seville. The Prado was now deserted at night, as the air was too sharp for evening walks, and the afternoon promenades had begun. But how tame it was after the moonlight nights on the Plaza Isabel and the banks of the Guadalquivir! and the Madrileñas, handsome as they had seemed to me just from London and Paris, were not to be mentioned in the same day with the warm-hearted, graceful Andalusians. The city began to wear, however, more of the aspect of a great capital. Summer absentees were returning with a fresh stock of health to undergo the winter labors and dissipations. The diplomatic corps were already established in their old quarters, and the Court was soon to follow. The best evidence, however, of a renewal of life was the throng in the Puerta del Sol. The snatches of conversation which saluted your ear were upon every imaginable topic. The Morocco expedition, the English note, the visit of Marshal Pelissier, the funds, the loan, the circus, *el grillo*, the next bull fight, mingled up, of course, with an immense amount of scandal about everybody, from the Queen down, or up, according to the talker's standpoint in society. Madrid is almost the only place in Spain where there is any Government in the European acceptation of the term, that is, any organization of the controlling power, acting as a regulating and compressing influence. The garrison is quite numerous, and there is a respectable political police force, both open and secret. Not only is there a home police, but the French Government maintains one of its own to keep watch upon exiles and travelling Frenchmen. Perhaps it has an unknown similar establishment in other capitals, but nothing in Madrid can be kept a secret. One of the principal spies was pointed out to me. He was a young-looking man—a Frenchman—and from his appearance I never would have thought him engaged in such a detestable occupation. Happy is the nation whose Government has no political police.

The morning after my arrival I had an opportunity of judging of the efficiency of the municipal organization. Before day, I was awakened by a tremendous noise and the sound of heavy blows, and going to the window, saw the watchman breaking open the door of the next house. Thinking that some obnoxious person was concealed within, and that the police were in pursuit, I retired quietly to rest. The noise still continued, and in a few moments I felt a choking sensation. My American experience told me what was the matter; it was a fire, a thing of rare occurrence in Europe, and almost unknown in Spain. I dressed with speed, seized my dagger, letter of credit, passport and watch. With these one can confront any danger—without them, existence is worth very little abroad. The scene from my balcony was curious. First, the police stationed a force at each end of the street, to prevent circulation. Then the water carriers commenced making their appearance, each with his cask of water—this being a condition of exercising their calling; then a company of soldiers to preserve order. In the meantime clouds of smoke were rolling up, and the balcony became too hot to hold us. The utmost commotion reigned not only in our house but in the whole neighborhood. I am sorry to say that my two fellow lodgers, one a Spaniard, the other an Englishman, had packed up at the first alarm, and incontinently left. With the happy indifference of a man who has little to lose, and cannot save even that, I remained alone to console the terrified women. An American can scarcely imagine how terrified people do become in Europe about an occurrence which is a matter of every-day life to us. My hostess wrung her hands dolorously, exclaiming, "*la bomba! la bomba!* Oh, if *la bomba* would only come!" Thinks I to myself, what the plague is *la bomba*, supposing in my innocence (for I had never witnessed a Spanish fire before) that it was a bomb, with some stifling gas to extinguish the flames. They were all too busy to explain, so that I awaited with some curiosity the appearance of the beneficent *bomba*. Presently came an order from the chief of police to prepare to leave; so everything was removed from my apartment in front to the back part of the house, and we remained awaiting the end. In the meantime the engines had arrived. This was *la bomba*, and small affairs they were, not yet grown to the full estate of fire enginehood, and rather resembling our garden engines. Nor was their advent marked by any unusual bustle; no shouting, no running with the "masheen." Drawn up in line of battle, they were deliberately filled by the gallegos—smoking cigarettes—and as deliberately pumped. They answered the purpose, however, and I went to the head of the stairs to inform the trembling assemblage that the danger was passed. While standing there we heard a noise that startled us all—a terrific thumping on the staircase, accompanied with the jingling of metal. It sounded as though the ancestral house ghost was taking his departure. The noise approached rapidly, and soon it appeared in the bodily shape of a tall, thin, half-dressed Pole, with an immense bundle on his back, leaping three steps at a time. Seeing us standing so quietly, he appeared confused and stopped short. It seems that he lodged in the seventh story to the rear, and in those sublimated regions the alarm had penetrated with difficulty. But he was determined to make up in speed what he had lost in time; so, throwing all his worldly possessions into a sheet, had presented himself before us very much in the costume in which he had retired to sleep. Of course, our party were surprised at his being so alarmed, and rated him soundly for his want of pluck. The poor Pole attempted to defend his conduct, but was no match for his opponents, and soon sunk, crest-fallen and envious of our superior courage, back to the heavenly regions whence he had descended.

The crowd below had increased; the Corregidor and the Governor of the Province were present in uniform with dress swords—both persons of high rank. It would have horrified an Englishman or an Austrian to see how practical an equality reigned between them and even the water carriers. The Captain-General was represented by a staff officer on horseback, who seemed anxious to do something, but as there were no fainting damsels to be carried away on the gallant charger, his office remained a sinecure. I had a fair opportunity of seeing our neighbors, who thronged the balconies in the sparse costume of six o'clock, A. M. They were doubtless amiable, very amiable people; more than that it would be hazardous to assert. They were engaged like ourselves in contemplating the spectacle below, which was now diversified by a fight—some astonished passer-by having received the contents of a hose in his stomach, and testily resented that want of respect by cracking the Gallician manager of it over the head, which the proud descendant of Pelayo took in very bad part. After separating the combatants, all hands smiled and refreshed themselves with a cigarette. In an hour more the street was washed, and primeval quiet restored.

My first visit on my return was to the Museo and the Academy of San Fernando, to see if my opinions remained the same after visiting the Murillos at Seville. It seemed to me that in the highest style of painting, in lofty conception and sublime purity of expression, there was nothing in Madrid to equal the famous San Antonio, or the Conception, or the Guardian Angel which form the boast of Seville; but in the semi-earthly subjects that are represented in the three Murillos of the Academy, Madrid possesses a treasure which the world of art cannot surpass, and it is strange that the hand-books of painting dwell so little upon them. Indeed, had it not been for the robberies of the French Generals and their imperial master, it is more than probable that the whole Spanish school—Murillo, Velasquez, Ribera and Cano alike—would have been considered a mere offshoot, with little general merit and still less originality. Whereas, individuality and originality, both of conception and execution, are its distinguishing traits. It is true that most of their painters repeat themselves, even to the extent of what may be called mannerism; but this springs from those very traits of character which prevent the Spaniard from copying foreigners even if he would. Every great artist has naturally some ideal which reappears in his different works. A statesman or a soldier has a few fixed principles, which must be applied to a thousand varying situations, no two of which are alike. The ideal of artistic beauty, though a mere phantom perhaps, in truth has a real existence in the conception of each great painter. The difficulty consists in the attempt to grasp it, to withdraw it from the misty regions where such conceptions must float, and transfer it visibly to canvass. It is probable that no such attempt will ever be completely successful, but the Conceptions of Murillo seem to be a nearer approach to it than anything else which we have. The mere style may change. This is an accessory of execution. The highest perfection is something independent of such aids. Surely no one would wish to see the Last Judgment of Michael Angelo in oil colors. A deficiency in these minor respects has blinded many persons to the great excellencies of some of the Spanish painters, of which Ribera is a striking example, as if he must necessarily enter the procrustean bed with Albano, whose subjects required a variety and exquisite finish that would have been misplaced and injurious to the other. The effect of this want of variety of style in Spanish artists is disagreeably felt when many pictures of the same person are collected in the same room. Even the gallery of Murillos at Seville makes this impression upon you. Inferior artists can stand the test, because they paint from without and not from within, and consequently vary as often as they paint, but the same cannot be affirmed of any of the great masters except Rafaelle. The collections of Rubens in Madrid and Paris, leave you with little variety of impression, and so do the Titians, and I doubt not the same would be said of Michael Angelo, if his productions were placed in a row, yet he was the grandest genius of them all. I have more than once been painfully struck with this in the works of Guido. A single Guido, such as the Annunciation or the Aurora, is beautiful. A dozen Guidos in a row, as they are placed at Madrid, are simply oppressive. Place a Ribera between a Titian or Rubens and one of Rafaelle's early Madonnas, and its unrivalled excellencies as well as its defects, would be visible to the most unskilled beholder. There is, moreover, very little universality or versatility of talent among Spaniards; they seem to devote themselves to some one subject, whether by taste or accident. Murillo embraced a greater variety than any other, yet his virgins and holy female subjects generally seemed to have been his decided favorites. Velasquez was a painter of living men, and the illustration might be continued through Ribera, Zurbaran and the whole school.

There is no one here like Rafaelle, or Titian, or Rubens, to paint everything in the heavens, earth, and the water under the earth, with equal facility and felicity.

To change the subject from paintings to bulls, I went one day to see the *Apartado*. There was to be a fight that afternoon, and three animals of the breed of Hernandez, and three of Bañuelos, were collected in the *corral* attached to the Plaza. Galleries are built around the *corral*, so that we could look down upon the operation, which consisted in enticing them separately into the *toril*, and enclosing them in apartments according to the order of their entry into the ring. The behavior of the bulls upon these occasions is a fair test of what their conduct will be in the fight. Every now and then they would rush at the herdsmen, who escaped nimbly behind barriers erected for the purpose, while the bull would vainly struggle to tear up the wall. The herdsmen were a desperately wild-looking set, and one would have found it difficult to choose between them and the bulls. I very naturally reflected upon the disagreeable predicament we would be in, if the gallery were to break. Some of the historic families of Spain would have been put in mourning, for the company, though small, was very select, consisting for the most of nobles and bull fighters. The animals seemed much astonished and rather depressed when separated. It is surprising that this exhibition should be open to the public, for the bulls must necessarily be somewhat disconcerted at finding themselves exposed to the general gaze of so many persons whom they could not reach. They were, after much scuffling, all duly separated, each one in his stall, and the fight took place in the afternoon, but offered no peculiar features.

During my stay in Madrid the Queen, who had returned from La Granja, was to make a procession to the Church of the Atocha, so a friend procured for me a place in a window upon the Calle de Alcalá through which she was to pass. As the hour approached, carpets and variegated cloths were hung over the balconies in honor of the *fête*, a custom originally derived from the East, though known also to the Romans. The garrison was soon under arms, a double line of sentries bordering the street. The infantry were good-looking men, larger than the French and far handsomer, but not equal in average size to our people. In style of marching they are between the English and French, without the accurate drill and step of the former, or the *abandon* of the latter—I think a happy medium. The cuirassiers were a particularly fine body and well mounted. Royalty was not punctual upon this occasion, and we were kept some time in waiting. The interval was not wholly lost though, for I had been joined by two young ladies of two opposite styles of beauty; the one blonde, the other brunette, with clear complexion, fine forehead, and an exquisite, velvety pair of eyes that sparkled as she spoke. Under the circumstances, her Majesty's speedy coming was not wished for. But at length the bugles up the Calle Mayor sounded the Marcha Real, and the escort appeared in sight crossing the Puerta del Sol. The ceremonies and the equipages carried one back to the days when Spain was a great monarchy, and her proud boast was uttered that the sun never sat upon her dominions. The pomp was the same, but the grandeur had departed. A number of high officers preceded the procession. They did not impress me half so favorably as the troops, and had rather the appearance of part of a show than persons for real service. Such appearances, however, are very deceptive. Then came antique carriages and four, and still more antique carriages and six, filled with the *Servidumbre,* maids of honor, gentlemen in waiting, ministers, etc. Four led horses had a peculiar significance, I forget what. Finally appeared their Majesties. The Queen is far from handsome; her reputation for beauty does not equal that for virtue, nor is she at all graceful. In truth, though Queen of Spain, she certainly is no Spaniard in person or character, and the contrast between her procession to Atocha and that of her former subject Eugenia to a Te Deum at Notre Dame, is too striking to be agreeable. The king consort is an uneasy-looking, insignificant personage, and, from his appearance, would much rather have been smoking a royal *puro* than seated by his helpmate. But grandeur as well as poverty makes strange bedfellows. The procession passed on, my companions gave me a graceful inclination of their fans and a *Vaya vm. con Dios,* and we severally parted to our homes.

An amusing quarrel took place at the Church, as I was told, next day. The diplomatic corps had been invited, but by some oversight no places had been reserved; every apology was made and other places were offered, but they insisted on remaining outside and airing their wrath, until a message was

brought from the Queen, begging them to take the seats reserved for the Infantas, with many apologies, which they at
last consented to accept. As those gentlemen were persons
skilled in ceremonies, the course they adopted was probably
right; but, according to a common man's idea, it would have
been much more dignified to go quietly home and receive their
satisfaction in writing, instead of making a scene at the door.
The more belligerent might have challenged the Minister of
Foreign Affairs, who is not a warlike character, and thus the
question might have been peaceably arranged. Foreign diplomacy seems to consist of this sort of thing, coupled with the
back-stairs intriguing, characteristic of nations who surrender
the government of their affairs into the hands of a minister,
instead of deciding upon their foreign policy for themselves.

It had been my intention to pay a visit to the Escorial, but
the queen's household had engaged the diligence for some time
ahead, so that there would have been some trouble in getting
there, and still greater in getting away. As the place presents
but the one attraction, I concluded, therefore, to remain content with the impressions of a former visit. I had seen it then
in the winter, when the surrounding scenery harmonized well
with the gloomy idea of the founder—an idea which the architect has embodied with singular felicity. The Escorial is certainly the eighth wonder of the world. It makes but one
impression upon a visitor, but that impression is so profound
that it cannot easily be shaken off. The exterior, the church,
the Mausoleum, are all alike grandiose and overpowering. It
seems scarcely possible that the mere arrangement of speechless stone and mortar could produce such an effect, or that the
work of human hands could so master and crush the spirit.
You are overwhelmed, and breathe, on issuing from beneath
the massive portal, as though a frightful load had been taken
off your soul. What are the Coliseum and St. Peter's compared with this? Among the thousand descriptions, I prefer
that of Mad. Calderon, as conveying more vividly and truthfully than any other I have read, the unaccountable effect it
produces. The gridiron shape seems absurd on paper, but no
one would discover it for himself, and the triumph of the architect is thereby rendered so much the more complete.

Having failed in this attempt, I took a seat for Burgos direct.

Chapter XX.

MADRID TO BURGOS.

Departure—The Country—Somo Sierra—View over New Castile—First Impression
of Spain—Aranda—Lerma—Burgos—Las Huelgas—Miraflores—Cardena—The
Cid.

There was an unusual collection at the office of the diligence
to bid farewell to their various acquaintances. The winter
population was evidently returning. The principal thoroughfares, such as Calle de Alcalá, de San Geronymo, and others
emptying into the Puerta del Sol, were thronged with well-
dressed crowds, and every now and then a fur tippet gave
evidence of the change in the temperature. Madrid was becoming again the centre of Spain. The hour appointed for
starting was six o'clock. The conductor desired to start a
quarter before the time, as all were present. Expecting a
message which was to be brought me at the bureau, I wished
to delay till the last moment. The conductor—a Basque—said
he liked to be punctual. I replied that punctuality consisted
in starting exactly at the hour indicated, neither before nor
after. He would not admit the general principle, but thought
I was right in this particular case. His error was on the right
side, as is usually the case in travelling arrangements in Spain,
notwithstanding the reputation which the Government has
acquired, and it may be deservedly, for dilatoriness. The
message I had been expecting soon arrived, and at five minutes
before six, amidst the usual shouting of postilions, the barking
of dogs and the gazing of idlers, the various diligences started.
We rattled across the Puerta del Sol, up the Calle de Fuencarral, and sallying out of the city gate, entered the desert
which separates *La Corte* from the chain of the Somo Sierra.
It may be laid down as a general rule that no stranger likes
Madrid. Its hollow, insincere society, its unpatriotic and

absurd efforts to engraft foreign manners and foreign modes of
thought upon the stern old Castillian stock, the vagabond character of a large portion of its population, and the absence of
all memorials of the past, combine to render it one of the least
agreeable and attractive cities in Spain, though as a great
capital, it necessarily offers many resources for aiding the time
to slip by. I was told by several gentlemen who had married
in Madrid and resided there, that it improved upon acquaintance. I asked them if they had any friends. The invariable
answer was that although they had many acquaintances, they
could scarcely advance any—beyond the circle of their marital
connections—to the higher rank of friendship. In truth a very
great proportion of those who compose society are attracted
hither by the Government, and an utter selfishness is the rule
of their lives. Yet there are exceptions; and on issuing from
the gate I did experience a sort of regret, or rather a sympa-
thetic feeling with a city where I had spent some pleasant
moments. The scene around and the prospect ahead were
calculated to awaken such a sentiment. To the west was the
setting sun just disappearing beneath the horizon; a lurid,
threatening glare attended his departure, and a few clouds
gathered above as if to do homage to the expiring king of day.
His last rays glittered upon a battalion of soldiers who were
drilling on the parade ground to the right, filling the air with
the clash of weapons and the sonorous music of trumpets. Far
off to the north-west extended the lofty Guadarama mountain,
already indistinct in the evening shade. All else was one vast,
cheerless, broken plain, over which the cold wind howled with
the fierceness of a winter's blast. It was well calculated to
make the traveller regret his well matted room and sunny
balcony, even in Madrid.

The road near the city was thronged with vehicles returning
from the baths and mountains. From time to time a coach of
greater pretension bore its noble occupant along, and once a
coupé with four horses, preceded by outriders in the royal
livery, and containing two very heavy individuals inside,
whirled by us in clouds of dust. Legions of donkeys and
mules were returning from the city to their respective villages,
but soon these disappeared, and we disposed ourselves to pass
the night as best we could. The other corner of the berliña
was occupied by a stout lady, a resident of Madrid, who was

going to Bayonne to visit a relative living there. She was talkative and good humored, and was entitled to the three F's, for though she might not have been strictly styled fair, yet she was as near it as most persons who have unwillingly attained the other two. In addition to her many agreeabilities, she had the tangible one of a large basket most bountifully furnished, of which she insisted that I should partake, and with such earnestness that I durst not decline. The only article of commissariat which my foresight had provided me, would have been much more appropriate in America or Ireland than Spain, to wit: a flask of brandy. I offered it with many apologies, but as the good lady had never tasted any before, she declined making the experience now, so that the entertainment, so far as I was concerned, repeated the fable of the stork and the fox.

The road to the foot of the mountain is uninteresting in the extreme, and two previous journeys having rendered me familiar with its weariness, there was no inducement to force nature by struggling to keep awake. Fuencarral, Alcobendas, the historical and exceedingly ancient city of Buitrago, were passed by unconsciously. A furious storm, fulfilling the prognostications of sunset, discharged its torrents in like manner, without disturbing our slumbers, which continued uninterrupted until daylight broke upon the summit of the Sierra hanging over our heads. The prospect descending this mountain toward Madrid is very impressive to those who are just entering Spain from Bayonne. It is one of those boundless, immeasurable, indefinite and apparently infinite views which I have so often noticed in this book as peculiar to Spain. Far as the vision can reach is rolled out the uneven, rugged plain of New Castile, offering no resting place for the eye save a few brown villages that can scarcely be distinguished from the thirsty earth upon which they stand. The pass itself is almost the only passage from Old to New Castile, and defended by a handful of determined men, is impregnable against any army that could be assembled, unless the accuracy of fire-arms be increased even beyond their present range. Yet Napoleon with a squadron of lancers put to flight a whole division, provided, so far as the externals went, with all the requisites of war. The Spanish character has unjustly suffered by this and similar occurrences, but the militia of America, whose individual bravery none would question, have furnished fully as lamentable instances of panic; and the battles of New Orleans and Buena Vista offered the strange spectacle of one portion of the volunteers contending with a courage and valor that no regular soldier could imitate, while on the same field another portion threw down their weapons and fled without a shot.

Descending the mountain, we changed horses at a hamlet where I had most unwillingly been detained twenty-four hours in the fall of 1851 by a sudden attack of indisposition. At that time all around me bore the impress of novelty as well as grandeur. Most of the day I had passed on the summit of a little elevation which afforded an uninterrupted prospect toward the snow-covered ranges that bound the horizon to the north and north-west. Scarcely a tree or a shrub was in sight to break the continuity of waste. Long trains of laden mules would wind along the dusty road with the well armed arriero trolling lustily some old ballad, perhaps of the Cid or Count Fernan Gonsalez, and from time to time a soldier belonging to the Guardia Civil would hurry past; otherwise no living thing disturbed the quiet of the solitude. The sun shone brightly, and the deep blue sky over head reminded one of other seasons, but the keen wind that pierced to the very bones dispelled all illusions. And, thought I to myself, can this be Spain? Is this the romantic land of poetry? It was not what I had anticipated. There were no green valleys, no warbling songsters, no gentle zephyrs, yet the scene had a strange fascination. And now this very loneliness, this grandeur of isolation, throwing the burthen of life upon the individual, and at the same time developing within him the qualities which enable him to bear its weight, seemed to me indispensable to the idea of Castillian chivalry, with its freedom from dependence upon bodily enjoyments. The hardy life of the peasant in these lofty regions may be imagined when I state that a fire was lighted in the village once a week for the purpose of cooking bread, and that during the rest of the time a few bushes to boil chocolate was the utmost that could be allowed, for there are no trees in Castile, and the peasants tear up even those that the Government plants lest they should harbor birds. Spanish bodies have immense vitality and power of generating heat, and appear to be quite independent of artificial warmth. In the morning the unoccupied portion of the population—which seemed to include the whole, except on the arrival of a diligence—were seated upon benches on the western side of the street, enjoying the genial rays of the morning sun. When I returned in the afternoon, the village presented identically the same appearance, except that the progress of the sun had caused a corresponding change of position; they had moved over to the eastern side. Being without occupation, I imitated the example, and we talked away, until, about sunset, those who had gone out into the fields to labor commenced returning, and a finer looking race of men I never beheld. Of the medium height, sinewy in their persons, of grave and stately demeanor, these ragged peasants threw their thread-bare cloaks over their shoulders and walked into this collection of mud hovels with an air of dignified, courteous self-respect which many a sovereign would give half his kingdom to possess. I must do Castillejo also the justice to say the Spains could not furnish more snowy linen or delightful chocolate than that which it afforded me. On the present occasion it presented a more cheerful aspect.

The journey to Burgos was without variety. A cold, bitter cold wind; extensive and even grand views of the plains, as they are called, bounded on every side by lofty Sierras; peasants wrapped in their dun brown cloaks; files of mules and country vehicles of all sorts, were its features. About noon we stopped for breakfast at Aranda, famous in the olden time for the glories of its Bishopric, and in modern for its collection of beggars. The purling waters of the upper Duero afford moisture for its Alameda, whose green was refreshing to the eyes after the morning ride. Aranda is the locality of a celebrated fair which was not long over, and workmen were engaged in removing the bull ring which had been extemporized for the occasion. The breakfast was the cause of bitter complaints among the French passengers in the interior. I found it very palatable after the fast of eighteen hours, and had the full worth of my three pesetas in garlic and other savory condiments. The vacant place in the berlina was here taken by an officer of high rank in the army, who prepossessed me in his favor by distributing a handful of coppers to the wretched beggars as he entered. He was a youngish man, from the province of Burgos, near the border of Alava, a true Castillian in every respect, having alike the virtues and the defects of that sterling

24

race; courteous, formal at first, until the proper relations are
established, but then genial, high toned, and, I doubt not, true
as the ore of his native mountains; of course somewhat prejudiced, and not very enlarged in his views, because, like most
of his countrymen, he had seen but little of the world. In
his youth he belonged to the anti-Carlist party, which is a still
living division of political faction along the borders that were
desolated by the civil war, and the battle is not unfrequently
renewed even at present, on a small scale, from the depth of
pure conservative feeling. Good Catholics as the liberals were,
they were determined to cast off the rule of the clergy, and my
companion broke forth in private against the whole party, upon
recognizing, in our fellow-passenger, a sister of one of its bit-
terest chiefs, who had been expiating his political sins in exile
at Bayonne for many a year. But to her his conduct was
marked by perfect courtesy of demeanor. While we were
standing a little distance from the diligence, he asked me, in a
joking way, if I thought her handsome. I replied that no one
could tell to what he would finally come, but at present six
arrobas (150 lbs.) was as much as my admiration could well
embrace, whereas our worthy companion would probably come
nearer ten. He seemed amused at this way of measuring
beauty, and thought she would hardly exceed eight. That
evening, while waiting in the bureau of diligence at Burgos,
the idea took me of being weighed upon a pair of scales that
were hanging idly near by. A few minutes afterward, hearing myself addressed, I turned, and imagine my horror to see
her balanced, exclaiming to me with a triumphant air, "*Mire
vm. Caballero, ocho arrobas, menos cinco libras*" (eight arrobas,
wanting five pounds). The officer looked uneasy; perhaps I
did too. I certainly felt so, for I have always been in doubt
whether the rascally wind had not borne our conversation into
the window.

In the due course of events, we reached the City of Lerma,
capital of the great country and dutchy of that title. The
famous minister of Philip III, its Duke, erected an Iglesia Colegial or Collegiata and a Palace, both finished in the
grandest style of magnificence, and worthy of the inheritor of
so great a name. They survive in a half ruined state, diverted
from their original purposes. The War of Independence con-
signed to the past many a relic of ancient pomp and grandeur,

and Lerma, in its green little Vega, will with difficulty recover its former importance. As something had broken about the axle tree, the delay gave us an opportunity of looking around the town, and even of walking on the Paseo that skirts the trout-bearing waters of the Alanza. A few leagues more, driven at a furious rate, brought us to the crest of a hill, whence in the twilight, we saw the venerable city of Burgos, its ruined castle, and the filagree spire of its Cathedral, projecting against the tawny mountain that bounded the valley on the north-west.

Burgos is emphatically the heart of old Castile, and here is to be found in all its excellence, extravagance, if you will, those characteristics which, in the opinion of the world, have constituted the Spanish character. Proud, obstinate, unyielding though they be, it is a glorious old race, somewhat behind the world at present, and belonging as it were to a past age. Still no one can contemplate the genuine old Castillian without admiration. The aspect of the city is consonant with what one might be led to expect, severe, bordering upon the demi-grand in its situation, maintaining in unabated magnificence a few relics of ancient times, but insignificant in the productions of the last two centuries. The old castle on the hill, survives after a fashion, and gives a panoramic view over the city and the valley of the Arlanzon, with its spacious promenades, pretty enough in the spring or early summer. But the historical absorbs every other species of interest. Every great city in Spain is the representative of some epoch and some civilization; Toledo of the Gothic monarchy, and subsequently of the Primacy of the Church; Leon, of the early struggles for existence against the invaders; Cordova, of the pride of the Moorish power; Granada, of its romance and fall; stately Seville, of the consolidation of the Peninsula into a glorious unity and its expansion over the world; and so Burgos is the representative of old Spain, of Spain of the reconquest, the city of the Alonzos, the Ferdinands, of the Cid, as it behooved the crown of Castile to be placed upon its head. The Charleses and the Philips, these Hapsburg and Bourbon hybrids have no place within her walls. She is the genuine, unadulterated embodification of Castile. Like her children, she is *vieja y rancia*, with no touch of Jewish or Moorish blood stagnating in her veins. Her recollections are of the chivalrous times—of the lance and the linked mail, not of the wig and the rapier. Several private houses of a date anterior to the sixteenth century yet survive. The site of the Cid's mansion is kept vacant, and marked by a pillar, that of Fernan Gonzalez by the arch. The old palace of the Velascoes is in a ruinous state of neglect, but exists. Time has hallowed much, destroyed something, rebuilt nothing.

The great architectural attraction of Burgos is the Gothic Cathedral. For grandeur, it is far inferior to that of Seville, nor can it rival the fairy grace of Leon, but in all the peculiar beauties of the Arabo-Gothic, in delicacy of delineation, in appropriateness of ornament, in general excellence, there is none to take precedence. It is more amply provided with spires and pinnacles than even most Gothic structures, and seen from the Castle hill, presents quite a forest-like appearance. The interior contains everything. Among the paintings of various degrees of excellence, is one of the Virgin and Child, which is ascribed to Michael Angelo, or as some suppose, the result of the joint labors of himself and Sebastian del Piombo. Others say it is simply a picture of the Florentine School. They are all agreed about its merits. Then there is the famous chest of the Cid, upon the pledge of which, and his honor, he succeeded in raising the Hebraic loan. Then there is a painfully vivid image of the Crucifixion, that spares none of the horrible details of death. The individual portions of the building that call for admiration are endless. The noble dome, the portals, the immense chapel of the great Velasco family, hereditary constables of Castile, the rejas, the tombs, would fill a volume of themselves. I have but one adverse criticism to make, which is that being built of white stone, the interior, like the Cathedral del Pilar in Zaragoza, is too full of light. The traveller feels painfully the absence of that solemn, sombre grandeur which overwhelms him at Seville.

The hotel was thronged with persons on their return from the sea baths upon the Bay of Biscay, which are much frequented. Opposite to me at the table d'hôte, was a family from Madrid, who were to remain the next day. One of its members has retained a place in my memory as the last individual I met of the unmistakable type of Spanish beauty. To say this much is to say nearly everything. A gentleman of Burgos, a charming old bachelor, to whom I had a card of introduction, fortunately recognized the party, by my vivid

description, as acquaintances, and I was kindly placed in relation with them. As our time was unoccupied, it was agreed,
much to my delight, to make an excursion to the surrounding
country together. A four seated vehicle, that Charles III
would have recognized, provided with an abundant apparatus
of bells, and fluttering pieces of bunting, was brought to the
door, and we started merrily on our way.

On the left bank of the Arlanzon—a short walk from the
city—lay the celebrated convent of Santa Maria, la Real de las
Huelgas, "Huelga" signifying "rest" or "recreation;" the
convent being situated in the midst of former gardens and
orchards. It was commenced by Alonzo VIII, certainly before
the year 1187;—why is not well known, though scarcely in
token of his humiliation for the defeat of Alarcos, inasmuch as
that battle was not fought till 1195. Before it was completed,
the great victory of Las Navas gave a death blow to the
Moorish power, and probably may have added gratitude to
other motives for finishing it in style of royal magnificence. It is an immense collection of different dates and
different orders of architecture. The church is a very fine
building, and has, in particular, beautiful aisles. But the interest which this famous convent inspires, like many other things
in Old Castile, is due rather to its past glories and grandeur
than to the decaying present, stripped of its cherished privileges. No convent had ever been possessed of such authority. Its lady abbess united feudal with ecclesiastical power.
Twelve affiliated convents, sixty-four towns and villages, besides other lands, acknowledged her as their feudal or ecclesiastical superior, with all seigneural and episcopal rights, among
them that of hearing and deciding suits, civil, criminal and
ecclesiastical, admitting to orders, establishing and changing
convents, subject to no bishop; and, in truth, a sort of floating
diocese and county. A century afterward, some difficulties
having arisen with respect to the royal prerogative, the char-
ters were inspected, and all the privileges therein granted were
confirmed anew in solemn terms by the king, delivering over
all suggesters to the contrary to the society of Judas. No
sovereign had ever before had such a subject, and it was irreverently said, that if his Holiness the Pope should take it into
his head to get married, the only woman worthy of the alliance would be the abbess of Las Huelgas. A position of such

power could only be intrusted to noble hands, and among the list of abbesses is found all the good old names of Castile— Guzman, Laynez, Velasco, Zuñiga, Mendoza, Enriquez, Sandoval. In addition, one of the Infantas enjoyed the nominal protectorate under the style of Lady Guardian. They said that even now none were admitted but ladies of noble blood. St. Ferdinand armed himself as a knight in the chapel which is called by his name, and Alonzo XI, the hero of Salado, together with Henry of Trastamara, imitated the example of their illustrious ancestor. In the Coro and Naves are many tombs of the founder and his wife, of Alonzo VII, of Sancho the Wise, and of various other personages of royal blood.

On the same side of the river, but further to the north-east, was the Carthusian monastery of Miraflores, or La Cartuja as it is generally called, whose name is evidence of its charming situation. Its cloisters and some of the ornaments in the church are not surpassed by any other existing remains of mediæval art, particularly the choir and the tomb of the parents of Isabella the Catholic, which are of an airy elegance that defies imitation. The Padre Florez narrates that when Philip II beheld these master-works, he exclaimed to the bystanders, "We have done nothing at the Escorial." I have already remarked how strange it seems to me, that the Carthusians, whose rule was, perhaps, the most stringent and mortifying in the Church, should have always selected the most beautiful sites for their monasteries. As nothing can surpass the view from the terrace of their establishment near Granada in the gorgeous beauties of the tropics, so may the Miraflores disdain comparison in its prospect down the flowery vale that extends to Burgos; but it must be seen at the proper season of the year, and on this visit it had already begun to put on the sober garb of winter.

A league or two to the east brought us to the monastery of San Pedro de Cardena, precious in the eyes of all readers of Spanish ballads as having been the burial place of Ruy Diaz de Bivar, the Cid—the honor of Spain, the terror of infidels, the delight of the world. The old hero was interred here with his whole family, his father and mother, his grandfather, his wife, his daughters, the Queens of Aragon and Navarre, his gallant cousin, Alvar Fañez, and various other relatives. His remains have had little rest, and like those of Columbus pay the penalty of immortality by perpetual transmigrations. Their first journey after death was from Valencia to Burgos, thence they were brought here. The French, among the few things they knew about Spain, had heard of the Cid and Doña Jimenez through the tragedy of Corneille. With the appreciation of true valor, and also that disposition for effect which are innate in the nation, they removed his sepulchre to the Paseo at Burgos. In defence of an action, almost sacrilege, they assert that unless this had been done, the bones of the grim warrior would have inevitably been appropriated by the English amateurs in Wellington's army, and there is more truth in it than appears at first. The witty *feuilletoniste* and traveller, Théophile Gautier, says that General Thiebault, who effected the removal, slept with the bones in his own bed, in order by such glorious proximity to elevate his courage—a precaution, the author adds, of which he stood in no need. The Spanish indignantly restored them after the expulsion of their invaders. But the sequestration of the convents, which followed the accession of the liberal party to power, caused the remains to be once more removed to the city, where they are preserved—if in veneration, certainly in no great state. The monastery of Cardeña was one of the most ancient in Spain; but apart from its historical associations, and unless in such agreeable company, one would scarcely have made it a second visit. It is mournful to see the desolation that envelops these relics of the past. No reverend monk seeks the evidence of truth in the black letter tomes of their libraries; no paintings smile from their walls; no full toned choir chaunts the echoing melody through their vaults; no blooming garden yields its perfume to the longing winds. Their glory is departed. Overgrown by weeds and clambering ivy, they await in silence the sentence of destruction, and the next generation of travellers will probably be moralizing over their ruins.

The shades of evening were gathering as we re-entered the Posada, and I, with many regrets, bade farewell to my companions. They were to leave for the South, and I for the North the same night.

CHAPTER XXI.

BURGOS TO THE FRONTIER.

The road to Pancorbo is uninteresting in the extreme, so far as natural beauty is concerned, and I was therefore not sorry to sleep through it. The diligence was late in arriving, and still later in starting, so that I composed myself immediately to rest, feeling renewed cause for gratification in the happy power which nature had bestowed upon me; and passed in unconscious slumber over the bare plains and bleak hills of old Castile, awaking only in the celebrated defile of Pancorbo, one of the most striking mountain passes conceivable—a Spanish Via Mala, where a couple of thousand men could protect this portion of Spain against any possibility of invasion from the north until it should be turned. Perpendicular rocks, five hundred feet high, of fantastic shape, tower above, and threaten to crush the traveller, almost excluding the rays of the sun. Between them flows the rivulet Oroncillo, and the road contents itself with a narrow ledge along which to pass. In a little chapel, hollowed out of the rock, stands an altar to our Lady of the Road, who preserved us through its dangers. During the night the clouds, collected upon the mountains, had condensed, and its wild grandeurs were enveloped in mist and occasional showers. The sun made faint efforts to struggle out, and spanned the valley with rainbows. But we were doomed to have sombre weather until we reached Vitoria. The appearance of the country beyond Pancorbo was entirely different from what I had been seeing the last two months. It presented the evidences of a reasonable temperature and a moist climate, and in consequence, the productions were entirely those of the temperate zone. Orchards, Indian corn—of a most insignificant size, however, compared with ours—and even green fields, at last reappeared. But the most charming sight of all were the woods, of which the Castiles are utterly denuded. The aspect of the population, too, changed in many respects for the better. There was a far greater appearance of well being, and every one had the air of a small proprietor, who has some interest in the country beyond his daily wages. The number of farm houses increased, each surrounded by the little ornaments which characterize a temperate region and a free country. Particularly was this the case when we entered the Basque province of Alava. The Ebro is the geographical line between it and Old Castile, and Miranda, the frontier post of the Spanish custom house. But if natural distinctions were allowed, the boundary should rather be marked by the Pass of Pancorbo.

Before reaching Vitoria we passed through the battle field of the same name, where King Joseph and Marshal Jourdan, in 1813, received one of the most disgraceful defeats that ever dishonored a General. A battle it can scarcely be called, so far as the leaders were concerned, though the loss of nearly ten thousand men on both sides proved that the common soldiers had stood bravely. The plunder was enormous, for Joseph spent the last moments of his pretended reign in despoiling the people whom he would fain call his children. Jourdan, like his brother marshals, had but one thought in Spain, that of acquiring riches by all means, whether fair or foul. So entirely was he demoralized, that he failed to defend with courage what he had procured by downright robbery. The general headquarters had more the air of an ambulating brothel than a centre of command. The British held on to all they took, stolen as they knew it to be, proclaiming it lawful plunder, though the process of reasoning I never exactly comprehended, as it seemed to me that the original right of the Spaniards revived upon the recovery of the property even by their allies. No age of the world has ever presented to history a greater average of military talent and gallantry, and at the same time a more complete absence of every trait that characterizes men of lofty honor and tone than that in which figured the marshals of Napoleon. They were for the most part children, not of the revolution of 1789 but of 1793; neither did they spring from the people, but from the dregs of the lowest society, forming their characters in a school which ignored virtue and futurity, and thought only of the sensual enjoyment of the moment. There was a marked contrast between the common soldiers and officers who represented the people on the one hand, and on the other the higher ranks of the army, growing up under the baleful shade of the Committee of Safety and the Directory. The former were far superior to any opponents they met, and the Englishman or Austrian was almost a drunken savage by comparison; but the latter were low indeed in everything but their profession. Like all parvenus, their great ambition was to be rich, as the acquisition of blood was impossible, and to this object they sacrificed everything, even military duty, as was painfully exemplified in the case of this very battle of Vitoria by Jourdan. That Napoleon was aware of it, and regretted these excesses in a military point of view, if in no other, is well known, but though in appearance absolute, he was compelled, like all other civilized despots, to satisfy public opinion around him. The war in Spain was universally unpopular with the army; it was the grave of reputations that had stood the test of fifty battles, and many a high renown was shattered against the walls of Zaragoza, the Guerilleros of Andalusia and the Pyrenees or the serried ranks of Wellington. If a victory were gained, the ceaseless efforts of the Guerilleros deprived it of all profit, and the Emperor's eye was not there to reward the gallant charge or the desperate resistance. He was therefore obliged to wink at the extortion and avarice of his Marshals by way of reconciling them to the painful duty which it was necessary that some one should perform. I had once thought that these disgraceful scenes were enacted only in Spain; but such was not the case. The rest of Europe bore abundant marks of their ravages when away from the master's eye. One of the worst instances of the conduct of this school is mentioned by General de Brack, who says that on the retreat from Moscow, he saw with his own eyes a General cause the horses to be taken from a cannon to supply the place of those which had drawn his baggage wagon, laden with luxuries and valuables plundered from the burning city. Most of us will agree with the General that this is the lowest depth of military infamy. Ney and Soult, among the best of the whole, still could not change their natures. Possessed of unquestionable military talent, the one a mere creature of impulse, betrayed first Napoleon, then Louis XVIII; the other was innately unreliable, and without the sense of honor or duty. So well was his character known, that before the battle of Ligny the private soldiers made bold to warn the Emperor against his treachery, and this was the universal estimation in which he was held. General Napier has kindly, and, we may say, gallantly concealed his defects from view—but they are too notorious to be forgotten. Though I have a much higher opinion at present of the French soldiers than of their officers, yet men like McMahon or St. Jean de Angely would never stoop to the commission of such acts as disgraced the children of 1793. The British officers in the Peninsula, however inferior to their opponents in capacity, were generally high-toned men, who would scorn to steal or rob. *Bon sang ne ment pas.* The Duke of Wellington fortunately united both moral and mental greatness, and the consequence was inevitable. Every Marshal, from Soult the best, to Junot the poorest, received defeat and dishonor at his hands, for the French soldiers themselves ceased to feel confidence in chiefs who were absorbed in their desire for amassing wealth.

The entrance to Vitoria, passing by the public walks, is very pretty. The Alameda and the Florida are scarcely surpassed in Spain; and the latter, with its flowers and healthy grass, and children running about in its alleys, possesses a new charm after the solemn stateliness of the rest of Spain. The town itself is divided into two portions, the new and the old. The new, glorying in its wide, clean streets and lofty houses, ornamented with balconied fronts, was a fair example of progress. There are churches and things to be shown, but the view from the tower of Sta. María over the plain, in the centre of which is the hillock that forms the site of the old city, is best worth the trouble. It affords a fine prospect over a well cultivated country, containing, it is said, more than one hundred villages and hamlets, scattered over the green expanse, and bounded in the distance by the Pyrenean spurs which separate it from the neighboring provinces of Guipuzcoa, Burgos and Santander. The population is lively, much given to dancing and playing all sorts of athletic games in the Alameda, which is crowded on a Sunday afternoon with as animated a collection of men,

women and children as the world can show. I speak this from
the experience of a previous visit; for, upon the present occasion, our delay was confined to an hour for breakfast, the
greater part of which I spent upon the Plaza, a fine square,
with arcades. I remember the place well, as having offered
to me the first sight of a mantilla worn in actual life. In
leaving Vitoria for Burgos our postilion had also sported a
calañes hat, both of which are properly parts of the Andalusian
costume, and seldom seen in the north. The costume of the
Basques and of all the north-west provinces is by no means so
gay as that of the rest of Spain. The damp weather would of
itself be enough to impose a more sober garb. The various
fancy head dresses are replaced by a flat woollen cap, the *bouina*,
such as is in favorite use on our plantations, being a kind of
hybrid between a Scotch and a sailor's, and the women content
themselves with the *trensa*, or plaited hair hanging down behind. The chocolate at the Fonda was another evidence that
we had left Spain proper; for it was *claro muy claro*, that is to
say, thin, as is the fashion in France, and to me, just from
Seville, almost without taste or substance.

The Basques are an enduring example of the length of time
which a people may retain their characteristic peculiarities.
Small in number, and inhabiting a country very limited in
extent, they have never been thoroughly subdued. Celts, Romans, Moors, Spaniards, French, have met them, with but little
reason to be proud of the encounter. For the maintenance of
their cherished liberties (fueros) they have shrunk from no
sacrifice. When the privilege of trading with America was an
inestimable boon, they refused to accept it at the price of the
surrender of these fueros, though among the best seamen in
Spain, and producing the very articles most needed for that
trade. The "fueros" consisted in the right of self-government
and freedom from the conscription, the customs, the excise on
stamped paper and tobacco, and from individual taxation. In
war they were to rise *en masse*, and their fair proportion to the
support of the central Government was to be levied by their
own assemblies. The King of Spain was Lord of Biscay, and
as such their leader. The oak of Guernica, under which the
assemblies were held, is the symbol of their freedom, and is
engraven on the heart of every Basque. This portion of the
Peninsula used to be treated as Tyrol, in the Austrian Empire.

But its extraordinary exemptions are quite against the spirit of modern monarchy. Any premature attempt, however, to incorporate it definitely with Spain must be followed by furious convulsions. They show the advantage of free government. Robbers and office seekers are comparatively unknown. A charming simplicity reigns in their life. The men are honest and industrious, the women virtuous and loyal; and, though they do not arouse your enthusiasm or touch your heart as the Andalusians, you feel they are fully entitled to your admiration and respect.

Soon after leaving Vitoria, we commenced ascending the Sierra of Elgu, for which it was necessary to hitch on three yoke of oxen, two under the charge of boys, and one conducted by a brisk, skinny old woman—all of whom worked with a hearty good will. The oxen were not large, but appeared well trained and intelligent, and their treatment was humane, which, in my experience, is always evidence of an enlightened system of agriculture. On the other side of the ridge is the province of Guipuzcoa, lying to the north of the great Pyrenean chain, or, rather, in the midst of it, and emptying its waters into the Bay of Biscay. The Deva rises at the foot of the pass, and rivals the streams of Switzerland in the purity of its waters. On both sides of the Sierra the scenery is entirely pastoral. The vast prospect-views of the Castiles and the grand inspiring solitudes of the Andalusian mountains yield to a country of unsurpassed beauty, in the style of the Pyrenees, whose precipitous sides are covered with the green of Ireland. Such scenery is certainly very pleasing; but your thoughts never rise to the height of sublimity, and your feelings are as circumscribed as your vision. Be that as it may, there are few prettier valleys than that of the Deva. The Celtic scholars say that Cantabria—Centiberia—the ancient name for this portion of Spain, is to be derived from Kent-Aber, the "corner of water," just as Celtiberia—Kelt-aber—the Celts of river, and Havre, or Aber, and Aber-deen, and various other places in Europe derive their names, *Kent* being the corner, as in the County of Kent in England, and Abero-Abro-Ebro, being the river itself, all of which would seem to be in direct conflict with Humboldt's theory that the Basques were the original Iberians; for, if so, they would never have allowed a foreign name to be given exclusively to the country of which they only

were in possession. The appropriateness of the name would
seem to justify the Celtic derivation; for, while the rest of
Spain has always suffered from want of moisture, and oftentimes been desolated by droughts, there is a never-failing supply of rain in all the north-west corner, and the purest trout
streams are in superabundance. This continuation of the Pyrenees, parallel to the Bay of Biscay, seems naturally to attract
the clouds, but all on the northern side. The Basques have
generally much fairer complexions than is usual in the other
portions of the Peninsula, a circumstance which some have
attributed to the influence of Norman blood, whereas, following the universal law of nature, it is caused simply by the
moisture of the climate. Remove them to La Mancha for a
few generations, and all distinguishing marks of complexion
would soon disappear. Lieutenant Gibbon, in his exploring
expedition over the Andes, notices the same fact that on the
west of the Cordilleras, where it seldom rains and the sky is
unclouded, the ladies resemble the Spanish in complexion;
whereas, on the east, amid the continued showers and dampness
brought over by the south-eastern trade winds, they are as fair
as in Germany.

Our company had been reduced to a good lady of some fifty
years "*y pico*" in the berliña, who appeared the soul of kindness, and another lady and a French Commis in the interior.
Part of our way lay upon quite a steep precipice overhanging
the river without a parapet. As luck would have it, the postilion's horse was a miserable-tempered beast, which took a
fancy of stopping short at occasional intervals and kicking the
rest of the animals toward the river. Every such performance
produced a volley of oaths in three languages from the banquette, and considerable commotion in the interior, with the
protrusion of an alarmed physiognomy at each window. My
companion's equanimity began to give way at these signs of
fear, and though she had instructed me in the morning upon
the subject of rainbows, informing me gravely that they sucked
up the water, her philosophy failed to give her assurance upon
the edge of a precipice. In response to her inquiries as to the
danger of an upset, I gave her the Turkish consolation that
we could die but once, and that it was the mayoral's business,
not ours, to guard against accidents. Half convinced, she
recovered the natural courage of a Spanish woman. Not so,

however, in the interior; once we approached nearer than
usual to the edge, and suddenly open flew the door, outburst
the lady, followed by the Commis, *sacré-ing* most fearfully, and
vowing that he was not in the least frightened for himself, but
only for "cette pauvre dame." With difficulty they were persuaded to enter again, the Frenchman swearing that at the
next station he would give the postilion a bit of his mind,
which he did in desperately bad Spanish, opening the attack,
however, very finely, by calling him a *p-ñ-t-rro*. But was there
ever such a Tartar! The postilion, as soon as he comprehended the object of his assailant, gave back as good as he got,
repaying his debt with such interest that the capital seemed
to double with every ten words. Fortunately, the road-bed
was not shaken, and we continued the journey in safety.

It was Sunday, and the road was thronged with persons well
dressed and of pleasant countenance. Numerous solidly-built
villages, with sounding names—Castañares, Escoriaza, Arech-
avaleta, Mondragon, were scattered along the valley. At Vergara, celebrated for the Convention which put an end to the
civil war and procured for Espartero the title of Duke de la
Victoria, we left the Deva, and, appealing again to oxen, crossed
the ridge which separates the valley from that of the Ureta.
On my first entry into Spain in 1851, the only other passenger
was a political exile, an old Carlist and a thorough Biscayen,
who was returning after a long absence, his heart filled with
the glories of his native land, upon which he dwelt with much
emphasis, pointing out the various things worthy of admiration. While ascending this ridge we had stopped at a farm-house
to get a glass of milk, which was really very fine and worthy
of all praise; but, in the midst of his eulogy upon Basque
milk and butter in general, my attention was unfortunately
attracted by a wooden plough, a sort of stick, the precise
counterpart of the one represented in the school picture history as held by Cincinnatus. He was a little confounded when
he caught sight of this implement, but soon recovering, waved
his hand majestically toward the obnoxious object, exclaiming
" the classic plough!" I was puzzled at first to know whether
he was serious or jesting; but never was a man more in earnest. This was only patriotism, a very good quality in itself,
carried to an exaggeration, for he was not only polite but even
kind, considering that I was a young stranger, not very famil-

iar either with the language or the people, and, at his home in
Vitoria, he afforded me opportunities of seeing the working
of things, which a formal letter of introduction would scarcely
have procured.

At Villa-real we dined or lunched upon a superb dish of trout,
just caught before the village inn and scarcely dead. How
many an old epicure would have made the journey expressly
for that enjoyment! Appealing once more to our oxen, we
crossed into the valley of the Oria, passing by the village of
Ormaiztegui, where Zumalacarregui, the Carlist General, was
born. This remarkable man is little known in America, and
as he supported an unsuccessful cause, his reputation in Europe
is waning, but there were few greater born in the eighteenth
century. A larger field or more romantic times only were
requisite to make him a hero in the history of the world. An
officer of the army at the death of Ferdinand, he espoused the
cause of Don Carlos and was its main support. Taking his station in the Basque provinces and gathering up a handful of
peasants, he cast cannon, armed his troops from the spoils of
his enemies, and subjected every army that approached to igno-
minious defeat. The laurels of Mina himself, the invincible
Mina, wilted in this contest. But the hand of resistless fate
was interposed to arrest his progress, and when he was preparing to march upon Madrid a stray ball at the siege of Bilbao
relieved them from the unconquerable foe. Had he been disposed, like most leaders of civil war, to accept a compromise,
he would have received dukedoms and countships without
number; yet the chieftain who wielded, one may almost say
the destiny of his country, left scarcely enough to inter him.
This is the stuff of which true heroes are made. The high road
from Vitoria to Ernani, near San Sebastian, passes through a
country every foot of which was contested, not once only but
frequently. One of Zumalacarregui's greatest victories was
just here about his birthplace, by which he foiled the well laid
plans of four times his number, led by the best of the Chris-
tianist generals, to envelop him in a trap. After his death the
Carlist army continued to resist with like success. Even the
British legion of auxiliaries, commanded by General Evans,
which were to sweep them off the face of the earth, met
nothing but humiliation. At Ernani it made a *"reconnaissance
poussée un peu trop loin"* and was utterly defeated. Several other

"*reconnaissances*" were made with the like result. The surprising resistance made by the Basques in their mountain fastnesses against the united opposition of Spain, France and
England, finds its only parallel in the exploits of Marion among
the swamps of our own country. Between the two heroes there
was a striking resemblance of character. Both were upon the
highest tone of honor. Chivalrous, unselfish, indifferent to the
charms of wealth or luxury, they moved with a single purpose
of patriotism. Appearing upon the theatre of action in the
midst of prostration and despondency they restored confidence,
created armies, and with naked, starving soldiers gained victories over troops who enjoyed every advantage that money
could procure. Whether Marion would have displayed also
the talents of a General is not known, as his force was always
small. Zumalacarregui was more fortunate in opportunity,
but both will fill an enviable place in history, and in their deeds
will offer fit subjects for the Muse of succeeding generations.

The sky had now cleared, and the whole population were out
of doors amusing themselves. The men gathered at the fives
court, which appears to be a universal amusement here, as it
used to be in the Carolinas; the elderly females seated around
little tables playing cards. I tried, but without success, to
make out the game. The sin was doubtless venial as the
stakes were decidedly low, seldom exceeding three coppers.
An abundant fund of good humor seemed to be at the disposal
of the players. The valley of the Oria is densely populated,
and contains a very considerable number of manufactories and
forges, the iron being plentiful and good. These mountains
abound in it, and that of Somorostro is, I believe, the most
malleable in the world. The country is distinguished throughout by marks of prosperity and content. Tolosa, its capital,
is a beautiful town, beautifully situate, and is becoming an
excursion city for fishing parties from the watering places
around the Bay of Biscay. Several fat Frenchmen were walking about, looking exceedingly foreign and un-at-home.

After leaving Tolosa, we enjoyed the pleasure of hearing a
quarrel in the Basque tongue, the veritable Euskara, between
our mayoral and some lazy fellows who had been swinging
behind the diligence. Of all the incomprehensible sounds that
ever issued from the throat of man these were the most
astounding. First one, then another, then altogether, com-
25

mencing in a high key, and ending in a low one or vice versa. Broadsides of consonants were discharged against each other, with destructive effect, at least so far as regards the distortion of the countenance. Once a bomb, thirteen inch at least, burst in the mouth of one of the mortars, and produced a violent fit of coughing, which was music compared with the noises that had preceded. It is said that the devil was piqued, about the time of the birth of Abel, with an ambition of learning this language, for which purpose he resided at Bilbao seven years, and in all that time acquired three words. His children have succeeded no better. The Basques say that it was the honeyed phrases of the Euskara which Adam whispered into the listening ear of Eve. It has certainly puzzled philologists, and the learned investigations of Humboldt, Larramendi and others, have only established that it is a fully, nay exuberantly developed language without a cognate upon the earth. Like all languages which have ceased to convey the mandates of political power, it is doomed eventually to disappear. In some parts of Biscay it is still the only speech, but the Spanish is creeping in. On the French side of the Bidassoa, the progress is even more rapid. A gentleman from that part of France told me that he and his brother had established a prize for improvization in the Euskara, but the tendency to extinction could not be arrested. In the mouths of the mayoral and his opponents, however, it gave no signs of decay. Our quarrel had continued some minutes, when the passengers, apprehensive lest so much thundering might cause a shower, insisted upon proceeding, and comparative quiet was re-established in the valley of the Oria. Another mountain ridge was then crossed into the valley of the Urumea, which we descended until, about dusk, a castle-crowned eminence was descried rising steeply from the waters of the Bay of Biscay, and a few minutes afterward we entered the fortress gate of San Sebastian.

The situation of San Sebastian is commanding, both in a military and commercial point of view. Sebastian and Cadiz, at the two extremities of Spain, have both been appropriately compared to Venus rising from the sea. It is built on a narrow neck of land connecting the immense rock—some four hundred feet high, called Mount Orgullo, upon which stands the castle—with the mainland. The French seized it during

the Peninsula war. From them it was taken by the British by
storm. Though an allied town, being Spanish, and though the
Spanish contingent at that very time were nobly protecting
the besiegers against the efforts of Soult at San Marcial, it was
sacked with a ferocity unparalleled even among savages, and
was finally burnt. The English officers did their utmost here,
as at Badajoz, to restrain the excesses of the soldiers, but in
vain. At the latter place, the Duke of Wellington was compelled to flee, lest he should be shot by the infuriated demons.
As may be imagined, the English are held here in utter abomination, and are considered the Cagots of the world. The
burning had, however, the good effect of causing the town to
be rebuilt in fine style, with clean streets and regular houses,
though the confined space causes them to be rather higher
than consorts with Spanish customs. The harbor is very secure but rather small, and, they say, difficult of access. As
a military post it is of the first importance. No enemy could
safely invade this portion of Spain without first securing possession of it. The view of the Pyrenees and of the sea from
the castle in the afternoon, when the peaks of the giant chain
are tipped with fire, and the little town at its foot, with the
placid harbor, are shrouded in vast shadows, is indeed magnificent. The people of San Sebastian being engaged in foreign
commerce have not so many prejudices as their neighbors, and
are quite disposed to give and receive. I speak again, however,
from the recollections of the previous visit, for upon this occasion my view did not extend beyond the street, and my conversation was confined to the landlady and her daughter, a
buxom, bustling lassie, with health and energy enough for a
dozen lives.

After an hour's delay we repassed the fortified entrance, and
whirling along the Alameda, over which swept a delicious
breeze from the sea, commenced ascending the high country
that lies between this and Irun. We wound around the Bay of
Los Pasages, which is so completely land-locked as to appear a
lake, and finally came to the little town of Irun, the last in
Spain, situate upon a lofty hill that overlooks the opposite
shore of the Bidassoa. For the first time since my entry by
the Puerto de Benasque, I heard the word "passport" from the
mouth of an official. I handed it to him. It was an old one
well supplied with visas of a past generation, a couple of hun-

dred or more, and seemed to puzzle him amazingly as he turned it first one side and then another, but there had not been the scrape of a Spanish pen within the last six years at least. He looked at me, and then thought of the little fee which he demands of travellers on their leaving Spain, as though that of itself did not render one sufficiently miserable, and finally concluded, with the help of a small boy and a dim lantern, that all was right. It was formerly the habit, also, to search the baggage at Irun, lest specie should be carried out and the country thus impoverished, but sounder teaching has shown that nothing is so useless to a country as the overplus of coin, so that we were allowed to carry out all that we might have the good fortune to possess.

The whole population of Irun seemed to be in the streets or on the balconies. As it is the first town upon entering Spain, and offers a marked contrast to the Bayonne side, travellers are apt to remember it. Some difficulty had, on my first visit, detained us there a couple of hours, and in that time I became practically acquainted with several little Spanish customs which I have since put to good use. One was, that on wishing to pay for my chocolate, I found the debt had been discharged by an unknown friend. I had forgotten this peculiarity of Spanish manners, and for some time could not comprehend why the Mozo would not receive my money, thinking there must be some mistake. In our own country, I fear the waiter would have condescendingly received pay from both parties. My companion in the berliña was acquainted in the town and proposed that I should accompany him on a visit, which I, nothing loth, agreed to. An elderly lady and a younger one called at the house while we were there. The latter smote me through at once. She was of medium height, beautifully rounded form, regular features, dark hair, and pearly teeth peeping from behind a pair of rosy lips. As her large, lustrous eyes fell upon me, I thought I had never seen anything to resemble her upon earth, and began to fear that a death stroke had at last been received. But Andalusia had not then been seen. I would have been glad to meet once more the fair maid of Irun, in order to compare her with the daughters of the Guadalquivir. Perhaps, though, it was fortunate that I did not, as the sight of half a dozen young additional Basques would have spoilt, or at least marred the romance sadly.

The diligence rattled down the steep eminence to the Bidassoa, which we were to·cross on the famous frontier bridge that, could it speak, might tell such eventful tales. How many a steel-bristling battalion and plumed squadron passed that bridge never to return! How often has the tide of battle raged over this very little stream, now so placid, with the thousand stars of the milky way glittering from its bosom! and all to gratify the selfish ambition of worms like themselves! But these are trite reflections, though peculiarly appropriate to the locality. To say that I regretted the necessity of leaving Spain would be superfluous. Seven times had the orange bloomed since I first set foot upon her soil, yet it now seemed to me as of yesterday. Enjoyment, far beyond the most sanguine expectations, had fallen to my lot. The romantic dreams of youth seemed to be half fulfilled, and no subsequent events of life, however untoward, could deprive me of those pleasing recollections. As we approached the bridge, a *guardia civil* opened the door with "*Hágan me vvm. el favor de sus pasaportes.*" Satisfied with the inspection, they were returned. At the entrance to the bridge stood the Spanish sentinel in national yellow and red, with dark eyes and moustache. A couple of dozen steps brought us to another, a sandy bearded sentinel in familiar red pantaloons, the imperial eagle spread upon his hat; at the same moment the door was opened again, but this time with "*Vos passeports, Messieurs, S. V. P.*" We were in France.

GENERAL.

The Spanish Empire was compared by Edmund Burke to a
whale stranded upon the sea-shore. In his time, the comparison
was not inappropriate. Exhausted with a life of unwonted
activity, it lay supinely inert, scarcely heeding the current as
it whirled past. But the present century has witnessed the
passage of fearful storms over the political surface of the Peninsula, which have lashed its waters into fury, and seemingly
threatened the destruction of all existing institutions. Since
1833 many revolutions have taken place, whose causes and
results have seldom been accurately comprehended by foreigners. Here, as elsewhere, rages the conflict of two ideas—
the one that mankind are made for government, the other that
government is made for mankind; and were Spain isolated from
the rest of Europe, the troubled waters would soon subside
into reasonable quiet. But the neighborhood of France intro-
duces two other ideas, antagonistic in themselves, which have
small following, yet whose adherents take advantage of every
commotion to make themselves felt. These two latter schools
resemble each other in this, that both, nominally democratic,
undertake to shape the destiny of every citizen through the
agency of a great central power—prescribing what he shall
do, and what he shall not do, and for the free will of the individual substituting the opinion of an Emperor or of a committee
of safety. It is difficult to say which of them is most in con-
tradiction to the sentiments of the great body of the Spanish

nation; yet that they exert considerable influence by getting upon the end of the lever is undeniable. Sartorius was a disciple of the first, and attempted, by means of a coup d'etat and force, to rule through the mere edicts of a sovereign. His ministry was overthrown by counter violence at Vicálvaro and in the streets of the capital, and it is to be hoped that he and his followers are buried for ever. The mob of Madrid, headed by Pucheta, the bull fighter, attempted the second by similar violent means, and were similarly overthrown. Neither had the slightest sympathy in the heart of the population, who silently looked on rather as spectators than as participators in the drama.

If there be one trait in the Spanish character more strongly developed than another, it is self-esteem, a conviction of his rights, and his dignity as a man and a Spaniard, and for that reason alone. In comparison with this, all the accidents of birth, wealth and office are as nothing. A certain degree of respect is acknowledged and paid to some of these accidents, but it is a respect of form, and confined within very narrow limits. Hence comes the practical equality that reigns among all classes, manifested even in the jealous application of *Usted*, a contraction of *Vuestra Merced* (your worship), as a style of address which is used to Counts and street sweepers alike, though the title may be recognized occasionally as an appellative—a strange contrast to the Teutonic nations, where French is sometimes found convenient to avoid the eternal recurrence of Durchlant, Hoheit, Excelenz, Grace, Lordship, and other relics of a barbarous social system. In the Austrian service I believe the proper use of "Du" and "Sie" is made a matter of military regulation. Even in Italy, the distinctive styles of addressing equals, superiors and inferiors is still to a certain extent retained. All this is utterly unknown in Spain. If a Spanish boot-black were addressed as "Thou" instead of Usted, "your worship," he would be at a loss to comprehend the use of a grammatical form, which is expressive only of tender affection, and would attribute it to an ignorance of the language—not to an assumption of superiority. The origin of this external quality must be sought in their history. From the time of Pelayo, personal slavery among Christians was scarcely known in the Castiles, unless it were in the Seigneuries bordering upon France, where the feudal system took some root. The nature of the religious wars, carried on unceasingly with the Moors, rendered impossible any other distinction of persons than that of faith and of individual prowess. The road to wealth, power and reputation was open to everyone who chose to make a successful foray against these invaders. The downfall of the Moorish power was followed by the discovery of America—a still wider field for natural talents, where every European was 'a demi-god, and mere pig-herds, such as Pizarro, could acquire kingdoms. To this sense of personal dignity, the pre-eminence of their country under Charles and Philip, added a national pride, little in harmony with its fallen fortunes of the present day. An amusing instance is narrated of this during the reign of Louis XIV. When the Spanish nobles were signing their adherence to his descendant, their King, they respectively affixed to their names the words "as noble as the King," and one added "y algo mas," at which a horrified French courtier exclaimed, "Surely you do not think your family more ancient than the Bourbons?" "You forget, sir, that *I* am a Castillian," was the reply.

The States rights principle is profoundly ingrained in the Spanish heart—far more than in the United States. Though the foundation of their character be the same, the differences are striking, and are marked by the boundary lines of the provinces, which seem to be moral as well as geographical frontiers. Nor have these differences as yet yielded to the influence of railroads and mutual emigration. The Catalans are industrious, energetic and rebellious. The Aragonese, pertinacious, firm, even obstinate, and at times quarrelsome. The Valencians, hard working, fond of amusement, full of genius, but pass quickly from one extreme to another, and are prone to the shedding of blood. The Gallicians and Asturians, well disposed, industrious, honest as the day is long, and easily satisfied. The Castillian, serious, formal in demeanor, dignified, consistent, and worthy of entire confidence. The Andalusian, gay, graceful, imaginative, enthusiastic, exuberant in genius, a charming companion, and entirely opposed to unnecessary labor. There is little love lost between these various provinces. Spain has felt in her civil wars the evil effect of this want of unity, for every such difference is apt to assume a sectional aspect. Thus the party of Don Carlos was almost confined to Biscay, Navarre and Aragon. But, on the other hand, it saved the

country in the great contest with Napoleon, who vainly thought
Spain conquered with the capture of Madrid, just as Kossuth
mistook the mob of New York, yelling at his carriage wheels,
for the great American people. The necessities of modern
times have required that the bond of union should be drawn
closer, but Narvaez and his successors proceeded too far in
that direction, and one of the good actions of the present
Ministry has been to undo their work and to restore vigor to
the extremities. Such is evidently the path of true statesmanship. Unity to a certain extent is consistent with the feelings
of the nation, and having a natural, not an artificial origin, can
be preserved without violence. Commerce, aided by railroads
and the telegraph, will bind it firmly enough without recourse
to the vulgar acts of force and the army and navy; the great
postal and railroad lines in which the central government is
interested, the immense herd of officers, who derive their
appointment from the same source, will consolidate its power
sufficiently for all purposes of good, while the strong local
attachment and intense personality of the Spaniard will prevent him from becoming a floating Proletariat, and justify a
considerable delegation of provincial powers. He is intensely
conservative also, and much more disposed to submit to the
past than to the varying whim of any man or set of men,
however great their pretensions to wisdom, which disposition
is, indeed, an invariable characteristic of those who prize individual liberty and hate despotism.

Of all the countries in Europe, therefore, Spain seems to me
the best fitted for a republic, and the Spaniards to possess most
happily the combination of national, local and personal pride,
which fits men for living in an organized community, with the
advantages of self-government. Yet the chances for any such
results are small, for though the present Queen has lost all hold
upon the respect of the nation, the Spaniard is by nature
loyal. Attachment to the sovereign is essentially a part of his
character, and it is surprising with how much leniency they
treat her frailties, and with how much delicacy she is spared
even in the Puerta del Sol. I was at Seville when Merino
attempted her life. There was but one sentiment in the population high or low; the word "infame" resounded throughout
the city, though the government was at the time tending in a
most unpopular direction, and peculiarly odious to that prov-

ince. The idea of a republic enters into the heads of very few. Indeed, the conduct of the so-called republicans of the Faubourg St. Antoine, in June, 1848, has brought discredit upon the very name, and frightened or disgusted all except the followers of Espartero and Cavaignac, who are really republicans, that is to say, they believe that liberty consists in the absence of tyranny and unnecessary control, not in a mere change of masters; that power begets oppression, and that that government is best which governs the least—necessary to preserve the·society for which it was established. It may be said that the whole of French politics vibrates between the two extremes, and the sole question is, who shall rule us? For as De Tocqueville truly remarks, the only effect of the frequent revolutions of the last half century has been to substitute the red cap, the golden and the iron crown successively for each other. Every party as it ascends the seat of power, adopts the same means and manner of government. The Bibliotheque Nationale becomes the Bibliotheque Royale or Imperiale; otherwise little alteration is visible. In Spain there is no question as to who shall be King. Nearly all have settled down upon the present Queen and the Cortes. But the question warmly contested, is *how* shall we be ruled? and this involves the practical distinctions of Spanish politics.

The patriots of the War of Independence, who found themselves at Cadiz deserted by their cowardly monarch, and charged with the duty of governing the country, at least the portion of it which was preserved from the invader, set about forming a constitution rather in the spirit of philosophers, dealing with abstract principles, than as statesmen, and gave birth to the instrument of 1812, which might have answered the purpose well enough had they also enjoyed the power of creating a nation to suit their constitution. But taking the Spaniards as they were, hampered with the relics of ancient and irreconcilable institutions, it was utterly unfitted for the purpose, and has always failed when put in practice. Upon his restoration, Ferdinand, who, if devoid of the courage of his great ancestors, inherited their arbitrary nature, Bourbon-like, forgetting nothing and learning nothing, subverted their labors and treated the members of the convention as his greatest enemies. Persecution became the order of the day, and every evil thing that a contest of six years had swept away was restored; even the Inquisition resumed its authority. In 1820, a reaction took place, and the pendulum swung to the opposite extreme. The philosophic hands of Martinez de le Rosa, pure as snow themselves, were unable to restrain the violence of his party. This charming writer, and excellent parliamentarian, was deficient in the stern determination of a revolutionary leader, imposing the law not only upon his enemies but his friends. Personally brave himself, and ready to die at any moment, in defence of the good cause, he yet belonged rather to the class of martyrs than of heroes. Disorder ran wild. The blood of innocent priests and helpless old monks defiled the garments of liberty, until the Duke of Augoulême cantered through the Peninsula, without a hand being raised in defence of this abortive revolution. From that time, until the death of *el Rey absoluto*, a perpetual gloom overhung the nation. Whatever it possessed of intelligence or virtue languished in exile. At length, to the inexpressible relief of humanity, el Rey absoluto was gathered to his ancestors in the Escorial, and then arose a civil war, which, in the origin of its parties and the various motives of the combatants, was unique. The King, in dying, bequeathed the realm to his daughter, for the sham Cortes is not worthy of mention. His brother, Don Carlos, claimed the throne by virtue of the fundamental salic law, which had been established upon the entry of the Bourbons. The Liberal party supported Christina and her daughter; the Absolutists, Don Carlos, so that, according to appearances, the *rôles* were reserved, those who were in favor of a free government shedding their blood in defence of the right of Ferdinand to will away the country at his death, and the Absolutists upholding the established law against the despotism of this royal prerogative. But the contest was really very different. Christina having neither law nor reason to sustain her, was compelled to court the men of 1812, who with their sympathizers, accepted the overture, bringing to her support nearly the whole of Spain. The Absolutists were soon subdued. But the Basque provinces, seeing in the centralizing tendencies of the new government, a danger to their local and ancestral liberties, rallied under the heroic Zumalacarregui around their *fueros* to which, as well as other existing institutions, the programme of Don Carlos offered protection. With these went Aragon and Catalonia rather from a general disposition to rebel, than from any sympathy with absolutism. The loss of Zumalacarregui by a chance shot before Bilbao, was a death blow to the hopes of Don Carlos, and the convention of Vergara completed the ruin of the Absolutist party, with their ideas of Divine right. The victors gradually fell into the inevitable division of those who are almost content with things as they are—the Moderados—and those who are in favor of a steady progressive movement—the Progresistas. Of course, the extreme Moderados were so apprehensive of going ahead, that they went backward, and the extreme Progresistas were in favor of dispensing with every thing except the locomotive itself. In the course of events, all reasonable apprehension of the Carlists having disappeared, the Moderados became more decidedly pronounced for their favorite policy of guarding against the dangers of license by strengthening the central power, and gradually absorbed the outskirts of the Carlist party. Success crowned their exertions. Espartero fled for his life, and Narvaez, a man of consummate ability, finally assumed the reins. Things went on steadily in this direction until Sartorius made a deliberate attempt to overthrow liberty and re-establish the government of Philip II. The revolution of 1854 hurled him into the abyss of infamy. The revolution was commenced by O'Donnel and the other military chieftains, but they having failed in their first effort, the mob of Madrid took it in hand, and the Government, true to its centralized imbecility, having nothing to rely upon but unreliable soldiers, and still more unreliable officers, succumbed to the *populacho* of the capital, as such Governments always will do, sooner or later. Sartorious and Christina escaped paying the penalty of their treason. The life of the one and the ill-gotten wealth of the other were justly forfeited to their outraged country. O'Donnel, doubtless much to his disgust and astonishment, found himself the hero of a mob. But the universal voice of the nation called for Espartero, who, with unfeigned reluctance, left his retirement at Logroño, and attempted anew to shape the destinies of his country. Old General San Miguel had by his personal popularity arrested the mob when, in their thirst for blood, they marched to the palace demanding the lives of the royal family. But the task of stemming the current, finally and effectually fell to Espartero, who with infinite difficulty, succeeded in so doing, and in mooring the storm-tossed vessel once more in safety. This done, the wheel of fickle fortune again revolved, and he was relegated to his mountain retreat. O'Donnel stepped into the vacant place, and thus far has managed to sustain his position.

The life of Espartero has been a chequered one. With none of the usual advantages of fortune or birth, he has twice been hailed as the saviour of his country, and twice has he been driven from almost sovereign power without in any degree forfeiting the esteem of the nation. He possesses the two virtues, rare among European statesmen, of truth and honesty. Sincerely attached to the principles of constitutional liberty, he has endeavored, when elevated to office, to carry them into practice. I am sorry to believe that Napoleon was half right in saying that this is not the age for Washingtons. Europe seems to need and to desire the hand of iron, even if the velvet be somewhat worn off the glove. Espartero resembles rather the early statesmen of our republic, who were content with serving their country without the prurient ambition of wearing the livery of office, and whose intellectual statue did not require the advantage of a pedestal in order that it might be rendered visible to the world. Such ideas of self-abnegation are not in vogue beyond the water, and those who are governed by them can with difficulty contend against the palace Camarillas that undermine the ground beneath their feet. The general disposition is in favor of a unity of arbitrary power.

O'Donnel's character is in better harmony with the prevailing opinions. Unscrupulous as a politician and in fact little more than an adventurer, he has sufficient wisdom, or perhaps patriotism, to see that downright absolutism does not accord with the necessities of Spain, and has succeeded in rallying to his administration the enlightened liberals without forfeiting the support of the conservatives. His policy seems to be that of the moderate Progresistas. At least they have supported him. Order and security are maintained, while the tendency is to restore to the Ayuntamientos as much liberty as is consistent with the necessities of national defence. Yet, during the whole of my sojourn in Spain, his tenure of power was very precarious, and I would not have been astonished at any moment to hear that he had been deposed. An attempt at a military insurrection was actually made at Seville, but without success. The execution of the offenders gave opportunity for

many biting comparisons between the revolution or successful
rebellion which had elevated him to authority, and the rebellion
or unsuccessful revolution which had sent them to the block.
In America, where every measure is subjected to the scrutiny
of an Argus-eyed press, and the country resounds with the din
of a presidential contest, waged for many long months before
the reins are changed, we can form no idea of the thousand
secret and personal machinations which are here made to put
the "ins" out, and the "outs" in. One prominent objection
made to the administration of O'Donnel is that he has bestowed all the honors of the country upon the Vicalvarists.
After a revolution, it is but reasonable that the successful
party should seize the vacant spoils, and provided the best
men, who are really competent, be selected, this is hardly a
fair ground of complaint. Whether O'Donnel has so acted is
a much more doubtful matter, and there is perhaps too much
reason for believing that he has sometimes gratified his personal and party feeling, to say no more, at the expense of his
country. His enemies charge that he considers the Vicalvarists to have saved the country, and consequently entitled to
divide it among themselves, not being content with a reasonable salvage. The breaking out of the Moorish war was a
fortunate occurrence for his administration. Nothing could
have been more popular with the mass of the nation. The
stirring ballads of the Cid have lost little of their interest in
the hearts of true Spaniards by the lapse of ages, and the song
of the solitary muleteer yet makes the Sierras echo with the
romantic adventures of the re-conquest. The terms of the
peace do not appear to have found favor with the nation, and
the probabilities are that hostilities will again be resumed
sooner or later; but as the Moors are without naval power, the
evil consequences, if any there be, will fall upon the army
alone, while the glory will be of the whole nation. It will
moreover arouse the dormant national pride as it has already
done, and cause them to feel that their country is once more
entitled to occupy the attention of the world. If victory follow their standards, it is possible that O'Donnel may continue
for some time longer to rule, though Spain is doomed to undergo many changes yet ere she settles down into stability.
The whole condition of affairs, at least so far as the external
form of government is concerned, is transitory, so that it is

scarcely worth the trouble to describe it more minutely. It is better to speak of the various classes and institutions which will influence any crisis and any form of government that may arise.

The nobility naturally occupy the first place, and though by no means so influential as the similar class in England or Austria, is yet not without its importance. The feudal times, when rank and wealth were so inseparably connected as almost to be synonymous—when the Count was the ruler of a county and the Duke of a dutchy—have passed away in the greater part of Europe, and a nobility of birth has taken their place. The remains of the old system still linger in Spain, and there are certain lands, the ownership of which gives by courtesy the right to be distinguished by a title. It is needless to say that such titles are little respected, and confer about the same importance which the rank of a colonel or major of militia used to do in the ruder settlements of America. The real nobility, recognized by the law, is one of descent, as distinguished from an aristocracy, a *nobleza de Sangre*, comprehending the various grades known in other countries, with the exception of the one of prince, which is not a Spanish title, the only exception I remember being that of Godoy, Prince of the Peace. Nor is the importance of these titles measured by the grade, but rather by the antiquity of their origin; for there are many persons, uniting all grades, who yet select, in preference, some ancient title of Count, thus affording another exemplification of the independence of the Spanish character, for, though the Government was apparently an absolute despotism, the monarch was thus virtually denied to be the sole fountain of honor. In England, the title of Duke conferred upon a nobleman would immediately, like Aaron's rod, swallow up all his other distinctions, and on the morrow the humble backs would be bent still more humbly before the new dignity. Such is not the case in Spain. Nor, indeed, does a title of itself give any acknowledged pre-eminence over a simple gentleman; the very excess of Spanish pride thus correcting itself. There is, however, a distinction among the nobles of an acknowledged pre-eminence, viz.: the grandeeships. All grandees are practically equal, whatever may be the class of grandeeship, though there are formal differences among them as to the time of covering themselves; and individual ones are entitled to certain empty privileges which have been inherited from the middle ages, the most honorable being that exercised by the Duke of Medina Celi of claiming the crown at every coronation, in his right as representative of the Infants de la Cerda, who were dispossessed by their uncle Sancho el Bravo in the thirteenth century. Those whose families date from the great feudal chiefs, by no means admit a social equality with the new men of the last two centuries; and so strict was this formerly that the old grandees refused to address the new by the familiar appellation of "tu," which was given to each other as being all cousins, as in fact they were, and even of the king, he being only *primus inter pares*, and intermarriages between the royal family and those of his companions, the counts, being of frequent occurrence. The power of the sovereign himself was unable to break down this barrier. It was *la crême de la crême* of Vienna. By intermarriage and otherwise, many of these nobles are possessed of immense estates, and unite in themselves several grandeeships. The Duke of Ossuna, for instance, is ten times grandee of Spain, besides possessing various other titles. The remainder of the titled nobility are styled *Titulados del Reino*. As I have said before, the feudal system proper was never introduced into the greater part of Spain, so that the idea of the utter nonentity of younger compared with older sons, or of daughters compared with masculine collaterals, formed no part of their civilization. The entail of a title to the male descendants only was seldom made. This explains how in Spain the loftiest honors frequently descend to daughters, and by marriage pass over into different families. Such was, in fact, the Spanish development of the Teutonic idea as distinguished from the feudal, which latter proceeded entirely upon the notion of actual service in the field. When the Goths adopted the idea of hereditary descent, they carried out the principle to its legitimate deductions, while the English, under the feudal law of William the Conqueror, introduced from France, reached the opposite conclusion. The most honorable of these titles are those derived from the great warriors before the age of the Catholic sovereigns, such as the Mendozas, the Guzmans, the Velascos, Sandovals, Zuñigas, Pachecos, the Girons and those conferred during the three succeeding reigns, when merit was necessary to distinction. In the last hundred years the privilege of thus ennobling has been used unsparingly.

General San Miguel, a most worthy old gentleman, was made a duke for arresting the mob. Espartero, Narvaez, Palafox, Castaños, Tacon, received the same distinction for services which we would scarcely think worthy of such honors. The Moderado chiefs seem to have a particular fancy for that of marquis. As the value of the decoration decreases, the facility of acquiring it increases in proportion, and *vice versa*. One title is actually del Socorro, because the recipient, like Prince Torlonia, in an opportune moment, replenished the coffers of his sovereign. Thus has the sentiment of aristocracy undermined that of nobility. Yet with all this, the number is not greater than in other countries. At present, there are about seventy-nine dukedoms, six hundred and sixty-five marquisates, five hundred and thirty-eight countships, seventy-three viscountships, and sixty-one baronies, held by eight hundred and eighty-four individuals, one hundred and nineteen of whom divide among themselves one hundred and ninety-seven grandeeships. The number of untitled persons claiming gentle descent, with huge coats of arms over their family mansions, is much greater. Their abundance is very natural when it is considered that every man, during a contest lasting from 711 to 1492, was a soldier, and many must have honestly and honorably won their spurs. Those who were in the battle of Las Navas placed a chain or a cross upon their shields in commemoration of the event. Others derive the scallop shell from the battle of Clavijo, in which the forces of Spain were led by Santiago. The cross of St. Andrew represents the battle of Baeza. The memory of Salado and other battles is in similar manner perpetuated. Perhaps the most appropriate and soldierly of them all, unless it be a fiction, was the device of the Count of Barcelona—four upright bars formed by drawing the fingers, dipped in the blood of the wounded Wifred, down his shield. As I have before mentioned, the inhabitants of certain provinces in a mass are nominally noble, which does not, however, prevent them from being the most industrious in Spain.

Most travellers are profuse in their condemnation of the Spanish nobility. Certainly, an aristocracy of any sort, whether of money, blood or intellect, is absurd in our age of the world. But considering the circumstances in which they are placed, the nobility in Spain, notwithstanding some very poor specimens, is about as good I suspect as in other countries.

26

Persons endowed with an attribute or a distinction, which is respected, are apt to respect themselves, and to become worthy to a certain extent of the respect of others; at least such should be the rule. If mankind in their wisdom had agreed to revere long noses, long nosed people would probably be higher toned than before, and a family who had possessed this attribute for generations, would be a great family. This I take it is the only sensible foundation for the principle of hereditary honors. But the Latin nations have been weaned from the idea of an aristocracy, and consequently the difference between their aristocracy and their commonalty has ceased to be so great in appearance as that of some other nations still enveloped in the fog of mediæval barbarism. The closing of the interval between them is due as much to the elevation of the lower as to the depression of the upper classes. The effect of this progress of ideas, though by no means so great as in France, is yet visible in Spain. The number of men who, since the constitution, have risen from the humblest ranks to the head of the government, without objection on that score, is a fair example of it. As a body, the nobility is without distinctive influence, because without cohesion. Any such government as that of England, where both parties unite in reserving the honors and emoluments of office for the younger relatives of their leaders, would not be tolerated a week. Indeed, one of the most furious radicals in Spain is a marquis. But family and wealth are not without reasonable influence, and individuals of the higher rank of nobility, if competent, can easily obtain any position they may covet. As a class, they have always been in favor of liberty whenever it was not brought into too direct opposition to loyalty, nor is it unnatural that gentlemen, who consider themselves by their birthright the equal of any human being, however surrounded by the externals of power, should desire the privileges of freemen. The majority of the aristocracy certainly do not make great exertions on ordinary occasions. Why should they? They carry out one of our maxims, that the post of honor is the private station, and are content with the position to which they are entitled by birth. If any value is to be attached to antiquity of descent, they are certainly entitled to it in its fullest extent, for there are really some, in comparison with whom Henry V is a *novus homo*, a mere upstart. Men deducing their origin from individuals who were great personages when Spain was a Phenician colony, and who are honorably mentioned by the Roman historians, not to speak of the descendants of Geryon, may be excused for holding themselves a little higher than others in Europe that pride themselves upon an inferior degree of the same distinction. Unfortunately for our day they rely too much upon the past. There is one exception, however, even among the grandees, a gentleman who would be an ornament to any class·in society, and I have heard of no English duke worthy of a comparison. Among other accusations against them, is their want of corporal weight, few reaching two hundred pounds avoirdupois. This is true, but size is a poor measure of greatness. Napoleon I, Napoleon III, Cæsar, Alexander, would have fared badly by this standard, nor would Marion and Hamilton, two undoubted geniuses, have thought it less strange to be weighed in such scales. One hundred and seventy-five pounds is well enough, but fifty or a hundred more are not necessary to nobility. Spanish men are elegantly formed and muscular, and Spanish women are beautiful, but there are few leviathans of loveliness in the Peninsula. Adipose matter is rare, the only fat things I saw being the hogs, which, during the sweet acorn harvest, present a rotundity truly aristocratic.

I have heard foreigners sneeringly say, what kind of a nobility is this which does not spend money, gives no grand dinners, few balls, and eats no more than common mortals? Such manifestations of excellence are not in accordance with the customs of the country, and another fact is that the fortunes of the great families are eaten up by their stewards and retainers, who form a part of their family, and who are supported out of the common fund. Such was always the case. Nor were they mere servants, but included men of learning and literature also. The necessity for these great armies of retainers has passed away, but the retainers remain, sometimes to the number of thousands, and neither they nor their children are ever discharged. Then again the loss of the South American provinces and the invasion of the French and the British, in the War of Independence, have caused a great diminution of their formerly inordinate wealth. Many of them are comparatively poor, for the effect of progress in increasing the value of landed property has not yet made itself very sensibly felt. Furthermore, to

restricted means, is united the recollection of the great era when
a Spanish grandee was acknowledged throughout Europe as
second only to a reigning prince. It may easily be conceived
that they are not anxious to make a display of their altered
fortunes. I should be sorry to advocate the Spanish aristocracy
or any other aristocracy, but all aristocracies alike, that is all
who live upon the labor of others without contributing their
proportion to the advancement of the common country are
drones, and it is hardly fair to select this as the scape-goat of a
general principle. The length and breadth of the wide world
do not offer a finer example of nature's nobility than a true
Spanish gentleman, whether of great or humble family. It is
true that the old Scotch maxim about declining families is applicable to Spain, and that the women of distinguished origin
are better than the men, since the one are formed and educated
at home, the other abroad. But this, though the misfortune of
the latter, is the glory of the former, and I freely confess that
when the fairer part of creation—to the charms of personal,
moral and intellectual beauty—unite an untainted descent from
the stalwart knights, who in the mist of ages defended the outpost of Christianity against its enemies, I do find an additional
reason for worshipping at their shrine.

The people of Spain are really worthy of admiration. The
tyranny and corruption which have enervated the higher
classes passed lightly over them. Their manly but uneducated
virtues ceased to arouse jealousy in the gloomy despot of the
Escorial, whose most sincere ambition was to check the progress of liberty and inquiry, and to retain the human intellect in
fetters which it had outgrown, and whose pressure was wearing away the very substance, so that the nation presented the
spectacle of an unexampled oppression upon the one portion,
while the other enjoyed a liberty practically without bounds.
One can thus comprehend how they so long submitted to a
government in appearance the most absolute of Western Europe. Here are found those virtues which eminently characterize the nation—courage, fidelity, temperance and dignity.
Whatever may have been one's anticipation of their character,
it is fully realized in the peasantry of Old Castile. By no
means so brilliant as the inhabitants of some of the other
provinces, they possess more solidity, and when well officered
make superb soldiers, the last to complain on a march or to

boast in the camp. They consider themselves the heart of the earth, and cannot conceive that other nations should be put in comparison with them. But as a set-off to their pride, they aspire in their deportment to be worthy of their position. Taciturn, grave in demeanor and dignified in gesture, they are yet by no means averse to amusement if confined within proper bounds, and are the type of Spanish courtesy and loyalty. Like most persons whose friendship is worth possessing they are reserved upon first acquaintance, but when once friends no steel can be truer. In this respect there is a marked difference between them and the English, whose reserve is attributable to their want of sociability. I have already alluded to the different characteristics of the various provinces, more decidedly developed among the peasantry than the Hidalgos, who naturally resemble each other. The Andalusian will ever be enthusiastic and graceful, nor can anything eradicate obstinacy and tenacity from the Aragonese; but, with all these variations, the foundation of their character is still the same. All classes of the population, unless perhaps in the extreme north-west, which I have never visited, are distinguished by a dignified courtesy of manner. Something of the same sort still lingers in the peasantry of the south of France, but it is there owing rather to good nature and a certain species of gallantry that have always distinguished the French. In Spain it springs from a genuine self-esteem, a feeling of what is due to the person himself rather than a disposition to please another. A muleteer will, therefore, offer his meal to the passing acquaintance with all the air of a grandee, and beggars salute each other with regal majesty. People endowed with these personal qualities are capable of any elevation. As yet no great effort has been made to eradicate the vices of a past age, but the work of amelioration is commencing. The necessity of diffusing education is acknowledged, and the number of persons who can read and write compares favorably with any country in Europe except Prussia and Scotland. I did meet at Turin a scion of a noble house in Seville, who not unnaturally thought the world had better remain as it was, but the journey had opened his eyes to the necessities of progress, for subsequently in Andalusia I found his ideas had undergone considerable change. There are scattered here and there a few of the same opinion; the vast majority, however, are warmly in favor of entering the great race of national improvement. If the effect of this movement is to be the destruction of their noble, chivalrous sentiments, I should prefer them as they are, but there are good reasons for hoping better results. Spaniards are by nature conservative. If they run into excesses, it will be only for the moment. Their formal manners, grandiloquent style and antiquated notions of honor may seem ridiculous in the eyes of foreigners, who are unable or unwilling to penetrate into the recesses of their character. So, too, may their sincere religious faith appear absurd to those who have emancipated themselves from every control except that of pure reason. Yet who would cast this ballast over for the pleasure of being tossed about by every contrary wind that blows? The example of Cervantes has not been followed with sufficient discrimination. Don Quixote was a satire upon the unnatural romances of chivalry; his imitators have held up to laughter and ridicule every disinterested sentiment which does not look to some material reward as its legitimate object. The lofty inspiration which inculcates a contempt for bodily enjoyments, and prompts its subject to defy the perils of sea and land in the accomplishment of an ideal object, is scorned as vulgar fanaticism. If the result of progress is to be the elimination of this element from Spanish character, better a thousand times for them to remain as they are.

For a long time Spain suffered under the usual want of a middle class to interpose between the nobility and the people, sympathizing in many respects with both, yet opposing the preponderance of either. In the middle ages the cities fulfilled this function. With the consolidation which took place in Europe during the fifteenth century, their political influence disappeared. But some such class must exist in every society, otherwise there would rage a perpetual conflict, resulting alternately in a victory of the one and the slavery of the other. For three centuries the Church was the safety valve of Spain. Now that its power is broken down, a middle class, similar to the English, and founded mainly on property, is beginning to rise and to assert its claims to a share of power.

By the side of these is gradually springing up another, known in France by the appropriate designation of "Industriel." It is the growth of this class which has added most to the progress of the age, and at the same time, has caused most of its difficulties. Whether the solidity and severity of the Spanish national character will control its manifestations of discontent, or whether it is doomed to be here also a hot-bed of revolution, time alone can show. At present it is confined almost exclusively to a few of the northern provinces. The traveller frequently meets its agents in the shape of Commis, who are certainly not calculated to make a favorable impression. Though without the impertinence of the Parisian, they are far inferior to the German or English employee of the corresponding rank, and display a taste for eating and drinking, a forwardness of manner, and a general disposition to mere sensual enjoyments, which show how far they have departed from their countrymen. They are evidently a foreign importation, and their parasitical union with the sturdy Spanish oak has not a very congruous appearance.

Foreign commerce is slowly reviving, but many years must elapse before it can rival its former pre-eminence. The honor of the Spanish merchant in old times was proverbial. Voltaire has preserved a beautiful instance of it in their refusal, during one of the wars of the seventeenth century, to allow the debts of the French creditors to be confiscated by the Government. Of their integrity now I know nothing of my own experience. Foreign merchants have complained of them, but that is the same everywhere over the world. There is no good reason why Spain should not be a commercial nation. The present flourishing condition of English commerce did not always exist, neither were the harbors of Italy always surrendered to fishing smacks. Why nations should thus rise and fall is beyond the-reach of human ken. Tyre, Carthage, Greece, Italy, Spain, Holland, England have all had their day, and the trident is now passing to America in obedience to some law not revealed to statesmen. There is, therefore, no reason in the nature of things why those nations which once whitened the sea with their fleets may not do so again. But it cannot be accomplished by the wave of a magician's wand. Commerce no longer depends upon the mere carrying trade; it is one of the consequences of a general internal development, and Spain has just entered upon this new direction.

There are certain defects in the Spanish. character, whose salience exposes them to the view of the most hasty traveller. One of these is their pride, which is excessive, and coupled

with an unconquerable tenacity of purpose, exercises great
influence over their conduct.   It exists in all classes of society,
home and abroad.   Even the Spanish Jews in London, as I
have already mentioned, who have little reason to remember
their former country with pleasure, have always held themselves aloof from association with those of other nations.
There is much to be said in excuse for this sentiment.
No nation in modern times has possessed so proud a past.
Nor is it possible to write the history of any country in America, Europe, Asia or Africa, unless perhaps it be Russia, without assigning a place of more or less prominence to the Spaniards.   During a considerable portion of this period they have
stood in the first rank, and have been the principal support of
a religion which rules the consciences of the greater half of
the civilized world.   Their ancestors were enjoying the advantages of enlightenment at a time when the bare-legged princes
of the north were living the life of semi-brutes in straw hovels.
True, their country no longer occupies the same exalted position it once did, but those who are concerned actively with the
present have little time to think upon the subject, and secret
pride dwells more complacently upon past than present glories.
This quality produces in some respects injurious, in others,
beneficial effects.   It certainly does elevate their tone, preserve
their antiquated, perhaps, but still lofty notions of honor, and
guards them from the commission of many a deed of low vil-
lainy.   On the other hand, it frequently prevents a poor gentleman from engaging in honest industry, and causes him to
prefer lounging about some plaza, enveloped in a thread-bare
cloak, and pinched with want, rather than stain his lineage by
embracing a plebeian occupation.   However much one may dis-
prove of such prejudices, there is nothing ludicrous about these
relics of the past.   For my own part, I consider all honest
occupations alike honorable, and cannot conceive why a capitalist is more respectable than a street ditcher, provided they
be otherwise equal.   No doubt such will be the opinion of the
world at some future day; it certainly is not at present, and a
laugh or sneer at these old Castillians comes with a poor grace
from us who are daily committing the same errors on perhaps
a minor scale.

   But the general idea which prevails of Spanish indolence is
grossly exaggerated.   No doubt there is a vast quantity of

idleness there as in other countries, where the rewards of labor
are not sufficient fully to develop its energies; and it must be
admitted that it is delightful to sit upon the edge of an Andalusian fountain, beneath the orange groves, watching the shadows as they pass over the face of the dial. But to attribute
this indisposition for labor to the enervating effects of the
climate is absurd, if for no other reason simply because the
climate is not enervating. Very few people labor for the
amusement of laboring. The whole arrangement of our life
and actions proceeds upon the opposite supposition. There
must be an inducement, consisting for the most part in the
gratification of wants and desires. In addition to natural
wants and desires, civilization creates artificial ones which are
more imperious still. In Andalusia the delicious climate and
the temperate, enduring character of the people reduce the
reasonable wants of man to the smallest compass. Fuel is
supplied spontaneously by the sun, and food by the earth.
Doctors, carriages, and other necessities of northern life, cease
to be so regarded here, and most of the artificial enjoyments,
such as eating, drinking, rich furniture, equipages, are positively penalties. Art and skill can offer no gratification equal
those which are furnished them by nature. In the north
nature does nothing; cold and dreary, she frightens and repels
rather than attracts. Industry is a relief from the ennui of a
leisure which offers no pleasure in its inanity. The primeval
curse, " Thou shalt earn thy bread by the sweat of thy brow,"
falls heavily upon its inhabitants. Their wants are natural,
their pleasures mostly created, and constant labor is requisite
to prevent society from relapsing into semi-barbarism. The
same pressure of necessity elsewhere will stimulate the same
industry quite independent of climate. Thus the population
of Valencia, where the sun darts down his rays with African
intensity, is yet exceedingly industrious, for the soil, though
fertile, absolutely requires the labor of irrigation, and the
crowded numbers impose the necessity of exertion. They
seem to appreciate, also, one of the most sensible tribunals
in christendom, that of Los Alcaldes de'las Aguas, who sit once
a week, without lawyer or law beyond justice, to decide disputes about irrigation. For this, however, they are indebted
to the Moors. In Andalusia, these great incentives are wanting. The soil is fertile as the banks of the Nile. Benignant

nature has poured out the last contents of her Cornucopia. There is a deficiency rather than a surplus of population. Its inhabitants are therefore neither driven to toil by want, nor enticed to it by the prospect of some higher gratification. Set forth an adequate inducement, create some want, such as a taste for the arts, a thirst for glory which nature cannot grati- fy, and no people are more energetic than these gay loiterers of Andalusia, who will frequently undergo more fatigue for the purpose of attending a dance or bull fight than would suffice to gain a small livelihood. Their lack of industry is the fault of their civilization, not of themselves. It will be said that men make civilization, which is partly true, but so is the con- verse, and it requires generations to effect a change. Many races are industrious by inheritance and habit. The Andalu- sians are not; their ancestors returned to their long lost homes as conquerors, who considered mere labor inappropriate to a soldier. They subsequently became the recipients of a wealth, which was hardly their own, and for fifty years of this century it has scarcely been worth while to sow, since it was far from certain who would reap. That there is vast room for improve- ment, south of the Sierra Morena, none can doubt, but it is tiresome to hear the reiterated platitudes about the climate, as if laziness, like malaria, were inseparable from certain coun- tries. As for the rest of Spain, and particularly Gallicia, the Basque Provinces and Catalonia, I think the peasantry are in an eminent degree hard working, when one considers that no amount of labor can, except in rare instances, elevate them much above the position in which they were born.

There is another defect in the Spanish character, a very serious one—their want of appreciation of human suffering. If cruelty means a pleasure in inflicting pain, I do not think it a characteristic of the Spaniards, but there certainly is vast indifference to suffering and even to life. If a Spaniard pro- poses to himself the accomplishment of some end, the fact that a certain number of lives must be sacrificed is a matter of small consideration. The doctrine that the least possible amount of pain is to be inflicted, which is sufficient to the attainment of the object, is scarcely recognized in practice as an acknowledged rule of action. It is the same with beasts as men. To tell a Spaniard that his bit was too powerful and inflicted unnecessary pain, and should, therefore, be changed, would be an unknown sort of language. If it injured the horse, that would be another matter. By not making this distinction travellers have thought that Spaniards positively enjoyed the sufferings of the animals at a bull fight, whereas they are merely indifferent. They go to see the contest, and if allowed to choose, would probably prefer that the animals should be insensible to pain. But there is none of that restless sentiment upon the subject here which characterizes the modern French, or the better class of the German or English people, though the brutal disposition of the lower class of the latter is alike without a counterpart. It may be said, too, by way of palliation, that the Spaniards have no more respect for themselves than for others, and never complain of suffering. If any suppose that the Spanish race is essentially cruel or indifferent it would be an error. Our ideas of humanity are entirely things of the last hundred years. For two centuries the Spanish people have been very little influenced by external nations, and to a considerable extent retain their old ideas unchanged. Up to the agitation of the rights of man in 1789, it is amazing what cruelties were perpetrated everywhere by those in power. So completely has the change of society altered the relations which exist between man and man, that we think the Spaniards ferocious because they act pretty much as their and our ancestors did a half century ago. But the hand of progress and reform has seized them with a firm grasp. The rays which formerly illuminated only the loftiest peaks are now penetrating into the valleys, and we may reasonably expect to see the day, and that shortly, when their darkest recesses will be filled with light.

There is one feature which distinguishes Spaniards from all other nations in Europe—the absence of that respect and adoration for the mere possession of wealth which is the moving spring of society elsewhere. Men are not ranked according to the length of their purses, and poverty is neither a sin nor a disgrace. The poorest beggar feels his full dignity as a man, and maintains, by his conduct, the apparently self-evident truth that the earth was made for man and not man for the earth. Their habits of life and even their dress are admirably calculated to uphold this independence of worldly means. The enjoyment of intercourse is mostly out of doors, on the Paseo, at church, in the theatre. The house is really a home not intended for the display of vain glories, but for the charms of domesticity and that privacy which is incompatible with the presence of mere strangers. In countries not blessed with so fine a climate, a different style of life is forced upon the inhabitants; the sacred enjoyments of home are sacrificed for the absorbing ambition of display; men spend their time in amassing the means, and wives become indexes to the capacity and liberality of their husband's pockets. The national costume in Spain is simple, and the distinction consists not so much in the costliness of the dress as in the elegance of the wearer, so that this fruitful source of ruin to families does not exist. It would puzzle the most keen-eyed tax assessor to detect the various grades of rich or poor among the happy throng. Even in the deportment of the fair promenaders it is difficult to distinguish the different ranks. In England or Germany there is an unmistakeable difference between the higher and lower classes, not only in dress but in manner; this latter has as little existence in Spain as the former, all are gentlemen alike, and it is often impossible for a stranger to judge of the exact social position of the parties even after a slight acquaintance.

But this virtue, when carried to an excess, produces practically an evil effect in encouraging beggary. The Spanish beggar is a very different person from the English, Italian, or even the German, where the children carry their mama's compliments on the fine weather to a neighbor, and ask if she will not go out a begging. He is proud and dignified; suggests the propriety of alms, but does not insist, because such a course would be shocking to his Castillian pride. He sees nothing humiliating in the occupation itself, but only in the manner of exercising it. There are various classes, some are really objects of charity, honest persons reduced to want, who would work willingly were there any to employ them. Heaven forbid that these should be received with a sneer, or that we should adopt the religion of Ch. Jus. Montague, and let them starve in God's name. But there are others, beggars by profession, sons of beggars and beggaresses, inheriting poverty from a long line of mendicant ancestors. A part of the Scriptures is carried out by them in strict obedience, for they take no heed what they shall eat, nor what they shall drink, nor wherewithal shall they be clothed. The sight of these produces no indignation in the minds of Spaniards, who give or do not give as the fancy strikes them, always with courteous speech and without that exhibition of contempt which foreigners display. The *perdone me vm. por Dios* is an effectual guard against them. This hereditary race of beggars will disappear very soon. In the days of convents and monasteries they found a steady though humble support, and whatever they obtained from strangers was considered the legitimate fruits of their industry, so much clear gain to capitalize; but general charity is too uncertain a reliance to marry upon, and future travellers will regret the absence of a characteristic if not very ornamental feature of Spanish scenery.

CHAPTER XXIII.

GENERAL CONTINUED.

The Church—Reforms—Religious Sincerity of the Spaniards—The Army—The Press—Internal Improvements—Police—Political Wants.

The Church has always exercised a prominent influence in the government of Spain, and the prosperity of the country has depended in no small degree upon the character of its ecclesiastical population. A considerable part of its history has been engrossed by contests in which questions of faith were involved; first, with the Moors, then with the Turks, and, finally, with the Protestants. It is, therefore, natural that the whole nation should be overspread with a religious hue. More than that, the Spanish character is essentially religious. Their fervor, devotion, their indifference to most of the pleasures of the body, their poetical temperament, attract them toward some influence beyond the earth. Spain has, therefore, always been the home of enthusiasts, and though we may, perhaps, never again behold Loyola and Santa Teresa, the same spirit survives in all departments of human life, and requires only the influence of propitious circumstances for its development. The extravagances, therefore, which have appeared in connection with their prominent institutions must be looked upon with some allowance, as they are the legitimate fruits of the national character. There is nothing mediocre in the country. Everything is in the superlative either for good or evil. More particularly is this the case with regard to the Church. The horrors perpetrated by Alexander VI and Torquemada are more than counter-balanced by the virtues of Las Casas, and an infinite number of others, who have given a lustre to humanity by their brilliant qualities. The fierce, unanimous, undying resistance offered to the invasion of Napoleon, was due, in no small degree, to the patriotic efforts of the priest-

hood, who surrendered everything for the maintenance of the
national honor and the national religion. Cross and sometimes
sabre in hand, they animated the defenders to the breach.
Often defeated, they yielded not to their oppressor, and with
their last breath still maintained the rights of the coward
prince who had ingloriously acknowledged himself a subject
of the great tyrant. Of course their enemies stigmatize them
as fanatics. By the same rule of logic Marion was a fanatic,
Washington a fanatic, and every other patriot who weds himself to his country's cause for weal or for woe. Where education is so much neglected, the lower ranks of the clergy must
frequently present lamentable instances of ignorance, but the
world cannot show a nobler body of Christians than the Spanish prelates. Secured as they are by their religion against
most inducements to nepotism, and deprived by the late reforms
of the means of gratifying that unworthy sentiment, their lives
are devoted to the duties of their station. Amid all the scandals
which are uttered indiscriminately by natives and foreigners,
I have never heard a breath whispered against them. The
political influence enjoyed by their predecessors no longer
exposes them to the temptations of worldly ambition. Nor is
there any such division of parties as calls for their interference; so that religion, in its strictest sense, engrosses the
whole of their thoughts. Would that the same could be said
of other countries.

The history of the Spanish Church is a noble monument to
the independence of the nation. From the earliest times it
was distinguished for its resistance not only to the encroach-
ments of the Papacy, but to the introduction of foreign doctrines, come they whence they might. In becoming members
of the great Catholic Hierarchy they never ceased to be Spaniards, and asserted the independence of the national church
upon all suitable occasions. These events, from a false shame,
were concealed by those who wrote in later days, after the
establishment of the Inquisition, when any departure from the
established rule, whether in matters of principle, or practice,
or prejudice, was visited with fire and sword. But a more
enlightened spirit has been awakened, and their early ecclesiastical will soon be as great a source of pride as their profane
history has been. The hard, material features of the feudal
age, subordinating man to man, or still worse to a mere clod

of earth, were relieved by the preponderance of the theocracy, which spread its protecting wings over the oppressed, and taught the haughty baron that there was a living spirit in whose eyes the rich and the poor, the powerful and the obscure were equal. With the extension of its empire in the sixteenth century, Spain became the most powerful son of the Church, and almost the Church itself. Unfortunately with it came the baleful Inquisition, stifling every thing generous. It is not strictly correct to lay the bloody monster at the foot of the Catholic faith, for none resisted its introduction more sincerely than the secular clergy. It was at first, at least in Spain, essentially a political institution, both within and without the Church, intended to prevent freedom of thought and discussion everywhere. But it soon sought a new theatre of action. Protestants there were none; Jews and Mohammedans, except a few in secret, had been banished, and for want of proper aliment, like the fabled monster, it devoured its own entrails. It is difficult to speak with moderation of an institution, one of whose rules of action was never to confront the witness with the accused, and which treated the suspected with a severity surpassing that of the condemned. The silent effect which it produced upon the Spanish character has seldom been exaggerated. It nearly destroyed their natural Southern frankness, for what heart could expand when the bosom friend, the father, the wife, might, perhaps, be one of its accursed spies? Whatever of suspicion yet lingers about them may be justly traced to this source.

The enormous wealth of the Spanish clergy was formerly a great cause of scandal to the world, and it was reasonably and truly affirmed that the quantity of lands held in mortmain opposed a serious obstacle to the progress of the nation. The clergy were naturally poor administrators of their property, and felt none of that necessity for enlightened economy which struggles to increase the interval between receipt and expenses. In the middle ages the lands of the Church were, comparatively, the garden spots of the kingdom, because cultivated by a peasantry whose mild servitude enabled them to feel the energy of freemen. In the progress of events, the balance of the scale was turned, and they eventually became the very worst cultivated of all. Whatever evils may have flowed from this source, have now ceased to exist. The ecclesiastical property has been absorbed by the State. Monks and friars are matters of history. The salaries of the clergy are paid by the Government. There are no bishoprics of Durham or Canterbury, no sinecures, no pluralities. The emoluments of their office are barely sufficient to support them and to cover their private charities, and the Spanish Church, so far as its government is concerned, is really a reformed church. The change was inevitable, for it is impossible long to resist the progress of ideas; the new wine threatened to burst the old bottles. In the days of aristocracy, the church government naturally accommodated itself to the condition and exigencies of society. The laws of primogeniture secured the pre-eminence of the heads of noble houses. Bishoprics, masterships, abbeys, offered corresponding positions for the younger members of the family, and for great intellects born out of the privileged classes, whose efforts might otherwise have been directed to revolution. In a word, they were the safety-valves of the system. The philosophers of the eighteenth century struck a death blow at the root of aristocracy, by preaching anew (with very little religion it must be admitted) the doctrines of the New Testament as to the natural equality of man, which had, during seventeen centuries of violence and oppression, been practically forgotten. The acknowledgment of the new system involved the destruction of the old. It was no longer necessary to society that the Church should be a great civil institution, standing between the class of wealth and power and those who possessed neither. In England and Austria only does it still maintain its civil influence and unnatural prerogative. In Spain they have utterly disappeared, almost as much so as in America.

Still the Catholic is the established religion, and the exercise of any other is strictly forbidden. Persons of different faith cannot even intermarry within the territorial limits, though provided with the papal dispensation, and Gibraltar or Bayonne used to be the Gretna Green for impatient lovers. Such is the law of the land. Religious liberty, therefore, in its largest sense does not exist. The United States of America proudly stand alone in the world as the only country where the privilege is allowed to every one of selecting and supporting the form of worship or the faith most congenial to his convictions or prejudices, which is certainly the beau ideal of religious liberty. No such thing exists in Europe. The French system

27

is enlightened in so far as it supports all religions—Catholic Protestant, Jewish and Mohammedan. The other countries for the most part tolerate a difference of faith, but impose restrictions and taxes upon dissenters for the maintenance of a creed which they sometimes regard as little better than heathenism—the very worst species of oppression, admitting as a theoretical right what it refuses in practice. The denial of toleration in Spain is practically productive of little hardship. There are no Protestants in that country, and probably never will be any, for the heart of the people is essentially Catholic, and the age of profound religious conviction, and consequently of conversions, is almost gone. The dominant religion, too, has been shorn of its power to oppress. So far as the rights of the Spanish people are involved, therefore, it is a matter of supreme indifference whether other religions be prohibited or not, and the few strangers who travel among them seem either not to suffer very much from the want of spiritual consolation, or have laid in such a supply in advance as would last them during the journey, the latter probably, as their religion would otherwise be a poor reliance. The resistance which the Government for a long time made to Protestant burying grounds should not be passed over so lightly, as it was a relic of bigotry unworthy of a great nation and disgraceful to the age. A Protestant, Jew or Mohammedan, who had the misfortune to depart this life within her borders, was buried in an old field with the horses from the bull ring, or cast into the sea, if upon the coast. Even now any public religious ceremony at the funeral procession is prohibited. This privilege, thus jealously restricted, was most grudgingly yielded after a series of persevering applications on the part of Lord Palmerston.

So many years have elapsed since the abolition of monasteries, that a new generation has grown up. Their restoration, therefore, is impossible, and it is time that history should begin impartially to balance the virtues and defects of these institutions, which played so important a part in the Christian world. Hitherto it has all been upon one side. Their worst and exceptional features alone have been brought into relief by the light of adverse criticism. They had undoubtedly lived out their lives, for there is a life of institutions as well as of men. The labors and sorrows of fourscore were upon them, yet their youth and manhood had been vigorous, and their old age not devoid of virtue and respect. If meddling and worldly brethren sometimes disturbed the peace of families, there are also innumerable instances of harmony restored, of wounded hearts healed, of broken-spirited and despairing victims soothed, which have been forgotten in the privacy of domestic events. That they have frequently nourished idlers is true, but it is likewise true that the most industrious and painstaking of Spanish authors came from the depths of a cloister.

The Spanish are sincere in their faith, and practice it as they understand its precepts. Mohammedans complain that the followers of Christ, having a very good religion, though a false one, utterly neglect its duties, and in general there is foundation for the criticism. The contrast between the two in any common meeting place, any neutral ground, such as Gibraltar, is very disadvantageous to the latter. The Spaniards have very justifiably the same opinion of Protestants, judging them by the travelling public, who, to all appearances, are without any religion whatever. It is a vain-glorious boast to exalt the precepts of our faith when those precepts are systematically overlooked in practice. That there are great moral defects in Spain every traveller must see, but they are derived from the false system of government under which they have so long suffered, and not, according to my experience, from their religion or from any extraordinary disobedience of its injunctions. Certain of the Commandments are never broken, and if some of the rest are infringed, it is to a much less extent than in other European countries, and may be explained by the lack of industrial employment and the consequent habits which idleness engenders. That superstition still lingers in remote localities, and that mere symbols of faith have frequently been confounded with the faith itself, is true, but the advancing tide of free thought is rapidly sweeping all this into the past, and of the two evils it is certainly the less. The spirit of the age is entirely against not only superstition, but, I am sorry to say, religion, that is a religion in the vital sense of the word, and the real ground of apprehension at present is from a deficiency, not an excess of belief. The atheism, deism, and philosophistic religion, so prevalent in the *soi-disant* enlightened countries, and which once threatened to invade the Peninsula, have disappeared here now that the success of the liberal party is assured and the material power of the Church placed under reasonable restrictions by the concordats of the past ten years. Priests and monks have always furnished objects for the witticism of Spaniards, frequently for their abuse, and sometimes their violence, but woe be to the unwary anti-Catholic who confounds this with any want of respect for religion itself. The Spaniard may jest about the housekeeper, nephews, kitchen and good wine of his spiritual guide, but doubt as to the propriety of his belief in the purity of the Church and the immaculate conception of Our Lady would be perilous in the last degree. There would be about as much chance for a Protestant propagandist as for a Mormon prophet.

In another point the prevailing opinion of outsiders about this country is equally at fault, viz : in their estimate of the efficiency of Spanish soldiers, simply because they persist in regarding Spain as a country still profoundly asleep. If her army is to be judged by that of the eighteenth century, they are of course correct, but Spain of the eighteenth and Spain of the nineteenth centuries are very far apart, and in no department more than in the military. She has fared badly at the hands of foreign historians. The English writers, and at their head Sir Charles Napier in his admirable history of the Peninsular war, have studiously striven to deprive her citizens of all credit during the War of Independence, whether for skill, organization, courage, or general efficiency, and their statements have poisoned the public mind wherever the language is spoken. The French, with characteristic impartiality, have been more disposed to do them justice, but the great mass of our countrymen do not take the trouble to seek for truth when hid under the bushel of a strange idiom. The Spanish accounts are unknown, and so are the histories of the German officers serving in those campaigns, who were, by the nature of their position, the most unprejudiced observers. The erroneous opinions thus formed have remained fixed in the general mind with unshakeable tenacity. Yet the evidence of every traveller during the last ten years, capable of forming a judgment upon the matter, is otherwise. If it be possible to estimate the efficiency of troops by their appearance in time of peace, I should have no hesitation in assigning the Spanish army as high a rank as any in Europe, except the French, and the experience of the Moorish war has certainly not been inconsistent with that position. The Spanish infantry and cavalry were once

the best in the world. The latter were entitled, by their chivalric genealogy to be the worthy representatives of a nation
where caballero and gentleman are still synonymous. The latter, until the fatal battle of Rocroy, made Europe tremble at
the sound of their approach. The same individual qualities
exist, the same muscular strength, the same physical endurance, the same activity of person, the same temperate life, the
same excitability of disposition, the same tenacity of purpose,
the same pride of character continue to distinguish them. The
curse of Spanish armies, for the last two hundred years, has
been the inefficiency of their battalion officers, but this evil is
rapidly disappearing, and with its disappearance the horizon
will once more become bright to them.

The conscription for a service of eight years is the usual
method of recruiting. At first it was odious to the last degree,
and was styled "the contribution of blood," but the nation is
gradually getting used to it, and the service is, moreover,
becoming more popular, so that, in 1859, a large proportion
of those who were discharged re-enlisted immediately. The
infantry has been lately organized into forty regiments of the
line, each with two battalions of eight companies, one *regimento
fijo*, at Ceuta, of three battalions, twenty battalions of cazadores in imitation of the *chasseurs à pied*. There are, in addition, eighty battalions of "milicias provinciales" as a reserve.
The former organization was somewhat different, the number
of the companies being less and that of the battalions greater.
The Royal Guard is abolished, as giving rise to unjust preferences, and the only household troop are the Halbadiers. Their
uniform is not so showy as the Austrian, nor so ugly as the
French, but combines suitability with a reasonable amount of
good looks. The movements of the drill occupy, in like manner, a medium place between the French and English, not so
board stiff as the one, nor so entirely nonchalant as the other.
The men are larger than the French and much handsomer fellows, though without that good humored expression which pre-
possess in favor of the latter. The cavalry is divided into
nineteen regiments. They are, of course, fine riders, and
manœuvred well enough, but I was somewhat disappointed in
the horses. The pride of the army, however, are the artillery
and engineer corps. In addition to the ordinary artillery, the
Spaniards, like ourselves, have been compelled by the nature of

their country, intersected as it is everywhere by steep valleys and rocky Sierras, to develop the system of mountain batteries with three mules to a gun—one to carry the piece itself, another the carriage, and a third the ammunition. It is precisely what is required for the country, and there is suitable material at hand. The paths, though narrow and steep, are firm; the mules, large, sure-footed, quick-moving and hardy, and the activity of Spaniards in climbing hillsides was proverbial even in the days of Muza, who, in his report to the Caliph, pronounced them to be "cabras para escapar en los montes." Marshal Pelissier paid a visit to Madrid while I was there, and after reviewing the garrison, expressed, warmly, his surprise and satisfaction at the efficiency of the artillery. During the War of Independence this branch of the service was always well conducted. In our day it has kept even pace with the progress of improvement, and seems to have been the principal cause of the victories in Africa. Of the engineers I can give no opinion, but they rank even higher in the estimation of those who are capable and have had opportunities of forming a judgment.

The preponderance of officers in the Spanish army is surprising at first glance. That there should be a larger number in the lower ranks than is usual in other countries may be desirable, for the men see little actual service, and when the contingency comes it is therefore necessary that they should have a sufficiency of leaders educated in the science of war to direct them. Such is the case with our volunteers, who will follow if well led, but certainly not otherwise. The objectionable feature in Spain is the vast number of generals. The highest rank is that of captain-general, corresponding to marshal, of whom there are a dozen or so, some of them merely honorary. The title of captain-general, as the ruler of a province, is very ancient, and until this century their powers were very great, in fact almost sovereign, imitated probably from the Walis of the Cordovese empire, who united all sorts of functions, even dispensing justice, just as the captain-generals of Spain used formerly to preside in full uniform over the Court of Chancery. The kingdom is still divided off into capitanias-generales, but they are mere military districts, and the officers in command have been shorn of all civil authority. Next come sixty-seven lieutenant-generals, one hundred and

fifty-seven mariscales de campo, four hundred and one briga-
diers—numbers perfectly preposterous upon the footing of actual service. The rule of advancement is, I believe, nominally
that of seniority, but this rule is enforced only in some departments, such as the artillery and engineers, in which the examinations are very strict; whereas, in the infantry and cavalry,
such is not and could not be the case. A friend at court, therefore, is worth more than any amount of capacity. The consequence is that comparatively young men, if supported by
palace influence, are early advanced to the highest places in
the military hierarchy. After that there is no object in the
department to which they belong to concentrate their ambition. Their rank has been obtained without any distinguished
deed of valor which could sanctify it in the public respect.
They are surrounded by a collection of persons as little distinguished as themselves, and if they desire to occupy a place in
the world, to rise from the common herd of generals, they
must needs enter the field of politics. It is very difficult to fix
upon a system of promotion which does not produce injustice
practically. Nothing can be more unfair than that men of
energy, industry and capacity should be compelled to wait the
slow revolution of the wheel, while their seniors, without perhaps a single recommendation, are mounting. At the same
time it is equally demoralizing to see an undeserving junior
pushed up through all the grades by the supple adroitness of
some friend, male or female, about the court. The system of
advancement by seniority tends to overflow the higher ranks
of the army, which, however, is a minor evil, if the departments of military and civil life are kept distinct. But such is
not the case in Spain or Europe generally. They sit in the
Cortes or ministry partly as soldiers, partly as civilians. If
their adversaries maintain too firm a grasp upon the reigns of
power, they appeal readily to pronunciamentos and revolution,
and hence for the most part spring the various commotions
which have agitated the Government since the peace of 1814.
It is honorable to them that in the majority of instances the
army has pronounced for liberal government. A despotic central power can hold out to them no prospect of glory, such as
gilds the bitter pill beyond the Pyrenees, and they consequently follow their natural bent which is for freedom and equality.
The people of Spain have generally taken little part in these

demonstrations, but the nation is becoming tired of them; there is a universal desire for stable peace if it can be purchased on reasonable terms. The Morocco war, too, has withdrawn the attention of the army chiefs from domestic concerns, and offered a more honorable object for their ambition; and the late renunciation of the Count of Montemolin has removed a standing source of dissatisfaction, so that there is ground for hoping that the day of organized military insurrections is passing away.

The press, as usual in Europe, is mostly concentrated at the capital. The centrifugal tendency of Spaniards prevents such an entire absorption by the metropolis as happens in France and England, but very few provincial journals venture to have a policy of their own. Being a thing of comparatively late introduction, and its birth occurring in the midst of revolutionary throes, it is essentially and bitterly partisan, and directed heart and soul to the establishment of the principles it may espouse, yet in the midst of the most violent excitement it never, so far as I have seen, descends to personal abuse. There were a number of ephemeral charivaris, such as *el grillo*, during the past summer, which gratified the taste of the *Madrileños* for wit and satire to its full extent, but the established organs hold themselves above this style of argument. In fact, the principles involved in their contests are too important to be overlooked in the mere scramble about men, and the point of honor is too high to permit those personalities about the candidate, his wife and children, grandfather and grandmother, his nativity, the length of his body and his purse, which form the charm of our dailies. All such are considered private matters. Nor would it be consistent with Spanish ideas of propriety for George Washington Wormwood to convert the Squash Town Harbinger into a machine for the ventilation of his personal malignity. The editors are almost always gentlemen, and many of the most distinguished men in Spain were connected in youth with the press, it being quite the fashion at that day. It does not follow, however, that this system is the best because it may be the most gentlemanly. The press is a terrific power in its very nature, and when it adds the weight of respectability to its already almost irresistible influence it assumes proportions that endanger the stability of government. The London Times is really a fourth estate, and more potent in Great Britain than any common ministry. In fact, if the House of Lords were to declare war against the Thunderer, as the latter during the Crimean war once dared it to do, the result is far from being certain. So long as the master of this power is right all goes well; but an editor is not necessarily right, because he is decent or honest. In France the editors are obnoxious to punishment for publishing false news, *Saxonice* "lying," but what would become of the American press if any such law were enforced with us?

Our system of license is beneficial in one respect, since it destroys the influence of the press as a press. What persons read in the Times they believe, which is far from the universal case in America. This minute distribution of its influence among small, if sometimes not respectable recipients, is also favorable to the rights of minorities, which it is the object of constitutional government to protect. Every clique of a thousand voters can make itself heard throughout the land, and generally does, for the smaller the minority the louder the trumpet blast which frightens the old fogy organs into silence. If these ends could be attained consistently with a high editorial tone, of course it would be better for individuals and the country, but then the laws should be enforced more rigidly to counterbalance its power. In England the jury never hesitates to give damages even to a candidate who sues for a libel. Unfortunately in America we have too much chivalry to justify such a mode of seeking reparation, yet not enough to frown down the offender who thus oversteps the boundary of propriety and abuses his trust. But upon the whole our plan seems to be the best, even if we should have to adopt Franklin's idea—unrestricted liberty of the press, together with unrestricted liberty of the cudgel, by way of constitutional limitation, for thus every class of society, however exalted or however debased, finds a suitable organ for the expression of its wants and sympathies. European statesmen have yet to learn what a safety valve this is in a free government, or in any government. An excitement commences; the partisan press takes it up; things look squally; penny newspapers commence to blow; inflammatory speeches are made; rusty muskets cleaned up; ferocious meetings held; Fourth of July orators have to be held down by the seat of their breeches lest they should go off into infinite space and dislocate the solar system. By and by

subscribers begin to exclaim on opening the morning paper—
"What! the same old thing!" the waters subside rapidly; the
Jericho rams' horns are put away for a more propitious occasion, and the country is spared. Every few years the same
thing happens again, with this difference, that the *blowers* generally change sides with the *blowees*. As a sensible German
once said to me: "In 1849 a disappointed Republican rose in
a bilious mood, fit for treason and revolution, ready to over-
turn the Government in a twinkling. He read the National
Zeitung and found an article abusing Manteufel roundly as a
traitor and a despot, reflecting his own sentiments exactly.
Quite satisfied, he went down to his work and thought no more
about politics for the rest of the day; now that is all gone."
And it is true. The top of the pot is kept down so tight in
Europe that sooner or later it must burst, and then comes all
the trouble of making a new one. In Spain the pressure is by
no means so great as in some other countries, and a very fair
share of liberty is allowed. To descend from the essential to
the material, the paper and typography are unexceptionable,
by far the best in Europe, except, perhaps, the Sardinian.

Spain has not yet reached that height of improvement where
individual energy develops the country without governmental
aid. Nor do they comprehend our system of building roads by
anticipation out of the future, relying for eventual payment
upon the ten-fold increase of general wealth caused thereby.
The House of Austria did nothing whatever for the internal
communication between province and province, in a country
where, owing to variety of climate and production, such facilities were of all others necessary. The Bourbons, and particularly Charles III, made most of the magnificent *caminos reales*,
which are inferior to none in Europe. Yet so unsatisfactory
was the system as a whole, that even within a score of years
the necessaries of life would be at famine prices in one locality
and not a hundred miles off almost worthless from want of the
means of transportation. The Government and the nation
have now become fully impressed with the urgency of a complete system, and are carrying it out as vigorously as they can
in a country where coin is not in superfluity. The railroad
from Madrid to Alicante is finished, and branches will soon be
extended to Valencia and Cartagena. One is in operation from
Cadiz to Cordova, by Seville. It is in contemplation to con-

tinue it to Madrid over the Sierra Morena, but that will be of difficult accomplishment. The connexion between Madrid and Bayonne by Valladolid and Burgos will soon be finished, and that passing by Zaragoza to Barcelona is in progress. A connection between Madrid and Lisbon is also to be made. Besides these, there are some local roads and a vast number of projects in embryo. Spain contains within herself everything requisite for these works, except, perhaps, the timber. There is an abundance of capital hoarded away or invested in foreign securities, but a general want of living confidence in the stability of institutions and the continuity of progress prevents its application to useful works. The confidence requisite for that purpose is indeed a plant of slow growth and does not attain maturity in a day, but it is growing, and the causes of uncertainty in the political future, and the apathy of the nation in regard to civil commotions, so ruinous to steady progress, are disappearing. The depreciation in the value of gold coin, caused by the late discoveries, is a boon to a country so deeply involved in debt as Spain, and will enable her before long to acquit herself of the burthen that presses down her finances. This weight removed, the natural consequence will be the accumulation of capital, and then we may expect to see the Peninsula rank, as it once did, among the most favored regions of the earth. Nothing else is wanted to render it such.

The Spanish government, under Ferdinand VII., scarcely deserved the name of a government, if the attainment of the ends for which government is established be a criterion, that is to say, it utterly failed to protect life or property against such as made a determined effort to violate the laws. It was merely a political machine to put down free thought and free speech. The improvement since then has been immense, but there is still room. Great difficulty was experienced in introducing the requisite reforms. The whole system of police is entirely against the national prejudices; and much ridicule was at first made of the institution. The functionaries were nick-named " hijos de Luis Felipe," being an importation from France, but the nation has become reconciled to them by conviction of their necessity. The country police is, without exception, the finest and most respectable body of police I have ever met in Europe. Physically strong and enduring as all Spaniards are, they have not yet been so long indulged with the luxury of arbitrary power as to cultivate a spirit of insolence and tyranny, which is beginning to be dreadfully complained of in France. But a considerable portion of Andalusia, in particular, is too sparsely settled to enable them to afford protection against all evil-doers, and nobody in Europe considers himself as belonging to the police, or interested actively in the preservation of order, except such as are enrolled and paid. During the past summer, that province rang with complaints of violence committed not upon travellers and diligences, but upon respectable persons, who were seized and concealed until a certain amount should be paid as a ransom. It was always famous for such misdeeds. There are no means of extirpating the evil, but the development of the country itself and the education of the common people, which will cause them to regard these acts in their true light, rather than as a species of adventure excusable if successful. Indeed, the present generation in certain parts of the mountains were so wholly inured to a life of violence in their youth, that there seems to be but little hope of reforming them, and it is only left to imitate the example of Moses in patiently awaiting their extinction. The next generation may prove more pliable.

For such as do not quarrel, life is now about as safe in Spain as elsewhere, at least as safe as it is in America, but harsh words are a dangerous luxury, and are apt to be followed by something more serious. Spaniards do not understand the art of angry talking. After a certain point it is the knife and nothing but the knife. The revolver they do not fancy, because they are not used to it, but with an Albacete they are at home. There is a defect in the national character in this respect. On serious matters they cannot agree to disgree, that is they cannot talk about it. A Spanish gentleman once accounting to a friend of mine for the fact that the jury system had never been tried in Spain, explained it by saying that if twelve of his countrymen were shut up in a room to discuss a given subject, only one would come out alive, and there is some truth in the explanation. The duel is frequently appealed to by gentlemen to settle points of honor, for, like ourselves, they are very sensitive to hard epithets, which heal more slowly than wounds.

> Una herida mejor
> Se sana que una palabra;

or, as the old maxim has it, "*heridas sanan pero no malas palabras.*" The parties are well criticised by their circle of acquaintances, unless everything be conducted strictly according to the old chivalric rules. The challenger of course chooses the terms, as they have not yet been able to understand the right of the offender to entrench himself behind a favorite weapon. Not only the contest itself, but the subsequent intercourse of the parties is upon the same high tone, and I have heard great stress laid upon a certain distinguished gentleman's neglecting or refusing to inquire after his opponent's health. The abominable American habit of converting the scene of the tragedy into a cock-pit, and of publishing a long correspondence, wherein the parties or their friends try to get the advantage by technicalities, is quite unknown. The pen is hardly resorted to at all on ordinary occasions, in accordance with the feudal state of society, in which a man might be a gentleman of rank, and entitled to satisfaction, although he could not write well enough to demand it, chirography being considered an accomplishment of clerks, not of warriors. There can be no doubt that duelling is a relic of barbarism, and should be abolished, but so should the causes which furnish occasion for it, or else enlightened public opinion should afford some satisfaction for the insults which now drive gentlemen to this antiquated and absurd remedy.

There is another passion which leads to much bloodshed in Spain—jealousy. There can be in the nature of things but one way of settling such a difficulty. As a theologian, and a follower of the precept which bids the sufferer to turn the other cheek, the traveller may condemn them, certainly not as a human being.

In one particular the Spaniards are in advance of us, viz., in adopting the decimal system of weights and measures. It is outrageous that in the middle of the nineteenth century, the United States of America, claiming, with some justice, to be the most enlightened nation in the world, should be still struggling with the confusion of troy, penny and avoirdupois weights, not to speak of rods, perches and barleycorns.

Upon the whole the thing most needed in Spain is a ministry, virtuous enough to distribute its official patronage, even if among their partisans, yet according to merit and capacity, and strong enough to be able to do so without fear. Napoleon I is entitled to the credit of having introduced the system into France, impelled, perhaps, by the necessity of his position. If the Spanish Government copied this feature of the Napoleonic policy, they would give more satisfaction to true patriots than they have yet succeeded in doing. One day the conversation happened to turn upon the mismanagement of the royal property, by which the Queen was wofully cheated. A Frenchman present expressed his indignation, saying that if he were in authority he would reform such abuses immediately. A Catalonian replied to his indignation by a significant gesture, to the effect that the Camerilla, standing upon prescription, would prove more than a match for any officer, however right he might be, and such would undoubtedly be the case. No decidedly reform ministry could hold its own in the present condition of affairs. But there is, after all, a vast difference in this respect between a military despot, relying solely upon energetic and capable subordinates for the solidity and stability of his authority, and a constitutional chief, shaken by every breath of public opinion. And then, perhaps, America may not be the most suitable place whence to cast the stone of condemnation.

Chapter XXIV.

POLITICAL.

Our Troubles with Spain—Anglo-Saxonism—*Entente Cordiale* Directed Against us by England—Filibusters—Spanish Political Desires—Means of Acquiring Cuba Honorably — Standing of Americans in Europe—Influence of our Diplomatic Corps—Our Position in Spain—Adios.

There is no earthly reason why Spain and the United States of America should not be the best friends in the world. With many differences, there is yet a striking resemblance in the better points of character, to some of which I have made passing allusions in the preceding pages. Our commercial interests do not clash, there is no legitimate occasion for rivalry between us, and when we stood most in need of a friend she was by our side to aid us. Our most gifted authors have found her history a congenial field for the exercise of their talents. Yet somehow all this seems to be overlooked, and politicians and newspapers speak as though we were natural enemies. The rise of this spirit seems to have been simultaneous with that of Anglo-Saxonism. No longer feeling the honorable pride of independent nationality to which we are most justly entitled, there has sprung up a class, proclaiming that we are only an offshoot of the Anglo-Saxons, and that the Revolution cut no cord but the umbilical. There is, doubtless, a sufficiency of Anglo-Saxon blood in America; but there is probably a still greater amount of Celtic and Teutonic. We speak, too, their language; and a very poor one it is, fit for serpents only. We derive from them the feudal institution of trial by our peers, which continental nations, owing to their necessity for standing armies, have not been able to retain. Beyond this there is little to remind us of the former dominion exercised by the English over the American Continent. Almost every State in the Union has in substance rejected her laws, and substituted the civil therefor. We have adopted the French military system, with scarcely a variation. With the Germans, we sympathize in the freedom of intellect and the inquiring spirit that characterize the race. We have developed a liberty purely our own, which England has timidly copied. We have taught her the folly and cruelty of those ferocious laws which annually covered her island with gibbets—that men, as men, have some rights, even though they be not equal in worldly position. We have taught her how to clear the wilderness of Australia; how to educate her ignorant subjects at home. Finally, we have set the example of so elevating the laboring classes, that no one in America must be vicious or degraded because of his rank in the social scale; that all, even the poorest, feel an interest in the preservation of order and the well being of society, and we have thus rendered the phrase "*bas peuple*" inapplicable to any honest portion of our population. And yet we are told that we have done nothing, that this is the legitimate and inevitable fruit of Anglo-Saxonism which we have only developed. If such talk were mere sentimentality no one would care. But the unfortunate effect, in the eyes of the world, is to abnegate our proud position as a new nation, receiving and assimilating the energetic spirits from every country in Europe, and moulding them all into gigantic proportions for the secondary one of a member of the Anglo-Saxon race, of which England is the head, and our respected selves the tail. "An two men ride of a horse, one must ride behind." It does not follow, though, that the latter position is to be coveted. Nor can I imagine why we should mount the same animal at all.

All this talk is beginning to make the Europeans believe that we consider ourselves under some obligations to sympathize with and sustain Anglo-Saxonism, the real truth being that there is a far greater sympathy between the French and us, than between their neighbors and us. We are essentially democratic; they abhor and detest the idea. The most miserable creature in England would spurn liberty if accompanied by equality; for he thinks there must be some poor devil, more miserable than himself, over whom he can tyrannise. We acknowledge and are in favor of securing to every one his just rights in the political system; whereas, exactly the contrary holds in the Anglo-Saxon, who follows the old parable of giving to him that hath, and taking from him that hath not, even that which he hath. The universal tendency is to yield power to those above, and to keep the lower class pressed to the earth. I therefore see little to justify the attempt of Mr. Bright to transplant our institutions into England. He forgets that the Americans—it is useless to investigate the causes why—are a race of a higher and more delicate organization, and can be entrusted with liberty because they can appreciate it. The common Englishman would only covet the privilege of suffrage in order that he might sell his vote at its market value. He needs a sort of master, and delights in having one. Universal suffrage in England, with due submission, seems to me the craziest idea that ever entered into the brain of a statesman. But Mr. Bright has a meagre following, for the English people know themselves too well to indulge in such a Eutopian experiment. Not content with this, they kindly volunteer to lecture us upon the errors of our system of society,—for it is a difference of society as well as of government,—and pronounce republicanism a failure because we prefer to confine government within the strictest limits necessary for the objects of its institution, and perhaps find King Log more suitable for the purpose than King Stork. Even Mr. Macaulay has favored us with a "preachment," which is founded upon such a strange confusion as to seem to belie the aphorism that history is wisdom teaching by experience, and that its votaries should consequently be the wisest of statesmen. England is a conglomeration of monopolies. The land is a monopoly of a few thousands; the Government of a few hundreds. The whole number of capitalists does not exceed a few millions. All below is a toiling, ignorant, vicious, discontented multitude, who know not one week where they will find bread for the next. Such is their system, and were America like England, Mr. Macaulay would be justifiable in supposing the cause of republicanism hopeless. But what class in America enjoys a monopoly of the pleasures of life? Is not every avenue open to the most unfriended capacity? Do not all receive the benefits of education? Can not, and have not, the poorest boys occupied the chair of the Presidency? Have our great statesmen, our millionaires, been, for the most part, the children of even competency? Owing to the equality which reigns throughout our ideas and institutions, is it not in the power of every honest laborer, and do not the vast majority, lay up a provision against the contingencies of

28

old age? Whence, then, is to come this army of grim, despairing, famished workmen, who, having nothing, hoping nothing,
without past or future, are to wage an eternal warfare against
the order of society? Is there, then, no middle ground between
a savorless communism and the despotism of capital? Are
there no checks and balances in nature? Do freedom, equality,
education, an honorable inculcation of industry effect nothing?
It is provoking to hear such solemn inconsequences from a
really great man.

The disposition, too, to place a money value upon everything,
the real cause of their difficulties, is peculiar to the Anglo-Saxons, and an anomaly in the present age of the world. In
the military profession, where, of all others, individual merit
should be the sole passport to distinction, commissions are still
bought and sold. Throughout the country money is imperatively required for every position of eminence. The records
of the House of Lords contain the strange case of a duke who
was expelled for no other crime than his poverty. Men of the
first abilities are deterred from accepting the peerage, because
they have not amassed money enough to save them from the
humiliating and disgraceful position of a poor gentleman. We
Americans like money, not because it is money, or because it
brings position or respect, but because it gratifies bodily desires. It would be thought an astonishing thing with us if
the presidential electors were to inspect the pockets of the
candidate rather than his head and his heart; or if, in 1848,
Mr. Cass had been recommended on account of his wealth, or
General Taylor had sold out his commission—things perfectly
consonant with Anglo-Saxon ideas. Yet the greatness of England is due in considerable part to this very state of affairs,
and any attempt to alter it may involve the downfall of her
power. The natural rulers are the aristocracy, and the Anglo-
Saxon gentleman is certainly one of the best qualified persons
in Europe to govern Anglo-Saxons, but all below bear the
impress of an inferior class, a strange combination of servility
with tyranny. That there should be any real sympathy between the great body of the two nations is as little to be
desired as expected.

Having thus spoken of the want of sympathy between us in
the weaker points of character, justice requires me to confess
that there is an equal absence of resemblance in the virtues.

The Englishman certainly does possess bull-dog courage. His officers may be ignorant of the science of war, but he, nevertheless, fights to the last, nor is he subject either to the exhilaration of success or the depression of defeat. He is conservative by nature, and abhors humbugs and humbuggery. The middle classes, and particularly the country gentlemen, are worthy of their position. The men of this rank are true and the women virtuous. Reserved in intercourse and unamiable toward their own countrymen, they seem to be courteous to foreigners and even to each other when the social barrier is broken through; but they do not compose the nation. In discussing national relations it is not the merits and demerits of one class alone that are to be considered, but the bearing of the whole.

The increase of steam and financial communication, and the little leaven of Anglo-Saxonism unfortunately left among us, has of late years caused many Americans to look up to England as the mother *country*, according to the phrase. Though, perhaps, not one in ten of those who use the expression so frequently has any great amount of the much prized fluid in his veins. The manner in which the homage is received beyond the water depends very much upon the state of relations with France. As the one goes up, the other goes down. The difference between the conduct of the English toward America now, and what it was in 1850, is astonishing. Then France was torn internally, scarcely able to maintain domestic tranquility, and powerless for any offensive action. Europe was just beginning to stagger weakly along, as if from a bed of sickness. England and Russia alone, of the great powers, had stood the storm unbent. Under this state of things America was a presumptuous youngster, to be snubbed upon every opportune occasion. The Yankees (as they persist in calling the whole nation) were described to Europe as lank, nasal-twanging barbarians, very good for accumulating money and manufacturing wooden nutmegs, but worthy only of a place in the kitchen of the civilized world. The Brusselled parlor of Christendom was not to be defiled with their presence. The newspapers never wearied of ringing the changes upon American short-comings. Our self-government and liberty were held up as empty bubbles on the point of bursting. The plain and unflattering truth being that the English have a profound contempt for us, and it is impossible to blame them for it, when we remember the servility and utter abnegation of manhood that characterize so many of us in the presence of a live lord. They have eagerly embraced every opportunity of kicking and cuffing us, yet we whine at their feet. How could they do otherwise than despise us? Since that time, however, certain changes have taken place in the world. The distracted French republic has given way to a powerfully organized empire, with a chief capable of planning, and an army and navy capable of executing any enterprize, however gigantic. The first warning given of this change was in 1851, on the Greek question, when the President of the French republic checked Lord Palmerston, and gave England to understand that her course of proceeding in foreign domineering must be altered, or a war with France would follow in a fortnight. We all remember the salutary effect of that warning, and Palmerston's capital "bottle-holding" speech. The doctrine of a balance of power upon the ocean as well as the land has been again spoken of in high places. The ghost of Waterloo, from being a source of unmingled pride and gratification and boasting. has come to cause as many terrors as that of Banquo. An unexpected consequence has been that the manner of speaking of America has altered apace. It is "our cousins beyond the water" and "Brother Jonathan." An American is appealed to whether we will allow the "mother country" to be crushed, the "Protestant religion to be destroyed," etc. All this has happened before, and if the government of Louis Napoleon were supplanted by a weak monarchy, the present good feeling of our "dear cousins" would disappear as rapidly as their fears. In truth, opposition to the advancement of the United States, whether materially or intellectually, is the normal condition of England. We have suffered from it ever since the foundation of our Government, and will continue to do so, except when the fear of invasion causes a temporary change in her policy, for selfishness, an utter, unholy and inconceivable desire to sacrifice the happiness and prosperity of every other country to their own even most trifling advantage is their invariable rule of action. They quarrel among themselves about the length of a bishop's gown, or the cut of a guardsman's hat, or great constitutional questions, but there is never a difference of action on this point; and any statesman who dared to raise a voice in behalf of jus-

tice and honor in foreign relations could not be returned from
a single constituency in England. Witness poor Bright and
Cobden in the Chinese war. Woe to any nation that trusts
her friendship!

There can be very little doubt that one great object of the
British Government in forming the *entente cordiale,* was the
regulation of affairs in the western as well as the eastern world.
Lord Clarendon was awkward enough to betray this in 1854.
They have fallen finely into their own trap. I was told, upon
good authority, in Madrid, that Louis Napoleon, conversing
with an English friend before 1848, remarked that, in pursuance
of his destiny, he would some day be Emperor of France. "In
that event," says the Englishman, "you will, I hope, be on
good terms with England." "Certainly," replied Napoleon, "I
will make an alliance with England." Subsequently, in the
course of the conversation, he continued: "There will soon be
but two nations in Europe—France and Russia." "But how
do you reconcile that with what you have just said about the
alliance?" "It is by means of that very alliance that I will
reduce England to the second rank," replied the far-seeing
statesman. If this be true, the plan has certainly succeeded to
admiration. Every year he has imposed new humiliations
upon his ally, while remaining punctilliously faithful to the
bond. The Crimea destroyed its military reputation. The affair of the "Charles et George" showed what reliance could be
placed upon its friendship, and the Italian war has been a grave
for what remained of its diplomatic prestige. Even the sarcastic letter to the famous Liverpool brokers, was not without
its effect. Yet the conduct of Napoleon has been unexceptionable. He sought her co-operation in Italy, which was con-
temptuously rejected. He subsequently offered her an opportunity of participating in the peace, which was declined. He
agreed to co-operate with her in Central America; but I am far
from supposing that he could be seduced into an active opposition to us, unless we attempted to monopolize all the Isthmus
routes. England feels that her greatness is fast being overshadowed by the growing Empire of Russia on the one side,
and the growing Republic of America on the other, and
clutches at every straw which may save her, as she seems to
think there is not room in the world for herself and any one
else. In this position of affairs, it seems to be the true policy

of the United States to maintain steadily the Monroe doctrine, not as it was first intended, but as it has been subsequently interpreted. That England can be persuaded by peaceable means to cease intermeddling with the American continent is not to be supposed, and in case Napoleon is overthrown, it is possible her influence over the succeeding dynasty will be so great as to revive into existence the one-legged *entente cordiale*, and then no bounds could be set to her pride, so that sooner or later force must be employed. The only other European power which exerts a perceptible influence on North America is Spain, and this brings me again to the beginning of the chapter.

The public sentiment in Spain was outraged in the highest degree by the successive invasions of the Island of Cuba, and the destruction of the Consul's house by the mob in New Orleans. I was told in the winter of 1851–'52, that upon the reception of this latter piece of news it was proposed in Madrid to reciprocate violence by mobbing the residence of our Minister, which probably would have been attempted had it not been for the universal and well-deserved popularity that Mr. Barringer enjoyed. We cannot deny that the Spaniards were perfectly justifiable in their indignation. And if we judge them by ourselves, they might have demanded, with arms in their hands, indemnity for the past and security for the future. But the nation became still more indignant at the offer to purchase. The other was a mere exhibition of popular phrensy; this a deliberate insult by the Government. Castillian honor was touched to the quick at the insinuation that Spain would part with her territory for money, and the fact that such an idea was seriously entertained by our Government at all betrays a lamentable ignorance of the real character of the Spaniard. I have never seen one of any rank who did not express himself in the strongest language upon this indignity. That money would be of great use in furthering any necessary intrigues is unquestionable, and had the negotiations with the Sartorius Ministry and Queen Christina been skilfully conducted, the desired end might have been attained. For there is little doubt that these parties would have betrayed the country willingly, nay eagerly, for a few millions privately transferred. The revolution of 1854 restored the liberal party to power, and no liberal party in any country can venture to make the national

territory a matter of bargain and sale.   The first motion of the
Constitutional Cortes was one adopted unanimously against
the transfer upon any conditions.   So long, therefore, as attempts are made to take the island by force, or to threaten the
purchase of it with money, we may count upon the determined
opposition of the Spanish government and the Spanish nation.
But the Spaniards themselves are becoming rapidly convinced
that the age for colonies has passed away.   Cuba is fertile, and
produces a large revenue, but the expense of administration is
very great.   Its proximity to our coast entails the necessity of
a large garrison, composed of the best troops in the army, at
an increased rate of pay.   Then there is a host of other functionaries to be supported, and they must either be paid enormously or allowed to peculate upon the revenue, generally
both.   Under the present restrictive system, Cuba is of some
value as a market for the Northern provinces, but this cannot
continue long, for the whole policy of commercial restrictions
is against the spirit of the age, and must eventually disappear,
when no reason of opposition will be left except national pride.
If then, the Island is to be acquired with the consent of Spain
(and no other method would be consistent with our national
honor), some means must be suggested of soothing the Castillian
pride.   Several times have gentlemen suggested to me this
summer a plan, which would, it is true, involve us perhaps in a
war, but it would be a war with a great power, in which glory
might be gained, and not in pitiful filibustering, as barren of
tangible advantages as it is of honor.

During the days of its weakness and internal distraction, Spain
has been compelled alternately to seek the aid of France and
England, and not unfrequently each of its two parties had, at
the same time, enlisted respectively the moral aid of one of
these nations.   They have no reason for loving either.   In earlier
times their coasts were ravaged by pirates, such as Drake,
whose rule was fire and slaughter.   The present century commenced with the invasion of the country by Napoleon, probably
the most shameful outrage that was ever perpetrated, inasmuch as it was a persistent attempt for five years, first to conquer, and that failing, to ravage and destroy an unoffending
nation.   The English landed an army ostensibly to sustain
the Spaniards, but, in truth, to fight their own battles, and the
outrages committed by them were unsurpassed save by those

of the French.   Speak to a real Spaniard of the sacking of Ciu-
did Rodrigo, of Badajos, of St. Sebastian, and as, with flashing
eyes, he details the foul deeds of his pretended allies, you will
see what sympathy he has for England.   The French demolished fortresses lest they should fall into the hands of the English, and the English the same lest they should fall into the
hands of the French, so that between the two Spain was left a
mass of ruins.   The fortifications before Gibraltar are an amusing instance of the latter.   Anterior to the War of Independence, the Spanish had erected lines in front of the Rock of Gibraltar.   One fine morning the British, pretending great apprehension from the French, sallied forth and blew them up.
After the war was over, the Spaniards were naturally disposed
to restore things to their original condition, when, to their
astonishment, their dear allies received the working party with
a discharge of cannon, and have never since allowed the lines
to be re-constructed.   Several occurrences of this sort, together
with the brutality and drunkenness of the British soldiers,
caused their departure from the soil of the Peninsula to be
longed for almost as much as that of the French.   And yet
English books are full of the ingratitude of the Spaniards, and
claim the merit of expelling Napoleon's numberless legions
entirely for the fifty thousand British.   In the northern provinces, the Provincias Bascongadas, Navarre, Aragon and
Catalonia, the feeling is intensified by the remembrance of the
Carlist War and the question of a protective tariff.   Notwithstanding all this, England, even more than France, has pre-
sumed upon the weakness of Spain to use a dictatorial tone in
diplomatic intercourse, not merely as to external relations, but
even the management of their internal concerns.   The sum-
mary ejection of Sir Henry Bulwer from Madrid, in 1848, was
a slight check upon their impertinence, but the old tone was
quickly resumed.   Of late years French influence has increased,
and English waned in proportion.   This result is natural when
we contrast the policy pursued of late by the two nations.
England has been guided entirely by self-interest.   Napoleon's
conduct toward the so called Latin nations, at least, has been
marked by an unheard-of generosity.   The Morocco affair has
been the finishing stroke.   That the Spaniards were justifiable
in demanding satisfaction from the Moors, to any extent, will
scarcely be questioned.   Yet so determined were the English

to maintain sole command of the Straits of Gibraltar, that an armed intervention on their part was impending, and would, doubtless, have occurred had it not been for the prompt action of the French in sending a fleet and an army near the seat of the conflict. Unfortunately for the reputation of England, about this time occurred the San Juan difficulty, rather a high-handed proceeding all must admit. The contrast between her deportment toward Spain and that toward powerful, bellicose America, was a matter of sarcastic laughter to all Europe. At present, therefore, French influence is in the ascendant, but it is not in the Iberian heart to like either of these nations.

Now the Spanish have two political desires to gratify, for which they would make any sacrifice, however unreasonable. The first is the expulsion of the English from the Rock of Gibraltar. No American can comprehend what a continual eye-sore this fortress is to every inhabitant of the Peninsula, except the smugglers at Ronda. Imagine that the British, in some successful foray, had obtained possession of Key West, commanding the coasting commerce between the South and the East, and blockading the entrance to the Gulf, and we can appreciate the scowling countenance of the old Castillian when he first sees the British flag waving over the soil of Spain, for Gibraltar is always so described in Spanish geographies. No length of time can ever reconcile them to this occupation, and if a successful party were to scale the rock, as they almost succeeded in doing one night, the act would be enthusiastically sustained by the whole nation, and its heroes loaded with the highest rewards which the Government could invent.

The second wish of the Spaniards is the re-union of the whole Peninsula under one Government. How two people differing in so many respects, and agreeing in so many others as the Spaniards and Portuguese, could have sprung up side by side, and remained in a state of quasi enmity in the Peninsula, is a mystery. . The difficulty of intercommunication has had much to do with keeping them apart, for highways in Spain must be made by the Government or not be made at all, such is the enormous outlay requisite. Yet, to look at the map, the country lying upon the upper waters of the Tagus and the Guadiana would seem much more naturally connected with the country lying about the mouth of these rivers than with Andalusia, which is separated by the lofty Sierra Morena.

The Spaniards are unanimous for the union of the two, and a majority of the Portuguese could be converted to the same policy, but the interests of England render her an active and uncompromising opponent of the project. Portugal, as a portion of Spain, would be really independent of England; as a nominally independent State, England, the predominating maritime power, is her sole efficient protector, and a safe entrance is thus secured to British troops at any moment they may choose to make a diversion against Spain. The inherent difficulties about the satisfactory arrangement of the details of the project are so great, that very little diplomacy is requisite to baffle any scheme that may be proposed.

I have been frequently told by Spaniards, and, I believe, such could be made the general sentiment of the nation, that our energetic aid to the successful accomplishment of either of these projects would reconcile them to the transfer of Cuba, provided, of course, that the Cubans were willing to be transferred. We should thus incur the mortal hatred of the "mother country" which we have enjoyed for a century past, and, in all probability, will enjoy for a century to come, for even natural parents are pained to see their progeny step forth into the world; but the grief of a step-mother must be intense, when the rebellious infant not only makes his own clearing and sets up for himself, but bids fair to get along better than the good lady herself. On the other hand, we would have the satisfaction of acting a manly, dangerous part, and of generously aiding a noble nation, that has always been our friend, to re-assume her place at the great council table of the world. In the mean time we might regulate our little matters over here to our satisfaction. It is not probable that the Emperor Napoleon would maintain England in her opposition to America. If such should unfortunately be the case, the issue must be met in a suitable manner, by force if we be strong enough, otherwise by diplomacy, but met persistently, for no plan has been suggested for many years so fraught with danger to the real independence of nations as the *entente cordiale*, with its English interpretation. Napoleon has used it only as a defensive means of protecting nationalities; he thus secured independence to Turkey, and attempted to do so to Italy. Whereas, the English statesmen have regarded it as an offensive organization for the general purpose of regulating the world to suit their own interests or fancies. Russia was to be driven to the wall; the peace of Villafranca was a shameful treachery, because Austria was not crushed. China ought to be invaded by joint forces and annexed, and a good curb bridle should be placed upon Young America, with one shank resting upon the Island of San Juan. Thus all the barbarians, east and west, would be held in check. Should internal difficulties arise in the United States, it is possible they might find a pretext for interfering. And all this, as their orators proclaim, is required by the interests of civilization! Anglo-Saxon civilization! Certainly our civilization is bad enough, but it is a doubtful matter whether we would be benefited by exchanging it for that which flourishes beyond the sea. The sympathies of the American people in behalf of Russia during the Crimean war were in obedience to the instinct which frequently prompts nations to proceed in the right direction, when their reasoning powers would probably have led them astray. It is almost to be regretted that we did not take a more decided part in that contest. Russia and America are allies by the force of our position, and there is scarcely any conjuncture of affairs which could place our interests in opposition, while we seem condemned to an eternal enmity with England. So long as their feeling to us is silent, it matters little, but no manifestation of it should be permitted. In truth, the relation which America occupies to England is that of a great Mississippi, daily receiving fresh accretions, on its way to the ocean, and yet daily impeded in its course by little dams, that our *soi-disant* cousins, with an industry worthy of a better cause, are continually erecting in every quarter of the globe to impede our progress. In youth it may not be good policy to complain too loudly, but so soon as the nation has attained full size, it seems to me that we should put an end to the system. It is not only our policy but our duty to refrain from all participation in European politics. Their ideas of liberty and despotism are, happily, unknown here. But we must enforce a reciprocity, and, above all, unsparingly destroy anything like a coalition. Now, the filibustering upon Cuba has been the excuse for the present one so far as it concerns us, and the most appropriate revenge would be to acquire the island at the expense of the guilty party herself. It might be difficult to find a reasonable subject for quarrel, yet we have been respectively so much in the habit of speaking ferociously of each other, that one might probably be discovered. The siege of Gibraltar would certainly be no trifle, but modern improvements increase every day the chance of success. No masonry can withstand the rifle cannon or the tremendous bombs that are coming into fashion. The Rock of Gibraltar might defy an escalade, but it is not a Sevastopol. There is no earth for works, and there are no engineers in the English army to make them, as the Russian war conclusively proved, so that it could be taken sooner or later, and six months in camp on the Bay of Algeciras, within three days' horseback of the marvels of Andalusia, would not be the most disagreeable lot that could befall an American volunteer.

Notwithstanding the little disagreement we have had with Spain, I am of the opinion that Americans are better received here than in any other country of Europe, even than in France. For some reason or other our position throughout the world is not so good as it was at an earlier date. Perhaps they know us better. Formerly, to be an American was, of itself, a passport; now, it is rather the contrary, and the traveller finds that the announcement causes a slight prepossession against him. If Europeans are questioned as to the cause of this prejudice, it is generally found traceable to two circumstances. The first is the character of some of the men who are sent abroad to represent us in an official capacity. This, however, is much exaggerated. The majority of them, though not men of great education or elegant manners, are pleasant enough in their way, and good-hearted, unaffected gentlemen. Our own newspapers are full of complaint on the subject, written frequently by individuals who have sought to use the embassy as a means of forcing them into good society, and who avenge themselves by abusing the minister, when, poor fellow, he is frequently quite guiltless, for how in the world could he give them the *entrée* into fashionable circles if he has it not himself? Their ignorance of the language of the country is much harped upon, whereas nothing has saved us from so many difficulties as this very ignorance. An incompetent or evil disposed person is comparatively harmless if he be denied the power of speech, and if the Government will send such men abroad, ignorance of the language should be an indispensable qualification. Another mistaken idea is that the minister should live in grand style, than which there can be no greater error. The Government of the United States will never consent to put our representatives on a footing with the ambassadors of great nations, who, to a princely fortune, unite salaries of fifty thousand dollars a year, and it is well known that those of our ministers who have reflected most credit upon the nation were persons of very moderate means, living in the simplicity and integrity of true republicanism, and therefore depending for position entirely upon social and intellectual accomplishments, which, in our country, are not often united with large fortunes. It has always seemed to me, therefore, that our diplomatic corps is far more respectably filled than we generally suppose. There are exceptions, and it must be admitted that you do occasionally meet with a person whom you would be surprised to find in a gentleman's house at home, and whom you are horrified to hear held up as a representative of society in America. The only practical remedy for this evil is to abolish the corps altogether, and to send envoys extraordinary when anything especial is to be done. These men would necessarily be fit for their place, and the ordinary duties might be discharged by consuls-general, quite as effectually, in the majority of cases, as at present.

The other great cause of complaint is the private conduct of some of our countrymen. It is utterly impossible to make Europeans comprehend that pecuniary competence or even great wealth is not evidence of education or social position in America. Any person who has means enough to travel for pleasure is supposed to be a fair specimen of the better class at home, and inasmuch as some of our fellow citizens at Paris indulge rather freely in slings, cocktails, whiskey-straits, cobblers, brandy-smashes, white-lions and similar " refreshers," and expectorate copiously upon the carpet, the interior of private houses in America is supposed to resemble, on a small scale, the larger bar-rooms, and our only music to be the national oath uttered in every note of the gamut. But in the midst of all this hoggishness, there is a certain foundation of good feeling and strong character, and I can vouch for my own experience that, with one exception, I have never known a deliberately mean action committed by an American, and that, I regret to say, was by a person whose position under the Government would have led me far from such a suspicion.

The American character has, fortunately, suffered little in

Spain from either of these causes. Our ministers have, for the most part, maintained a respectable standing. The social position and personal influence of Mr. Barringer and his accomplished lady, in 1852, were such as the country might be proud of, and though Mr. Soulé did arouse the hatred of the nation, yet his unquestioned talents and elegant manners secured their respect. As few of our countrymen wander among the barren Sierras and scanty *posadas* of the inland, we are received at least upon terms of fair curiosity. They will make the mistake of calling us Anglo-Americans, which I utterly repudiated, claiming to hail neither from Spanish America nor from Anglo America, but from American America—a distinction, in my opinion, to be rigidly enforced, as the populations on this continent, which are of pure Spanish, French or English descent, are utterly insignificant and have never made any solid progress. Canada, by the force of our example, has commenced to make some improvement, but the colonies farther removed from our settlements furnish striking examples of the rule. Otherwise, I have never found cause to complain of the deportment of Spaniards toward us. Indeed, if an educated American will resolve to give up creature comforts and to take Spain and Spaniards as he finds them, there is no more agreeable country in the world. For my own part I confess to a decided partiality for many things in it. I like the flowery vales of Andalusia and the tawny mountains of Aragon. I like to kneel in its Cathedrals and to promenade by moonlight upon its Paseos. I like to ride in its diligences when I have a place in the berliña. I like its prancing horses and pawing bulls. I like its fandangos and its olés, its guitars and its wild, plaintive melodies. I like its oranges and its pomegranates. I like its marble courts and sparkling fountains. I like its dry, invigorating climate. I like its language. I like its punctilious, brave and elegant men. But far above all these do I adore its women—the immortal, the ever-beautiful!

Con que adios! y que se descanse bien.